MW00785633

Winning at War

Winning at War

Seven Keys to Military Victory throughout History

Christian P. Potholm

ROWMAN & LITTLEFIELD PUBLISHERS, INC.
Lanham • Boulder • New York • Toronto • Plymouth, UK

Published by Rowman & Littlefield Publishers, Inc.
A wholly owned subsidiary of The Rowman & Littlefield Publishing Group, Inc.
4501 Forbes Boulevard, Suite 200, Lanham, Maryland 20706
http://www.rowmanlittlefield.com

Estover Road, Plymouth PL6 7PY, United Kingdom

Copyright © 2010 by Rowman & Littlefield Publishers, Inc.

All rights reserved. No part of this book may be reproduced in any form or by
any electronic or mechanical means, including information storage and retrieval
systems, without written permission from the publisher, except by a reviewer who
may quote passages in a review.

British Library Cataloguing in Publication Information Available

Library of Congress Cataloging-in-Publication Data
Potholm, Christian P., 1940–
    Winning at war : seven keys to military victory throughout history / Christian P.
Potholm II.
        p. cm.
    Includes bibliographical references and index.
    ISBN 978-1-4422-0130-9 (hardcover : alk. paper) — ISBN 978-1-4422-0132-3
(ebook)
    1. Military art and science—History. 2. Military art and science—Case studies. I.
Title.
    U104.P835 2010
    355.02—dc22   2009029750

∞ ™ The paper used in this publication meets the minimum requirements of
American National Standard for Information Sciences—Permanence of Paper for
Printed Library Materials, ANSI/NISO Z39.48-1992.

Printed in the United States of America

To Ted Lyons,
who first encouraged me to write this book

and

to Will, Noah, and Aiden;
may your world be freer from war

Contents

Preface

To take up a pen is to be at war.

—Voltaire

I have been studying war for almost sixty years.

I was only ten when the Korean War broke out, but I carefully read the papers daily. The first phases of that war were highly mobile, with the map positions of the armies changing almost daily. It was exciting, although a bit disturbing, to see photos of American GIs in action, but in almost constant retreat, and I followed the action with both interest and concern. That summer, I remember one July day running next door to my godmother, Connie Parmelee, and saying very excitedly, "We knocked out five tanks today." She, who had lived through World War II with a naval husband who had fought on a destroyer in the North Atlantic and in the Pacific in some of their most important battles, including Leyte Gulf, gave a trenchant reply. I have never forgotten it: "Those poor boys."

This dichotomy between war-generated excitement and the underlying pathos and ultimately more important element of human sacrifice and suffering is, of course, never far from the study of war—let alone its practice. The tactics and strategy of war always have illuminated that dichotomy for me.

In those years, I was also stimulated by the interest in World War II, which my cousin Charles Petersen studied carefully and widely. Being able to read and speak German, he introduced me to the great sweeps of that titanic struggle, especially the war on the Eastern Front, which at the time was little known or studied in the United States. With considerable excitement, we read dozens of books about the war, especially that excellent series of paperbacks by Ballantine Books featuring many accounts by Germans, Russians, Americans, British, and Japanese participants. For me, Benno Zieser's poignant memoir *The Road to Stalingrad* was particularly influential.

Later, in college and graduate school, I became interested in the malleability of history and the alternative possibilities of different outcomes. The Battle of Stalingrad, the Battle of Lepanto Gulf and the struggle for the Horn of Africa during 1936–1941 all provided me with interesting examples to investigate, as did the science fiction writings of Poul Anderson and Ray Bradbury, which stressed alternative historical outcomes throughout time and space, as did the later novel by Orson Scott Card, *Ender's Game*.

Especially illuminating and stimulating to me was Robert Sheckley's 1957 short story, "Pilgrimage to Earth," in his book by the same name.[1] In it, the distant future has many humans coming from all over the galaxy to enjoy the two things Earth has always done best: provide a wide range of love and war experiences. The visitor, Alfred Simon, from Kazanga IV, has come to Earth for "love," not "war," but he reminds himself "that he must not judge Earth by his own standards. If people on Earth enjoyed killing people, and the victims didn't mind being killed, why should anyone object?"[2] He seems prescient for, as Rudyard Kipling once put it, "Two things greater than all things are, the first is Love and the second War."

As an undergraduate at Bowdoin, I was exposed to the writings of Homer, Thucydides, Herodotus, and Xenophon; gave my first college lecture on the Battle of Lepanto Gulf; and did my senior honors thesis on the Battle of Stalingrad, much to the disgust of my history professors, who couldn't imagine wasting a year of my scholastic life on a "mere battle." I believe that, unfortunately, as Max Boot suggests, this bias against battles and wars (indeed matters military) is still manifest today in much of academia with, I would argue, students being the intellectual losers:

> History is driven by many factors, but while academia focuses on economics, race, class, sexuality, geography, germs, culture, and other influences on the course of human events, it would be foolish and short-sighted to overlook the impact of military prowess and especially aptitude in taking advantage of major shifts in war-fighting.[3]

It seems obvious that it is not the study of battles *qua* battles that is important, but the insights into the nature of Mars that they reveal. The proper study of important battles can offer not only a window into the nature of warfare of that era, but also a view of the contemporary societies that produced their concomitant dedication, or lack thereof, to the ways of war.

After receiving my PhD from the Fletcher School of Law and Diplomacy, I taught at Dartmouth and Vassar before returning to my alma mater, Bowdoin, as a professor of government. In my courses on international relations, I concentrated on the causes of war—which would turn out to be virtually without number, ranging from love and lust (the Trojan War) to attempted world conquest and personal aggrandizement (Alexander the Great, Napoleon, Genghis Khan), the struggle for raw materials (Japan in World War II), and so on.

While teaching at Dartmouth in 1966, we used Raymond Aron's monumental *Peace and War*,[4] which used historical description and analysis to project more universal themes. Hans Morgenthau's realist textbooks also held sway during that era.[5] Their ruminations and insights led me to the conclusion that human beings have waged, and will continue to wage, war for such a broad spectrum of goals and motivations that the study of war must look far beyond its multiplicity of causes. The causes of war are simply too numerous to offer meaningful insights into any general theory of warfare. There are so many reasons why people go to war that it is almost counterproductive to spend time looking at one cause versus another or one cluster of causes versus another cluster. Human beings have simply gone to war over virtually anything.

This period in scholarship was also the era of intense speculation about the ultimate nature of humankind and the causes of war from a biological or evolutionary perspective. Konrad Lorenz, Robert Ardrey, and Desmond Morris all stimulated widespread debate about the relationship between human beings and the animal kingdom.[6] At the time, much was made in their works about the fact that humans seem to be one of the few species that kills their fellows on purpose. Ironically, the symbol of peace among humans, the dove, turned out to be another of those aberrant species. Of course, today, further studies of animals implicate lions, leopards, gorillas, chimps, and some of the other great apes in intraspecies killing as well.

There was also the concomitant scholarly and not-so-scholarly debate over the nature of humankind and the causes of war. Was (and is) war in our genes or our cultural learning process? Many, such as Alexander Alland and D. Hard and R. W. Sussman, were highly motivated to recoil from the notion of "Man the born killer."[7]

Yet such influential thinkers as Sigmund Freud, Carl Jung, and Albert Einstein all thought the urge to warfare was intrinsic to human nature. Freud, in particular, contrasted the warring impulses of Eros and Thanatos. For his part, Albert Camus also saw war as central to being human, "We used to wonder where war lived, what it was that made it so vile. And now we realize that we know where it lives, that it is inside ourselves." Much earlier, Thucydides saw war as an intrinsic and ongoing punishment for man's hubris. Readers interested in a current and thought-provoking overview of the nature versus nurture debate with regard to war should consult the recent work of David Livingstone Smith and his stimulating *The Most Dangerous Animal, Human Nature and the Origins of War*.[8]

Alas, at the end of several decades worth of academic, scientific, and popular debate, the answer seems almost irrelevant. Since humans have fought so often and so ubiquitously throughout recorded history, what does it matter from whence war comes? The fault may not be in our stars, but truly in ourselves—as painful as that may be to accept. But either way, peace is best perceived as the period between wars, not the state of natural or learned or expected grace. As Winston Churchill put it so simply and elegantly, "The story of the human race is War. Except for brief and precarious interludes, there has never been peace in the World."

David Livingstone Smith, in fact, makes some interesting calculations indicating that over the last century or so, upwards of 200 million people, mostly civilians, have been killed in war, from World Wars I and II through the regional conflicts in Angola, Rwanda, Bosnia, Liberia, Burundi, Afghanistan, the Sudan, Cambodia, Iran/Iraq, Congo, Laos, and so forth. For Smith, this amounts to 1.7 million dead a year, or 4,630 a day during this period.[9] These statistics, in and of themselves, seem to undercut the implications of the current politically correct assertion that 95 percent of human history is not war, hence war is overstudied. That may be, but the 5 percent or 10 percent (or whatever the percentage) that is war certainly seems to have a cataclysmic impact on humankind.

Moreover, since these cosmic questions seemed beyond answering and, at least after several decades of study, beyond my continuing interest, I turned to a more narrowly focused set of interests dealing with war. What contributes to success in war? What, if anything, guarantees it? Why do some states or countries or peoples succeed in war and others fail? Why do some peoples emerge so consistently triumphant in warfare during some eras and fail ignominiously in others? What are the independent variables that determine success in war? Are there any truly objective factors that can be examined and *a priori* determine the likelihood of success in the wars of the future?

These are not easy questions to answer, and many contemporary students of international relations are not interested in them, or even believe we can answer them. But I was—and remain—convinced we must explore them and that a search for a template to explain them was attainable. For a long time, the task seemed monumental, even overwhelming, and quite frustrating, both for its complexity and for the difficulty of the challenges of finding some overarching theory or theories into which to contain the myriad examples and principles.

But when I encountered the writings of Geoffrey Parker, Victor Hanson, and especially Williamson Murray, I was stimulated to redouble my efforts.[10] While Parker and Hanson tend to focus on the rise of the West and its worldwide prominence based on technological and war craft superiority, they did help me tremendously in narrowing the scope of my inquiries in a major and very useful way. Nevertheless, even as I began to see with much greater clarity the process of success in war, wherever found in time or space in human history, I still hungered for some additional overarching themes that were less Eurocentric, or at least more capable of helping me understand success in battles and in war, in localized conflicts and areas beyond the scope of Western success, or failure.[11] I wanted to create a conceptual framework that could be truly cross-cultural in nature and that could take into account the significant successes of non-Europeans in making war.

The Mongols, for example, were never exposed, as were the Meiji rulers of Japan, to the innovations of European-type warfare or "WestWar" as Geoffrey Parker terms it. Nevertheless, they practiced extremely successful and very "modern" warfare. Indeed, one could argue that between the Romans at their height and the rise of the West in the sixteenth century, the Mongols were the most efficient and successful war makers of their time and for centuries.

Finally, I reexamined the way in which the early Greeks and Romans themselves looked at warfare and its relationship to the nature of humans. Somehow, I now realized, for all these years I had been diverted from the true essence of understanding war.

Rethinking the nature of war and success in war, I ended up back with a classical image—Mars the god of war. If there were a real god of war, what actions would he reward across time and space? What dimensions made success in war more rather than less likely? This book is the result of asking those questions.

We should never forget that war is terrible, but we should acknowledge also that it fascinates us and is such an intrinsic part of our total human heritage that it cannot be ignored. For as Leon Trotsky put it a century ago, "You may not be interested in war, but war is interested in you."

The enormous and enduring legacy of war, and its intrinsic centrality to the human condition can disturb one greatly. And studying war in an objective way can be debilitating and draining and, ultimately, extremely sobering. To write about a conceptual framework that, in so far as possible, tries to operate in a moral vacuum, without judgments about war as war, is very difficult. But over forty years of academic study and discourse have led me to undertake this effort. I hope it will stimulate others who study war to look at it anew and perhaps challenge some of their own long-held assumptions.

In this regard, I have been very fortunate to have had excellent students and colleagues over the years with whom I have shared comments and controversy, and by whom I have always been stimulated and challenged. I am most grateful for their contributions of the following to this volume.

I have especially benefited from the input of several generations of Bowdoin students who took my courses, "Government, War, and Society" and

"Conflict Simulation and Conflict Resolution." A number of them helped considerably in the putting together this book: Ann Zeigler, Mike Corbelle, Ingrid Anid, Courtney Eustace, Arnab Quadry, Jessica Lian, Ian Merry, Jack Dingess, Matthew Lentini, David Sokolow, Nate Tavel, Craig Hardt, Emily Straus, Eamonn Hart, and Jeff Lin.

Very effective also was copyediting done by Brandon Mazer, Rebecca "Becca" Van Horn, and Tim Fuderich. They deserve considerable credit for making the work both more understandable and more relevant to today's generation. Brandon Mazer was highly dedicated and incisive and often challenged both prose and content. Tim Fuderich assisted nobly in the research of many historical notes and did an outstanding job with the entire manuscript—even while deploring my efforts to develop a framework in a "moral vacuum." When it comes to proofreading, Becca Van Horn is in a class by herself.

But none of their excellent work could have been possible, let alone probable, without the superb direction of our departmental coordinator, Lynne Atkinson, a true treasure of the college. Special kudos also, to Joe Calvo of the Bowdoin Copy Center for his untiring efforts to reproduce the many versions of individual chapters as well as the entire manuscript.

A special thanks also to Barry and Karen Mills, who have made Bowdoin such a wonderful and scholarly rewarding place to teach, and to Cristle Collins Judd, who continues to accent the importance of scholarship at the college, especially through her participation in the Faculty Lecture Series. The best days of the college lie ahead thanks to their hard and dedicated work today.

As always, I owe an enormous debt of gratitude to Sandy Quinlan Potholm, who has read this manuscript and edited my previous books without complaint and with great insight. Her intellectual and proofreading contributions remain invaluable.

I would especially like to acknowledge the intellectual stimulation and support of David "Broo" Parmelee, Lyle and John Gibbons, as well as the contributions, stimulation, and input over the years of Bruce and Heather Davis, Erik Potholm and Chris Averill, Ann and Dennis Kimmage, Steve Cerf, Dan Levine, Admiral Greg "Grog" Johnson, Will Buxton, Sharon Merrill, Bill Utley, Keith Brown, Bob Tyrer, David Hecht, Brigadier "Knobby" Clarke, William S. Cohen, Bernie LaCroix, Fred Hill, and Stan Wakefield, as well as to the various professors and practitioners who have stimulated and challenged my assumptions by commenting on my lectures and chapters and providing needed information from their areas of specialty: Jim Higginbotham, Henry Laurence, Allen Wells, Shelley Deane, Thomas Conlan, David Gordon, Alan Springer, and Leslie Shaw.

David Emery was of enormous help in providing important insights during the entire process, while Tim Woodcock provided a number of historical additions and amendments. The entire manuscript was greatly improved by the intellectual and analytical contributions of Amos Eno, while Jeff Selinger brought important comments to the early chapters. Gil Barndollar always continues to amaze with his in-depth knowledge of matters military, while Claude Berube was most helpful in suggesting useful changes and positive direction. Also I owe special thanks for the careful reading, important and far-ranging insights, and judicious editing of the final manuscript by Williamson "Wick" Murray, as well as the questions, corrections, and suggestions of the various anonymous referees.

Richard Morgan has long been my mentor in many things, and over the years has taught me—against my earlier naive assumptions—the validity of the introductory quote from Voltaire.

Thanks, too, to the Bowdoin library staff who have assisted me and others so ably over the years, especially Phyllis McQuaide, Barbara Harvey, Patricia Myshrall, Leanne Pander, and Carmen Greenlee, as well as head librarian Sherrie Bergman. On more than one occasion, I'm sure I taxed their patience as well as the Inter-Library Loan system. Barbara Harvey, in particular, went above and beyond all calls of librarian duty.

Scholarship remains a most collective enterprise, and I am very grateful for all the help I have received from students, colleagues, and friends alike. Any remaining errors obviously are solely my responsibility.

Finally, I want to thank Jed Lyons, friend, publisher, and editor of note and his fine staff at Rowman and Littlefield, especially Jon Sisk and Melissa Wilks. Jed is an author's best friend.

1

Introduction:
The Template of Mars

The judgment of history is without pity.

—Raymond Aron

War is a violent teacher.

—Thucydides

There are many books about the reasons humans go to war.

There are many books about the nature of humankind and the causes of war.

There are many books deploring war as a human institution.

There are many books glorifying war and warrior-hood.

There are many books arguing for the cultural determinants of success in warfare.

There are many books declaring that war is but an aberration in human history.

This book fits none of these categories.

Instead, it seeks to develop and utilize an analytical framework enabling readers to compare and contrast success in war irrespective of culture or time period—a framework that can be applied to wars throughout time and space, and across cultures and societies.

It asks: What contributes to success in battle and war? Why do some states, countries, or people succeed in war when others fail? Why do some emerge so consistently triumphant in warfare during some eras and fail ignominiously in others? We often focus, as we should, on the important role leadership plays in warfare, but in this volume we hope to look beyond this factor except in chapter seven where it appears as a function of will.

Are there objective factors that can be examined in order to explain who won in war and who lost, and that can a priori determine the likelihood of success in wars in the future? Are there independent variables that determine success in war?

These are not easy questions to answer, and many contemporary students of international relations are not particularly interested in them, or even convinced we can answer them. But a useful, transcultural conceptual framework that will help us explore and understand the mysteries of war can and should be created and serve as a basis for future intellectual exploration and application.

As indicated in the preface, for a long time this task seemed to be monumental, even overwhelming, both for its complexity and for the challenges involved in finding an overarching set of variables that accommodate the myriad examples and principles related to warfare.

Yet it remains important to see how states achieved success in war—who wins wars and why. These overarching themes should not be as Eurocentric as are many in the existing literature. Rather, themes and categories dealing with success in war need to be more capable of helping us understand success in conflicts and areas beyond the scope of Western success or failure, contact or noncontact. The combination of these themes should also be able to provide an analytic screen that can have predictive capacity as well as explanatory properties.

THE CENTRALITY OF MARS

In creating such a transcultural conceptual framework, the notion of Mars, the god of war, proves to be of enormous help. In fact, Mars can be seen as the key concept to understand war, for Mars remains—in glorious simplicity—the essence of war and can lead to a set of variables that transcend individual cultures.

It was clear that the ancients, particularly the Greeks and Romans, correctly understood Mars most profoundly and insightfully. They, and others in many other societies, saw the god of war not simply as a deity to be worshiped, but also as a way to understand both humans and war in its various dimensions and characteristics.[1]

Mars and his parallels throughout human cultures encapsulate the various aspects of war, including its ability to overwhelm the hopes, dreams, and plans of humans. This awesome power of the notion of a god of war remains intact today, and the elegant simplicity of the concept of Mars can bring us useful insights and explanatory aspects if we will just utilize it as a unifying concept.

Simply put, in the worldviews of the Romans and many other societies, the god of war made the rules that dictate outcomes of human conflict, without regard for the hopes or fears or goals of the participants. This perspicacious insight found in so many previous human collectivities gives us a powerful and useful stimulus to examine war in a very different way from that which we are used to. We need simply to explore these notions from a somewhat different perspective, with an often very different intent; but the basic idea of a god of war remains central to the endeavor.

The Compost of Ptholomeus, for example, describes Mars thus: "He is red and angry, and a maker of swords and knyves, and a shedder of mannes blode." The Greek Heraclitus put our joint heritage even more starkly: "War is the father of us all."

For the ancients, then, there was a god of war, and he provided instruction for all of us, whether we wanted that instruction or not. By creating a god of Mars, and personalizing him, the ancients invented an archetype that isolated war and its dimensions from human values. They, in fact, decoupled war from other aspects of human activities and motivation. Ethics, morality, causality, and other dimensions all fell away in import, except in so far as these aspects of humankind impacted the ability of people to follow the ways of Mars.

But why utilize Mars, especially, in this day and age? What purpose would be served? What could be the case for using the term *Mars* with intellectual profit in the twenty-first century?

Using the notion of a god of war can provide an analytic construct that can free us from the cultural norms that can often detract from creation of a true archetype of success in warfare. This dimension is very conducive to the development of the notion of a "Template of Mars," a set of elements that those who would gain the favor of Mars must emulate.

Mars, the ultimate metaphor for human conflict, thus can provide a paradigm that will enable us to look at human conflict throughout time and space without subjective cultural variants and constrains, without notions of good or evil, and especially without the situational ethics of right or wrong (again, except as simple multipliers of will). By using Mars as that metaphor, one can create a framework in a moral vacuum, unencumbered by notions and encumbrances of "just" or "unjust" wars.

If, for example, there were a real god of war, we would not be constantly debating the nature of humankind and/or worrying about our collective guilt in fratricide. Instead, we would be trying to understand what he (or to add a degree of political correctness unknown to the ancients, "she") rewards when we enter his or her realm.

Of course, one does not have to believe in a literal god of war to adhere to the concept of an ultimate Platonic universal archetype of successful warfare regardless of culture or time or place. But Mars as a concept becomes a most useful way of understanding war from the perspective of war itself. Used simply as a transcendent concept, Mars is thus a means of understanding the nature of war and of analyzing the ingredients for success in war or battles.

In the end, therefore, it does not matter if there is no literal god of war; it only matters that we use the concept of one as a way to analyze success or failure in war. In this way, Mars can serve both as a simple conceptual framework for comparison and, in some cases, more ambitiously as a heuristic and hermeneutic tool that will enable us to move across cultures and time to compare success in warfare with far less emotional and cultural baggage than that which normally accompanies such an endeavor.

Hopefully, the framework will lead to greater objectivity precisely because it is being used in what is an absence of moral consideration, a moral vacuum. Studying war in a moral vacuum may be repugnant to many, but it can nevertheless yield important conceptual advantages. If we can analyze war in a moral vacuum, for example, then the myriad discussions of who's "right" and who's "wrong" in war fall away, as do notions such as "my country right or wrong" or even "my country always right" (or "always wrong!").

This is very hard to do in the present climate with political viewpoints often overriding other elements, even in scholarly journals and books. But I believe such an approach can also help students of war and international relations to avoid the menace of causality and moral interpretation in any given war situation. Used properly, it will free us up to appreciate the trenchant insight of Alex Comfort, "The smell of burning flesh will not sicken you if they tell you it will warm the world."

With such a framework, the concerns about labeling "modern" versus "ancient" forms of warfare, or "Western" versus "Eastern" or "oriental" forms of war are likewise moved into a secondary, subordinate position, especially if the concept of Mars can lead us to the elements that explain success in warfare wherever found. Even some widely assumed notions about success in warfare being tied to specific cultures and cultural values become of much less ultimate importance if we look at the collective elements of the Template of Mars as the independent variable, not the cultures themselves.

One would hope it is obvious, but using the concept of Mars in no way absolves humanity of its long-term obsession with war, its repeated follies in beginning and prosecuting wars, or the horrible and devastating consequences of those wars.

On the contrary, by using Mars as an analytic construct, we are freed up from trying to distinguish this war or that war on the basis of some moral or ethical variable, or from even spending time decrying that there is war in the human experience. There are only, some would argue, necessary wars and unnecessary wars, but the practices that produced success in war throughout time and space, both within and among human societies, can be analyzed and appreciated, and ultimately applied to human conflict wherever it occurs.

The Template of Mars can thus serve as a trop or sturdy metaphor, a rhetorical device that enables us to examine war without necessarily believing in a literal or real god of war. Thus, occasionally the Template narrative that follows may lapse into intellectual shorthand by asserting that a society or nation "worshiped Mars" or that "Mars rewards" or "Mars dictates." Obviously, we are not talking about actual worship, of course, but rather better adherence to the set of rules and practices that lead to success in warfare. "Mars" simply becomes a literary device to avoid endless repetition of phrases such as: "they followed but two of the seven dimensions of the conceptual framework we deem central to the success of war."

Let us now take a cursory look at the seven elements of the Template of Mars that will form the essence of our examination of war in a moral vacuum. In the process, we will discover that the god of war turns out to be a most jealous god indeed, insisting on adherence to virtually all of the elements in most situations.

FORMING THE TEMPLATE

In this effort, the term *template* signifies a pattern in warfare that must be followed in order for one to be consistently successful at war. The construction of the template should produce characteristics that explain—and even predict—success in warfare, just as the lack of those ingredients predicts and explains failure in warfare. It is also imperative, of course, to see the interactions between and among the different elements of the Template of Mars as essential to the overall outcome.

Why is this interplay between analysis and practice important? Because they have always been and indeed remain closely related. As Mao Tse-tung reflected, "Unless you understand the actual circumstance of war, its nature and its relations to other things, you will not know the laws of war, or know how to direct war, or be able to win victory."

Looking at the vast literature on war, one finds that there are many possible elements for the Template that already exist and could initially be included in any comprehensive examination of war. Some writers mention one, others several. In fact, the various overviews of war are replete with some common and important denominators.

It is useful here to briefly chronicle the process of finding what would eventually become the principal ingredients of the Template of Mars as cited by students of war through the ages.

There was, for example, considerable agreement in war literature on the importance of weaponry and weapons technology. *Superior weapons and/or weapons technology* (as found in any part of the world and relative to those one is fighting) gives whoever possesses superior weaponry one important advantage over their military rivals.[3] This superiority may be relative or absolute for any given situation or time, and today, with the Internet and a freer flow of knowledge, relative technological advantages may be less enduring.

When one thinks of some of the weapons—such as the wheeled chariot, the stirrup, the broad sword, the composite bow, breach loading artillery, and the submarine, all of which have changed the course of warfare (when they were both invented and subsequently utilized in battle), this notion seems relatively straightforward: armies and peoples with superior weapons have usually held an advantage over their opponents.

Indeed, sometimes that advantage may seem to be small or subtle, but nevertheless it can have a major impact, as when Philip of Macedonia lengthened the basic spear of the Greek phalanx from eight or ten feet to fourteen feet, giving the Macedonians a considerable advantage during the period of classical infantry warfare.

In another example, the Mongols, with their rapid firing and powerful recurved bow, had an advantage over those peoples who had slower firing, less powerful bows. The composite bow simply had greater distance, greater accuracy, and a greater rate of fire than other bows and even early muskets.

With regard to firearms, it should be noted that Hans Delbruck, in his *The Dawn of Modern Warfare* indicates that for 150 years after their invention firearms and gunpowder did not have much of an impact on warfare.[4] The role of weapons and weapons technology and its relationship to the Template will be examined in chapter two.

In the vast literature about war, there is also widespread support for the notion of *superior discipline*. Antoine Henri de Jomini, for example, writing in the early nineteenth century, speaks of the need for "a strict but not humiliating discipline, and a spirit of subordination and punctuality, based on conviction rather than on the formalities of the service."[5] More recently, Williamson Murray persuasively argues that discipline is the "glue" that holds armies together: "Without that discipline, armies were not armies, but armed mobs, inseparable of maintaining cohesion, tactical formations, or obedience."[6]

In chapter three, we look at how superior discipline is highly regarded by scholars and practitioners in many cultures alike. We also focus on the fact that the lack of superior discipline, especially a lack of *relative* superior discipline, is often one of the most telling ingredients in both explaining and predicting failure in war.

Additionally, other students of warfare have focused on *receptivity to innovation* as a key to obtaining an advantage in warfare, especially over time. They rightly argue that new weapons and disciplined troops are not enough, but rather that there has to be an ongoing receptivity to both those new weapons and the tactics and strategies used to maximize their effectiveness—or to reduce their effectiveness in the hands of one's opponents.

Different cultures at different times and places are clearly more receptive to innovation than others. Jeremy Black, for example, documents the acceptance of flintlock muskets by the Indians but not the Chinese during the late eighteenth century.[7] For his part, Geoffrey Parker combines the triad of technology, discipline, and military innovation as explaining success in warfare.[8] Also, as Walter Millis points out in *Arms and Men*, the receptivity to innovation involves a managerial revolution along with technological and mechanical revolutions in arms.[9]

Whenever the degree of that change is substantial, many authors refer to it as a "revolution in military affairs," or RMA.[10] Various societies differ greatly in their ability and/or willingness to adapt to new military technology, tactics, or strategies. In chapter five, we present a number of situations where societies proved to be receptive to military innovation and others where they did not.

In addition, a great deal has been written about the need to be *ruthless and persevering* in order to succeed in warfare. It turns out, as we explore in chapter four, that it is very important to qualify the word *ruthless* by connecting it to two attributes: "sustained" and "controlled."

Thus, superior military weapons and, later, technology, superior discipline, receptivity to innovation, and a willingness to do whatever it takes to defeat one's enemy rather easily show their importance to the notion of success in war and become early and important dimensions of the Template of Mars.

Yet another theme important to the study of war, but one not as often examined as superior technology or superior discipline, is that of a focus on the dedication of scarce resources to the preparation and conduct of war. Many historical accounts rightly focus on the size and richness of the societies in question and their ability to conquer in order to acquire raw materials. Indeed, there has always been a historical interplay between the high actual costs of war and the often mistaken notion of "war paying for war." John Hampden put it succinctly many years ago:

> Great sums of money . . . are the sinews of war, and all other business. Our dear-bought experience has taught us what vast taxes are absolutely necessary to maintain the armies and fleets, which are requisite for our security; and for the defense of our religious and civil rights and provided we attain those ends, it will not be thought at [the] long run, we have bought them too dear.[11]

In any case, there is an element of societal and political sacrifice that is required to satisfy Mars. It is necessary to pay and keep paying, not just a blood price but also a price in gold to be worthy of success. But in addition to these obvious and important aspects of the relationship between the wealth of a society and its potential for success in warfare, the protection of those scarce resources that are needed to be spent on military training, equipment, and the development of a strategic vision turns out to be of considerable import.

A country's capital can be spent on civilian goods at the expense of military necessities—equipment, training, pay, and hospital and rehabilitation expenses. That is often understood by students of warfare. It is vital, as noted in chapter six, however, that this percentage of the capital of a society necessary for success in warfare be protected from the mishandling of rulers (including the military elite), as well as from the people.

But even with the elements of technology, discipline, receptivity to innovation, sustained ruthlessness, and the commitment of scarce resources to military affairs, there remains a need to emphasize additional dimensions, which seem, over time, to lead to success in war regardless of the society or culture.

In order to understand all the dimensions of Mars, it is also necessary to answer the question: "Why do some inferior-sized and -equipped armies and peoples often overcome superior opponents?" This addition of *"will"* as *a power multiplier* is a necessary and very powerful ingredient and explanatory factor in the Template. Chapter seven explores the many wellsprings of superior will in war, underscoring its power, for will can often be something of an independent variable in determining success or failure, and its sources are many.

Not only are there individual motivations at play, such as greed, the fight for freedom, or primordial attachments, but also, there can also be a multiplicity of motivations involved in a people armed and at war. In this regard, obviously, there are power-multiplication possibilities in having more than one source of will strength involved in the motivation process. For example, during the Chinese revolution, Mao Tse-tung accented Chinese nationalism as a weapon against the Japanese, as well as revolutionary rhetoric and goals, and intertwined these elements with those of working for a better world and making an end to all war as part of his holistic exhortations.[12]

Finally, to understand fully the power-enhancing nature of the Template, there needs to be an additional element of great import: *the assumption that there will always be another war*. Such a dimension is seldom mentioned in the literature of war so starkly, but surely if there were a god of war, he would insist on a society or a people always preparing itself for the next war instead of resting on its previous military laurels or assuming the time for war had passed. This concept and some prominent examples, such as the Romans, occupy our attention in chapter eight.

In this regard, Clausewitz famously observed that war is an extension of policy by other means and thus a reflection of goals, needs, and merits of policy. Kings and congresses, presidents and peoples care about the merits of the policies or reasons that make them want to go to war. Mars, however, if he existed, would be totally indifferent as to the merits of those policies. His only concern would be whether commitment to a particular policy by a belligerent inhibits or facilitates that belligerent's observing his rules.

Taken together, then, these seven dimensions forming the "Template of Mars" will, it is to be hoped, enable students of war to look at success in warfare freed from some cultural constraints. It is my belief that warfare, in addition to being conditioned by culture, is also conditioned by adherence to the requirements of Mars. Different societies at different stages of threat and involvement in war may change their willingness and ability to follow one or more of the elements of the Template, but the Template changes not. To that extent, the Template may prove, in a number of circumstances, to be transcultural in nature.

During World War II, for example, the mass killing of civilians, especially by strategic bombing, became an accepted means of warfare by such different societies as the Germans, the British, the Soviets, the Americans, and the Japanese. However heinous the killing of innocent civilians may be, in World War II, the use of that method of warfare became perceived as an important determinant of success by all sides, irrespective of how this element was regarded prior to the war by some of the societies involved. In short, various cultures adapted to this dimension of the Template, not the other way around. One could also argue that by 2010, many of these same cultures had reversed themselves and all decried this method's continued use.

In using the Template, then, we are interested in the constants of success in war, not its morality. This is not, of course, an exercise to glorify war or to advocate war over peace. Rather, it is a concerted effort to understand what leads to success in war, no matter where that war is found in time or space.

In the chapters that follow, we examine how each component of the Template is integral to the overall pattern. Many societies, many peoples, many cultures, many religions, and many ideologies may manifest one or more of the ingredients. But true success in warfare over time seems to require exhibiting a multiplicity of ingredients. Indeed, these seven components overlap and mutually reinforce each other when the Template as a whole is followed by a society or a people.

In this, Mars turns out to be a jealous god, requiring a truly staggering amount of devotion and attention in order to receive his rewards consistently, at least on a comparative basis, depending on one's opponents at any given time. Whether one thinks following such a path is worthwhile, it is hoped that this exploration will stimulate further thought and discussion about the nature of a war in a culture-free context.

DIMENSIONS AND DYNAMISM OF
THE TEMPLATE OF MARS

In the subsequent chapters, there will be an in-depth examination of the seven critical prerequisites or elements of the Template of Mars, providing important insights into the question of success in war.

To recapitulate, the dimensions are:

1. Superior Weapons and/or Technological Entrepreneurship
2. Superior Discipline as an Organizational Principle
3. Ability and Willingness to Practice Sustained but Controlled Ruthlessness
4. Receptivity to Military and Organizational Innovation
5. Ability and Willingness to Protect Capital from People and Rulers
6. Superior Will (however generated: nationalism; ethnicity; racism; religion; ideology; manifest destiny; leadership; freedom; or simply a search for glory, space, or dominance)
7. An Ongoing Assumption That There Will Always Be Another War.

A word of caution is needed at the outset. These ingredients of the Template are not introduced in any particular hierarchy. Moreover, because a society or a people or a state exhibits one or several of these ingredients—perhaps even excelling at one element—does not mean that it will be successful in warfare. As a conceptual framework, the Template offers categories of comparison that will facilitate an examination of those ingredients in action.

Over time, a people or nation or state must exhibit most or all of the ingredients at any one time in order to be consistently successful in interstate warfare. And while it is true that a deficiency in one element may be compensated for by excellence in another, on balance, all are needed for sustained success over a long period of time. Obviously the resulting composite will exist relative to the opponents an entity chooses.

These ingredients taken together constitute the Template, a pattern that stands above and beyond individual societies as a Platonic ideal of what ingredients are necessary for success in war. As we proceed, it is imperative that while we are describing one specific feature of the Template we must be reminded that they are all related, often overlapping, and mutually reinforcing.

It is very important to note that it is their interlocking nature that gives the Template its power and enduring relevance. It is the total mix of ingredients that gives the Template its strength as a power multiplier, obviating any single element being definitive. For example, "Superior Weapons and Technological Entrepreneurship" needs to be framed somewhat differently here than when this element has been examined in the context of warfare by others.[13] The side with the superior technology overall, or in specific societal elements, is often seen to have an advantage at a particular time and place. But one can argue that it is not superior technology *qua* technology or its possession that are critical, but rather it is the ability and willingness of the society and its military to both recognize the value of that technology and to utilize it in the most efficacious way.

Superior technology entrepreneurship is vital to success in war, and it is not a single constant but rather a multiplicity of "plays within plays" within warfare. During the insurgency in Iraq, the United States enjoyed a huge technological advantage overall over the forces of al Qaeda and the various sectarian militias. But with their use of improvised explosive devices (IEDs), those same forces integrated a most useful preexisting technology that initially gave them a decided advantage over the United States and Iraqi forces in certain battle situations and that allowed them to enjoy technological superiority in that space—at least briefly. Over time, as one would expect, a broader array of superior technological entrepreneurship ended up favoring the larger, richer adversary—but only because that adversary had the will to press home those advantages over time.

Take also an example from World War II. It is widely accepted that the Germans had superior technology in many areas: jet aircraft (ME-262), cruise missiles (V-1), rocket interceptors (Komet), ballistic missiles (V-2), the snorkel-equipped submarine (XXI U-boat), and highly advanced tanks (Panther and Tiger). Yet these inventions and refinements, while giving the Germans the potential for greater military success overall, did not prove decisive in the broader perspective of World War II. These new weapons often came to the battlefield too late or in insufficient numbers to affect the outcome of the war and were themselves countered by technological advances among the Allies.

For example, initially German U-boat technology exceeded the comparable antisubmarine technology of the Allies, but the Allied advances in radar and sonar, improvements in the long-distance flying capabilities of Allied aircraft, and especially in code breaking, eventually resulted in Allied success when merchant and other surface ships battled submarines.[14]

In a different way, the Battle for the North Atlantic was the result of two related aspects. First, the Americans developed the ability to manufacture Liberty ships and other merchant vessels faster than the Germans could sink them. It is often overlooked that for much of 1942 and 1943, the Germans were actually sinking British and American ships faster than new ones could be built. The same thing was true with regard to armor. In World War II, American tanks were inferior to some of their German counterparts (such as the Panther and Tiger), but American factories could produce many more than German factories so that even with a negative tank kill ratio of one to five, the Americans eventually overcame the German quality advantages. For their part, the Russians already had a technological advantage over the Germans with their T-34 tank, arguably the most important armored vehicle of World War II.

Second, the British and the Americans eventually developed and put into use superior technology for finding and destroying German U-boats at a catastrophic rate, a rate that was faster than Germany could replace them. In fact, by the end of the war serving in the submarine service (the *Kriegsmarine*) ended up being more dangerous than serving on the Eastern Front against the Soviets. The British were also highly successful in breaking the German military code and thus were privy to operational details and locations where the Germans were contemplating using their U-boat packs.

Conversely, prior to the German assault on France following the "phony war" of 1939 after the invasion of Poland, the French had better tanks and more of them than the Germans, but they failed to concentrate those tanks in any meaningful way. The French Char B1 series, for example, was superior to the German Mark III or IV, and the French had 400 of them. But instead of concentrating their tanks, the French scattered them piecemeal across a broad front and thus ignored a very important concept of Carl von Clausewitz. For Clausewitz, the key to victory in battle was to use as many of one's forces as one could at the "*Schwernpunkt*" or decisive point. The notion of "The Superiority of Numbers," at the decisive point lies at the heart of his theory of battle.[15]

The Germans massed their smaller number of tanks and developed a battle plan that gave them a local tactical superiority that eventually turned into a huge strategic superiority when the French failed to adapt to the changed world of German strategy. Using massed armor and aircraft known as blitzkrieg, the Germans avoided a rerun of their World War I lunge through Belgium.

This was not, of course, the only reason the French were defeated so rapidly and decisively in 1940—poor French generalship was a factor as well—but it was a very important element in their defeat. Therefore, we must always realize that it is not simply the technology in and of itself, but also the willingness and ability of the society and its military leadership to use the technology to its maximum effect and to recognize the dynamic battlefield realities the new technologies and their new usages provide.

In subsequent chapters, we will be exploring each element in turn, but it is important to realize that these characteristics are, from the perspective of Mars:

1. constantly evolving
2. interlocking and interrelated
3. mutually reinforcing
4. relative, both in relation to others and to a temporal dimension
5. not confined by time or space

In short, although not a conceptual theriaca, these elements of success constitute a dynamic set of possibilities.[16] The Template of Mars thus provides not just a conceptual framework, but an ongoing mind-set. It is also important to recognize that although the impact and duration of particular elements may change or seem to change from era to era, the efficacy of the Template as an analytic device does not change.

In the example given above, the French made a number of strategic and tactical mistakes in the run-up to World War II. Those mistakes turned out to be magnified by the Germans' ability to take advantage of them. According to the Template, the French rightly assumed there would be another war. Unfortunately for them, they failed at another aspect of the Template: receptivity to innovation—relative to their enemy Germany.

Whereas the Germans were moving ahead with new battle plans to avoid the type of defensive, trench warfare of World War I, the French planned in large measure for just such a war. The heavy fortifications known as the Maginot Line were designed to refight World War I and once again bleed the Germans to defeat.

The French were not unmindful of the potential for mobile warfare, however, and indeed their Plan D (named for the Dyle River in Belgium) called for their advancing into Belgium to meet the Wehrmacht there. But when the Germans refused to repeat their von Schlieffen Plan from World War I and make Belgium their primary maneuver area, the French did not adapt.

Instead, the Germans attacked through the Ardennes, flanking the Maginot Line and preventing the French from putting Plan D into action.

Robert A. Doughty rightly points out that the French did not perceive how much warfare had changed since 1918, "Yet their errors came less from their stupidity, incompetence, or decadence than from their having come up with the wrong formula for the problem that appeared in 1940."[17]

CAUTIONS IN THE USE OF THE TEMPLATE

As we proceed further in our examination of "The Template of Mars," a few cautions are in order:

Caution: Trying to analyze war in a moral vacuum is not only difficult, it also cuts against many of our cherished preoccupations with "just" versus "unjust" wars. Even an attempt to do this makes many uncomfortable, and it is painful to move outside our moral comfort zone to even try. It is much easier to be against all wars—or almost all wars. But just because the Template is "uncomfortable" even "unlikeable" or even "horrible" does not mean that it is "wrong" as an analytical tool.

Caution: We are not equating success in war with moral superiority. In the nineteenth century, Europeans were fond of calling Africa "The Dark Continent," and ascribing to its peoples dire practices, uncivilized behavior, and values unworthy of enlightened humans. Yet it was Europeans—with the considerable assistance of many of the Africa peoples—who promoted and sustained the horrific trans-Atlantic slave trade that took the lives of and displaced as many as 20 million people. It is true that many African tribes basically only had a choice of participating in the slave trade as a victim or a perpetrator, but others participated in order to improve their competitive position vis-à-vis their hereditary opponents.

And it was the Germans in Southwest Africa and German East Africa who slaughtered thousands of Herero and Maji Majis. So too, it was European-on-European violence that brought the world to calamity in World War I and World War II, and it was a European people, the Germans under Nazi rule, who conceived and actualized the Holocaust. Much of what went on in Africa pales by comparison to those slaughters, indicating that cultural aspersions do not help us understand the true nature of warfare.

Caution: We are not talking about courage or about successful warrior-hood. This is true even though we believe that individual skill in battle and personal fortitude in the face of danger is what true warrior-hood is about. Yet, success in warfare often has less to do with individual values or abilities. Warriors against warriors create fine combats, and often produce heroic contests and literature, but warriors are at a significant disadvantage against soldiers. Long-term success in war requires making soldiers out of warriors, melding the courage of individuals to the cohesion and discipline of the unit and multiplying the power of the individual warrior, those who are trained to fight in battle.

Of interest in this regard, there are almost as many versions of warrior heaven as there are warrior societies, but perhaps the Viking warrior heaven, Valhalla, best exemplifies the values of true warrior-hood for its own sake rather than fighting for a larger cause or purpose.[18]

To the Viking warrior, there was a glorious life after death, but only if that warrior died with a weapon in his hand. Success in war did not matter for entry into heaven. Advancing one's clan or ethnic group did not matter. Advancing the Norse religion did not. To the Viking warriors, only death in combat mattered. After the battle, the Norse god of war, Odin, sent the helmeted maiden Valkyries to bring the dead warriors to the hallowed hall of the selected heroes.

Once in Valhalla, the warriors spent their days fighting and again killing each other; but at sundown, they all came back to life and could drink, eat, fornicate, and swap warrior stories with each other. The next days were a repeat of the previous ones, on and on, until the final judgment day when the dreaded Fenris wolf was freed and Odin led the warriors into a final battle.

Caution: We are not talking about the ability to make war or to fight or to love fighting. Despite the classical tradition, great individual warriors do not necessarily win most wars. As strange as it may appear, loving war fighting does not seem to be an essential for success in the world of Mars. Rather, we are looking at the notion of "soldier-hood." For, as Victor Hanson points out, there is a profound difference between a "warrior" and "a soldier."[19] Warriors are brave but fight as individuals, whereas soldiers fight as a collective body. In this regard, Hanson is particularly impressed with the "citizen warrior" in the Western tradition going back to the early Greeks.

Unfortunately, Hanson is so anxious to stake out the primacy of the European and American military core values (of discipline and technological innovation) that in one of his primary examples, the Zulu wars of the nineteenth century, he misses the independent variables that show the Template at work.

For example, Hanson dismisses the degree of discipline inherent in the Zulu way of war, a discipline required to envelop and hold the enemy in place. Such discipline is what enabled them to build their nation in the first place. Moreover, he fails to see the relative nature of the Zulu position. The Zulu accent on discipline, technological innovation, and sustained ruthlessness is what enabled them to triumph over their African adversaries and create a nation of a million where only a few thousand once stood. Hanson refuses to give them credit for this accomplishment of soldier-hood. However, it is their relative inferiority (when compared to the later

British invaders) in terms of military innovation (both their weapons and the process of using them), not their absolute inferiority that ultimately dooms them.

Overall, Hanson places a great stock in the superior dynamics of Western, capitalist societies that enhanced their ability to wage war successfully. This is a most valid point. However, it is Western capitalist societies' adhesion to the imperatives of the Template of Mars that gave them such an advantage. The case being made here is that it is the Template, not Western culture, that was and is the independent variable. When other societies followed the Template, they were successful because of it.

At the same time, it is important to note that in the eyes of Mars, there can be a blending of the virtues of soldier-hood and warrior-hood. There have been many human cultures (from Sparta to Nazi Germany or Imperial Japan) that glorified war and particularly honored war fighters since this joined the notions of "soldier-hood" and "warrior-hood" together to give them heightened societal value.

Caution: We are not talking about brave fighting men and women; we are talking about a commitment to the profound notion: "There will always be another war." Here we are simply agreeing with Thucydides when he said "Peace is an armistice in a war that is continuously going on." This is such a chilling and profound notion that it frightens us all, but it does get Mars's undying attention.

In fact, Mars demands nothing less. Some societies seek to create a sharp demarcation between needing soldiers for war, and constantly preparing those soldiers for war, as we will see in chapter eight. Mars appears to consistently reward these societies. This is true no matter how many people ignore the insightful assertion of George Orwell, "People sleep peaceably in their beds at night only because rough men stand ready to do violence on their behalf."

Caution: We are not about glorifying European values and promoting a Eurocentric analysis. The horrible price paid for European hegemony by the end of the nineteenth century was not just paid in other parts of the world. One has to see World War I and World War II in this context. Yet as the war in Kosovo showed, today the European countries do not have the ability or the will to stop wars and impose peace in Europe without a substantial U.S. presence. As Europe passes from the favor of Mars (as well as from favoring Mars), we ask, what are the reasons for this decline? Does it have anything to do with the inability of more and more Europeans to see war in a moral vacuum?

Caution: We are not talking about fixed places in history. Many societies and people can produce good warriors and wage successful wars in one age but fail to succeed in another. There is no reason why a people once skilled in war craft and adherence to Mars cannot lose that commitment, or why a people thought to be unskilled and incapable of sustained success in war cannot make that commitment and become successful in warfare. All it takes is a willingness to dedicate the country to the dictates of Mars.

Therefore, it is the willingness and ability to follow the dictates known as the Template of Mars that determine which states rise and which states fall at various periods throughout their history.

John Sowell gives us powerful examples of this dynamic aspect of the Template of Mars.[20] England was conquered by Rome and then by the Normans, but the English eventually went on to acquire and rule a huge empire. In 1914, the British Empire was the largest the world had ever seen, encompassing one quarter of the human race and one quarter of the earth's surface. At its height, just before its decline, it occupied an area six times the size of the Roman Empire and involved 500 million people, 400 million of whom were on the Indian subcontinent. And only a hundredth of that territory was the British Isles.

Much credit has been given to the rise of Britain as an industrial power, the first to undergo the industrial revolution, but first it had a commercial revolution. When Napoleon dismissively called it a "nation of shopkeepers," he missed the importance of capital formation for subsequent investment in both arms and industrial facilities, as well as infrastructure such as the railroad built in 1830. He also ignored the tremendous advantage the British already possessed in terms of naval technology and training. These technological advances are but one element that helps to explain why Britain won the Napoleonic and other wars.

There was also the question of British superiority in technological entrepreneurship. Subsequent chapters will highlight the role of capital, especially entrepreneurial capital, in the scheme of Mars, but here is a useful place to introduce it.

Indeed, the revolution in force projection that married the cannon to the ship and developed the broadside strategy to sink opponents without boarding them is seen by some scholars as only half of the explanation for European success. For others, such as Dennis Showalter, that force projection "rode an ebb and flow tide of mercantilism."[21]

Countries, peoples, and empires can also move in the opposite direction from the teachings of Mars. The words of Francesco Petrarca in 1360 capture the essence of military change and the fortunes of those who can adapt:

In my youth the Britons . . . were taken to be the meekest of the (Non-Italians). Today they are a fiercely bellicose nation. They have overturned the ancient military glory of the French by victories so numerous that they, who were once inferior to the wretched Scots, have reduced the entire kingdom of France by fire and sword.[22]

Or take the case of the Italians themselves. The Roman subjugation of Britain (beginning with Caesar's raiding expedition and leading to the golden age of the Roman Empire from 96 CE to 180 CE) represented the apex of Rome's imperial power. Much later, the Romans withdrew from Britain early in the fifth century to meet the growing military threats to the declining Empire on the Continent.

For much of their imperial period, the Romans were simply better organized and better equipped, better disciplined, and more committed to sustained ruthlessness than were their local adversaries, including the Britons. But if we look at Italy in the twelfth and thirteenth centuries, we see it as weak, divided, and subject to almost constant invasions and attacks. And if we fast-forward to Italy in 1940, we see the results of their continuing failure to follow the Template of Mars.

Symbolically, many Italian ships of World War II ended up being "sunk in port" as their naval war museum in Rome illustrates. In room after room, there are pictures of lovely-looking battleships, cruisers, and destroyers. On many is a small notation, "Sunk in Port." If one looks at the performance of Italy in World Wars I and II, one will be stunned at how poorly that country did, obviating any meaningful comparison with their Roman ancestors. This was not simply true for the Italian Navy, it was duplicated in even greater defeats by the Italian Army in virtually every theater in which they fought: the Horn of Africa, North Africa, the Balkans, Russia, Italy, and the Greek Islands.[23]

From the point of view of the Template of Mars, these wide ranging defeats occurred not because Italian soldiers' war-making DNA wasn't up to the task, but because its political systems—first the Royalist, then the Fascist—had great military deficiencies; and both failed to adapt to the new demands of war. The Italian military of the World War II era was deficient in many areas: especially in terms of capital, military leadership, training and organization, strategy, tactics, and logistics. According to MacGregor Knox, though, there was "not a radical decline in efficiency from 1918 to 1940 . . . but rather a continuity of radical deficiencies in military culture."[24] He sees a long list of intertwined deficiencies that were overwhelming in their impact on the ability of Italy to wage modern war:

> Parochialism; fragile military traditions; shortages of key technical skills; energy and raw material dependence; the regime's inability to mobilize effectively what resources existed; the incompetence and venality of industry; the deficiency in military culture that prevented the armed forces from imagining, much less preparing for, modern war; strategic myopia; dissipation of effort; passivity; logistical ineffectiveness and dependence; and the armed forces' greater or lesser degrees of operational and tactical incapacity were so interwoven that separating them analytically is a thankless task.[25]

Thus one could say that the leaders of the Italian armed forces—as well as of Italian society—avoided modernity in terms of military professionalism, and by not paying attention to the demands of the Template of Mars and all of its dictates, the Italians paid a terrible price, suffering over 440,000 dead (more than Great Britain) as whole divisions disappeared in Russia and North Africa or were killed by Albanians, Greeks, Americans, Poles, British, and later by the Germans.

Caution: This work focuses on the Template explaining the winning of wars within commonsensical parameters. As stated elsewhere in this volume, Iceland could have the most highly motivated armed forces in the world, but it could not defeat China if China didn't want to be defeated. So too, we have avoided looking at contests between states with wildly divergent gross domestic products, except to focus in chapter six on the importance of protecting that gross domestic product of any size from civilian overuse. Obviously a larger gross domestic product gives an entity the opportunity to marshal more scarce human and natural resources than a smaller one, but the intent of the leaders of the polity (and its military) makes a great deal of difference, often to the point of being an independent variable.

So too, the analysis that follows tends to isolate side one against side two in terms of a single entity. Obviously, a state can form an alliance that can either enhance its inherent power or reduce it.

For example, in the case of the Italians in World War II cited earlier, their presence in the alliance with Nazi Germany could have been an asset. Instead, it can well be argued that Italy on the side of Germany was a net detriment, leading as it did to a powerful strategic drag on the German military by getting it involved in noncritical sectors such as Yugoslavia, Albania, Greece, and North Africa and diluting its strategic focus, making it easier, not harder, for the Allies to defeat Germany.

Conversely, the ability of the American revolutionaries to make a wartime alliance with France was central to their eventual success. But alliance politics and the power enhancement and power diminution that it can involve lie beyond the scope of this work.

Caution: The Template of Mars is first and foremost a conceptual framework. While it is designed to provide insights into future wars and thus can have some hermeneutic properties, the Template of Mars recognizes the ultimate unpredictability of the *course* of any particular war. As Alan Beyerchen so ably warns us in demonstrating the nonlinear character of war, it must always be remembered that unpredictability in war inevitably stems from the Clausewitzian triad of "interaction, friction and chance."[26]

Finally, it should be noted that over the vast sweep of time, Mars (as the analytical concept), however, rewards those who follow a number of categorical imperatives over time: a successful state or people must have all the requisite qualities of the Mars portfolio, not just one or two. All the variables of the Template are relative throughout time and space, depending on the enemy of the moment and the future. All are dynamic and often rapidly changing. All are interrelated so that being good, or even great, at one imperative is not enough, you have to have all seven working together.

A great deal of writing on war tends to place European cultural forces as the independent variable, with their discipline, weapons, or technology superiority and/or will determining the outcome.[27] But often a reverse reading of the situation can prove insightful.

Take the example of the disastrous British landing at Gallipoli in 1915 during World War I. Most of the literature points to the lack of planning, divided command, and flawed strategy and tactics on the part of the British, or it focuses on British temerity in failing to force the Dardanelles with naval units.[28] Yet, a closer examination of that battle in its totality yields a more balanced perspective. British mistakes, errors, and blunders might have been compensated for if the Turks had not, in this battle and the run-up to it at least, followed the key ingredients of the Template of Mars.

The Turks had high levels of discipline, despite being technologically inferior in many instances (although their minefields were of high enough quality to cancel out much of the British naval advantage). They also had the superb leadership of Ataturk. The Turkish will to win proved to be superior, and, always believing that there would be another war, the Turks had heavily refortified the Dardanelles and the Gallipoli Peninsula after their defeats in the Balkan wars of the late nineteenth century.[29]

In the process of exploring the various elements of the Template, we shall attempt to abstract, wherever possible, war from its political, social, and cultural contexts by accenting these elements themselves and then looking for examples of these variables rather than trying to apply cultural values to those examples. This cannot always be done, and many will continue to make the case that culture is the independent variable, but in the chapters that follow, we shall attempt to show that cultures can change their military weapons and styles when faced with the demands of the Template.

For the reader, the use of the Template with all of its dimensions can provide opportunities to examine the notion of historical malleability and to see how one group or another could have changed history by more carefully adhering to its tenets. Conversely it can demonstrate how another group would have been less successful in a given situation had it not more faithfully followed those tenets than did its adversary.

A NON-EUROCENTRIC APPLICATION OF THE TEMPLATE

Let us look at one non-Eurocentric example to see how all these elements can come together and mesh to give one side a decided advantage over those who do not accent their efficacy.

Many European accounts of the Mongols treat them as savage anomalies, periodic eruptions coming out of the east, their depredations remembered and made mythic for centuries after they occurred.[30] Yet the Mongols ruled a huge area, much larger than that of the United States, and controlled a great variety of populations for seven centuries. Mongol war craft and treatment of their own soldiers were decades if not centuries ahead of their European counterparts.

Ironically, Marco Polo's visit to China was possible only because of the Mongol peace that enabled merchants to travel from Europe to the Mongol court.[31] In fact, for much of his travels within the empire of Kublai Khan, Marco Polo carried with him a *paiza*, the royal Mongol passport "that seemed to confer magical powers of protection" and that enabled him to travel far and wide unmolested and greatly assisted.[32]

Coming out of the Gobi desert in the twelfth century, the Mongols show how successful a power can be when following all the elements of the Template of Mars. Led first by Temujin (Temuchin), who became Genghis (Chingis) Khan (1162–1227), the Mongols were to end up being a historical astonishment. Temujin, like Chaka the ama-Zulu, created an army and led it to unify a nation out of the Mongolian tribes before setting out to conquer neighbors and later those living thousands of miles away.

I am indebted to Thomas Conlan for pointing out the importance of Genghis's integrative philosophy and activities, which made a workable amalgamation of so many different people and resulted in conquered peoples and their warriors being integrated into the "Mongol people."[33] Conlan observes that we need to think of the term "Mongol" as a cultural rather than an ethnic or biological affiliation after the original amalgamation of Mongol tribes early in their expansion. Anyone who acted like a Mongol and swore to obey a Great Khan could become a Mongol.

Some groups were assimilated, others broken up entirely and incorporated into the Mongol tribes. By contrast, the Kirghiz, who joined the Mongols, maintained some sense of identity because they so quickly and willingly joined the Mongols. Moreover, the religious toleration of the animistic Mongols often paid off militarily, as in the 1238 Battle of Baghdad where Shiite Muslims and Nestorian Christians aided the forces of Hulegu.

No army in history ever won more battles or captured more territories.[34] The Mongols defeated the peoples of what are now China, Afghanistan,

Armenia, Georgia, Poland, Hungary, India, Korea, Germany, the Ottomans, India, Iraq, Pakistan, Yemen, Persia, Russia, and much of the Eurasian Muslim world, and they ended up dominating the Eurasian heartland for 400 years. It was only Mongolian succession crises that saved Europe, with the deaths of Genghis (1227), Ogadei (1241), and Mangku (1259) calling the Mongol armies back to Central Asia after they were threatening the heart of Europe, having already defeated all the European armies which dared face them.

Similarly, the Mongols ruled Russia for 240 years (1240 to 1480), and they threatened to conqueror many of the countries in Europe until the fifth supreme khan, Kublai, became interested in China and in expanding his empire in Asia. Their Tartar affiliates controlled Southern Ukraine and Crimea until the eighteenth century. Let us take a cursory look at the Mongols' relation with the Template of Mars, taking each component of it in turn.

Superior Technological Entrepreneurship

Contrary to popular imagination and much writing over the centuries, the Mongol "hordes" were often armies of only 20,000–40,000 men, but Mongol discipline, firepower, superb tactics, and strategy made it seem as if there were many more of them. Also, the armies the Mongols defeated naturally claimed after the fact that they had faced much larger formations than they had and that these huge numbers were solely responsible for the Mongol victories. In fact, small groups of 500 or fewer Mongols could do great damage and have great success.

As an additional aid to mobility, the Mongols set up a vast network of post roads or "yams" with 10,000 men and 300,000 horses, each unit being responsible for twenty-five miles of trail, resulting in a safe universe that exceeded anything the Romans ever devised. It was said that "a virgin with a sack of gold could ride from one end of the empire to the other unmolested."

R. E. Dupuy and T. N. Dupuy make a strong case for the pacific condition of areas that fell to Mongol rule: "The Mongols absolutely forbade any continuation of local and internal squabbles in their conquered territory. Law and order were rigidly and ruthlessly maintained. As a consequence, regimented conquered regions were usually far more peaceful under the Mongol occupation than they had been before the invasion."[35]

The Mongol communications were the fastest in the world at the time and for hundreds of years afterward. For example, the Pony Express in America (1860–1861) never came close to the Mongols' daily distribution numbers and distances.

The recurved bow was the Mongols' major technological breakthrough, for it had a greater power-to-weight ratio than the Welsh/English longbow and was capable of very rapid fire. It was as effective as any weapon until the 1800s and the inventions of the repeating rifle. The Mongols also had light lacquered body armor with silk undershirts to help withdraw any subsequent wounding arrow.

Superior Discipline

At a time when Europeans were fighting as individuals or small groups (conrois) of twenty to forty knights, the Mongols at times mastered huge formations of 40,000 highly disciplined troops whose training was constant year-round. The Mongols divided their army into units of ten, and if any one in that small unit surrendered or fled the battlefield, the entire unit would be executed. One of their favorite tactics was to pretend they were losing and retreat in order to lure their opponents into a killing zone where they would be surrounded. To do this successfully required great discipline, command, and control.

When not on military campaigns, all soldiers took part in "Great Hunts," a method of hunting called a *nerge*, which encompassed huge areas 80–100 miles wide. The area to be hunted was cordoned off and gradually constricted, with all animals inside killed. If any animals got through the cordon, the soldiers in the nearest units were punished.

Indeed, so central were these hunts to the Mongol military experience that in his later years, Genghis Khan continued to participate as an example. He had two serious falls in the hunts of 1223 and 1225, dying from injuries suffered in the latter.[36] Training during peacetime for the Mongols had many of the hallmarks of actual battle—discipline, danger, accuracy, cooperation, and coordination.

For his part, during his 1391 four-month struggle with Tokhtamish, Khan of the Golden Horde, Tamerlane stopped in the middle of his campaign to stage a "Great Hunt" in order to replenish his troops with fresh meat after they had exhausted the supplies they had brought with them. In the aftermath of the subsequent feasting from the hunt, Tamerlane and his forces crushed Tokhtamish.

The use of the nerge as an actual battle tactic is documented by Timothy May, who notes that in the Mongol invasion of Russia in 1237 it was used to encircle a number of Russian smaller cities and drive their populations into the center, spreading panic and undermining the defense of the larger cities.[37]

The Mongol emphasis on speed, great horsemanship, and deception in battle was to become their hallmark. They much preferred to win by trickery, feints, and deception than outright combat. Whenever possible, they used some newly accumulated allies to do the close hand-to-hand fighting or to storm the city walls. Contrary to many accounts, the Mongols much preferred to use nonviolent means to achieve their objectives rather than to fight for their conquests.

The Mongols' devotion to military discipline was critical to their ability to defeat their many enemies, almost all of whom greatly outnumbered them.

Receptivity to Innovation

The Mongols proved to be adaptive and receptive to innovation, adopting any technology necessary to win. For example, the Mongols saw that iron embedded in leather armor protected better against arrows and spears, so they adopted it. Also, when they were initially frustrated by the walled cities of the Chin, they soon adopted siege equipment (such as the catapult and ballista), made it highly mobile to fit the Mongol style of warfare, included Chinese engineers in their war plans, and eventually were able to penetrate and overcome cities everywhere. The Mongols also copied the Chinese in their use of gunpowder in bamboo to blow up city gates.[38]

Wherever they went, whenever possible, the Mongols simply captured and utilized the equipment and personnel skilled in its use and integrated them into their army. Confronted with new technology, the Mongols recruited local artisans (first Chinese and later Arabs and other peoples) and made them part of their armies. For his part, Tamerlane reused captured war elephants from India as well as "Greek fire," a deadly combination of naphtha and a petroleum base.

Later, in the sixteenth century, when Zahīr-ud-Dīn Muhammad, "Babur the Tiger," was fighting to subdue the Delhi sultanate, he integrated musket fire and especially cannons to defeat Ibrahim Lodhi in the crucial 1526 Battle of Panipat. His demi-cannon weighed 6,000 pounds and shot a 30-pound ball, while his "whole" cannon weighed 7,000 pounds and fired a 40-pound ball and his cannon "royal" weighed 8,000 pounds and fired a 60-pound ball. These cannons were particularly effective against the elephants of the Indian forces. Babur's skillful integration of firearms where appropriate again underscores continued Mongol willingness to adopt in order to succeed in warfare.

But equally important, Genghis Khan adopted a policy of religious toleration and promoted absorption of conquered peoples into the Mongol fighting force. He also revolutionized warfare by fighting through the winter and created a most modern army, closer to those of the twentieth century than those of the Europeans of that era. The Mongol army had unity of command, boasting very coordinated activity and a sophisticated but simple signal system of flags that enabled the leader in any particular battle to exercise control over his forces in a way not seen since the heyday of the Roman legions.

The Mongol army was also a national army, a national professional army. The empire was a holistic enterprise in which all males were considered to be in the army (from ages fifteen to seventy) except priests, physicians, and those who washed the bodies of the dead. Genghis Khan organized his soldiers into *tumens* (10,000 men), which were in turn divided into units of 1,000, 100, and eventually 10 men (an *arbat*).

Unlike contemporaneous European armies, the Mongols placed enormous emphasis on intelligence gathering. Before they invaded Europe, for example, they scouted it for two years, and used diplomacy and statecraft of the highest order to put themselves in position to win their next war.

The Mongol intelligence-gathering system was something the European countries would not achieve until centuries later, for as Tamerlane would subsequently put it, "One skillful plan can perform the service of a hundred thousand warriors" and he would send spies on ahead years in advance of his armies.[39]

For generation after generation of Mongol rulers, tricking the enemy was even more satisfying than beating them in battle, as the Mongols echoed the belief of Machiavelli as stated in *The Discourses on Livy*: "Although the use of fraud in every action is detestable, nonetheless in managing war it is a praiseworthy and glorious thing, and he who overcomes the enemy with fraud is praised as much as the one who overcomes it with force."[40]

Sustained but Controlled Ruthlessness

Perhaps until the American XXI Bomber Command under General Curtis LeMay burned Japan to the ground during 1944–1945, the Mongols set the gold standard for ruthlessness in warfare. When necessary, they routinely boiled human captives to render incendiary fat when they wanted to burn out an opponent's city. They even catapulted plague victims over the walls to use biological warfare to their advantage.

In fact, the earliest recorded use of the bubonic plague in warfare was during the siege of Kaffa in the Crimea by the Tartars in 1347.[41] After the outbreak of the plague in China in 1334, the "Black Death" moved inexorably west. In 1346, the Tartars, backed by the Venetians, invested the Genoese trading city of Kaffa. The city of Kaffa soon felt its effects during the siege in 1347 as the Mongols catapulted the bodies of plague victims into the city. Eventually, Genoese ships, returning to Italy brought with them the "Black Death," which would reduce the population of Europe by one-third or more.

The Mongols were truly relentless, keeping up attacks continuously and giving opponents no respite until they succumbed. The Mongols used captives as shields to walk ahead of them toward fortified positions so their opponents would use up arrows and crossbow bolts by killing non-Mongols.

Yet cities and rulers were almost always given a chance to accept the overlordship of the Khan. Usually only if the Mongolian ambassadors were harmed or the city or ruler in question refused to submit did the most draconian of punishments result. Then the Mongols attacked with no holds barred, often turning the defeated areas into "Cities of Sorrow" by killing every inhabitant and razing the city to the ground.

Moreover, as their reputation for extreme cruelty and widespread massacres spread far and wide, they made great use of these techniques in order to discourage resistance from the next target and to ensure that their subsequent foes saw giving up as a better alternative than fighting the Mongols. Contrary to popular opinion, the Mongols loved to win battles and take cities without fighting, by trickery, by reputation, and by cunning. They delighted in getting inside the enemies' heads to confuse, frighten, and outwit them.

Genghis Khan called himself "The Scourge of God." After seeing him destroy whole cities and all of their inhabitants, some of his future opponents vowed to fight to the death, but many more surrendered. In that superstitious age, it was very easy to believe that he was, in fact, "The Scourge of God." When he sacked Bukhara in 1221, for example, he declared, "I am God's punishment for your sins."[42] The dead, dying, and enslaved could hardly have doubted it. Certainly the inhabitants of nearby towns did not want further examples that showed whether he was divine-sent or was not.

A hundred years after the death of Genghis, Tamerlane was born and took the Tartars to great conquests in Central Asia and the Middle East. Like Genghis, he accepted the fealty of people without bloodshed wherever possible, but when challenged, he destroyed whole cities, killing and enslaving all of the inhabitants and planting barley all over the ground where the cities had been.[43]

Protection of Capital from People and Rulers

Most Mongol leaders shared the spoils of war with their followers and invested scarce resources in new techniques and equipment as required. Winning the battle and the war were paramount, not achieving personal wealth. In fact, Mongols were strictly forbidden from looting during battle. Indeed, the punishment for looting was the same as that for desertion: death. Once the battle had been won, spoils were available to all the winning troops. After the fighting was complete and punishment meted out, the Mongols turned to reconstruction and indirect rule, seeking to allow the captive peoples to become productive parts of the Mongol empire.

It is true that by the end of his life, Genghis had over 400 wives and massive horse herds, but he shared the wealth throughout his career and let nothing stand in the way of military success. Indeed, some scholars have pointed to his sharing of spoils as one of his major strengths; it served as an integrative mechanism for those who joined from other groups.[44] That is why indiscriminate pillaging of conquered peoples and cities was forbidden.[45] Tamerlane too was to make sure the spoils of conquest were divided among those who had fought.

Genghis also opened up the entire military enterprise, raising to command those who proved successful, regardless of their birth. In fact, the best of all the Mongol war leaders was Subutai, the son of a metal worker who advanced through the ranks until Genghis entrusted him with the command of huge armies. This was an unusual approach, and it served the Mongols well. Military careers open to talent meant that superior military process and leadership were rewarded and failed kinsmen were demoted. The best of the Mongol leaders would follow Genghis and his policy of military meritocracy.

Like Napoleon, Genghis issued a set of rules, the first Mongolian law code. He adopted the written script of the Uighurs so that the Mongols could become literate. He also insisted on something close to national health insurance to help disabled or impoverished old soldiers. At the end of their fighting career, Mongolian soldiers were infinitely better treated by their leaders than were their counterparts in Europe during the same time period.

The Mongolian army could travel self-sufficiently, which meant that each soldier had enough provisions on his three horses for several days of fighting. Mongol horses were very well trained as foals, and each warrior brought three horses to battle so they would always have one that was fresh.

The Mongol empires also were famous for making trade secure and thus providing their rulers and their military with an ongoing source of capital for future wars: "The Mongol hegemony had fostered a relatively peaceful environment over much of Asia and had reduced bandit harassment of caravans. With less fear of plunder, the costs incurred by the merchants were lowered and became more predictable."[46]

This expanded trade produced considerable dividends. The more stable the economic climate, the more predictable the trade, the greater the amount of capital that would be available to the Mongols to finance the next military campaign.

Superior Will

Why did the Mongols fight? For the spoils of war, for ethnic and "national" pride, and later for and with a sense of invincibility. They believed they were "Heaven Sent" and had been placed on Earth to wage war continuously and successfully. The Mongol's will was thus enhanced by an amazing combination of religious inspiration and sheer professionalism.

In virtually every battle, the Mongol soldiers' will to win was more powerful than their opponents. The Mongols may have been suspicious about the workings of the universe, but when they went into battle, they expected to win, trained to win, and couldn't believe that they would lose. Indeed, the Mongols seldom did, except when fighting each other.

Justin Marozzi also observes that Tamerlane was skillful in masking his personal ambition and that of his warriors with the cloak of Islam, creating "ideological propulsion" that served him well.[47] This served to give their war making greater power.

Belief That There Will Always Be Another War

The belief that there would always be another war was, of course, the raison d'être for being a male Mongol. Warfare was their way of life. They were born into a culture where it was the only fit occupation for men and warrior-soldiers were the envy of the entire society. Their whole lives were built around war, and they expected to go to war again and again. Mongols didn't expect to lose, and they usually didn't.

They eventually conquered a territory much larger than the United States and held major portions of it for 400 years. They conquered the largest population in the world—the Chinese, and most of the rest of the Eurasian land mass.

To appreciate the scope of Mongol successes, one must accent the space-time continuum that includes Kublai Khan (1215–1294), Tamerlane (1336–1405), Babur the Tiger (1483–1530) and Akbar the Great (1542–1605). The latter two's triumphs with the First and Second Battle of Panipat (1526 and 1556) led to the Mongol takeover of the Delhi sultanate, a takeover that lasted until Bahadur Shah II, the last Mughal emperor, was deposed in 1858, bringing most of India under the direct rule of the British Crown.

John A. Lynn is most persuasive in arguing that the writings of Parker and Hanson, by failing to take into account the enormous success of the non-Western armies from the Central Asian steppes, greatly suffer from their omission.[48] He correctly points out that the Germanic tribes—the Huns, the Avars, and the Magyars—all preceded the Mongol invasions of Europe from the depths of the Eurasian land mass.

Note also that while it is convenient to look at the Mongols' leadership in terms of the great personages who followed Genghis, it was really the Mongol military organization that formed the basis for their subsequent success with many other leaders.

How did these acolytes of Mars eventually lose and the Mongol Empire decline? They were checked on some occasions: two attempted invasions of Japan (1274 and 1281) were thwarted, not just by typhoons but the resistance of the Japanese samurai, and the Mongols also failed to subdue Java (1292). The Mongols were also defeated in Vietnam and at the battles of Ain Jalut (1260) and Second Homs (1281) in the Middle East. Ironically, their defeat at Ain Jalut was caused by a short-term alliance of convenience between the Mamluks and Christian crusaders (who were themselves later defeated by the Mamluks).[49]

Eventually, the Black Death killed millions in the Mongol-controlled cities, but it was primarily the internal dynastic struggles among the Mongols, especially after the death of Mongke Khan in 1259 and later those of Tokhtamish and Tamerlane during the decade of 1385–1395, that ultimately weakened them. It was not until 1388, however, that the Ming dynasty defeated the Mongols and overthrew them in China.

When the Mongols were united and when they collectively worshiped at the feet of Mars, they were an unparalleled force, and their success in warfare was truly legendary. They followed the Template of Mars and were successful to a degree seldom duplicated in history. After Genghis, the most continuing threat to the Mongols' continued supremacy came from internal rivalries and the division of his vast empire after his death.

Kublai, for example, controlled the empire of the Chin, while others occupied Persia, Mongolia, and Russia. Their views, goals, and actions were often at odds, especially at the peripheries of their separate territories. Also, Amy Chua is quite persuasive that the further the various Mongol leaders strayed from Genghis Khan's inclusive, unifying, and absorptive model of tolerance, the more likely would be their subsequent failure to maintain their empire.[50]

But the Mongols firmly establish the non-Eurocentric applicability of the Template of Mars. In this way, the Mongols demonstrate that the Template of Mars transcends the familiar categories of "East" and "West" war.

2

Superior Weapons and Technology Entrepreneurship

You can't say civilization don't advance, however, for in every war they kill you in a new way.

—Will Rogers

Over time, Mars rewards societies that develop or acquire superior weapons, superior weapons technology, and superior industrial processes and then use them in making war. Here are a few obvious examples of peoples and their superior weapons and integration into warfare: The English at Crecy, Poitiers, and Agincourt in the fourteenth century, the Mongols in the thirteenth century, the Romans during the expansion of their empire, the Zulus in the early nineteenth century (but also the British against Zulus a few years later), the Japanese in 1905 (but also the Soviets against the Japanese in 1939), and the Prussians in the Austro-Prussian War of 1866.

During the American Civil War, the introduction of ironclad warships (although since both sides developed them at the same time, there was little net advantage to either side), repeating rifles and pistols, and even the revolutionary use of railroads all show the entrepreneurial impulse in warfare. It is important to point out, however, that this is not simply an advantage in terms of basic equipment, but also what has been integrated into weapons systems and the training necessary to take maximum advantage of the new weapon. Mars rewards those militaries and societies that are willing to try new weapons, that are willing to improve upon them, and that integrate their advantages into existing military practices by developing new tactics to optimize the new gear.

Also, sometimes the technological breakthrough is simply one of greater reliability, as in the automatic rifle known as the AK-47, which was far more reliable than the existing automatic rifles of the 1950s that jammed easily and were susceptible to dirt and mechanical difficulties. Because of its superior lethality, ease of operation, durability, and low cost, the AK-47 turned out to be the weapon of choice for insurgents and regular armies alike across the world for the next fifty years. Designed to be maintained by illiterate and untrained soldiers, it is easily copied and manufactured. Its subsequent spread throughout many of the world's failed states (and its ubiquity in those societies) often makes any subsequent national reconstruction very difficult, since so many are armed with it. It would be hard to argue that this mass dissemination (over 100 million produced) or "democratization of access" has not had a major effect on the world's military situation.[1]

As a military change agent, the AK-47 would be challenged by other more sophisticated weapons systems that also have dramatically altered the course of warfare or its prevention over the past decades: intercontinental ballistic missiles, nuclear submarines, the Nimitz class nuclear aircraft carrier, the B-52 bomber, the Soviet BMPI armored personnel carrier, the F-117 Stealth fighter/bomber, and many others.

But having technological breakthroughs is no guarantee they will be maximally utilized by the society's military. For example, the Chinese, Muslim, and Indian seafarers had far more advanced naval technology than their European counterparts in the fifteenth century, but it was the Europeans who pushed out of their hereditary sphere of influence by taking maximum advantage of that technology that had been discovered by others.[2]

NEW WEAPONS IN HISTORY

When we speak of "technology" we often have a modern, industrial, mechanical bias. We think of spears versus Maxim guns and repeating rifles. But we start here with a different example of superior military technology, for Mars rewards not superior technology in the abstract or overall, but within the battle space of a particular time and place.

In the eighteenth century, the Nguni-speaking peoples continued their centuries-old movement south from central Africa onto the high plains of southern Africa. Warfare among the competing ethnic groups or tribes usually consisted of warriors from each taking long, javelin-like spears, hurling them at the enemy and then closing in to do further battle with clubs and small shields. Usually most battles were over quickly, with one side running away as soon as they felt they were losing the battle.

However, in a small clan, the Ama-Zulu, there was a warrior chief who revolutionized warfare by developing a locally superior method that enabled his clan to grow from 1,000 or so people to over 1 million in a relatively short period of time through conquest and absorption.

Chaka the Zulu was his name, and his technological revolution was simple yet profound. He forced his warriors to cut their spears in half so they would no longer sail straight, far, or true through the air. Thus there was no point in throwing them. Instead, the warriors were forced to hold on to their shorter, stabbing spears. When the Zulus closed with the enemy, they still had their spears, so they were better armed when it actually mattered at the climax of the battle.[3]

In addition, Chaka developed a much larger cowhide shield to protect his warriors from the initial spear throws of his opponents. These new shields also served to protect his warriors in the hand-to-hand combat that followed. Arranged in a strong line with overlapping shields, the Zulus were able to stab in between the shields with great effect to destroy their opponents.

Moreover, taking his ideas from the very cattle upon which his people depended for their livelihood, Chaka also developed a battle formation with the "head" and the "chest" of the steer moving forward to confront the main line of defense while its "horns" went around the flanks and encircled the enemy so they could not escape after they had been defeated. Adapted from the image of a bull, this formation was to prove revolutionary and devastatingly effective in the warfare of southern Africa, not only in defeating enemies in battle but in capturing large numbers of prisoners. Zulu tactics and their weapons thus blended to make a far more powerful military process with which to win battles.

Chaka's simple, but revolutionary, set of war-making changes, and the war craft that subsequently developed from them, enabled the Zulus to defeat dozens of enemies. Additionally, under Chaka's integration strategy, defeated enemy warriors could join the Zulu nation (or be killed, for Chaka was not at all averse to bloodletting). Thus, over time, the nation grew in size and military power.

Combined, these new weapons and new tactics changed the nature of warfare throughout southern Africa. The Zulus are believed to be the first of the Nguni-speaking peoples to have maintained a standing professional army.[4] While other tribes soon copied these innovations, none were ever able to defeat the Zulus decisively. It was not superior technology alone that explains the rise of the Zulus; it was the driving genius of Chaka to turn the new weapons into a viable tactical and strategic innovation.

Indeed, the Zulus defeated the British in the later Battle of Isandlwana in 1879, and were themselves only overcome when the British brought their enormous technological advantages of field artillery, Maxim guns, and larger and more tightly disciplined formations into play against them in subsequent battles.

In this case, we can see the relative aspect of technology in war and the Template of Mars. The Zulus had superior military technology versus their Nguni neighbors, but eventually were at a technological disadvantage when they came up against the British.

Much earlier, the wheeled chariot that carried an archer dominated the Late Bronze Age (1550–1200 BCE) in Asia Minor. It was the centerpiece of military force projection for the Assyrians, the Egyptians, and the Hittites. Around 1200 BCE, however, the Sea People began entering the region from the Balkans. They arrived in the eastern Mediterranean with new weapons, new tactics, and a new warrior class.

Armed with long swords, circular shields, and most important, light javelins, these invaders used their javelins to kill and wound the horses of the charioteers, greatly reducing their mobility and leaving them vulnerable to infantry attacks.[5] Moreover, the Sea People were ethnically diverse, suggesting a military revolution that was able to get different peoples into using the new technologies. This interplay between new weapons, new styles of warfare, and political change is a constant and important theme throughout the history of warfare.

The Romans and Mongols, among many others, were also very adept at developing or acquiring superior weaponry and using it. The Romans adopted the short, heavy, double-sided sword of the Spanish tribes and increased the size of their shields to cover their soldiers in the hand-to-hand fighting that was so deadly to Rome's opponents. The heavy sword with its capability of lopping off limbs and heads was terrifying in action. They also replaced the fourteen-foot-long spear, which was so essential a weapon in the Macedonian heavy infantry phalanx, with several lighter javelins (known as *pila*) that could be thrown from afar and that bent on contact so they could not be thrown back.

The technological progression of weapons throughout history is thus seen to have a life of its own. However, it is what Jeff Selinger calls "superior technological entrepreneurship," delineating not just the possession of weapons but also the ability or the desire to integrate them into one's armed forces, that is the controlling factor of superiority. The society and its political and military leaders must *want* to use the new technology and be willing to risk opposition in order to ensure that they are adopted by their armed forces. It is the "entrepreneurship" that is so vital to the process of upgrading one's military in an ongoing way.

Often it is a matter of seeing the advantage of the new weapons and deploying them first. For example, Ben Kiernan points out that the adoption of the Ming-dynasty technological revolution at the end of the fourteenth century by the Dai Viet (including war rockets using bamboo rather than iron, musket volley fire, and flame throwers) enabled them to crush their long-term adversaries, the Champa. It was precisely because they were open to the new weapons and their integration into Viet war making that they succeeded.[6]

For Mars, every new weapon and weapons system seems to morph into another more lethal adoption, or to provoke a counterdevelopment from one's opponent.

THE SPREAD OF WAR TECHNOLOGY

Many writers such as Victor Hanson and Geoffrey Parker have pointed out that the armed forces of the West have always relied on superior technology, usually to compensate for inferior numbers. Yet the West has not always enjoyed universal superiority, and in fact often has adapted weapons from other cultures for their own use. For example, the highly effective siege engine, the trebuchet, was invented in the fourth century BCE in China. Later it came to Greece and Rome, but was then lost as a technology in Europe until the Crusaders again encountered it in the Middle East.[7]

Also, until the advent of musketry volleys and field artillery in the early seventeenth century, the recurved bow used by horse archers all over Asia proved far more effective than any Western weaponry. It enabled Asiatic people such as the Mongols to defeat their enemies, including those in the West when the Mongols invaded the West's battle space. Likewise, the stirrup (which made possible the viability of the heavily armed mounted feudal knight of the Middle Ages) and gunpowder were invented in the East.

Across the world, other societies were exposed to firearms, but many chose to disregard their war-changing potential. They simply didn't use firearms long enough to start a revolution. Because the introduction of guns would destroy the existing social and military hierarchy of the battlefield and would have replaced the military elites, the military in many societies (such as Japan and China) spurned their widespread use, whereas in European countries guns were to play a central role.

Or if these other societies used them, they did not fully appreciate the need to develop a weapons system for using them. When the British fought in Burma, for example, the Burmese had not only swords and spears, but also firearms in the form of matchlocks and flintlocks. However, the individual Burmese soldiers were expected to make their own gunpowder as opposed to having the army supply it, thereby drastically reducing its effectiveness. Clearly the new weapons had not been adequately integrated into Burmese war making.

Societies and their militaries that adopted firearms had to be receptive to change, otherwise the military would resist using them. One military open to innovation was the Almoravids in the late sixteenth century. Starting from what is now Morocco, they launched an expedition against the savanna empire of Songhai in 1590. Led by Jucar Pasha and his 2,500 musketeers and 1,500 cavalrymen, and armed with a few cannons, they defeated the much larger forces (20,000) of Songhai commanded by Askia Ishaq on March 12, 1591, thus breaking the centuries-long hold of the savanna kingdoms over the very lucrative gold and salt trade routes of the western Sahara.[8]

By contrast, in the West, the Europeans made the most out of gunpowder and cannons, and married both to the fort and to the ship. Here, as Geoffrey Parker points out, there was a great deal of competition among European countries that led to advances in gunpowder weapons.[9] Parker believes that it was the competition itself that spread the military revolution, first across Europe and then across the globe.

Especially when added to the steamship (invented at the end of the eighteenth century but perfected in the nineteenth century), gunpowder weapons became formidable. The heavy naval gun could now travel up rivers deep inland into India, China, Burma, and Africa. Cannons married to ships changed the face of human history and resulted in a huge revolution in force projection. European imperialism depended on this revolution in order to maximize their international power.

In fact, although the states of the West seem to have often shown themselves extremely willing to adapt to new military technology, it is, as Parker notes, only after 1500 that we see a big explosion in that weaponry entrepreneurship. Yet even in the closed, medieval societies of Europe, new weapons of war were readily assimilated by those who practiced warfare the most.

This veneration of weapons and fighting occurred despite the efforts of the Catholic Church to ban the crossbow and to eliminate fighting on holy days and Sundays. Those who worshiped Mars were impervious to the counterdemands of a more peaceful god. Instead it has been suggested that the Crusades were an attempt on the part of Pope Urban II to give the Christian warriors an outlet for their violence beyond their European kingdoms.

Whether the new inventions of warfare came from inside their societies or outside, the Western countries have often been receptive to military innovation and technological upgrades, and this helps to explain European supremacy over many of their contemporaneous adversaries.

Moreover, by the end of the fifteenth century, the Portuguese were able to sweep around Africa and into the Indian Ocean. Along the way they crushed Swahili city-states, defeated Arab and Indian fleets, and ended up controlling the Indian Ocean. The Portuguese were later themselves defeated successively by the Dutch and English, who had taken that naval revolution to new levels with more rapidly firing naval weapons and superior discipline, which produced a distinct advantage for these later arrivals.

Peter Padfield, in his useful *Maritime Supremacy and the Opening of the Western Mind*, suggests moreover that "In the great wars of modern history, maritime powers have always prevailed over land-based empires . . . because of their liberty, flexibility and enterprise."[10]

Of course, one of the negative features—from the point of view of the rest of the world at least—is that the West, or at least many people in the West, equated technological superiority with racial and cultural superiority (Social Darwinism). The Template would say that during the period of imperial expansion, Westerners were more adroit and successful at worshiping Mars, not because they were "better" due to their cultural values.

THE RISKS OF ENTREPRENEURSHIP IN WAR

There is another dimension to technological advantage that is often overlooked: adopting new technology means taking risks and paying a great cost. Societies and militaries must be willing to underwrite often great expenses. Therefore, there must be a willingness on the part of civilian and military authorities to become weapons entrepreneurs.

One example studied by John Keegan is particularly telling: during the American Civil War with the arrival of the ironclad ship the *Monitor* and its competitor, the *Merrimac*, the admirals of the British Royal Navy saw that the age of sail (which had lasted 400 years) was now over.[11] In terms of military technology, the British suddenly went from having 149 first-class warships to having only two, the *Warrior* and her sister ship, *Ironside*. Their first steam-powered warship, the *Warrior*, represented a new and vastly more expensive age, one in which new technology changed the rules of the military game.[12]

This was quite a wrenching business, not only for the military culture of the British navy but also within Britain as a whole, since the previous naval culture so permeated many dimensions of British society. Nevertheless, the British ruthlessly built new steam ironclads after 1861 to replace their sailing vessels, reconstructing their entire fleet. The British were not only willing to try innovation, but they were also willing to pay the price to create that new military technology, and then to pay again to integrate that technology into war craft.

Naval designs changed with almost bewildering rapidity between 1860 and 1914, as the location of guns went from broadside to central battery to turret arrangement of guns, and propulsion went from piston to turbine engine, from coal propulsion to oil.

Then came the *Dreadnought* of 1906, which was as revolutionary as *Warrior* had been earlier because it made all other previous battleships obsolete. The dreadnought utilized new steam turbines, would be powered by oil instead of coal, and carried only heavy, long-range guns. It changed forever the nature of naval power, but as John Keegan writes: "Only a nation as rich, as fiscally efficient and as committed to its maintenance of maritime predominance as Britain could have taken such a risk and only a navy as technically adaptable as the Royal Navy could have seen the need to do so."[13]

For his part, Andrew Gordon sees something of the same dynamic at work, but provides insights into the extent to which battleship and battle cruiser (faster but with lighter armor plate) designs eventually led to the "fast battleship." Keegan stresses the difficulties Great Britain had in continuing to compete due to "Britain's relative economic decline and her competitors' absolute increase in wealth and productiveness."[14]

France, the United States, Japan, Germany, Russia, and Italy all followed suit—they had no choice if they were to remain competitive. Each military revolution again asserts the primacy of the phrase, "the weapons themselves speak."

Of course, nations and peoples can go backward and reduce their commitment to newer technologies. The failure of the United States to maintain existing military advantages is one such negative example. Upon taking office, President Thomas Jefferson and the Republicans reduced the size of the army so that "the result was an expensive economy for the army which was rendered so small as to be ineffective and nothing was provided in its place."[15]

Even more damaging, in 1801, Jefferson, believing navies "were more of a menace than a boon," insisted that many of the country's best force-projection weapons, the oceangoing frigates (which at the time were considered among the finest light warships in the world), be put in mothballs and replaced with smaller, ineffective gunboats that were only fifty feet long, of shallow draught, and limited to one or two small cannons.

He also cancelled the larger seventy-four gun ships of the line begun under Adams's presidency. Together with Madison's similar distrust of the standing military, these steps, Forest McDonald believes, "reduced the military capacities of the United States to virtually nothing," so that by 1811 the United States Navy had only five frigates, three sloops, and seven brigs in service.[16] Stephen Budiansky puts it even more starkly, pointing out that the United States started the War of 1812 with fewer cannons (447) than the British had ships (1,048), a frigate advantage of 250 to 7 and 72 ships of the line to 0.[17]

In addition to failing to accent initially the need for advanced weaponry, Jefferson and the Republicans simply ignored the dictum, "There will always be another war." Also, neither he nor President James Madison believed in a professional army with its advantages in discipline; instead they preferred to rely on militias.

The citizen militia supposed to defend Washington fled when the British attacked them at Bladensburg in 1814 using professional soldiers and (to the militia) a frighteningly new technology, Congreve rockets. Although U.S. sailors and marines fought bravely in that battle, they were flanked and overcome, enabling the British to set the capital on fire. Citizen militias did fight well in a number of battles, however, from Baltimore to New Orleans, although they proved to be no true substitute for a regular army.[18]

NEW WEAPONS CALL FOR NEW TACTICS

We can see that the society, the military, and the political leadership can all stand in the way of military innovation or promote it. But even if new weapons are accepted and integrated into the country's armed forces, it is by no means certain that military tactics or strategy will keep up with the technology.

For example, by the time of the American Civil War, rifles were now able to kill opponents at ranges of 250–300 yards, but the tactics of both the North and the South were based on the era in which muskets, with killing ranges of 30–40 yards had been used. The mass slaughters of the Civil War battles were caused in large part by the continuing use of musket volley tactics that put men in harm's way, forcing them to stand up in too closely packed ranks for longer periods of time. And these longer periods of time were spent in a greatly increased storm of projectiles, a most lethal combination.

The development of the bolt-action, breech-loading "needle gun" by the German craftsman Johann Nikolaus von Dreyse in the 1820s was eventually adopted by the Prussian Army over a twenty-year period, giving its riflemen a three-to-one firing rate advantage in the critical Battle of Koniggratz in 1866 during the Austro-Prussian War. Not only was it more rapid firing, but also the rifleman did not have to stand upright to load it in the midst of battle. As Max Boot points out, when the battle was over, modern Prussia was born and the Austrian empire was headed for the beginnings of its eventual disintegration.[19]

It should also be noted that the Prussians also had a major technological advantage in utilizing breech-loading artillery in this campaign, while the

French still primarily used the older muzzle-loaded variety. In any case, by 1914 all the major powers would be armed with similar breech-loading, bolt-action, rapid-fire guns. These advances in rifled artillery technology and increased rates of fire would greatly add to the casualties of World War I.

Although all of these were to be integral parts of the increasing lethality of the twentieth-century war, in the run-up to World War I all the major armies stayed with tactics that were in place at the 1815 Battle of Waterloo. For example, Boot estimates that a Napoleonic battalion with flintlock rifles could fire 2,000 rounds effective up to fifty yards, or 2 shots per soldier per minute in any attacking cohort. But by 1915, armed with magazine rifles and machine guns, a comparable unit could unleash 21,000 rounds per minute, or 200 shots per soldier in any attacking cohort; yet generals still sent soldiers forward directly into this lethal lead fusillade.[20]

There was an ongoing and sustained revolution in hand-held weapons from 1860 to 1890. By the end of the nineteenth century, a European or an American could lie down and fire fifteen rounds in as many seconds at targets a half mile away. But the military tactics had not taken this increased lethality into account, and the result was the greatest of slaughters.

For example, prior to the Anglo-Boer War, the Boers purchased 30,000 Mausers from Krupp in Germany, thereby equipping the Boers with a field rifle that was at least the equal of the British Lee-Metford rifle. Not only were the British unprepared to face an enemy with modern weaponry, including rapid-fire artillery, but they stubbornly refused to alter their usual battle plan of frontal infantry assaults against a force that was entrenched, dispersed across the battle space, and all the more difficult to target due to the use of smokeless powder.[21]

The failure to follow sound classical tactical principles, even with equivalent or superior technology or manpower, can produce defeat where it might be avoided. Clearly the British officers in charge of the assault had not remembered Sun Tzu in his *The Art of War*, "It is a military axiom not to advance uphill against the enemy, nor to oppose him when he comes downhill." This is a maxim Robert E. Lee might well have followed during the Battle of Gettysburg as well.

In other words, just as weapons do not just appear on the battlefield in "finished" form, neither do new, modified tactics automatically accompany them. Instead, there is long-run progression as from the harquebus to the musket to the rifle (and the progression of each from matchlock to wheel lock to flintlock to percussion cap to needle gun), from muzzle-loading to breech-loading rifle, from single-shot to magazine to automatic firing to machine gun. A comparable revolution would also take place with the bayonet, from muzzle fitting to ring to socket to eventually the ability to launch a grenade.

A corresponding or comparable revolution in tactics was a very long time coming. It is military technological entrepreneurship that propels positive change, but often war craft follows significantly behind the pace of new weapons invention and acquisition. This was certainly the case in World War I, when it was only late in the war that the tank and small unit "storm trooper" formations began to change the way attacks on fortified positions were made. Even then, it seems clear that what Williamson Murray calls the "infantry-artillery paradigm" was what carried the day.[22] For most of the war, the perfect storm of defensive lethality only resulted in mass slaughter, not strategic gains of any magnitude.

MACHINE GUNS

From the perspective of Mars, the machine gun can be both the embodiment of, and a metaphor for, modern warfare even though rifled artillery probably killed more combatants during World War I. It really began as the Maxim gun and the Maxim's predecessor, the Gatling gun. The Maxim machine gun was invented in 1883 by Hiram Maxim from Sangerville, Maine.[23] An interesting footnote to the story of the Maxim gun asks: "Why did Hiram Maxim go into arms?" When trying to decide what to do, he was told, "Hang your chemistry and electricity. If you want to make a pile of money, invent something that will enable Europeans to cut each other's throats with greater facility."[24]

The Maxim was a huge improvement over the previous multibarreled rapid-firing Gatling gun, which used a hand crank and often jammed.[25] Also, it was light enough to be carried by foot soldiers and thus provided a huge advantage to Europeans in Africa in the nineteenth century and also by the United States forces during the Spanish-American War.

The Maxim gun fired a staggering 666 rounds per minute and was quickly adopted by most of the armies of Europe. In fact, Maxim set up a factory in England to produce it, and was, in turn, knighted by Queen Victoria.[26] Ironically, although the most famous automatic rapid-fire weapons were invented by Americans, the American army initially wasn't interested in them (see chapter five).

The Gatling, Maxim, Browning, and Lewis machine guns were all invented by Americans, but the American military was not receptive to the changes these inventions represented and they were integrated into European armies before they were adopted in the United States.

There can be no question that this technological advantage assisted the small number of Europeans who set out to conquer most of the globe. On one occasion, for example, four Maxim guns killed and wounded 3,000 Zulus in less than ninety minutes during the conquest of Zululand. It was also used to devastating effect against other African peoples such as the Ashantis (in what is now Ghana), the Sudanese (Sudan), Fulani (the Sahel), Matabele (Zimbabwe), and Herero (Namibia).

Africans were very quick to see the quantum leap in carnage the Maxim gun represented. A Fulani warrior said with considerable insight:

> War now be no war. I savvy Maxim-gun kill away. . . . It be no blackman, white man fight, it be white man one side war. It no good. Big battle where white man kill black man long way away. Black man not get come near kill white man. If he come near, he die.[27]

At the Battle of Omdurman in 1898, the forces of the Mahdi fought incredibly bravely, but over 6,000 were killed, even while earning the praise of their British opponents. British officers commented on the fallen Africans: "Surely there never was wilder courage displayed."[28] However brave and courageous these African troops were, though, as the British writer Hilaire Belloc put it, they were at a most serious disadvantage because "We have got the Maxim gun and they have not." Ironically, even as this race for colonies proceeded, the arms race forged ahead in Europe, setting the stage for the European-on-European bloodletting that would be World War I.

The increase in the numbers of machine guns was staggering. For example, the British manufacturer Vickers boosted machine gun production from 2,405 in 1915 to 7,429 in 1916 to 21,784 in 1917 and to 39,473 in 1918, underscoring the new, heightened lethality of World War I where 63 million men were mobilized, 8 million were killed, and 22 million were wounded.[29] Ironically, the United States didn't adopt the machine gun as a normal part of its armament until after World War I; and during that war, U.S. troops had to be given machine guns by the British and the French.

So there can be no question but that the acquisition and utilization of superior technology (not just in the form of machine guns but artillery and rapid-fire small arms) is a critical ingredient in the Template of Mars. Of course, George Raudzens and others are correct that better weapons don't always win battles, especially when both sides (as in World War I on the Western front) have roughly the same panoply of weapons.[30] It is situations in which one side has technology the other does not, or in which one side has more thoroughly integrated that technology into its military strategy and tactics that we see the force-multiplying effects of superior technology.

Not only does superior technology usually give an advantage to its possessor, but it should also be noted that superior weapons also give confidence and a sense of invincibility to the side possessing them. A soldier's and even a society's fighting spirit can be tied to their weapons, and how they think those weapons can help them win. Many times they will win battles because they think they can, and many times they do because they simply believe in their superior weapons. And, as we shall see in chapter three, the mere possession of superior technology is not enough to ensure victory. In fact, we will be making the case that superior discipline (and training) are critical components in making it possible to use that technology in the madness of battle.

There is also one final important point with regard to the Template. While it is true that many European countries were the quickest and most devoted in their commitment to an ongoing arms race, there is nothing "European" about the adoption of superior technology. At the 1896 Battle of Adowa, for example, the Ethiopians under Menelek II, using repeating rifles, cannons, and machine guns, were able to defeat over 20,000 Italians and Eritreans.

Although Japan resisted firearms and their increased lethality for a long time, they eventually became experts with them. They defeated China in 1894 over Korea, and then crushed Russia in the Russo-Japanese War at the Battle of Tsushima Straits in 1905 and the earlier siege of Port Arthur in 1904.[31] These victories were a stunning conceptual challenge to the notion that receptivity to innovation was strictly a European characteristic.

The Japanese, having failed to follow the Template of Mars for many centuries, finally realized when Commodore Matthew Perry shelled Yokohama that superior firepower technology was a real threat of foreign domination, and they decided to modernize their military apparatus. With their societal discipline, will to win, and tactical creativity, they were able to modernize their military rapidly, and on February 8, 1904, having conquered Korea, they decided to challenge Imperial Russia. The Japanese attacked the Russian Fleet at Port Arthur, Manchuria, beginning the Russo-Japanese war. They were extremely successful in defeating their previously powerful European adversary.

Contrary to contemporary assertions, the Japanese did follow the dictates of Mars. They accepted the need to be receptive to innovation and upgraded their navy and improved their military capability on land and sea.

For their part, the Russians assumed that as a European power, they would triumph against the Japanese and sent their fleet from Petrograd around the world to confront the Japanese. But the Japanese were not what they had been a hundred years before. They had modernized their army and their navy, and when the Russians arrived in their home waters after a long and debilitating journey, they found a most formidable foe.

In fact, Admiral Heihachiro Togo of the Japanese Imperial Navy had enormous technological advantages over his Russian counterparts. The Japanese had modernized their entire fleet. Their new battleships had advantages in armor, speed, and guns. All of their ships could use the same ammunition, and all had better range, speed, and discipline than their European counterparts.

If we look only at the Template of Mars, the Japanese victory at Tsushima was guaranteed. They had adopted new gunpowder, thin-skinned shells (which would kill the crews of the opposing vessels), and new fuses.[32]

Moreover, while the Russians were disorganized and ill trained and also fatigued from traveling halfway around the world, the Japanese were extremely well trained and had very high small-unit cohesion, where each ship was designed as a single integrated fighting unit.

Looking at this situation, if there were a Mars, he could ask a simple but very important question, "Why wouldn't the Japanese have prevailed?"

The Russian Baltic Fleet had sailed around the world only to go down to a crashing defeat. The Russians may have been a European power with a larger gross domestic product than their Japanese opponents, but the Russians did not follow the tenets of the Template as skillfully as the Japanese.[33]

AIR WAR

By World War II, however weak they might be in terms of small arms and armor, Japan had significant technological advantages over even the United States in some crucial areas. For example, when the attack on Pearl Harbor came, its Mitsubishi A6M "Zero" fighter was far superior to anything the United States had; the Nakajima B5N "Kate" was the best carrier torpedo plane in the world; and the supposedly "obsolete" dive bomber, the Aichi D3A1 "Val," sank more Allied warships than any other Axis aircraft. Japan's top-of-the-line battleships and aircraft carriers were also equal to if not superior to those of the United States or Great Britain.[34] Also, when World War II began, Japanese aerial torpedoes and bomb release mechanisms were much more accurate and reliable than those of the United States.

Japanese pilots were also better and more extensively trained and, however dastardly one believes the attack on Pearl Harbor was, it represented a magnificently choreographed accomplishment and a significant recognition of the latent power of aircraft. As we shall see in chapter nine, however, Japanese technological superiority in these areas did not carry over to artillery, armor, or small arms.

In addition, superior technology can save one side's warriors as well as kill more of the enemy. For example, during the Vietnam War, the Thanh Hoa (Dragon Jaw) bridge in North Vietnam was consistently attacked over a seven-year period. There were 873 sorties sent by the United States forces against the bridge. It was never destroyed by these unguided iron bombs, although the United States lost over 100 planes within a seventy-five-square-mile radius of the bridge in an attempt to do so. Then in 1972 two U.S. precision-guided bombs did so. How different the United States fortunes against North Vietnam might have been had these weapons come on line even five years earlier.

This last example is very important and worth further examination. When the United States conducted its air war against North Vietnam, it suffered greatly from a flawed strategic battle plan. It also suffered from inferior relative technology in areas such as some aspects of air superiority. The North Vietnamese not only had a better air-superiority fighter (the MIG-21) than the Americans' F-4 Phantom and the F-105 Thunderchief, but for some of the war they also had better weapons systems on their aircraft (machine guns and 20 mm cannons versus often ineffective American air-to-air missiles).[35]

Also with Soviet help, North Vietnam instituted and maintained a sophisticated and technologically advanced antiair defense system aided by Russian trawlers carefully tracking American aircraft from their ships and, in the case of the B-52 bombers, from the island of Guam. Thanks to the Russians, the North Vietnamese boasted the most sophisticated antiair defense the United States had ever encountered. American pilots faced an integrated air defense system that used radar and telecommunications to coordinate missile firing intercepts with SAMs and by radar controlled flak guns of various calibers.[36]

Faced with this range of North Vietnamese technological advantages and the mistakes in U.S. strategy, it is not surprising that the net result was, as Marshall Michel puts it, "when the air war over North Vietnam ended at the end of December, 1972 only the most ardent chauvinists could say that the U.S. fighter force had achieved air superiority."[37]

Take also the example of the Stinger missile and the role it played in the Afghan war against the Soviet occupation. The Soviet armed forces and their Afghan allies had huge material and technological advantages as long as they enjoyed complete air superiority. The Soviet Hind helicopters and fixed-wing aircraft became machines of great devastation and also made convoy traffic possible in remote areas.

The Afghani mujahideen fighters were brave and energized by both religion and a strong will to expel the invaders. But they had been put on the defensive, and their insurgency seemed contained until the United States, working through the Pakistani military and intelligence services, introduced the Stinger missile into the battle space.

Relatively simple to use, handheld and light in weight, the heat-seeking Stinger was able to home in on the aircraft's engine exhaust. It proved to be extremely deadly against helicopters and aircraft, and with it, the mujahideen were able to shoot down so many Soviet helicopters and fixed-wing aircraft that their air superiority diminished month by month until they could no longer provide the necessary cover for the Soviet and Afghani government troops on the ground.

As George Crile indicates following the initial shoot-downs of Soviet aircraft, "Until this moment the three-man crew that flew the Hinds had never known fear. Never in the six years of the war. They could kill at will, and no one would kill back."[38] The use of the Stinger, together with the Vickers conventional antiaircraft guns, seemingly turned the course of the war around and paved the way for the eventual Soviet withdrawal from Afghanistan. The Stinger missile in other hands might not have been so revolutionary in its impact, but in the hands of the mujahideen, with their overpowering will to succeed, it proved conclusive.

While this example perhaps claims an extraordinary effect, the Template of Mars suggests that superior technology is of great importance in determining the winner on the battlefield. But we must never forget that the arms race is never ending and if the weapons could speak, they would say simply, "There are better ones than us coming." Ironically, once the Soviets were driven out of Afghanistan, the United States had to pay $100,000 per missile to get most of the remaining Stingers back.

NEW DEVELOPMENTS

We leave this chapter with two more examples of the ongoing changes that require not just new technology but also ongoing integration into the practice of warfare.

Fire Power

According to Max Boot, in World War II U.S. tanks fired seventeen rounds to destroy one opposing tank. In the first Gulf War, it was close to one round fired to one opposing tank destroyed. In World War II, the United States needed to drop 9,000 bombs to be sure of hitting any particular target, since the average bomb dropped missed by 2,300 feet. And during World War II, the United States risked 1,000 aircraft and 10,000 crewmen to hit a single target. In the first Gulf War, the F-117, a single plane with 2 crewmen, dropped 1 bomb to destroy 1 target—representing a 10,000 percent improvement. This exponential improvement is simply part of Mars's progression.[39]

Of course, even the latest technology fails if improperly used, as in 1999 when the Chinese embassy in Belgrade was hit by an American bomb during the war in Kosovo because the CIA maps used for targeting purposes were out of date. One has to have the target correctly identified in order to strike it. It also suggests that there are very powerful inertial forces propelling nations and people toward newer weapons systems. Those who do so gain in the favor of Mars.

Drone Warfare

To take one more recent example of this process: over the last ten years, the United States Air Force has demonstrated both the challenges and the payoffs for superior technology entrepreneurship. While it and other services have used small, pilotless drones for years, the major breakthroughs to develop a true pilotless weapons system required both new technology and a new appreciation of how to combine elements to make a new battlefield weapon of impact.[40]

First flown in Bosnia during 1996, the MQ-1B Predator is a large, high-flying drone that enables its operators to see the battle space undetected from a high altitude. The first versions were helpful in providing real-time imagery, albeit only along a sight path to their nearby base. But the accelerated pace of technological entrepreneurship was just beginning.

By 2003, advances in fiber optics made it possible to put the ground-control station (where the two operators and their screens were located) anywhere in the world. After 2006, the primary operators of the Predator would be based at Nellis Air Force Base outside Las Vegas, even though the Predators were flying thousands of miles away. Seeing images in various battle spaces, the Nellis pilots could call for air strikes from other aircraft. Air Force crews service, as well as launch and land, the drones in Afghanistan and Iraq or wherever they are needed.

But the true revolution was accomplished when the Air Force put a Hellfire missile on the Predator to make it a true weapons system that could be fired in real time. Instead of remaining just an intelligence-gathering platform in the sky, the Predator became a multipurpose weapons system, capable of striking a foe half a world away.

The Predator and its larger successor, the Reaper (which can carry four Hellfire missiles and two 500-pound bombs, the same total payload as an F-16) give battlefield commanders unprecedented and very low-cost alternatives to manned aircraft plus the addition of unseen targeting and long-time loitering. Predators and the Reaper can stay aloft for twenty-four hours at a time.

It is the ongoing mixture of drones, armed drones, and fiber optics that when combined as a technology platform provide a true revolution in battlefield capability. For example, it is now possible for an American or NATO ground commander when facing an entrenched enemy to call for helicopters and feint an assault. When the enemy seeks to slip away, the

Predator is available to kill from afar without risking any troops on the ground.

This quantum leap forward has astonishing economic realities as well. As the global war on terror and the other demands on the U.S. military budgets increase, this weapons system begins to look both more efficient and more cost effective. The Predators cost only $4.2 million apiece and, according to Robert Kaplan, "A third of that $4.2 million was spent on 'the ball,' a rotating sphere on the bottom of the plane where the optics, lasers, and video cameras were located."[41] By contrast, for the price of one F-22 fighter, you could have over forty Predators.

So valuable are these new weapons systems proving to be that during the spring of 2008, Secretary of Defense Robert Gates had to urge the Air Force to speed up deployment of additional Predators and Reapers by letting non–Air Force pilots operate them.[42]

Yet, and here is another dimension of both this leapfrogging technology and the notion of receptivity to innovation, in this particular case, it is not that the American military is resistant to the new drone technology—the Army, Navy, Marine, and Air Force branches of that military *all* see its potential. Instead, it is bureaucratic turf wars among the services that are preventing the rapid deployment of these astoundingly effective new weapons.

As of mid-2008, there were only twenty-five Predators actually flying in Afghanistan and Iraq (and only a few Reapers in Afghanistan, none in Iraq); given the long undefended borders of both countries, ten times that number could be used effectively. By insisting that only full-fledged rated or "real" pilots can "fly" these craft, the Air Force is expressing its service's culture and trying to maintain control over what will be a long-term, and extremely important segment of America's weapons panoply. Thus we see a truly revolutionary and battle-changing weapon held back from optimum use by bureaucratic infighting.

While the Predators are "real" aircraft, they can actually be "flown" by someone far from highly qualified in conventional aviation but proficient in the skills of reading video, flying by joy-stick, and other simulators. A combat-ready F-16 pilot may take several years and $10 million to produce, while a Predator operator can be developed in several months at a fraction of that cost.[43] For the troops on the ground, in daily combat, the question is, how long will this debate delay the battlefield implementation of these revolutionary weapons?

Even now, the army is seeking to develop its own de facto air arm, as in Task Force Odin now operating in Iraq, which is using a combination of civilian aircraft and Army surveillance vehicles to circumvent Air Force control and speed up the battle-space use of these newer technologies.

According to Mars, new weapons continue to require new ways of operating them and new ways of enhancing their utility, requiring the military to constantly learn, relearn, and apply new knowledge. It is important to remember, therefore, that the latest technology is only as good as its application and, as we examine in other chapters, not a substitute for all the other elements in the Template.

3

Superior Discipline

The only difference between an army and a rabble is discipline.

—Anonymous

Discipline cannot possibly be maintained without revolvers.

—Leon Trotsky

Mars also rewards societies that produce soldiers who have greater discipline than their adversaries. Having superior discipline has long been linked to small-group cohesion and the training that it requires. In truth, in many war and battle situations, superior discipline may be more important than superior technology and weaponry.

Virtually everyone who studies wars can cite the example of the 300 Spartans at the Battle of Thermopylae (480 BCE) who were heavily outnumbered by tens of thousands of Persians but who held out for days until finally betrayed and outflanked. Their superior discipline and warrior spirit (as well as a careful selection of the battle space to contest) accounted for such a stand.

Xenophon also wrote in his *Anabasis* about the discipline and professionalism that saved a Greek expeditionary force trapped in Persia as it fought its long way back to Greece.

Chapter 3

WHAT IS MILITARY DISCIPLINE?

Although many writers on warfare have stressed military innovation and superior technology, others have rightly pointed out the key role superior discipline provides. Williamson Murray, for example, rightly sees discipline as the central core ingredient for success in war, "the glue" that holds armies together: "Thus discipline was the glue then that made the individuals composing an army stay on the field of battle, no matter how terrible the conditions of fear, death, and mutilation might be. Without that discipline, armies were not armies, but armed mobs incapable of maintaining cohesion, tactical formations, or obedience."[1]

Murray argues that the writings and actions of Machiavelli, Maurice of Nassau, Gustavus Adolphus, and Frederick the Great, for example, simply revitalized the tradition of the centrality of discipline in warfare that was so important to the Greek phalanx and the Roman legion and that was lost during the feudal period in Europe as the continent was overrun by successive waves of invaders and dispersed into small feudal states.[2]

Felix Gilbert makes a similar point; however, he points to the importance of discipline in the military thought of Nicolo Machiavelli, especially in his *Art of War*.[3] For Gilbert, it is Machiavelli who, by looking back at the successful—and timeless—Roman military institutions, again arrives at the importance of discipline, training, and civic pride as the cement holding armies together.[4]

As Gilbert interprets Machiavelli, "Training is never finished or completed. . . . But even the bonds of that training cannot guarantee obedience. They must be reinforced by fear of harsh punishment. Severity and harshness are needed to hold a political body together."[5]

Machiavelli adds further, "But when a Prince is with his army, and has many soldiers under his command, he must needs disregard the reproach of cruelty, for without such a reputation in its Captain, no army can be held together or kept under any kind of control."[6]

Indeed, in the last analysis, superior discipline in warfare may well be more important to success in war than any of the other elements of the Template. Superior technology, for example, is of little value if one's soldiers are not trained to use it and are not able to maintain their cohesion under fire, under attack and near defeat.

But what is superior discipline? It is more than obeying orders or marching smartly. It involves small-group solidarity and individual devotion to the unit. It is about following orders, and in the absence of those orders, obedience to what they would have been. It is about over-learning tactics and group actions and using weapons over and over so that in the stress of combat, rote muscle memory takes over in order to help the individual

function in the horror of battle. Keeping formation, cohesion of movement, and staying a part of a unit under duress are learned abilities, as is
the need to go into danger rather than away from it.

For those of us who have never been in combat, it seems incredible that
any human could stand the noise, the confusion, the danger, the stress,
the fear, and the overwhelming sense of one's mortality as fellow soldiers
are dying all around you and death is coming at you from all angles. That
maelstrom of danger and death is one reason Napoleon often said that the
key virtue for a soldier was not courage, but fortitude.

To stand in the face of such carnage and perform your task of firing at
the enemy and not run away takes enormous courage *and* discipline. Even
more incredible is the need to force oneself to charge *toward* the enemy
who is firing at you. These reactions require courage and commitment, and
the training to make your muscles obey your command when your brain is
screaming at you to flee.

Only by being rigorously disciplined, trained, and overtrained and bonded
to their unit is it possible for soldiers to perform under those circumstances.

For Martin van Creveld, the difference between one army and another of
comparative size consists of what he calls "Fighting Power" which "rests on
mental, intellectual, and organizational foundations, its manifestations in
initiative, courage and toughness, the willingness to fight and the readiness,
if necessary, to die."[7]

THE VALUE OF DISCIPLINE

The Macedonians under Philip and Alexander the Great succeeded in large
part because of their superior discipline and fighting power. Likewise, the
fighting power of the Romans and the Mongols many times defeated numerically superior militaries by dint of stronger discipline (and, over time,
more receptivity to weapons innovation).

With superior discipline also comes an added bonus: greater flexibility.
The complex Roman and Mongol battle plans, with considerable and complicated battle movements, including feints and maneuver changes in the
middle of the battle, were only possible because of the outstanding discipline of their forces.

The Romans remain synonymous with discipline and training, for as
Josephus put it, "The Romans are unbeatably strong especially because of
their obedience and practice at arms," and further noted:

> To the Romans the beginning of war is not their introduction to arms. . . .
> Instead, as if they had grown with weapons in their hands, they never have an

armistice from training, never wait for crises to arrive. Their exercises lack none of the vigor of true war, but each solider trains every day with his whole heart as if it were war indeed. . . . He would not err who described their exercises as battles without blood, and their battles as bloody exercises.[8]

The blood spilled during training is an important part of the process, for casualties are the cost of good and hard training. "Training accidents" should be minimized by careful planning and operations, but they cannot be eliminated.

This training and discipline, when combined with superior command and control, enabled the Romans to field very large, organized formations. For example, in early Rome, the legion formations (usually 4,500 men, a unit ten times the size of the normal heavy horse knight formation during the European Middle Ages) were arranged in battlefield formations looking like a checkerboard with three separate lines of infantry (the *hastate*, the *principes*, and the *triarii*) arranged in cohorts with space in between them so that units could move forward and backward without getting in the way of the other lines. Throughout history, only a few militaries, such as the Mongols, showed this degree of superior discipline.

Such a complex but flexible formation required great precision, outstanding discipline, and constant training and practice to make it work in battle. It required ongoing training to make sure that soldiers did as they were told, even in the middle of a battle when they were confused, demoralized, or panicked.

After the reforms and innovations of Gaius Marius (157 BCE to 86 BCE), when property qualifications for membership were eliminated, the Roman army accented even more discipline, more regular training, and more standardization of weapons provided at state expense, and they replaced the myriad legion standards with eagles (instead of different animals for symbols) for greater cohesion and small-group solidarity. Even today, eagles remain a powerful symbol in military imagery. Marius also was instrumental in moving from the maniple formation outlined above to the more cohesive cohort (480 men) formation.

Discipline was very harsh. Collective punishment was meted out to units that were defeated or behaved disgracefully. In the widespread practice of decimation, one in ten offenders were killed or harshly punished while the rest of the unit had to camp outside the Roman fortifications until they were able to reclaim their honor.

Training, training, and more training was the essence of Roman success. As Vegetius wrote in the *Military Institutions of the Romans*, "What is necessary to be performed in the heat of action should constantly be practiced in the leisure of peace." However, as J. E. Lendon rightly points out, there was always a tension in the Roman tradition between its two ancestral military values: *virtus* (courage) and *disciplina* (discipline), which when combined produced the best results.[9]

With the decline of the Roman Empire, this commitment to discipline was lost and "not until the late 17th century did western military organizations punish individual soldiers for cowardice and breaches of military discipline and not until the 20th century with its mass armies and totalitarian states, do we see the capacity to inflict collective capital punishment on a similar scale."[10]

As indicated in the previous chapter, in the Mongol armies of the twelfth and thirteenth centuries, the collective punishment of failed units was even more draconian than that of the Romans. If a single man fled the battlefield, his entire ten-person unit was punished by death, so it was not surprising that small-group solidarity became the premier value for both individual and group.

Superior discipline as well as year-round training for war resulted in Mongol armies of unprecedented quality and flexibility in battle. The greatest Mongol general, Subotai, was able in 1223 to direct a battle with two army wing formations hundreds of miles apart as he conquered what is now Russia, and defeated large European armies in Poland and Hungary before returning to Mongolia upon the death of the Khan. Later, the Mughal, Zahīr-ud-Dīn Muhammad (often referred to as Babur) used strong discipline to defeat a much larger Indian force of the Delhi sultanate in 1526 at the Battle of Panipat.

With regard to discipline, Gunther Rothenberg is most helpful in suggesting the ongoing revolution in European war making that arises in the seventeenth century under the Dutch Maurice of Nassau, the Swedish Gustavus Adolphus, and the Hapsburgs' Raimondo Montecuccoli. This revolution is the direct result of reintroduced discipline, small-unit cohesion, and repetitive training of citizen militias.[11] For Rothenberg and other students of this transition, it is not simply the revolutionary impact of the effective mixture of gunpowder and pike, but the discipline to make that mixture work in the heat and stress of deadly action.

In particular, John A. Lynn accents the way drill—"the repetitive practice of rigidly prescribed movement in marching and in the manual of arms," enhances effectiveness and control of the battlefield by giving commanders control over their men.[12] Further, Lynn rightly underscores the importance of the seventeenth-century introduction of the regiment system (an updated version of the legion) whereby men joined units that were permanent and that outlived their service.

These new regiments had a strong chain of command, accented common discipline and drill, and produced a strong sense of identity, small-unit cohesion, and tradition.

Certainly this element helps to explain why the Puritans fighting against the army of Charles I during the English Revolution initially had a difficult time coping with royal forces until Oliver Cromwell created his "New Model Army." Cromwell subjected his men to discipline and training until eventually his army was superior to that of the king, defeating royal forces, despite being outnumbered two to one, at the critical Battle of Naseby in 1645.[13] Later, the better disciplined troops of the Duke of Cumberland would enable the English to defeat the Jacobite rebellion in 1746.

In the eighteenth century, the Prussians under Frederick the Great defeated much larger Austrian and Russian armies with superior discipline, which, as Frederick stressed, came from "making the men more afraid of their officers than of the enemy." And as he suggested in his *General Principles of War*: "The wars that I have waged have made me reflect profoundly on the principles of this great art which has made and overturned so many empires. The Roman Discipline now exits only with us in following their example we must regard war as mediation, peace as a rehearsal."[14]

Carl von Clausewitz put it best in his monumental and enduring *On War*. War, he said, was different from every other human activity; the enormous stresses and concomitant friction which battles produce were overwhelming: "Everything in war is very simple, but the simplest thing is difficult. The difficulties accumulate and end by producing a kind of friction that is inconceivable unless one has experienced war."[15]

The only way to prepare the soldier and the army for this overwhelming friction is to provide discipline, training, more discipline, and more training, and then more discipline and more training, until the individual becomes part of a unit and that unit is subjected to the rigors approximating war itself.

For Clausewitz, the only solution to the frictions of war is constantly exercising armies in time of peace and making training as realistic as possible to prepare troops for "the unbelievable physical effort of war." He goes on to say, "Small unit cohesion is not only the central ingredient for warfare, it is the central ingredient for the preparation of war."[16]

It is important to note that the highly praised battle actions of Colonel Joshua Chamberlain and the Twentieth Maine regiment at the battle on Little Round Top during the Gettysburg campaign were only possible because of this martinet's fascination for drill and more drill. To execute a complicated military maneuver in the middle of a hard-fought battle with your soldiers out of ammunition requires prior training of the highest order.

MILITARY DISCIPLINE IN HISTORY

The Conquistadors

Discipline thus turns out to be critical throughout time and space. For example, Jared Diamond in his chapter, "Collision at Cajamarca," asks how could fewer than 200 Spaniards defeat an Inca army of 80,000?[17] As Diamond describes that collision, on November 16, 1532, Atahuallpa the Inca was the absolute monarch of the largest and most advanced state in the New World, with an army of 80,000 men. Into his world came Francisco Pizarro with 168 Spanish soldiers, only 62 of whom were on horseback, a small group of adventurers, unfamiliar with the terrain, ignorant of the local inhabitants, 1,000 miles from the nearest Spanish base in Panama, and armed with unreliable muskets.

Diamond puts the case simply and firmly: Atahuallpa was in the middle of his own empire of millions, surrounded by his army of 80,000 warriors, fresh from defeating his foes, and unlike Montezuma in Mexico, he was aware that the Spanish were not gods but men and knew they possessed firearms, firearms he hoped to get for himself. Yet Pizarro captured Atahuallpa within a few minutes of meeting him, held him for ransom, got history's largest treasure trove and, enough gold to fill a room twenty-two feet by seventeen feet wide to a height of eight feet. Then Pizarro simply executed Atahuallpa and took over his empire.

At the time of the seizure, the entire Inca army panicked and ran away from the Spanish. Discipline—or the lack thereof—on the part of the Inca military was a hugely determining factor. The Inca soldiers were so afraid of the Spanish guns and horses that they fled madly and climbed on top of one another, forming mounds of dead and dying soldiers, trampling and suffocating many of their fellows. All told, at least 6,000 of them died as the Inca army disintegrated. There was no evidence of discipline, let alone military discipline.

Diamond points out that horses provided a huge advantage to the Spanish, probably at least as important as their guns in terms of frightening their opponents. The Spanish also had steel swords and body armor while Atahuallpa's troops with no animals on which to ride, had only stone, bronze, or wooden clubs and quilted cotton armor. The Spanish thus certainly had some technological superiority, but that, in and of itself, should not have enabled them to defeat a force 500 times their own. There would simply not have been any valid reason for an army of 80,000 to flee ignominiously when a few dozen or hundred of their fellows had been shot *if* they had been properly trained.

As one of the stunned Spanish eye-witnesses put it, "Truly it was not accomplished by our own forces, for there were so few of us. It was by the grace of God, which is Great."[18]

Rather, students of the Template would argue, it was the very poor discipline on the part of the Inca military, and the relatively better discipline on the part of the Spaniards, that accounts for the catastrophic outcome of the battle. Indeed, battlefield discipline among the Incas continued to be extremely poor in the subsequent battles of Jauja, Vilcashuaman, Vilcaconga, and Cuzco, where equally tiny numbers of Spanish soldiers again and again defeated Inca armies ten thousand strong. Of course, Spanish discipline was not the only factor at work, but it was certainly the sine qua non for their survival in those settings.

Diamond asks an additional important question: Why didn't Atahuallpa come to conquer Spain instead of the other way round? The Inca may have been the largest empire in the world at the time. More importantly for this discussion, why didn't his hundreds of thousands of warriors have the discipline and training to overwhelm less than 200 invaders? These are fascinating questions.

Think of the small numbers of Europeans who conquered huge numbers of Native Americans and other peoples of the world. Only with greater discipline would they have been in position to use their superior technology again and again and could they take advantage of the disunity among the Indians.

British Discipline

Much is made of the fact, for example, that Britain's successful actions in the nineteenth century against various peoples on three continents were made possible by advanced technology and possessing superior weapons. In part, this was true, but in situation after situation, from the Sudan to the Gold Coast to southern Africa, it was in larger part because of the iron discipline of the men in the square, the basic British infantry battle formation.

British training and discipline were as big a key as their firearms. Surely the Duke of Wellington was not totally serious when he claimed, "Waterloo was won on the playing fields of Eton." It was, in fact, won on the harsh training grounds of contemporary England. Far more important for the success of the British in war was the truth of the soldiers' saying, "Sweat saves blood." That is what was and what continues to be at the true heart of military success.

On balance, superior discipline is as important, if not more so, than superior technology, for it is what keeps units together so they can *continue* to employ their superior weapons. At the Battle of Omdurman, the British did use Gatling guns and heavy rifles to mow down the Sudanese followers of the Mahdi. But keeping the British in their military formation—the square—was the key. By contrast, in an earlier battle against the Zulus at Isandlwana in 1879, the square with its concomitant cohesion advantages never got a chance to form, and the British were overwhelmed and killed to a man. But the British square was rarely broken in all of its African campaigns. In fact, one prominent example of a "broken" square was at Abu Klea in the Sudan in 1885. It is true that the British square dissolved in that battle, but then it reformed and won the day.

The British in India were not only outnumbered, but in many cases, also outgunned. In the Mysore Wars (1767, 1778, and 1798), British armies of 10,000–15,000 men defeated Indian forces seven to ten times larger, even though these Indians had equally good muskets, cannons, and ammunition, as well as French advisors. However, the Indian forces often lacked the discipline and the bureaucratic organization of the British armies.

The Maratha Confederacy in early nineteenth-century India was a huge human collectivity with 40 million people and a larger gross domestic product than Great Britain.[19] It possessed a large army of 11,000 infantry and 100 pieces of artillery, and it armed its soldiers with muskets. Yet the forces of the Maratha Confederacy were defeated by General Arthur Wellesley (later the Duke of Wellington) and a force one-third their opponent's size (with only twenty cannons) on August 8, 1803. The victory was due not to superior arms or numbers, but to the discipline and tactics and will of the British and their native sepoys.

In fact, when properly trained and led, the Indian sepoys were what eventually enabled the British East India Company to conquer so much of India. By bringing close order drill, uniforms, a strong command structure, and the regiment system to India and grafting them onto the South Asian sepoys' motivation and morale, the company multiplied its ability to project power across the subcontinent.

Without its extensive Indian levies located at Calcutta, Madras, and Bombay, the company's conquests would have been impossible. As Lynn puts it, "These Western military practices and institutions, which were more important military innovations than weaponry were soon grafted onto the subcontinent."[20]

The English thus maintained a long tradition of discipline in its successful foreign adventure armies. For example, in 1415, Henry V won the battle of Agincourt with steely discipline as much as with the technology advantage of the longbow over the French crossbow and the lance. He kept his army together on the long march from Harfluer to Calais, through hostile countryside, in the pouring rain, with many soldiers suffering from dysentery, while having to prevent them from looting along the way. It was not by chance that Shakespeare immortalized the principle of small-unit discipline and cohesion when in his play *Henry V* he has the King say, "We few, we band of brothers." It was the enforced discipline of the band that made victory possible.

While much is made of the supremacy of the longbow at Agincourt, its advantages depended on a great deal of practice and discipline. For this, the entire kingdom was turned into a training ground for the weapon. No other "sport" was encouraged by the King; few were even permitted.

There was also the role of hunting as a method of inducing peacetime training, during which many of the same skills were employed. As Alfonso XI of Castile put it,

> For a knight should always engage in anything to do with arms and chivalry, and if he cannot do so in war, he should do so in activities which resemble war. And the chase is most similar to war, for these reasons war demands expense, met without complaint, one must be well horsed and well armed, one must be vigorous, and do without sleep, suffer lack of good food and drink, rise early, sometimes with a poor bed, undergo cold and heat, and conceal one's fear.[21]

In England, William Beckford agreed, writing: "Hunting is a kind of warfare; its uncertainties, its fatigues, its difficulties and its dangers rendering it interesting above all other diversions."[22]

France under Louis XIV was the strongest of the European powers, and its armies were the largest. Not by chance, Louis XIV was an ardent hunter, often hunting with portions of his court 110–140 days per year.[23] Moreover, the practice of hunting was widespread throughout the court. The Prince de Conde's chief huntsman, for example, kept a record that listed 924,717 items of game killed between 1748 and 1785, a total Tim Blanning wryly but correctly notes was "scarcely credible but authenticated." A lot of practice there.

Louis XIV's army was also famous for its mastery of fortifications and its harsh, rigorous military discipline. His General Jean Martinet's very name later became synonymous with such training.

FOR THE GOOD OF THE GROUP

Having a technological edge is not in and of itself enough to ensure victory. In short, it simply doesn't win battles alone. Technological advantage needs superior training and discipline to maximize its impact.

In all societies that seek Mars's favor, individual soldiers must give themselves over to the greater good of the group or cohort. In true soldier armies, individual survival doesn't matter. Survival of the group does. By training soldiers to obey orders *and* to protect their comrades, individuals become integrated into the unit and fight for the greater good of the whole.

This principle remains the same: superior discipline and small-group cohesion enable armies to endure incredible hardship and danger.

Two thousand years after the Romans trained for war so vigorously that, to them, subsequent actual warfare was like training, 20 million German men passed through the Wermacht during World War II. Their training put an inordinate accent on character, will power, mental stamina, courage, loyalty, independence, and obedience.

Reading today "On the German Art of War Regulation 300" of 1933, we find the echoes of the Greeks, the Romans, the Mongols, and the others who made discipline the key to success in war in the following sections:

> #5 War subjects the individual to the most severe tests of his spiritual and physical endurance. For this reason, character counts more in war than does intellect.[24]
>
> #13 Units that are only superficially held together, not bonded by long training and discipline, easily fail in moments of grave danger and under the pressure of unexpected events. . . . Discipline is the backbone of an army.[25]

There are many examples of German discipline and will enabling them during the latter stages of the war to take great punishment and still function as cohesive units. Their discipline, decentralized leadership, and group solidarity and flexibility enabled the Germans to inflict greater casualties on their opponents than they received in virtually all battles they fought during World War II. But it should also be noted, as Jon Latimer correctly points out, that contrary to popular opinion, German army subordinates were not only highly disciplined but also were encouraged to react creatively to changed conditions: "Commanders issued directives, but subordinates were allowed wide freedom of action to secure their commander's intention. Thus whenever a fluid situation emerged, they had a great scope for thought and action."[26]

Overall during World War II, German soldiers consistently caused higher casualties among their American and British opponents, regardless of whether they were on the offensive or the defensive; and as Max Boot wrote, "The German soldier was in all likelyhood the best of the war."[27]

This imbalance in casualties suffered versus casualties inflicted was even truer in their battles against the Soviets. At the very end of the war, when Germany was on the brink of total destruction with grossly undermanned units, the German soldiers inflicted massive casualties during the Red Army's offensive to penetrate the Seelow Heights east of Berlin as late as 1945. Of course, the Germans had the additional motivation of not wanting to be punished for their previous excesses against the Russian soldiers and civilians. Also, the higher Soviet casualties were also due in part to the reckless, headlong offensive pushes of the Soviet generals, who preferred wasting the lives of their soldiers to risking Stalin's wrath.

But take also the situation of the First Panzer SS Corps in the battle of Normandy 1944. Two of the best-trained and most fanatical German formations, the First SS Division Liebstandarte Adolf Hitler and the Twelfth SS Division Hitlerjugend, fought extremely well in the face of Allied naval artillery and air superiority, which caused them 40–50 percent casualties. Few army units had ever sustained such a killing aerial bombardment before they got to the battle space and yet were able to fight as well. As Michael Reynolds notes:

> How was I SS Panzer Corps, with one Division which would have been considered unfit for operations in other armies, and another made up from untried soldiers who were little more than boys, able to perform so dramatically and effectively in Normandy—particularly since it was operating without air support? Without going into too much detail, four factors are significant—tactics, morale, leadership, and equipment.[28]

The essence of the Template of Mars thus lies with its regimen of discipline and training. The South Korean General Paik Sun Yup, perhaps the best general of his generation in that country, put it simply and directly: "Discipline is the military's heart and soul. An army that suffers from lax discipline is nothing more than a mirage."[29]

Training and discipline bring to individual soldiers an enhancement, a power multiplier that benefits the entire army. Putting his finger on this intangible, Antoine de Saint-Exupéry wrote, "An army, if it is to be effective, must be something other than a numerical sum of its soldiers."

Repeated group activities, whether directly related to combat (firing practice) or not (drill) all have the effect of creating artificial kinship groups, some of them, such as the cohort, the company, and the platoon, are further reinforced by the creation of small fellowships within the unit in order to increase cohesion and therefore combat efficiency even further.

It is not just military thinkers and army commanders who recognize its importance. The soldier too recognizes the element of cohesion that comes from the shared experiences of training. Marine Sergeant Brad "The Iceman" Colbert, in combat in Iraq for the first time during the drive on Baghdad in 2003, relates, "It was just like training. I loaded and fired my weapon from muscle memory. I wasn't even aware what my hands were doing."[30]

During peacetime, soldiers, sailors, marines, and airmen must be trained and overtrained. They must be forced to replicate as near as possible the battle situation and to overcome fear and disorientation. In combat, it means performing the commonplace under uncommon conditions. For professional soldiers, it is preparation for combat that instills a sense of "rightness." Take John Ferling's apt description of a British captain on the eve of the Battle of Pell's Point during the American Revolution:

> This was to be a day of battle. It was not an unwelcome prospect for Evelyn. He was a soldier, a regular, a professional. Fighting was what he did, why he was in America, why he had chosen to remain in America. . . . Within moments of hearing the gunfire, the entire British force started inland. Their comrades needed help. There was a job to do.[31]

Today's American Special Forces have a saying, "Embrace the suck," meaning to accept, even glorify, the terrible conditions, not only of war but, more importantly, of the prelude to war as a way of bonding within the group. The worse the conditions, the tighter the bonds within the group and the higher its confidence to take whatever will come in the battles that lie ahead. These soldiers dedicate themselves to accepting hardship as the price of true soldier-hood.

Training and discipline also provide a resulting precious element of "belonging," which increases that group solidarity. You become part of a family, part of a "band of brothers." Or as Jean de Bueil puts it, "It is a joyous thing, war. You love your comrade so much in war. A great sweet feeling of loyalty and of pity fills your heart on seeing your friend so valiantly exposing his body. And then you are prepared to go and live or die with him, and for love not to abandon him."

Stephen Crane, likewise, called it "a mysterious fraternity born out of smoke and the danger of death." Such a mystical, spiritual closeness is much like love and comes from being with your unit in combat where everyone depends on everyone else. Nathaniel Fick in *One Bullet Away* describes that feeling, "Together we passed the test. Fear didn't beat us. I hope life improves for the people of Afghanistan and Iraq, but that's not why we did it. We fought for each other."[32]

Those who have been in battle and succeeded immediately draw a distinction between themselves and those who have not. Fick's highly disciplined and cohesive Marine reconnaissance platoon later ran into an army supply column coming down the highway with a hand-drawn map and no tank or artillery support. They were lost and bewildered and the Marine commander responded:

> "Stay the fuck away from me. You guys have no maps, no weapons, no fucking clue where you are. I don't want to be around when you get hosed." I hated feeling that way and tried to make a joke of it, but I couldn't. Sometime in the past month, we had become veterans. And like the veterans in every war, we didn't want to be near the new guys. New guys got themselves killed.[33]

For those of us who are civilians, this is superficially easy to understand, but grasping why men and women in combat go back into combat after they are wounded, who volunteer for front-line duty instead of staying in the rear, and who risk and even give their very lives for their comrades is much harder. Yet these selfless acts for the group are the essence of true warrior-hood.[34]

William Manchester, writing in *Goodbye, Darkness*, explains why he left the hospital to return to his unit even though he faced "almost certain death":

> It was an act of love. Those men on the line were my family, my home. They were closer to me than I can say, closer than any friends had been or ever would be. They had never let me down, and I couldn't do it to them. I had to be with them, rather than let them die and me live with the knowledge that I might have saved them. Men, I now knew, do not fight for flag or country, for the Marine Corps or glory or any other abstraction. They fight for one another.[35]

Even today, wars are decided less by technology than by superior will; better war plans; the achievement of surprise; greater economic strength; and, above all, superior discipline and training. Standard operating procedures require that one must stand and watch those around you being killed and still perform your assigned task and mission. The group depends on you and you on the group.

This has not changed, as Sharron French points out, since the Spartan mother first said to her warrior son thousands of years ago, "Come back with your shield or on it," meaning that she expected him to win or die honorably. The young warrior was being told "to fight bravely, maintain his martial discipline, and return with both his body and his honor intact. If a warrior came back without his shield, it meant he had laid it down in order to break ranks and run from battle."[36] Honor, discipline and group solidarity were—and are—inextricably intertwined in the shield wall of classical infantry warfare.

FLEXIBILITY IN DISCIPLINE

Taken together, then, there are three aspects to the element of superior discipline: The first critical element is the ability of a formation to stand fast in the face of the enemy, whether being attacked or attacking. The second is to withstand losses amid great carnage without losing the cohesion of the group. There is also a third important ingredient to small-unit cohesion, and that is the degree of autonomy given to junior officers. Flexibility and initiative, over time, is of enormous importance in maximizing the opportunities of small groups to achieve their objectives. Decentralized leadership enables small units to show flexibility and responsiveness to changed conditions on the ground as the battle develops.

This is especially true with forces like the German elite units in World War II and the U.S. Marines today, which allow junior officers to command effectively and be decisive and grab opportunities when senior officers are not present or are incapacitated.[37] This flexibility is key to success in warfare. As the German *Truppenfuhrung* of 1933 suggests, "The emptiness of the battlefield requires soldiers who can think and act independently, who can make calculated, decisive and daring use of every situation, and who understand that victory depends on each individual."[38]

It is interesting to note that although Clausewitz and the Swiss writer and theoretician Antoine Henri de Jomini both stress the importance of flexibility of overall command and the importance of the "decisive point" in the battle, neither places a great deal of emphasis on small-unit flexibility or junior officers responding to local "decisive points."[39]

But it is flexibility among junior officers that helps to maximize the advantages of small-unit cohesion. The German word *auftragstaktik* ("mission tactics") is most useful here. Because of the fast-paced, confusing, mechanized, and disorienting nature of modern warfare, it is essential that small-group leadership be prepared to lead at any time during the kaleidoscope of change that is a battle. Junior officers must be trained to take charge of their units and redirect their activities as the situation changes. Decentralization and small-unit cohesion are key.

As Martin van Creveld so cogently argues, the ability of the German armed forces to incorporate discipline, comradeship, and *auftragstaktik* resulted in a superior fighting force, and that in terms of "morale, élan, unit cohesion, and resilience, it probably had no equal among twentieth-century armies."[40]

Likewise, one can argue that Israel's success in its wars with the Arab states in 1967 and 1973 was due to higher motivation, better discipline, and especially junior-officer flexibility. In the Yom Kippur War of 1973, for example, the success of the Israeli counterattack (as seen in "Operation Gazelle") in the face of what had been up to that point a substantial Egyptian victory as the Egyptians broke through the Bar-Lev line (and had the Israelis on the run and sorely perplexed), derived from mid-battle decisions taken by officers who saw local opportunities in the midst of chaos and potential defeat, and who took them at the Chinese Farm and Tirtur Road. Their Egyptian counterparts, led bravely and competently in the initial phases of the war, were hampered as the battle went on by the hierarchical rigidity of their army and by the fact that battle decisions were made by their generals far from the front.

Conversely, after Hezbollah's considerable success against Israel during the war in Lebanon during 2006, Israeli officers complained about the rigidity of their battle plans and the fact that Hezbollah had greatly improved its discipline, training, and equipment so as to greatly reduce Israel's margin of technological superiority over its forces.

The creation of a climate of opinion allows for the creativity of junior officers, who are on the ground and facing reality in its sharpest dimension, and this creativity can pay big dividends. As General David Petraeus put it during the successful surge in Iraq during 2007–2008, the goal was telling military commanders "how to think, not what to think."

Echoing the apropos quote of Leo Tolstoy, "Battle is decided not by the order of a commander in chief, but by the spirit of the army," Bing West speaks to just this point and provides an instructive portrayal of American junior officers seeing the potential for turning around the counterinsurgency situation on the ground in Anbar Province during the fall of 2007 even *before* their commanders did.[41]

Small units who have trained and trained and overtrained, and whose junior officers and even noncommissioned officers are able to be flexible can thus respond better under pressure. Many authors such as Victor Hanson and Max Boot have rightly associated these elements most notably with the rise of the West. They see these elements as being present elsewhere, of course, but in the West, they have been underscored again and again by the primacy of discipline in the twin forms of drill and long-term service.

Nevertheless, it is easy to find non-Western examples where discipline and training overcame numerically superior opponents. In 1979, for example, the North Vietnamese defeated the Chinese invaders. The Vietnamese proved themselves to be better trained, better equipped, and better led, with an iron discipline that startled and dismayed the Chinese.

And of course in intra-European warfare, the side with the most training, discipline, and flexibility often succeeded against great odds. The English won at Trafalgar (off the Spanish coast) in 1805, defeating a much larger Spanish and French force with superior discipline that resulted in greater firepower. Boot estimates that British gunners were three or four times faster and more accurate than their Spanish or French rivals.[42] This was solely the result of superior discipline and training, not from any singular or a priori technological advantage.

Also in that battle, British junior officers were given the task by Admiral Nelson to "Engage the enemy more closely" and then were left to carry out that mission as they best saw fit. They were thus entrepreneurs in battle, and their discipline and confidence led to victory. At the end of the battle, the British had inflicted ten casualties for every one they received and lost no ships.

We will return to this element of junior-officer initiative in chapter ten, when we examine the role such officers played in turning around the progress of the war against the insurgents in Iraq.

Over time—and throughout time and space—success in war most often has come to those armies and those societies that accent discipline and training and small-unit cohesion. Discipline remains at the very heart of success in war and among the ingredients that Mars is most likely to reward.

But discipline in the army should, in order to satisfy Mars, also involve organizational discipline by the state. While the armed forces can in some fundamental sense renew themselves without a great deal of societal input (as happened in the United States after the Vietnam War), eventually the society and government must help to remake themselves in response to principles of discipline and order if they are to reach their maximum potential for future success in war.

In short, the society and the political system, as much as the military system, must be organized for success in the next war. This often considerable time and effort and may run counter to other societal values, as we will be discussing in chapter eight.

But however one puts together the elements of "success" in warfare, one must conclude that "discipline" lies at its heart, regardless of time or space or culture or situation. It is, simply, the sine qua non of success when Mars is overseeing the battle space. "God is on the side of the big battalions," Napoleon was fond of saying. Mars would, of course, argue that God is on the side of the biggest, best-disciplined battalions.

4

Sustained but Controlled Ruthlessness

War is cruelty. There is no use trying to reform it. The crueler it is, the sooner it will be over.

—General William T. Sherman

We must be ruthless, relentless, and remorseless.

—Admiral John "Jackie" Fisher

The third element in the Template of Mars is sustained but targeted and controlled ruthlessness. This is one of the least understood—and most abhorrent—of the Template's aspects because it so harshly assaults our assumptions about our own humanity.

Yet success in war has long been associated with this ingredient. Aeschylus gave praise for "victory in whose august glow all felonies are effaced." But that assumption is very hard for many of us to accept. There is something in most of humankind that abhors the death of many, let alone those innocent, for any purpose.

That is why this chapter is the longest in the book and perhaps its most controversial for the intellectual climate of our age. Yet for successful practitioners on the battlefield, the application of sustained but controlled ruthlessness is essential. For as important as superior technology or superior discipline and training are, there remain other vital prerequisites. To succeed in war, one must be willing to be ruthless and to maintain sufficient ruthlessness until the job is done.

Half-measures do not normally work for Mars. Without being able to apply and sustain ruthlessness, states and societies on the verge of success will lose wars, especially longer-lasting ones, as America discovered in Vietnam and might still in Afghanistan. In these cases, sustained ruthlessness may be practiced by the military but terminated by the civilian population, at least in a democracy.

Sustained but controlled ruthlessness means to use one's power, all the power at one's disposal, to impose your will on your antagonist before they impose theirs on you. It means to break your enemy's will before he or she can break yours.

Sustained but controlled ruthlessness is, of course, not simply gratuitous violence, but purposeful violence, applied for purpose and an end result. It is not uncontrolled vengeance or indiscriminate killing for its own sake. Rather, sustained but controlled ruthlessness involves a willingness to kill enemy soldiers even if it also means the death of innocent bystanders in order to be successful. This notion runs so counter to our basic sense of what humanity should be that it is very hard to accept.

As Confederate General Nathan Bedford Forest put it, "War means fighting and fighting means killing." Many rightly decry war as an instrument of national policy. Many also object to war on the more fundamental grounds of its killing aspects. For many, most disturbing of all is the killing of civilians. And many people and scholars alike have a reflexive, and warranted, distaste for war and the multiplicity of tragedies it spawns.

But from the perspective of Mars, it is of critical importance to look at war realistically. Unfortunately, inhumanity has often proved highly efficacious in warfare, and this military "realism," however distasteful, offers powerful insights as to which side wins in battle. Pattern recognition impels us to view the importance of sustained ruthlessness. As this chapter suggests, there is necessary versus gratuitous ruthlessness; there is also "smart" strategic use of ruthlessness and "dumb," or self-defeating, use of ruthlessness.

John McCain, no stranger to the horrors of war, puts it this way,

> War is a miserable business. The lives of a nation's finest patriots are sacrificed. Innocent people suffer and die. . . . However heady the appeal of a call to arms, however just the cause, we should still shed a tear for all that will be lost when war claims its wages from us. Shed a tear, and then get on with the business of killing our enemies as quickly as we can, and as ruthlessly as we must.[1]

Once one confronts the true realities of warfare, it is hard to get beyond this seminal truth and that stated below by General Matthew Ridgeway during the Korean War. After taking over the demoralized and defeated U.S.-led Eighth Army on December 26, 1950, an army that had just endured the longest retreat in American history from the Chongchon River to below the Han, General Ridgeway instituted major reforms and pushed his soldiers to simply "kill Chinese." When some reporters objected to his use of harsh names for his various offensive operations (such as "Operation

Killer" and "Operation Ripper"), he replied simply and cogently, "War is about killing."

Ridgeway did not mean to gratuitously kill Chinese civilians or those Chinese soldiers who had surrendered or who wanted to surrender. His point was that war means killing your opponents in order to force them to stop fighting, and no amount of glossing over of the notion can change that harsh reality. He insisted that killing is a necessary condition for success on the battlefield and that killing enough of the enemy in order to break—or at least check—their will is essential.

There was—and there remains—a clarity of vision echoed in the contemporary words of his adversary, Mao Tse-tung, who said in the same context, "The key lies in the number of Americans we can kill."

Carl von Clausewitz put it most aptly: "Kind-hearted people might of course think there was some ingenious way to disarm or defeat an enemy without too much bloodshed, and might imagine this is the true goal of the art of war. Pleasant as it sounds, it is a fallacy that must be exposed: war is such a dangerous business that the mistakes which come from kindness are the very worst."[2]

This is a rather consistent theme among men who have had the responsibility of waging war. British General Harold Alexander wrote of World War II after seeing it first hand, "War is homicide on a scale which transforms it into a crusade and an art, dignified by its difficulties and risks." Beilby Porteus put it another way, "One murder made a villain, millions a hero."

So it remains today and as it always has been. Despite how much we would like to hope and pray there are no more wars, or if they are to occur, that they do not kill innocent people, such a thing is not possible.

SUSTAINED RUTHLESSNESS AS A TACTIC OF MARS

For anything like an objective analysis of war qua war, we must leave aside the moral question, because Mars insists that we do so. War involves killing, and the killing of innocent civilians remains an intrinsic dimension of war. There is also great poignancy to the dilemma caused by those who routinely kill civilians as a way to achieve their goals or who deliberately mix with the civilian population so as to deter attacks upon themselves and/or to encourage the attacks in order to erode civilian support. Any efforts to kill or dislodge them, no matter how carefully executed, will mean the loss of innocent lives, precisely because opponents have put them in harm's way and mean to keep them there in order to attain their goals.

Throughout human history, unfortunately, success in war has often come to those armies and leaders who practiced sustained but controlled ruthlessness, and the killing of innocents has often been the means, if not the purpose, of the exercise. It was a rare army indeed that could win a war by being less ruthless than its opponent.

The Romans, Mongols, and many others are justly remembered as being brutal and savage to their adversaries, as brutal and savage as necessary to prevail against them. Yet not by chance they remain the epitome of success in warfare. When Cato declared in 150 BCE, "Carthage must be destroyed," he was not speaking metaphorically.

Cutting down the sacred trees of the Druids in order to break their spirit in Britain, destroying all traces of Carthage after the Third Punic War and plowing its fields with salt, and killing or enslaving the entire population during the 67–73 CE "Jewish" war are all emblematic of the sustained ruthlessness of the Romans. They did whatever was necessary to break the will of their enemy.

Josephus, who was an eyewitness to much of the fighting and slaughter, puts the total number of Jewish dead during that war at 1.1 million. Even allowing for some exaggeration, this is a staggering figure, accounting for half the Jewish population in Judea at the time.[3]

Sustained ruthlessness, the ability to project and use maximum force in order to prevail, is an intrinsic component in successful warfare.[4] During the Vietnam War, for example, the North Vietnamese practiced a most impressive form of sustained ruthlessness. Over the course of the thirty-year war, they proved they were willing to kill anyone—and in large numbers—who would prevent victory. This included the Japanese, the French, the Americans, and many, many other Vietnamese.

There was a strategic, not a moral, imperative that had them blowing up marketplaces filled with civilians and sending rockets randomly into population centers and especially targeting any and all opponents before, during, and after the Communist takeover of an area.

The systematic killing of civilians by the North Vietnamese and Viet Cong became a hallmark of that effort. R. J. Rummel in his extremely comprehensive and conclusive *Death by Government*, for example, believes that the Hanoi regime "wiped out about 1.1 million Vietnamese," including 95,000 of the over 2 million Vietnamese who passed through their reeducation camps after the war.[5] Note that Rummel does not include in this figure his own estimate (which he believes is conservative) of 250,000 of the boat people who died fleeing after the takeover of South Vietnam. As a fitting reminder of their ruthlessness, North Vietnamese even razed the South Vietnamese military cemetery in Saigon when the war was over.

However immoral these actions, North Vietnamese utilization of sustained ruthlessness was a key ingredient in their defeat of the Americans and the South Vietnamese. Their view of *Da Tran*, "The Long War," was also "The Most Ruthless War."

Regardless of "why" they acted so ruthlessly (or how they justified that ruthlessness), the important aspect is that the North Vietnamese did apply more sustained and effective ruthlessness than their American and South Vietnamese counterparts. They broke the political will of the Americans, and later militarily overran the South Vietnamese.

Conversely, while the U.S. use of defoliation, massive bombings, and other methods of warfare may look like sustained ruthlessness, it turned out—at best—to be misapplied or misdirected ruthlessness. To be successful, sustained ruthlessness has to be wisely applied, it has to be focused, and it has to be brought to bear upon the right targets. For much of the Vietnam War, the United States was sadly deficient in all three areas of ruthlessness.

Remember that during the Vietnam War, the United States dropped twice the explosive tonnage it had previously used in both the European and Pacific theaters during World War II. So harsh military power was applied. But the United States dropped 90 percent of that tonnage on South Vietnam, Laos, and Cambodia, not on North Vietnam—and mostly on jungle at that, thereby greatly dissipating the effectiveness of American firepower. For example, the U.S. heavy bomber, the B-52, flew over 130,000 sorties, but the vast majority of targets were other than the North Vietnamese Clausewitzian centers of gravity.

Recent studies have pointed out that of the incredible total of 1.2 million fixed-wing sorties and 37 million rotary winged sorties flown by the United States during the entire Vietnam war, 71 percent were flown within South Vietnam, leading C. Dale Walton to note wryly "Bombing friends is problematic."[6]

Incredibly in that effort, American pilots flying over North Vietnam were not even allowed to bomb North Vietnamese airfields for most of the war. The United States even suspended strategic bombing from 1968 until December 1972 when President Nixon finally took the war "downtown" to Hanoi and Haiphong. In the eleven days of that effort, when B-52s struck the capital, it was the first time Hanoi's principal power plant had ever been struck, and the first time the port of Haiphong (through which flowed 80 percent of its supplies) was hit. Of over a hundred key dikes and dams in North Vietnam, only eight were ever struck.[7]

Imagine Mars rewarding the use of force so ridiculously off-target and misguided—and "un-ruthless"! General Curtis LeMay perhaps put it best when he declared: "In Japan, we dropped 502,000 tons and we won the war. In Vietnam we dropped 6,162,000 tons of bombs and we lost the war. The difference was that McNamara chose the targets in Vietnam and I chose the targets in Japan."[8]

For LeMay, American decision makers were wrong in assuming that China and the USSR would enter the war if strategic bombing was used extensively against North Vietnam, citing as proof the fact that when the United States finally did during December 1972, neither came even remotely close to intervening.[9]

Not only would Clausewitz have cringed at the U.S. failure to discern the proper "centers of gravity," Mars would declare that the failure of the United States to apply sustained ruthlessness against those of their opponents who were directing and prosecuting the war was intrinsic to the U.S. loss in that war.

American bombing was so self-constrained and so carefully calibrated during 99 percent of the war that the United States lost virtually any chance to use its enormous advantage to be decisive in that contest. In short, the failure to sensibly apply sustained ruthlessness took away one of its greatest assets by using its air power in a most unstrategic way. Imagine having nineteen different bombing pauses during the Johnson administration alone. It is now obvious that no one in authority at the time understood the wisdom of Machiavelli when he said "Never do your enemy a little hurt."

Bombing a single truck on the Ho Chi Minh trail as opposed to the truck factory or the port where military trucks arrived by the thousands remains ludicrous in the eyes of Mars. It is truly hard to imagine Mars suggesting that a country at war should be rewarded for trying to destroy individual trucks along a 1,000-mile network of roads rather than preventing those trucks from being manufactured or imported in the first place. This was not "sustained ruthlessness," no matter how many North Vietnamese were killed as they walked or rode down the Ho Chi Minh trail.

As John McCain wrote,

> Most of the pilots flying the missions believed that our targets were virtually worthless. We had long believed that our attacks, more often than not limited to trucks, trains and barges, were not just failing to break the enemy's resolve but actually having the opposite effect by boosting Vietnam's confidence that it would withstand the full measure of American airpower. In all candor, we thought our civilian commanders were complete idiots who didn't have the least notion of what it took to win the war.[10]

Ironically, after the United States mined the harbor of Haiphong in 1972, not a single ship left it or entered it for the duration of the war. Indeed, no new trucks arrived at the port during the entire rest of the war until the United States Navy removed them as part of the peace accords. But it was too little too late and was applied after the war was lost at home.

We will be connecting sustained but controlled ruthlessness to national will in a subsequent chapter, but suffice it here to point out their intertwined nature. Mars punishes the opponent who does not initiate sustained ruthlessness or breaks it off before the other side.

From the perspective of Mars, therefore, the United States "deserved" to lose the war in Vietnam because it was unwilling/unable to sustain the application of ruthlessness—and also applied ruthlessness in a counterproductive way. The North Vietnamese were willing to use any means necessary to break the will of the American war makers and their efforts won the war.[11]

It should be underscored that the attribute of sustained ruthlessness is not senseless or wanton killing for its own sake but purposeful killing (accompanied by strong discipline) in order to achieve victory in war. Also, it is not a matter of scale but of consistent willingness to harm one's opponent, individually and collectively.

It is, in short, a willingness to properly use as much force and violence as necessary to prevail against one's foe, regardless of the nature of the opposition. It means prevailing whether the war is "limited" or "total." For Mars, war is never entered into unless the combatant is committed to using whatever is necessary to subdue the foe, irrespective of the context. Otherwise that war should be avoided.

In other words, many societies have brave warriors, but brave warriors do not in and of themselves make for a successful military strategy. Nor is it bravery that normally finds rewards provided by Mars. It is the applied and sustained ruthlessness of highly disciplined and focused military forces that Mars rewards time and time again.

Indeed, wherever we look in history—Greek, Roman, Chinese, Indian, African history—we find the Template of Mars replete with success engendered by sustained ruthlessness. Mars rewards armies and peoples that make war in order to win and that use virtually any means necessary to win, not those who seek to win by using the least amount of purposeful violence. Let us look first at the defeat of the Native Americans by their European counterparts. How and why did it happen?

THE INVASION OF THE AMERICAS

Caution: This is not an effort to blame the Native Americans for their own demise. Nor does it discount the major and even decisive contributing factors such as susceptibility to European diseases and inferior weapons technology. It is, however, to state firmly and categorically that the Native Americans' failure to make a united front against the European invaders *and* their normal preinvasion patterns of avoidance of sustained ruthlessness greatly reduced their margin of error in warfare and dimmed their chances for success, even for survival, when confronted with the European arrival. Fred Anderson captures many of the dynamics of this failure, and especially the reduced margins for political balancing by Native Americans after the Seven Years War.[12]

There were contributing factors beyond sustained ruthlessness, of course, especially those already mentioned—superior weapons technology and the introduction of European disease. Indeed, Charles Mann makes a convincing case in his revisionist book, *1491*, that the Indians of the Americas were older (25,000-plus years on the North and South American continents), more diverse (DNA from a variety of sources), and much more populous (over 24 million to 100 million) than previously supposed, so the impact of disease was truly considerable.[13]

Many of the Native American peoples were not hunters and gatherers but farmers, and with that Neolithic revolution, were empowered to create huge population aggregations. The Inca, Mexica, Aztecs, Amazonian, and Mississippian, were all civilizations based on farming. They invented or domesticated such crops as maize, tomatoes, peppers, potatoes, most types of squash, and manioc.

Mann rightly sees disease as a major culprit in the demise of Native American civilizations and peoples, although he also sees the vectors of disease moving both ways, from Europeans to Indians and from Indians to Europeans. While the Native American malaria, black water fever, and dysentery took a toll on the early explorers and conquerors, the European germs such as small pox, measles, and influenza proved much more destructive.

Of course, neither the Indians nor the Europeans had any idea of infection, so both suffered, but the Native Americans far more, as smallpox and other European diseases may have eliminated 50–60 percent of the total Indian population.

Leslie Shaw, for example, points out that a plague from 1617 to 1619 is thought to have wiped out 80 percent of the indigenous population from Cape Cod in Massachusetts to the Saco River in Maine so that the area was largely depopulated when the Pilgrims arrived. The Native Americans, she feels, while not initially connecting the disease with Europeans, felt that the European religions might be helpful in trying to cure them.[14]

Moreover, half the Huron people died when the disease spread from their enemies, the Five Nations of the Iroquois. The Wampanoag in Massachusetts were wiped out by disease and settler warfare. Ninety percent of them died, and nearly as many Pawtucket and Eastern Abenaki. In 1633, the Pequots, struck down by the same small pox epidemic that hurt the Huron and the Iroquois, went from 13,000 to 3,000 people. Of the 1 million Native Americans who may have lived east of the Mississippi before the arrival of the Europeans, only 150,000 survived in that location by the middle of the seventeenth century.[15]

There is, of course, enormous irony of the New World being exploited by the Old. Not only did over half the native population die due to diseases and warfare, but the Spanish ended up making the Native Americans pay the costs of the invasion with much of their gold, silver, and jewels.

Quite against their will, the Native Americans thus ended up being forced to become very good at gold and silver production. For example, in 1492, Europe possessed about $200 million in gold and silver. By 1600, that amount had increased eightfold.

Mann also rightly sees the Native American failure to form a united front as a major defect in their defense of their homeland against the Europeans, who set about dividing and conquering them. There is great poignancy, for example, in Tecumseh's (and his brother Tenskwatawa's) failed efforts to rally disparate tribes to fight against the Americans during the War of 1812. Tecumseh argued that the Indian lands were inalienable and could not be given or sold, and he urged all Native Americans to hold fast and resist the whites' encroachments. He called for all Indians, regardless of tribal affiliation, to join together to defeat the Americans.

Once again, however, there were many Native Americans, including many of the leaders of Tecumseh's own Shawnee nation, such as Black Hoof, who favored cooperation with the Americans against the British and their allies led by Tecumseh. Ironically, Tecumseh was killed during the 1813 Battle of the Thames during the American invasion of Canada. Disunity among Native Americans prevailed over the course of white expansion, and those who opposed the Europeans and the Americans were often eventually done in by competing tribes. Victorio, the great Chiricahua Apache war leader, for example, was hunted down and defeated by the American military only with the help of Navajo and Coyotero Apaches scouts as well. When Amerindians stayed together and were united, they were able to maintain their independence, at least for a time. There were a variety of examples, such as the power of the Five Nations of the Iroquois in holding the Dutch, French, and English at bay. The Iroquois actually expanded in the seventeenth century and were later rejoined in the eighteenth century by the Tuscarora, who had been, and became again, the sixth nation of Iroquoia. They also played the British and French off against each other until the end of the Seven Years War took away the French option. But this was seldom the case during the invasions of North America.[16]

Beyond these defects, what was also of great import in sealing the collective dooms of the Native American peoples was their inability and/or unwillingness to apply sustained ruthlessness to the invading Europeans. Of course, it is impossible to generalize about all Native American war making practices, and some exceptions should be noted as subtext. For example, the

United States had to fight three wars to subdue the Seminoles, the second of which lasted twenty years.[17]

Most Native American peoples produced brave and skillful warriors, but only rarely—and for very limited periods—did they practice sustained ruthlessness against the European invaders. It was simply not an intrinsic part of their war-fighting tool kit for most Indian societies. For the most part, in contrast with the invading Europeans, they were simply disinterested in sustained ruthlessness as a war-making skill.

Native American peoples practiced warfare on an ongoing basis, but it was most often of a very different kind than that practiced for centuries by Europeans. They could—and did—mount effective killing raids, they could be very cruel to their captives and on occasion devastate their opponents' homes and villages. But throughout most of their history they seldom practiced the warfare of devastation that was such an integral part of the European heritage.

By the time of the arrival of the Europeans, most Native American groups had evolved a series of war-making styles that fit their need. It is just that in the face of European invasion, they were up against a level of sustained ruthlessness that was, for most of their societies, extremely novel. The same thing, of course, would have been true if the Mongols had invaded the Americas first instead of the Europeans.

It should also be noted that while European societies had centuries to practice sustained ruthlessness in warfare, Native Americans did not have the luxury of much time in reacting to this new form of warfare in their midst. Among the numerous disadvantages they faced when dealing with the European invaders was their lack of unity and a lack of some of the essential ingredients of the Template of Mars.

Because of devastating disease and the eventual total "weight" of European numbers and technology, they might have been marginalized anyway. But whatever chance they may have had for a better outcome, that chance was greatly diminished by their failure to appreciate the importance of sustained ruthlessness in the worship of Mars.

Most of the devastation and ethnic-cleansing aspects of European/American interaction with Native Americans took place after the battles were over. Even if the Native Americans had to ultimately lose to the European invaders in some absolute sense, if they had utilized the very important dimension of "sustained ruthlessness" in their war making, they might have been able to carve out better terms for their defeat or at least staved it off for another generation or two depending on their location.

While neither Europeans nor Native Americans were free of ruthless and terrible behavior, one can more easily apply the term "savage" to the European rather than the Indian form of warfare, and certainly by the terms of the Template, Native Americans failed to live up to Mars's dictates. Therefore, in the eyes of Mars, the Europeans simply deserved to win.

For the most part, while it is impossible to generalize about all Indian war characteristics, war making among Native American peoples seems to have followed four major patterns.

First, there was the "skulking," or raiding pattern as practiced by the Eastern Woodland Indians.[18] Second there was the "capture for sacrifice" war as practiced by the Aztecs, Incas, and Mayans, who wanted prisoners for human sacrifice more than they wanted to kill their opponents. Since it is much harder to capture your opponents (even if you meant to sacrifice them later) than to kill them immediately—and their weapons and military tactics reflected this—Native American peoples were at a disadvantage when fighting against those who cared nothing about capturing but only about killing.

Additionally, Shaw suggests that there were considerable differences in the goals of these types of warfare. The Mayan peoples were often content with capturing the leaders of their enemies and then taking them back to torture and sacrifice them, leaving the subject population basically alone. The Aztecs, on the other hand, would seize whole populations and sacrifice some, even many, of their members over time, using these tactics as an object lesson to the next subject peoples. Additionally, the ritualized "Flower War" of the Aztecs, although not their only type of warfare, was the one they ended up favoring most prior to the arrival of the Spaniards. In these "wars," defeated opponents within the Empire were revanquished in order to obtain captives for human sacrifice.

Third, there were the raiding forms of the Plains Indians and those of the upper Mississippi. They carried out raids for revenge, horses, women, and simply for glory—the greatest glory in the rite of passage to warrior-hood was in charging into battle with a wooden stick and "counting coup" by striking an armed opponent with the stick or other object to show courage. This form of warfare flourished especially after the coming of the Spanish and their horses, and it flowered on the Great Plains with elaborate degrees of honor based on the type of coup struck and the degree of danger involved. Among the Pawnees, for example, the greatest honor in battle could come from an unarmed brave seizing a weapon from an opponent without killing him.

And fourth, there was displacement, the driving of one group away from their traditional hunting or living areas, as with the Comanches pushing out the Apache and the Ojibwa forcing the westward migration of the Santee, Yankton, Teton, and Lakota Sioux. It should be noted that Steven A. Le Blanc and Katherine E. Register also document conspicuous examples of both displacement and cannibalism among Native Americans prior to the arrival of the Europeans.[19]

There are also examples of extermination of one tribe by another (or at least of its male members), such as the Arawaks (Tainos) and Ciboneys by the Caribs; but again, the overwhelming majority of Native American peoples did not practice wars of annihilation. Rather, these examples are the exceptions that prove the rule.

Once the Europeans arrived there were massive, deadly, and sustained dislocations, starting from east and moving west as indigenous peoples moved away from European expansion and displaced existing populations in the territories into which they moved. The Mandan, for example, lived near the Great Lakes prior to the coming of the Europeans but ended up on the Great Plains. Beyond European removal of Native Americans, there was also the concomitant pressure from those tribes that had acquired fire-arms and thus were able to bring advanced technology against other Native Americans. This was especially telling on the Great Plains, where groups that acquired horses and guns first were at a considerable advantage.

Fred Anderson makes a most telling point, "Unlike Europeans, most Na-tive American groups did not fight to destroy their enemies but to take cap-tives, plunder and trophies by which they could gain spiritual power and prove their merit as warriors. What they valued most, therefore, lay behind them, the captives they had tied to trees, the wounded and dead who lay on the field of battle, and the abandoned equipment strewn everywhere about."[20]

For his part, Howard Russell also emphasizes the Indians "three chief tactics of surprise, ambush, and stratagem" rather than sustained ruthless-ness, while Colin Calloway asserts that "Native conflicts were ritualistic, intermittent, seasonal and far less bloody than wars common in Europe."[21] Russell also was one of the earliest writers to accent the fact that the taking of scalps was more likely to have come as a result of the demands of the English and the French for proof of death for European-offered rewards, rather than existing Native American practices.

In this he was only partially correct. The European powers certainly in-creased the scope of the practice, but it is well documented that among the Algonquin, Montagnais, Huron and Iroquois, and others, scalping the dead or dying existed prior to the arrival of the Europeans.[22]

On balance, all four Native American war patterns militated against a successful following of Mars, for all four failed to produce significant pat-terns of sustained ruthlessness. When confronted with European soldiers who thrived on sustained ruthlessness, the Native Americans could only suffer by comparison. The Spanish and the English and the French wanted to kill and conquer, the Indians capture. Who would Mars favor in such a contest?

Many Native American societies were as vicious and cruel to their cap-tives as any Europeans. Their methods of torture were horrendous, often involving deliberate slow and agonizing death, and appear to have been in place with some tribes for centuries.[23] Also, human sacrifice occurred on a huge scale among the Maya and Aztecs.

Nevertheless, the war craft of the vast majority of Native American peoples did not ever reach the sustained levels of ruthlessness Europeans routinely practiced in the Hundred Years War and Thirty Years War. Indeed, the very length of such European wars put them in almost another universe from the shorter, far less destructive wars of the Native Americans.

Many Native American societies found the European way of making war—the burning of crops and homes, the slaughter of animals, and the killing of women and children—most barbaric. Indeed, although Wayne Lee finds some scattered exceptions and cautions against pushing the notion too far, he does note the widespread patterns of "restraint" in most Native American traditions of warfare.[24]

Likewise, Francis Jennings makes a strong argument that the European colonies represented an "invasion" of the Americas.[25] Other writers such as Armstrong Starkey have correctly pointed out that the war for control of the continent, at base, was decided by Europeans fighting other Europeans, not Europeans fighting Native Americans. The treaties made by these European powers seldom took into account either side's erstwhile native allies—and were seldom abided by in any case.[26]

Fierce, self-righteous, and trained in seemingly endless warfare in Europe, these European conquerors could hardly be expected to be more loving and generous to the Native Americans than they were to other Europeans, and indeed, during the Wars of Religion, to their own people. Imagine, for example, how devastated the countryside of Germany was after the Thirty Years War. And how many thousands of French Protestants were killed by French Catholics and how many thousands of German Catholics were killed by German Protestants and how many thousands of English Catholics and Protestants were killed by English Protestants and Catholics?[27]

In this regard, it is perhaps also useful to examine some contemporaneous beliefs of the Europeans. Much recent writing about the interaction between the native peoples in America and the arriving Europeans has centered around notions of "racism." It is important to remember, however, that "racism" in the fifteenth and sixteenth centuries had more to do with perceived ethnicity than color or civilization.

People then thought of the English "race," the French "race" and the Spanish "race." Since they had practiced sustained ruthlessness on each other (and indeed upon their own "race") for decades or longer, it was not surprising that they practiced sustained ruthlessness on the Native Americans with even fewer qualms.

Moreover, it should be remembered that the European racism against Europeans that was exported to the Americans had its roots within European cultures for a very long time. Why, then, should the English, for example, have been expected to treat the Native Americans better than they treated the Irish or the peasants of France?

The early French and Spanish expeditions to what is now Florida and their settlements at La Caroline and St. Augustine not only massacred large numbers of Indians, they also slaughtered large numbers of each other. In this initial period, it would be hard to distinguish between their racism toward each other and their racism toward the first Americans.[28]

It should be noted that while there was European-American racism involved in the dispossession of Native American peoples, the savage ruthlessness was from Mars and not from racial animus per se. After all, the European nations of the exploration period were so effective against the peoples of Africa, Asia, and the Americas precisely because they had practiced on each other for centuries.

This is not to say that many or even most Europeans weren't "racist" by today's standard meaning of that word, but they were racist independent of their military tactics. The tactics of the Europeans were not "racist," even though they themselves were. They had perfected them for a long time while fighting among themselves.

Moreover, we must remember that the Catholic Church and many Protestant groups of the time sanctioned this European raw power grab and applied ruthlessness. Remember that the Pope "gave" the Spanish in the New World (beyond the Portuguese line in Brazil) a mission to civilize the Native Americans. The Spanish would then read a proclamation, called the "Requerimiento," or "Summons,"—in Spanish—calling on the Indians to recognize the Holy Catholic Church and the King and Queen of Spain as their lords, and when they, of course, didn't respond, they often were enslaved.

Spanish conquistadors also extensively used the tactic of *entradas*, persistent armed explorations of the interior, as the invading army lived off the land by demanding tribute— taking food, women, and anything else they wanted.

This mode of warfare was modeled after the *chevauchee*, the English and French medieval tactic of living off the land even as you attacked it. The slaughter of civilians was the point of such chevauchees, in order to draw out the defenders from their castles and strong points. Killing innocent civilians in order to shame the host country's rulers and bring them to battle was a time-honored tradition and practiced extensively in the Hundred Years War. Having slaughtered large numbers of European peasants, it certainly would have been a huge departure had the Europeans treated the Native Americans differently.

We have already mentioned, in chapter three, Francisco Pizarro's brutal subjugation of the Incas during 1531–1533, but Cortez in Mexico also practiced the same degree of harshness. As T. R. Fehrenbach notes:

> Cortez was the technically superior, self-assured, morally confident, energetic, single minded aggressor, able to play upon his opponents' weaknesses and fears; Montezuma was the highly civilized but superstitious potentate, swamped in fatalism, reared in a static universe unable to cope with blinding change. The very appearance of outsiders began to shatter his world. He began the game with the power to destroy these strangers on his shores but he could not find the will to use it.[29]

Of course it should be pointed out that Cortez could not have overthrown the Aztec empire without his many Native American allies. Native Americans persisted in aiding the new "devil" instead of supporting the known "devil." In addition to the inadequacy of their styles of warfare, many Native American peoples simply would not make common cause against the European intruders. Cortez and his 900 soldiers certainly could not have defeated the aroused Aztecs after the death of Montezuma without the assistance of their 100,000 Native American allies such as the Tlaxcalans of central Mexico who saw the Spanish as a way to escape the tyranny of the Aztecs and gain a better life.[30] The seizure of Atahuallpa by Pizarro and the subsequent subjugation of the Inca Empire was facilitated by the lengthy civil war that enervated it prior to the arrival of the Spanish.

J. H. Elliott in his *Empires of the Atlantic World: Britain and Spain in America 1492–1830* also cites many instances of Native American allies creating buffer zones to protect the nascent European colonies.[31] For his part, Armstrong Starkey sums up the debilitating nature of Indian disunity quite simply, "Division among the Indians facilitated European encroachment into native lands."[32]

Even in fictional accounts of European–Native American interaction, the "good" Indians are the ones who help the invaders and the "bad" Indians are those who seek to repel them. In this regard, James Fennimore Cooper's *The Last of the Mohicans* ironically underscores the actual as well as metaphorical predicament of the Native American.[33]

For Cooper, the "good" Indians, Chingotchkook and Uncas, are allies of the whites and convert to Christianity, while their opponent, Magua, is portrayed as "demonic," and as "this dusky savage, the Prince of Darkness" by the heroic white Hawk-eye, La Longue Carabine.[34]

But it is Magua, the "bad" Indian, who correctly saw the fate of his people if they did not crush the Europeans and drive them into the sea. It is Magua who should stand as hero for his resistance to those who would destroy the Indian way of life. If Native Americans failed to cooperate among themselves and failed to wage harsh, relentless war against the European invaders, they were truly doomed.

From the perspective of Mars, the ultimate failure of Native Americans was due to their inability or unwillingness to practice sustained ruthlessness. Their very patterns of warfare militated against their ongoing success against the invaders. Native Americans may have been doomed anyway, but their approach to warfare made sure that their continent was taken away from them sooner and more decisively than otherwise might have been the case.

It is startling to see how so many Native American peoples failed to see Magua's metaphorical point of view. One could argue this was the final fatal flaw in the Native Americans' efforts to cope with the demands of Mars. Looking back on the sweep of European–Native American interaction from the perspective of Mars, one is stunned by the overall pacific and trusting nature of so many Native American societies toward these rapacious newcomers. From the point of view of Mars, their reactions were debilitating, even fatal.

Why, for example, didn't Powhatan wipe out the first settlers at Jamestown when they were sick and weak but in the process of taking the land of his people in the seventeenth century? Why did the Native Americans make so few efforts to unite and drive the intercontinental invaders into the sea?

Though there were instances of success, of course, as when the Skraelings drove off the Vikings when they encountered them in Labrador, and the Native Americans' elimination of the first English settlement at Roanoke Island in 1585, but the pattern of Indian reaction was far more often one of cooperation and acceptance rather than sustained ruthlessness. Part of this was due, of course, to the enervating ravages of disease that weakened Indian resolve and made them question the efficacy of their gods who might have led them to success in battle.

But part of the problem was simply the Indians' failure to rise up once they knew what the Europeans were doing to them and their way of life. The Wampanoag, for example, waited from 1620 until 1675 to strike at the European invaders, and by then, it was much too late. The Wampanoag paid a horrific price for ignoring the dictates of the Template of Mars.

Much writing about Native Americans in explaining the "inevitability" of the European conquest of North and South America has centered around technology (the Europeans had better war-making implements) and the impact of disease, which wiped out so much of the native American population. Both factors remain contributory, albeit far less important than the weight that has been traditionally accorded them. But from the perspective of Mars, they alone did not seal the fate of the native American peoples. The inability and lack of desire to practice sustained ruthlessness, indeed both their methods of warfare *and* their goals of war, militated against Native Americans ever being successful when confronting people who truly and consistently worshiped at the Template of Mars.

For hundreds, if not thousands, of years, the warfare they practiced made them ill suited to long-term success when confronted with *any* enemy, European or otherwise, who did practice sustained ruthlessness. From the perspective of Mars, the war patterns of the Native Americans were simply detriments when they and their societies were pitted against enemies who had few qualms about practicing sustained ruthlessness—and who had practiced that sustained ruthlessness against their peers in Europe for hundreds of years.

The sustained ruthlessness of the Europeans turned out to be a significant advantage in the warfare between them and the Native Americans. It would have given the Mongols a similar advantage had they invaded the homelands of the Native Americans.

In any case, one could well argue that much of the sustained ruthlessness of the French and Indian Wars was the result of European infusion of "savage" values into warfare. Acting in concert with the French, the Wabanaki peoples of northern New England in 1688 attacked Andover, Massachusetts, and later devastated the interior frontier of Maine, resulting in the depopulating of much of its interior by driving the English settlers south to the relative safety of Massachusetts and southern Maine. Ironically, of course, one of the results of the eventual British triumph in 1763 at the end of the Seven Years War was to make the English settlers in the colonies feel as if they no longer needed the protection of the mother country.

Looking at the arrival of the Europeans through the lens of Mars, the Wampanoag under Massasoit should have assumed that the Pilgrims would eventually cause them harm, and therefore should have killed them and driven them into the sea, not brought them venison and fish for a "Thanksgiving" celebration.

As Adam Hirsch points out in his "The Collision of Military Cultures in Seventeenth-Century New England," the Eastern Woodland Indians tended to practice ritual, symbolic, self-limiting warfare among themselves. Although their torture of prisoners was horrific, their generalized style of warfare exhibited "martial temperance."[35]

By comparison, the Puritans at Saybrook (where Long Island Sound and the Connecticut River meet) reacted most violently after the outbreak of the Pequot War of 1636–1637. Under the leadership of John Mason, they sent an expedition to Rhode Island and linked up with the Narragansett Indians, enemies of the Pequot. They then proceeded to a Pequot village on the Mystic River and set the entire village on fire, killing every Indian who tried to escape. Over 400 lost their lives.

As Nathan Philbrick in *Mayflower* reports: "It was a fearful sight to see their dying in the fire and the fire being put out only by their blood . . . but the victory was a sweet sacrifice and they gave praise thereof to God."[36]

Even their Native American allies were not spared: "Voted, that the earth is the Lord's and the fullness thereof voted that the earth is given to the Saints; voted, we are the Saints," declared a Milford town meeting in 1640.[37] The justification was something of which Mars would have approved, "They act like wolves and are to be dealt withall as wolves."[38]

Unfortunately for the long-term relations among Europeans, Indians, and later Americans, massacres would be perpetrated by all sides. Among the most vicious were the Colorado militia attacks on the Cheyenne-Arapaho village at Sand Creek in 1864, which killed several hundred Indians, two-thirds of whom were women and children, and the U.S. Seventh Cavalry's attack on the Lakota at Wounded Knee Creek in 1890, which killed over 300 men, women, and children.[39]

At the time of King Philip's War, 1675, the Wampanoag sachem Metacom (known to the English as King Philip), who was the son of Massasoit (the very sachem who had welcomed the Pilgrims upon their arrival), led the bloodiest uprising of the period. But that reaction turned out to be too late to save the Native Americans of New England from their gristly fate. King Philip's crusade against the Europeans was further hampered by the failure of many other Native Americans to join his effort to drive the Europeans into the sea.

Tribe after tribe, including the Pequots, the Mohawk, and even the Niantic, refused to join him in his effort, some even siding with the Europeans. Nevertheless, this war may have been one of the few times that Native Americans came close to using the sustained ruthlessness model of warfare.

This inability and unwillingness of Native American peoples to band together to oppose the European invaders was a consistent and very disheartening aspect to their war fighting capabilities.

According to Nathan Philbrick, King Philip's War was amazingly destructive. While World War II killed 1 percent of U.S. adult males, and the American Civil War 4–5 percent (although the percentage was much higher among the Confederate male population than the Union), King Philip's war killed nearly 8 percent of the same population cohort. Out of New England's total population of 70,000 people, 5,000 were killed during the war, most of them Indians.[40] Moreover, many Native Americans, including some Christians, were sold as slaves after it was over.

James Axtell claims even greater devastation, suggesting that of the 11,600 Indians living in southern New England in 1675, 68 percent were casualties of the war, including 2,000 dead in battle and from wounds,

3,000 from exposure and disease, 1,000 sold as slaves, and 2,000 as permanent refugees.[41]

Later, during the French and Indian War (ending in 1763), the British soldiers often massacred whichever Indians they found and scalped them as well in retribution for the Indians who allied themselves with the French. Of course, the English forces of British General James Wolfe, moving through Canada on the way to Quebec, also reduced the prosperous farms of the French "race" to a "smoldering wasteland." Over 1,400 farms were destroyed. "No one ever reckoned the numbers of rapes, scalpings, thefts, and casual murders perpetrated during this month of bloody horror."[42]

Lord Jeffrey Amherst gave orders during Pontiac's War in 1763, "We must use every stratagem in our Power to Reduce them," this meant putting to death all Indians taken prisoner and trying to spread disease among the Indians by passing smallpox-infected blankets to them.[43] They have, of course, named a college and town in Massachusetts for this fine fellow, although without mentioning his role in early biological warfare.

The hypertrophy of European warfare was the epitome of Mars's apprentice. This is not to say that the Native Americans "deserved" to be conquered because they did not adequately worship at the shrine of Mars, but it is to say that this was another in a series of debilitating consequences when competing with Europeans.

THE AMERICAN CIVIL WAR

The American Civil War provides another insight into the importance of sustained ruthlessness as a contributing factor to success in warfare. There are probably more books and articles written about this phase of American history than any other. The myriad points of view and interpretations, the arguments about the failure of the South's rebellion being predestined, even the fundamental question as to whether military strategy or the outcome of battles was determinate all militate against clarity of causation. But the Template of Mars offers important insights when we apply the characteristic of sustained but controlled ruthlessness.

It is important to remember that before the middle of 1863 and the fall of Vicksburg, the South was winning the war in the east (although the North had made steady gains in the west). Forays by the Army of the Potomac into northern Virginia had been repulsed, and Lee was taking the Army of Northern Virginia into Pennsylvania, where a portion of it would get as far as Harrisburg before the Battle of Gettysburg.

Indeed, even after the Battle of Gettysburg, Lee's army escaped and once more made its way back to Virginia. But with the fall of Vicksburg, and

Lincoln's appointment of General Ulysses S. Grant to be the de facto field commander in the east, the nature of the war changed. Whereas previous Union generals had failed to adopt the dimension of sustained ruthlessness, Grant came out of the Vicksburg campaign convinced it was the only way to win the war.

Prior to the mind-set of generals like Grant and William Tecumseh Sherman, most Union commanders followed the position of General George McClellan, whose war policy was adamantly not ruthless: "Neither confiscation of property, political executions of persons, territorial organization of state or forcible abortion of slavery should be contemplated for a moment," nor were the Union forces to interfere with "the relations of servitude."[44]

But Grant and Sherman felt that removing slaves from the Southern economy was logical and sensible and would have a detrimental effect on the ability of the South to wage war. Mark Grimsley masterfully traces the evolution of Northern war-making policy from the more limited form to "the hard hand of war" as "Kill, Confiscate, or Destroy" became Union war policy, slowly and hesitantly perhaps, but most definitely under the direction of Ulysses S. Grant.[45]

Today there is still debate, with some authors arguing that the Civil War was less ferocious or total than others have asserted. But the counterarguments seem far more persuasive. With over 600,000 dead (died in battle, from wounds, and from disease) and 1 million or more total casualties, the Civil War was the most costly in terms of lives in American history. In fact, the casualty lists from that contest equal or exceed the casualties from all other American wars combined.[46]

And as Victor Hanson so vividly and insightfully indicates, the American Civil War was essentially a stalemate until Grant and then Sherman adopted sustained ruthlessness as their operational imperative.[47] But it is not fair to make Sherman some devilish cartoon character or to rely on a truncated version of his famous saying, "War is hell." The whole quote shows the true essence of his belief system. General William Tecumseh Sherman:

> I am sick and tired of war. War is at best barbarism. Its glory is all moonshine. It is only those who have neither fired a shot nor heard the shrieks and groans of the wounded who cry aloud for blood, for vengeance, for desolation. War is hell.[48]

Grant and Sherman began to follow the Template of Mars in their victorious western theater operations. It was after the bloody Shiloh battle that Grant said "I gave up all idea on saving the Union except by complete conquest" and asserted the connection between civilian goods and Confederate ongoing success: "Supplies within reach of the Confederate armies I regarded as much contraband as ordinance stores. Their destruction was accomplished without bloodshed and tended to the same result as the destruction of armies. I continued this policy to the close of the war."[49]

From then on, Grant and Sherman actively sought to make Southern civilians pay a price for supporting the Confederacy and thus turn them against it. It is true that Sherman did have a habit of making rather strident comments such as, "To secure the safety of the navigation of the Mississippi River I would slay millions. On that point I am not only insane but mad."[50]

It was Sherman who first actualized the harder form of war in which civilians in the South would be made to suffer for their support of the Confederacy. Infrastructure and means of production, therefore, became legitimate targets. "All the people are now guerillas," he wrote to Grant,[51] and he later wrote, perceptively gauging the center of gravity for the Confederacy, "The Army of the Confederacy is the South."[52] This accorded with Grant's view, and he urged Sherman to "leave nothing of value for the enemy to carry on the war with."[53]

Prior to Grant and Sherman, Union generals won or lost battles, but none ever pursued sustained ruthlessness to subdue those who had rebelled. It fell to Grant and his lieutenants to pursue sustained ruthlessness as they freed the slaves, burned the slave owners' homes, seized their crops and animals, destroyed their infrastructure, and pushed for the mid-nineteenth-century American version of total war.

Listen to Grant explaining his desires to the chief of staff of the army, Major General H. W. Halleck, to give the order to General Philip Sheridan concerning the Shenandoah Valley, the breadbasket of the South, and hear the chuckle of Mars: "Eat out Virginia clear and clean as far as they go, so that crows flying over it for the balance of the season will have to carry their provisions with them."[54]

Or hear General Sherman's anticipation for his great foray through the South, bringing the hard species of war, "I am going into the very bowels of the Confederacy, and propose to leave a trail that will be recognized fifty years hence."[55]

The history of Sherman's "March to the Sea" in 1864–1865, was indeed a Mars-pleasing sixty-mile-wide chevauchee, with 60,000 Union soldiers smashing their way through the heart of the Old South, confiscating, destroying, burning, and pillaging.

As long as the battles were between armies in northern Virginia, the South could and did achieve stalemate. But subsequent to Grant and Sherman's introduction of Mars's total war, that all changed. Sherman's "March to the Sea" was designed to penalize civilians as much as the Confederate military and bring the horrors of war onto the very Southerners who most adamantly supported it. As Victor Hanson has noted, it was a democratic people's army, freeing slaves and liberating territory and bringing destruction to the people who started and sustained that war.

As Hanson describes it, Sherman's march through Georgia and the Carolinas was a "huge blue tornado" that sucked up 100,000 hogs, 20,000 head of cattle, 150,000 chickens, 500,000 bushels of corn, and captured cotton that the Union later sold for $30 million. In the process, the Union forces also tore up 300 miles of rail lines.[56]

Sherman effectively destroyed the plantation culture, saying "I am prepared to demonstrate the vulnerability of the South—to the South" His, and his army's wrath were fueled by the horrors of slavery. Sherman sat in the slave quarters of a Georgia plantation and told his men and the freed slaves to take whatever they needed and "spare nothing."[57]

Rebel armies failed to stop him or even try very hard. The "cavaliers," who most wanted the war, simply ran away. For these 10,000 big plantation owners who had dictated the lives of 6 million people in the South and border states, this blitzkrieg of ten to fifteen miles a day was overwhelming as it moved too fast along too many roads for the Confederates to always know exactly where it was going.

"I practice the hard species of war," said Sherman, and he was right, and Mars rewarded him. Once Union forces took total war into the heart of the Confederacy, resulting in the burning of Atlanta, Columbia, and Richmond and capturing Savanna, Petersburg, and dozens of other Southern cities, the planter class saw that they had reaped the whirlwind: "They regarded us just as the Romans did the Goths and the parallel is not unjust."[58]

It is very important to point out that this ruthlessness was of the controlled variety. The Union forces were told to burn and loot civilian property, but not rape or kill civilians. This was not total war or indiscriminate slaughter of all they met. But it was controlled ruthlessness for a purpose, to break the will of the Confederacy.

This element of the Template of Mars undoubtedly saved Lincoln's presidency in 1864. Remember that Lincoln expected to lose that election, writing: on August 23, 1964: "This morning, as for some days past, it seems exceedingly probable that this Administration will not be re-elected. Then it will be my duty to so co-operate with the President elect, as to save the Union between the election and the inauguration as he will have secured his election on such ground that he cannot possibly save it afterwards."[59]

Charles Bracelen Flood, for example, writes that August, 1864 was the "darkest month" for the Lincoln presidency during the war, as the failed campaigns of General Benjamin Butler on the James River and General Nathaniel Banks in the Red River campaign, the threat to Washington by

Confederate Jubal Early, and the high casualties rates suffered by the Union forces at the Wilderness, Spotsylvania, Cold Harbor, and Petersburg, plus the rise of pro-peace forces in the North all threatened his reelection.[60]

But when Mobile was taken in the west, Atlanta fell and burned, and later General Philip Sheridan's scorched-earth campaign was successful in the Shenandoah Valley, the tide turned in the North, enabling Lincoln to be reelected over the peace candidacy of General George McClellan.[61]

The success of sustained but controlled ruthlessness as a tactic in the Civil War was soon projected elsewhere, and we find that the success of Grant and Sherman's hard war and the success of sustained ruthlessness would doom the remaining Native American peoples living in the western United States.

THE INDIAN WARS

Lance Janda astutely points out the extent to which the "hard" species of war was carried westward after the Civil War by the very people who had practiced it against the Confederacy. "In hindsight the tactics of the Indian wars bear a remarkable similarity to methods employed during the Civil War.[62] These leaders and their soldiers, who had seen the butchery and carnage of Shiloh and Petersburg and Cold Harbor, were not about to be less ruthless when "pacifying" the "hostiles" beyond the Mississippi and the Missouri.

"Kill the buffalo," as a policy, was therefore but a manifestation of the sustained ruthlessness already practiced on the South, where Sherman had destroyed hogs and cattle, freed the slaves, and liberated cotton. It was a way to destroy the Plains Indians' way of life and remove them from a position where they could no longer impede, let alone threaten, American westward expansion.

In fact, Janda points out that General Philip Sheridan foretold—and worked for—the total destruction of the buffalo herds, saying about the buffalo hunters, "Send them powder and lead, if you will, but for sake of a lasting peace, let them kill, skin and sell until the buffalos are extermi-nated."[63] Sheridan, who had burned out the Shenandoah Valley several times during the Civil War, was not about to treat the inhabitants of the Great Plains any better. Nor was he, or other American military command-ers, likely to stop making war in the winter just because the Cheyenne, Arapaho, and Mandan had traditionally done so.

Slaughter of buffalo greatly reduced Indian power as the buffalo herds declined from 70 million to fewer than 800 by 1895. First the southern herd was destroyed, then the northern herd, ending the economic and cul-tural system on which the Plains Indians depended.[64]

There would be no "Dance Back the Buffalo," no divine intervention for which so many Plains Indians desperately prayed. And as the buffalo herds were destroyed, warfare, starvation, and disease took their relentless and ghastly reapings. The number of Native Americans fell from 2 million at the beginning of the century to 90,000 by 1800. It was sustained ruthlessness that doomed the Plains Indians, just as surely as it had doomed the rebellion of the slaveholder planter class. In terms of human values, this was horrible. From the Template of Mars point of view, it also made perfect sense.

Interestingly enough, there had been a chilling precursor to what was to come to the Western Indians after the Civil War. In 1863, the year before Sherman's March, Kit Carson led a pacification effort against the Navajo, who had been raiding livestock and taking captives from the Mexicans, Spanish, and Americans. And a year later, Patrick Connor waged ferocious war against the Shoshones.

For the Navajo, even at this late date, some type of victory might have been possible. The Navajo had a huge territory that was very inhospitable to the invaders, but they existed in a fractured, very loose alliance of sixty clans, with political power diffused, so a united front against the invaders was almost impossible.

In addition, far from venerating Mars, the Navajo had a cosmology that made them terrified of dead people. This led to a cultural pattern in which they had to abandon their home hut, or hogan, if anybody died in it, for they feared "ghost sickness" above all. Whatever the metaphysical, ethical, or religious value of such a belief, it is hardly a recipe for military strategy on a grand scale or conducive of a spiritual underpinning for a warrior class, let alone a military policy of sustained ruthlessness.

Narbona, the leader of the Navajo, wanted to make peace and was killed by the whites for his trouble. His son-in-law, Manuelito, argued for fighting the Americans with every means at the Navajo's disposal, but he, like so many other Native American leaders, lost that argument.

In a true scorched-earth campaign, Carson destroyed the gardens of the Navajo and took their livestock or killed it. He even cut down thousands of fruit trees they had planted, and this sustained ruthlessness against inanimate objects helped to break the collective spirit of the Navajo clans.

Yet this was the same Kit Carson who objected when the former Methodist minister, Colonel John Chivington, slaughtered the Cheyenne under Black Kettle, killing men, women, and children in cold blood in one of the worst atrocities committed in all the Indian Wars. Carson favored the hard species of war, but he denounced wanton killing of Indian women and children and unarmed men.

Was the defeat of the Plains Indians and other western Native American groups preordained? Obviously, most of us assume it was, but as Bill Yenne writes in his inclusive study of the Plains wars from 1848 to 1890, that was far from clear to the people who lived in that era: "With hindsight it is easy to say that the eventual outcome of the Indian Wars in the West was inevitable, and perhaps it was. To those on both sides who fought bravely through most of the nineteenth century, though, it was not."[65]

NATIVE AMERICAN SUSTAINED RUTHLESSNESS

There were, on the other hand, some conspicuous exceptions to the pattern of Native Americans' avoidance of the demands of the Template of Mars. When Native Americans changed their war-making strategies and most closely approximated the dictates of Mars, they were startlingly successful. Take for example, the Araucanians in Chile, who, in the face of the Spanish invasion, changed many of their cultural values as well as their military tactics and strategies, adapting to the European way of war with skill and dispatch. As Robert Charles Padden so effectively describes, the Araucanians were remarkably successful in resisting the Spanish after their arrival in 1535 because they changed their political, cultural, and military systems in order to defeat the European invaders.[66] For over 200 years, they fought, and staved off, the Spanish invaders and kept their independence. Indeed, they did not formally acknowledge the authority of Chile until 1870.

Realizing the inferiority of their weapons against those of the Spanish, the Araucanians adopted new tactics of rushing at the Spanish and overwhelming them. In addition they accented weapons such as the lance and sword for close-quarter fighting rather than relying on the bow to shoot from afar, thus negating the advantage of Spanish firearms.

Viewing the Spanish as a threat to their very existence, the Araucanians sought battle situations that would reduce the advantage of the Spanish cavalry. They also created well-disciplined cavalry units of their own and formed other military units for specific purposes. Their youth began training with weapons at the age of six. Forming a unified political and military system, they carefully studied Spanish tactics and strategy, including the proper use of firearms. They also correctly saw the limits of European firearms—that their slow rate of fire could be overcome by charging directly at the Spanish and overwhelming them.

The Araucanians also came to believe there would always be another war, and they prepared accordingly even when the Spanish sought peace. In fact, according to Padden, "it was quite common for the warriors to kill any Indian who speaks of peace, or who was suspected of having the word in his mouth." David Weber goes even further, declaring, "The Araucanians came to see war as central to maintaining social, political, and even cosmic equilibrium."[67]

The Araucanians showed an impressive acceptance of the importance of sustained ruthlessness. Discovering the abhorrence with which the Spanish viewed cannibalism, they adopted it as "a cultural opposite, a symbol of resistance," eating those Spanish they captured, often after crucifying them on wooden crosses in a sickening parody of the Christian symbolism of drinking the blood and eating the body of Christ.[68]

As part of their very effective psychological warfare, the great chief of Arauco, Caupolican, told the Spanish governor, Garcia Hurtado de Mendoza, that he had eaten his predecessor and he would eat him as well![69] After 150 years of fighting the Araucanians, an expenditure of 50 million pesos and 25,000 recruits, the King of Spain declared that the Araucanian war "to be equal to those of Spain, Flanders and Italy," while the Araucanians still lived in independence and liberty.[70] Mars was very pleased.

Or take the case of the Comanche (originating as the Numunu in the Great Basin). They successfully resisted Spanish, French, British, and American forays into their territory and, after expanding militarily and commercially into the Southwest, remained dominant in the area for a century or more (1750–1850). Only in the 1870s, after losing huge numbers to disease, having the buffalo herds on which they depended destroyed, and suffering the full might of the United States after the Civil War, did they succumb. Their hundred-year reign suggests an alternative model to the notion of Native American decline in the face of initial European contact.

In fact, Pekka Hamalainen makes the case that they actually greatly expanded their domain during this time by skillful adaptation, shrewd diplomacy, and fierce war making.[71] The Comanches quickly adapted to horse warfare, made acquisitions of iron weapons, gunpowder, and high-grade firearms a very high priority and assumed there would always be another war. They also, like the Zulus and Mongols, were adroit at integrating non-tribal members into Comancheria.

Hamalainen also points out that Comanche ascendancy, and indeed Comanche imperialism, during this period, especially against the Spanish and then the Mexicans, helped the United States to eventually take over "Mexico's Far North" by expanding into Spanish territory and weakening it with over a century of wars and raids. And while one could agree with Larry McMurtry that it is hard to make the case that the diffused Comanche political system was an "empire" in the traditional sense of that term, it is startling to see how successful the Comanches were in following many of the tenets of Mars.[72]

For venerate Mars these "People of the Sun" did, in many ways. According to Hamalainen: First, they were very receptive to innovation, being among the first Indians to blend horses and mobile warfare and to trade whatever necessary in order to acquire iron for weapons and firearms, especially the most modern available, whether trading with the British to the north, the Spanish to the south, or the French and later the Americans to the east.

The Comanches' ongoing receptivity to innovation helped them to expand their empire even while comparable peoples were losing their own positions of prominence in the area. Their ongoing usage and expansion of the slave and horse trades further enhanced their ability to acquire equipment needed for martial supremacy during this period.

Second, they were widely regarded as the most ruthless of the western Native Americans, practicing whatever tactics were necessary not only to survive but to prevail. They even ended up pushing the Apaches west and out of their home territory, and they developed a complex, ongoing, and very lucrative trade in slaves that, along with their proficiency in horse raising and raiding, enabled them to pay for their new military equipment.

Third, the Comanches fixated on the notion "there will always be another war." Unlike many other tribes who hoped and even assumed the last war would truly be the final one with the Europeans, other Native Americans, or the Americans, the Comanches believed and lived and prepared as if the opposite was true.

Fourth, their emphasis on a continuing war and an expanding battle space forced them to find the economic means of sustaining that warfare, and they became very successful in protecting people from capital and constantly finding ways to control trade in order to gain wealth for armaments. Their imperial conquests grew until they were the principal power in the Southwest.

The Comanches and Araucanians were thus two exceptions that suggest how the ingredients of the Template of Mars relatively project what is necessary for a people to have the best chance of success in war against an implacable foe. In the case of the Comanches, their greater adherence to those principles enabled them to wax powerful against many other tribes, as well as the Spanish, the French, and the Texans. Only when they eventually came up against a more ruthless, more disciplined, more technologically advanced foe in the form of the post–Civil War United States did their relative position diminish.

WORLD WAR II

One final example of the importance of sustained ruthlessness can be seen in the conduct of World War II, for it provides us with some trenchant examinations of its efficacy even when both sides practice it.

Of course the horrors of Nazi Germany, Imperial Japan, and Mussolini's Italy are rightly criticized, and the monstrosity of the Holocaust gives ample testimony to man's inhumanity to man. But from the perspective of Mars, the sustained ruthlessness of the Germans and Japanese was subsequently countered by the Allies' own ferocity and ongoing pattern of sustained ruthlessness, which was the crucial ingredient for their success. This is an important calibration of the use of force, matching an enemy's effective ruthlessness with one's own ruthlessness, a dimension that is often over-looked in popular histories of the war.

The ferocity and adherence to the Template of Mars during World War II is often cloaked in the "righteousness" of the American cause after the surprise Japanese attack on Pearl Harbor and the subsequent declaration of war by Nazi Germany against the United States. Yet, in the European the-ater, Americans shot German and Italian prisoners in the battle for Sicily. And the British used German prisoners to clear mine fields in the Italian campaign.[73]

But it was the British and American bombing of Germany that really shows their dedication to sustained ruthlessness. Hanover, Cologne, Ham-burg, Dresden, and other German cities were heavily bombed, with con-comitant civilian casualties. Even Churchill, who favored the biggest and deadliest attacks, asked "Are we beasts?" Our hypothetical Mars would have answered, "Yes, but purposeful beasts."

The combined British and American firebombing raid on Hamburg for three successive days and nights in July 1943 illustrates this point quite well. Over 50,000 Germans, most of them civilians, were killed in Op-eration Gomorrah. As RAF Air Marshal Sir Arthur "Bomber" Harris put it, "their civilian population is the target." This sustained ruthlessness on the part of the Allies was not without cost, of course. In all, 143,000 British and American airmen were lost in the European theater.

Some have argued, of course, that the purposeful targeting of civilians is morally, ethically, and spiritually wrong.[74] Obviously such arguments lie far outside the scope of this work, but it might be worth suggesting that when confronted with an enemy who practices sustained ruthlessness and relies on it for success in war, there may be a humanistic argument for matching ruthlessness with ruthlessness. There, of course, is a counterargument as well, but it is not an argument Mars could accept.

Also, it should be noted that the unwillingness of many to accept the level of sustained ruthlessness practiced by the Allies might be due in part to the Holocaust, the inhumanity of which broke all bounds. From the perspective of Mars, however, the horror of the Holocaust has more than a moral dimension. In terms of winning the war, it made no sense for the Germans to kill so many of their most productive citizens and tie up such a great amount of manpower and transportation assets in order to accom-plish it while engaged in a major war whose outcome was uncertain.

For Mars, sustained ruthlessness on one side requires reciprocal sustained ruthlessness, indeed, as much if not more of it, if the opponents are to prevail. In the case of the Allied bombing of Germany during World War II, it was not only a signal that the Allies would fight until Germany was defeated, but also the strategic importance of the bombing—in and of itself—should not be overlooked. It was absolutely necessary to the successful outcome of the war for the Allies.

While it is true that the Allied air forces claimed greater potential—and indeed greater results—than were actually obtained, the importance of that bombing is succinctly captured by Williamson Murray and Allan R. Millett: "In the end, what is certain is that the Combined Bomber Offensive was essential to the defeat of Nazi Germany. It was not elegant, it was not humane, but it was effective."[75]

As J. Adam Tooze points out, German "Weapons and tanks reached their highest levels of the war in the last months of 1944" but declined sharply thereafter as the destruction of the German air defenses by deployment of thousands of P-51 fighters, which had accompanied American and British bombers in the spring of 1944, finally caught up with them.[76]

In the Pacific theater, there was at least an equal measure of sustained ruthlessness on the part of the combatants. In that battle space, the Americans initiated the targeting of civilian populations consistent with the dictates of Mars. To understand this phenomenon, we need to focus on the B-29 heavy bomber. It was the most expensive project of World War II, costing $3 billion compared with the Manhattan project's $2 billion. The B-29 was also the most complex plane ever built until that time and proved to be an awesome dispenser of sustained ruthlessness.

But bombing at 30,000 feet in the turbulent and fast-moving jet streams over Japan, the B-29's initial bombing raids were very inaccurate. It took the warrior genius of General Curtis LeMay to bring the bombers down to 5,000–8,000 feet, have them bomb at night (the Japanese night fighter capability was far less than that of Germany), and combine high-explosive with napalm bombs to literally burn Japan to the ground.

The spectacular firebombing of Tokyo on the night of May 9–10, 1945, killed between 84,000 and 100,000 Japanese, more than Hiroshima or Nagasaki.[77] In fact, the firebombing of Japan's five largest cities—Tokyo, Osaka, Nagoya, Yokohama, Kobe, and Kawasaki—alone killed over 126,000 people and destroyed over 100 square miles.[78] The firebombing campaign would subsequently turn sixty-six of Japan's largest cities to rubble.

The total devastation was considerable. At a cost of 359 B-29s and 3,415 airmen, the Fifth Air Force killed 330,000 Japanese, wounded 476,000, and made refugees out of 8.5 million.[79] General Curtis LeMay who planned and directed the air war against Imperial Japan by the Twenty-first Bomber

Command, put it quite forthrightly, "If we'd lost the war, I'd have been hung as a war criminal."

Interestingly enough, "Curtis LeMay regarded the Hiroshima and Nagasaki raids merely as an addition—a redundant and unwelcome addition—to a campaign which his B-29's were already winning."[80]

The Fifth Air Force, flying under LeMay's command and reflecting his views about the war against Japan and that country's public broadcasts calling for the total mobilization of the Japanese population stated simply, "The entire population of Japan is a proper Military Target. . . . THERE ARE NO CIVILIANS IN JAPAN."[81] Admiral William "Bull" Halsey was even more direct in his admonishment to "Kill Japs and Kill More Japs," adding, "Japanese will be spoken only in hell."[82]

To us, these are most cruel and racist notions, but they are music to the ears of Mars. And they put the decision to drop the atomic bombs in sharp relief. While much has been made of the "differentness" of nuclear weapons, it is relatively easy to understand how they might be seen as only slightly different when placed along the existing continuum of the firebombing of entire cities.

It could, of course, be argued that if the United States were not determined to obtain the unconditional surrender of Japan, but merely peace, with a Japan still in control of Korea, Manchuria, and large portions of China as well as its home islands, massive firebombing raids and the subsequent use of nuclear weapons would not necessarily have been required.

But the emperor and those closest to him were prepared for, and committed to, the notion of a final, climatic battle on the home islands. Given the goal of unconditional surrender—or even the dislodgement of the Japanese from foreign territories—it is difficult to see how American military and civilian decision makers could have—or should have—failed to use their most powerful weapons.

The American decision to drop the atomic bombs on Hiroshima and Nagasaki (which killed at least 70,000 and 36,000 people, respectively, according to the U.S./Japanese study from 1966) was but a continuation and a verification of its commitment to sustained ruthlessness.[83]

For many, there is no excuse for ever causing civilian deaths in wartime, but both the firebombing and the use of the two atomic bombs needs to be placed in context. Many critics of the use of the atomic bombs overlook the previous battle for Okinawa, one of the most savage and costly of the war for the United States in the Pacific. U.S. forces in that battle, which raged from March to June 1945, suffered 41,000 total casualties, or 35 percent of the U.S. forces engaged.[84]

In fact, March 1945 saw U.S. casualties at their highest monthly levels of the war to date: 20,325. No wonder President Truman stated that he wished to avoid an Okinawa "from one end of Japan to the other."[85] Far from slacking, Japanese resistance was increasing as the fighting came closer to the home islands.

Remember also that the U.S. Navy lost more ships (36 sunk and 368 damaged) during the two-month battle of Okinawa than it had lost in its *entire* history dating from 1776. Why would the Navy be arguing for an invasion of the Japanese home islands if it could be avoided?

But there was also another element to the moral and strategic calculations for dropping the atomic bombs, and that was the deaths of nearly 100,000 civilians on Okinawa, many of whom were forced to commit suicide by the Japanese military.[86] It was assumed, and correctly so, that Japanese civilian casualties of this type would have been much greater once the battles arrived on the Japanese home islands.

Okinawa was a bloody and deeply felt wake-up call to those Americans who thought the war was almost over. Military intercepts of Japanese codes indicated that the Japanese Imperial High Command was prepared to hurl 900,000 soldiers, and even more civilians, into the upcoming Ketsu-Go, which in their minds would be the ultimate and decisive battle. Operation Olympic (the first projected invasion of the Japanese main islands) was estimated to cost 140,000–160,000 American casualties.[87]

Moreover, the Japanese High Command had prepared a huge underground command center at Nagano in the central mountains of Japan from which to direct the war *after* the projected American invasions of Kyushu and Honshu.[88]

Additionally, a case can be easily made that even if the war against Japan only lasted a few more months, many more Japanese soldiers and civilians would have died than did with the bombing of Hiroshima and Nagasaki. For better or worse, Sherman's "hard war" and "soft peace" assumption saved hundreds of thousands—if not millions—of Japanese and American lives at the end of World War II. Estimates for the projected death rates for continuing the war ran as high as 250,000 a month, and Max Hastings offers the trenchant insight that it was "a delusion that the nuclear climax represented the bloodiest possible outcome. On the contrary, alternative scenarios suggest that if the conflict had continued for even a few weeks longer, more people of all nations—and especially Japan—would have lost their lives than perished at Hiroshima and Nagasaki."[89] For Hastings, "Such an assertion does not immediately render the detonation of the atomic bombs acceptable acts. It merely emphasizes the fact that the destruction of Hiroshima and Nagasaki by no means represented the worst outcome of the war for the Japanese people, far less for the world.[90]

In fact, one can point to the obvious alternative to the use of the atomic bomb—138,000 tons of liquid fire were scheduled to be dropped in March 1945, with 115,000 tons scheduled per month in the fall of 1945.[91] And recent scholarship has uncovered even more draconian plans to destroy the

Japanese civilian population should operations "Olympic" and "Coronet" have gone forward. Thomas B. Allen and Norman Polmar have highlighted the fact that U.S. war planners advocated the massive use of chemical weapons against all major Japanese cities, with projected civilian deaths of 5 million.[92]

Strangely enough, some critics of the decision to drop the atomic bomb quote Samuel Eliot Morison, but his words are either taken out of context or those critics remain oblivious to his definitive statements on the matter:

> It has been argued that the maritime blockage would have strangled the Japanese economy, and that the B-29's and naval bombardment would have destroyed her principal cities and forced a surrender without benefit of atomic fission. I do not think that anyone acquainted with the admirable discipline and tenacity of the Japanese people can believe this. If their Emperor had told them to fight to the last man, they would have fought to the last man, suffering far, far greater losses and injuries than those inflicted by the atomic bombs.[93]

Morison goes on to point out that the Japanese still had a million men under arms on the home islands, with over 5,000 Kamikaze planes left and:

> It requires no prophetic sense to foresee these horrible losses that would have been inflicted on our invading forces, even before they got ashore. After accepting these losses there would have been protracted battles on Japanese soil, which would have cost each side very many more lives, and created a bitterness which even time could hardly have healed.[94]

Only if the United States (after the horrific casualties it suffered on Okinawa and Iwo Jima) were willing to settle for a negotiated peace that would have left the Japanese undefeated and unoccupied could the war have ended without greater casualties than those suffered in the atomic bomb attacks on Hiroshima and Nagasaki.

In chapter seven, we shall be returning to the interplay between sustained ruthlessness and the role of superior will. Currently there is much tension between the use of sustained but controlled ruthlessness by democratic countries and the fact that sustained ruthlessness may backfire and cause the weakening of will on the part of the user. It remains to be seen how this will all play out in the future. For World War II in the Pacific, however, sustained ruthlessness—even sustained but controlled ruthlessness—and terror bombing arguably "worked."[95]

Of course, not every war, not every adversary, not every situation demands ruthlessness of the scale and magnitude and intent that we have examined in these examples. And sustained ruthlessness remains only one of the seven important patterns for success in war and should not be overestimated as an independent variable.

But the lessons of history clearly substantiate that Mars will eventually have the last word. Just because sustained ruthlessness—even ruthlessness applied in a controlled manner—is abhorrent to most of us, does not mean it wasn't efficacious in warfare in the past and won't be in the future.

Holocaust = evil but
→ controlled
"
relative
term

5

Receptivity to Military and Integrative Innovation

> The pulse of the God of War is hard to take.
>
> —Qiao Liang and Wang Xiangsui

Mars also is clearly partial to those societies and militaries that accept military innovation as a positive cultural value (both within the society and within the military itself). This may take the form of weapons development and the integration of them into the armed forces as well as tactical, strategic, and managerial changes to meet the ever-changing international environment and especially the integration of new knowledge.

We examine this element with some trepidation in light of Stephen Rosen's conclusion that it is difficult to find patterns in explaining innovation activities and Barry Watts and Williamson Murray's analysis that: "genuine innovation, like democratic government, is unlikely to be a tidy process—much less one that can be tightly or centrally controlled by senior defense managers. Indeed, attempts to eliminate the inherent messiness—including the tendency for adaption to proceed in fits and starts—may be one of the surest ways to kill innovation."[1]

But from the outset, we know at least that the attribute of innovation goes far beyond just acquiring new weapons. Here we are highlighting receptivity to innovation—innovation in equipment, logistics, processes, adjusting tactics and strategy to changing realities, management skills and training opportunities, even acceptance of new informational flows—which always needs to be part of a country's military tool kit. Yet for many militaries and societies, these innovations are missing. Why do some militaries accept innovation and others resist? Mars smiles on those who do accept innovation and, as some prominent historical examples show, over time frowns on and indeed punishes those who ignore innovation.

But not all societies accept the importance or validity of this paradigm.

There are some good reasons why military innovation is troublesome to many elites, both civilian and military, for as Holger H. Herwig puts it:

> Revolutionary change maximizes uncertainty and risk. Success is never guaranteed. New weapons demand new habits, new thinking, and new training. Enemy unpredictability, weather, friction, and the uncertainties inherent in battle are quite daunting enough without inviting further confusion through novelties of uncertain value.[2]

It is the thrust of this chapter that militaries and societies ignore military innovation at their own peril. We find many, if not most, militaries to be conservative and risk averse, quite resistant to change, often not prepared to fight the next war or wars. For example, in much of the history of the United States, the American society as a whole was generally more receptive to new technology than was its military.

In fact, many militaries in the world today seem designed not to fight wars against other militaries but to keep their own citizens in check. For them, following the dictates of Mars seems unnecessary and a waste of resources that could be better spent on the military elites themselves. Many of the world's military elites prefer to spend their country's money on their own creature comforts and lifestyle "requirements." These militaries simply represent pressure groups within their own societies. They wage "war" only on the national budget, and then spend most of those spoils not for training or technical innovation but on the military caste itself.

Thus it is not just the military's share of the national budget that matters to Mars, but what that share is used for. Looked at in this way, we can say that many militaries—and societies—throughout history have not readily accepted innovation, but have focused simply on keeping the top military officers happy. They often morphed into a ruling caste with no interest in military matters beyond staying in power.

In terms of receptivity to innovation, it is important to distinguish two dimensions to receptivity. The first is the more obvious, when new weapons appear (from somewhere, either from within the society or without), the military has a choice to accept, reject, or modify these innovations. But an important second dimension is the faith some societies and some militaries have in the value of expending scarce resources to develop new weapons that ultimately may or may not prove viable and useful.

Some examples of the failure to integrate existing new weapons and new technologies into the armed forces can underscore this point. But first let us look at the nature of successful military innovation.

USING INNOVATION SUCCESSFULLY

When Hannibal Barca led his Carthaginian, Spanish, and Celtic army to its overwhelming victory over the Romans in the Battle of Cannae, he stunned them with the audacity, discipline, and effectiveness of his Nubian horse cavalry. Hannibal's double envelopment and the destruction of 70,000 Romans should still be studied today by anyone wanting to learn about skill in battle and the importance of using military innovation.

Later tasked with bringing the war to Carthage, however, Publius Cornelius Scipio, having carefully studied the reasons for Hannibal's success, decided he could not to try match the Carthaginian cavalry with Roman horsemen. Instead, he recruited a North African king, Masinissa, whose cavalry troops were among the best in the Mediterranean basin. It is true that the Romans had long depended on foreign cavalry auxiliaries, but in this case, it was Scipio's decision to get the support of Masinissa and his cavalry that proved critical.

In addition, Scipio planned for the Carthaginian innovation of fighting elephants and introduced new, flexible infantry formations so that at the Battle of Zama in 202 BCE, when the Carthaginian war elephants charged, the Roman troops simply let them pass and even turned them against the Carthaginians by wounding them as they rumbled by.

The cavalry of Masinissa and the Romans' new anti-elephant tactics enabled Scipio to pull off a double envelopment of his own and defeat the Carthaginians. Tactical and strategic innovation by the Romans proved them worthy of Mars's honor.

Another example of classical receptivity to innovation and adaptation is Alexander the Great's reaction to encountering Indian war elephants at the Battle of Jhelum (326 BCE). Although the Macedonians won the battle, Alexander quickly saw the advantages of war elephants. First, they were effective killers that terrorized infantry. Second, the elephants would also scare cavalry horses. And third, they were far more difficult to stop with defensive stakes than horses. After the battle, Alexander had all surviving elephants rounded up and had the Indians train his men in their use. They remained in the service of the Greeks for generations afterward, even though Alexander's army refused to continue to campaign into India.

Much later, in the fourteenth century, the English discovered the value of the longbow after encountering it in their wars against the Welsh. The English saw how superior it was to their own crossbows due to its much higher rates of fire and ease of operation once one learned how to use it.

But as Clifford J. Rogers has so clearly indicated, it was not simply the weapon as a weapon, but the changes in tactics, strategy, and process that accompanied it that ultimately explains its success.[3] In the case of the longbow, it was not until masses of bows were employed by well-trained and proficient English archers that it became a war changing weapon. Then it became enormously important against heavy horse cavalry.

The English defeated the French at Crecy in 1346, and then again at Poitiers in 1356, in large part because of the longbow and its concomitant tactics, although as we saw in chapter three, discipline also played a major role. It is interesting to contrast the receptivity of the English to the long-bow when compared to that of the French.

The English kings saw the military potential of the longbow early and consistently. Various English kings such as Richard II, Edward the II, and Henry IV made its use compulsory. In 1339, for example, Richard II decreed that "servants and Laborers" needed "to obtain bows and arrows and to practice archery on Sundays and on holidays."[4] Again in 1410 Henry IV "Made archery practice compulsory for all able bodied men between the ages of sixteen and sixty," thereby integrating the use of the bow into the very society of the English.[5]

In this case, the receptivity to innovation had several dimensions, as the English accepted the longbow on various levels—military, political, and social—for as Hugh D. H. Soar indicates, "Monarch and commoner alike have recognized its power or used it to relax from life's stresses."[6]

RESISTANCE TO INNOVATION

Some militaries and societies throughout history fail to see the importance of innovation. parting the example above, even after they lost the Battle of Crecy due to the effectiveness of the longbow archers, the French nobility did not embrace bows as weapons of choice, preferring to hire mercenary crossbowmen from Italy. They lost again, this time even more decisively at the battle of Agincourt in 1415. For sixty years, the French steadfastly refused to "modernize" their weaponry in terms of accepting the efficacy of this new weapon, despite its proven advantages, including the fact that its ash arrows with bodkin arrowheads could pierce even steel helmets from inside 150 yards.[7]

As Philippe Contamine notes, even when in 1384, Charles VI of France prohibited playing at games other than archery and there thus resulted a vast improvement in the skills of those who worked with bows, the process was soon aborted: "But then there were fears of social subversion, for 'if they were gathered together they would be more powerful than the princes and nobles.'"[8]

French nobles simply did not want to risk their social or political posi-tion in order to integrate the weapon—and its concomitant weapons sys-tem—into their war-making efforts. To their detriment, they feared superior technology entrepreneurship in the hands of those they considered their social inferiors. Additionally, as Juliet Barker sums up the disdain of the French noblemen for the use of the bow, "I know little of hunting with the bow . . . . [I]f you want to know more, you had best go to England where it is a way of life."[9]

It is true that mastering the longbow took years of practice. Its use in battle also required bowmen to have the discipline to stand behind sharpened wooden stakes while human tanks in the form of armed knights bore down upon them. So again, it is not just the weapon but also the accompanying changes in discipline, tactics, strategy, and use that require flexibility. The longbow was an improvement on ordinary bows and crossbows (its rate of fire was six to seven times that of the crossbow), but it remained for the English to develop tactics (sending showers of arrows down upon opponents from longer distances of 250–300 yards and then straight on as they came closer) and refinements (the bodkin arrowhead could pierce armor plate).

Not only did the English accept the next technology, but they integrated it into a national production system. For his later campaign in 1418, for example, Henry V ordered his sheriffs to provide 1,190,000 arrows. This was a national appreciation of a new and very important military technological innovation.

Another striking example of the failure to innovate occurred in the Songhai Empire of western Africa, which occupied an area as large as the United States and controlled the lucrative salt and gold trades. Its various rulers were thus able to field professional armies as large as 30,000 warriors. As in medieval Europe, the Songhai armies at the time were dominated by "heavy horse"—mounted knights outfitted in chain mail and helmets. The Songhai kings were rich enough to afford all the new weapons then available, but they and their professional military were slow to see the advantages of the new firearms that were appearing around the Mediterranean basin and were reluctant to acquire them in any numbers.

In 1591, a Moroccan army equipped with muskets and artillery marched into the Songhai territory and soundly defeated them, with the new weapons providing a crucial role. The Songhai leaders and military had been rich enough and professional enough to have been likewise armed had they only chosen to do so, but the military was conservative and preferred the old ways. With their defeat at Tondibi in 1591 at the hands of the Moroccans, the Songhai Empire began a precipitous decline, with the subsequent loss of trade routes and the revenues they generated.[10]

By contrast, another African army, the Ethiopians under Menelek II, showed how having political authorities and the military hierarchy open to military innovation could prove extremely beneficial. During the latter decades of the nineteenth century, European conquest of the African continent took on increasing momentum as France, Great Britain, Germany, Belgium, Portugal, and Italy rushed to stake out claims to territory. Most African societies lacked the interest, the capital, or the access to the new weapons enjoyed by the Europeans. However, the Ethiopians, seeing the encroachment of the Italians, who occupied the Eritrean port of Massawa in 1885, decided to resist. Menelek's army invested in and adopted both rifles and rapid-firing artillery along with new tactics to meet the new European-style warfare.

At the Battle of Adowa, ten years later, the Ethiopians crushed the Italians and drove them back into Eritrea, saving the Ethiopian kingdom from colonial annexation for the next forty years. Only in 1936, and then only by using poison gas, machine guns, and aircraft, were the Italians able to overcome the Ethiopians. So Adowa stands as a very important exception in colonial warfare, where a dynamic leader moved outside the cultural norms to follow the Template of Mars properly.

The history of the United States military is also a veritable catalog of instances where those in authority refused to accept military innovations, even if they would change the course of warfare in the future.

In the middle of the American Civil War, for example, the Union's ordinance chief, James W. Ripley, refused to make the superior Spenser and Sharps breech-loading rifles standard, despite encouragement from President Lincoln to do so. Breech-loading rifles made it possible, for the first time in the history of warfare, for troops with long guns not to have to stand upright and be subjected to counterfire while they reloaded.

Ripley's reason for denying the new technology to his soldiers? He believed that the new weapons would use up too much ammunition. By 1864–1865 Union cavalry at least was reequipped with repeating rifles, and some have argued that this in and of itself constituted a "revolution in arms."[11] But the U.S. military also refused to purchase the six-barrel, multiple-projectile Gatling gun until 1866, when the war was over. Again, key elements of the American military were not receptive to the innovation it represented.

Let us also revisit the earlier example of the relationship between the United States military and the machine gun, which was to transform combat by the end of the nineteenth century. The Maxim gun, created by Hiram Maxim of Sangerville, Maine, in 1883—like the Gatling gun before it—had little appeal for the United States military. Ironically then, when the United States finally entered World War I in 1917, it had to get its machine guns from the French (and British) because it lacked sufficient numbers of them. Not surprisingly, the French equipped the American expeditionary forces with their cast-off Chauchat light machine gun—widely considered among the worst machine guns in any army during that period.[12]

By the time of their entrance into the war, the United States military was only beginning to integrate a few machine guns into its frontline units, while the Germans on the Western Front were thinking in terms of 1,000 interlocking machine guns per mile of front. How many Americans died charging into those fields of fire without any supporting machine gun fire from their own army due to a failure to appreciate receptivity to military innovation? We will never know for certain, but that number is undoubtedly very high.

Likewise, in terms of American failure to appreciate ingenuity, a U.S. inventor, John Deere, made the first tank. But the U.S. Army refused to consider it as an alternative to mounted cavalry. Even after World War I, and the successful showing of the fledgling U.S. Tank Corps in training exercises, the regular American Army eliminated the Armored Corps in 1920, and sent its officers back to the horse cavalry and the infantry.[13]

Between the two World Wars, the U.S. Army again rejected a homegrown innovation from American tank designer J. Walter Christie. Later, the Russians bought it and made it "the basis of the workhorse T-34 tank."[14] Although Christie's ideas were only a small part of the T-34's overall innovation, including its excellent weight distribution, the T-34 turned out to be arguably the most important tank (certainly the most important medium tank) of World War II in terms of its numbers and its durability, and a tank superior to any American tank of that era.

By contrast, the Sherman tank, the best American armored vehicle of World War II (at least until the M-25 Pershing with its 90 mm gun arrived in 1944), had but a one-to-five reverse kill ratio against the German Panther, Mark IV, and Tiger tanks, as in the European theater the German tanks knocked out five Shermans for every one they lost in tank battles. Its low-velocity 75 mm gun was one of the Sherman's weakest features and the bane of its crews when they encountered the more heavily armed German Panther and Tiger models. American tankers also often referred to the Sherman as "the Ronson" (the name of a popular cigarette lighter) for its perceived propensity to burst into flame when hit.[15] But because it was produced in prodigious numbers (all told 49,000) and was reliable mechanically, the Sherman had a significant impact on the battlefield.

For Mars, as Geoffrey Parker rightly claims, there thus is a challenge and response to weapons and process innovation that provides a dynamic that countries must accept. Not participating in the arms race is, of course, a choice. But since military technology is never static, no matter how much people and nations wish it were, there is always a new weapons system coming. While most societies around the world are satisfied with the military technology they have at any given moment in time, there can be a cumulating and detrimental effect on their relative position over time.

For example, the United States went to war against Japan in 1941 with 700 ships, of which only 8 were aircraft carriers. The Japanese had more carriers overall and better aircraft, and their air crews were better and more extensively trained. Ultimately, it would be the fast attack carriers that would provide the major force projection during the war in the Pacific, not the traditional capital ships of the previous war's navy, the battleship. Those who had promoted air power as the weapons of the future, such as the American General Billy Mitchell, were often ignored and criticized.

TWO INNOVATORS

By comparison, we can also look at innovation personified. A good example of receptivity to military innovation is the career of General Curtis LeMay. Although widely portrayed as a "warmonger" and "fascist," LeMay was largely responsible for creating a reliable deterrent for the United States during the Cold War. It is notable that two American presidents, Kennedy and Johnson, appointed and reappointed him to be chief of staff of the Air Force. Despite various assertions to the contrary, LeMay did not advocate using nuclear weapons against North Vietnam or Cuba, although he did urge that the United States invade Cuba during the Cuban Missile Crisis and use sustained ruthlessness against strategic targets in North Vietnam.[16]

LeMay not only pushed for the strategic importance of bombing, but he initiated processes and techniques to most effectively use the "new weapons" that came on line during World War II. For example, he personally mastered the B-17's revolutionary Norden bomb sight (which was one of the United States' greatest secrets of World War II), and, leading by example, initiated new bomber formations to reduce casualties in the air over Nazi-occupied Europe. But his greatest innovation was to switch the air war in the Pacific from the B-29 high-level bombing (30,000 feet), which was much less accurate over Japan than Germany due to the strong jet streams (often hundreds of miles an hour) over the Pacific, to low-level "firebombing" of Japanese cities. Since the B-29 was a very complex weapons system with 55,000 moving parts, vast supplies of those parts, fuel, and ordinance became critical to effect strategic bombing so far from America's factories.[17] But once in place, the B-29 became a war-winning weapons system.[18]

LeMay also went to the heart of strategic bombing and sustained ruthlessness when some questioned his approval of the killing of Japanese civilians. His logic was simple and most worthy of Mars, "Do you want to kill Japanese, or would you rather have Americans killed?"[19] To us, now at a safe distance from the horrors of World War II, this seems rather a simplistic choice, but to most Americans who fought in the Pacific theater, it was not.

After the war, he also built the Strategic Air Command integrating B-36s, B-47s, B-52s and mid-air refueling, and later intercontinental ballistic missiles into a seamless flow of weapons, training, and more training, keeping the United States at the forefront of military preparedness. LeMay insisted on the highest levels of training, with realistic missions done over and over again. For example, he had SAC bombers practice "hitting" every American city over 25,000 in population during thousands of missions. San Francisco alone was "bombed" 600 times in one month.[20]

While LeMay is a good example of top-down innovation, John Boyd is an equally fine example of a bottom-up innovator. One of the most revolutionary military minds in American history, Boyd is justifiably a legend for his innovative work, not just in one corner of the U.S. military but throughout its many facets and aspects.[21] A fighter pilot during the Korean War, he developed important insights into energy maneuver theory, which changed the way aerial dogfights were conducted. He also saw how the cockpit bubble canopy of the F-86 Sabre jet and better training enabled American pilots to score eight-to-one kills despite the speed and maneuver advantage of the Soviet MIG-15.[22]

Boyd would later be instrumental in the thinking that led to revolutionizing fighter aircraft themselves (including the F-15 Eagle and the F-16 Fighting Falcon). His sense of the importance of rapid movement, confusing one's opponent, and getting inside that opponent's decision-making cycle all recall the genius of Sun Tzu, whom he greatly admired.

Often working against the prevailing military ethos of the time, and in the face of savage opposition from some of his superiors, Boyd helped to inject into military thinking his monumental OODA process. In its simplest incarnation, OODA stands for "observe, orient, decide, and act." But, in fact and practice, it is a very elegant process consisting of a hundred feedback loops all designed for getting "inside" an enemy's decision-making loop and making your own decisions better and faster and more continuous.

His principles spread far and wide, from aerial combat to sustained aerial ground support (he lobbied to keep the Air Force in the close-support business and helped to design the A-10 Warthog), and from the Marine Corps and its tactics to the Army's Air/Land Battle, which so convincingly won the Gulf War of 1991. And as we shall see in chapter ten, his principles were also injected into the way successful insurgencies and counterinsurgencies are fought. Maximum flexibility, maximum speed, and constant movement are his legacy, for speed and maneuver become imbedded in all forms of warfare and lie at its heart.

RECEPTIVITY TO MILITARY INNOVATION

As in the "punctuated equilibrium" of biology, challenge and response in military practices stimulate action and reaction. For Mars to help any society maximize its success, the warriors in that society must override recalcitrant authorities when it comes to the introduction of military innovation. Often what impedes receptivity to the innovation impulse are the military leaders themselves. Many militaries are satisfied with the equipment, strategies, and techniques they have, and prefer to spend any additional funds on themselves. In other cases, it is the religious and cultural opposition that the military must try to override.

For example, in the Middle Ages, the crossbow was developed, but in 1139 Pope Innocent II tried to get it outlawed. Like the "Peace of God" and "Truce of God," these religious stipulations were never all-encompassing, nor did they lead to a freezing of innovation when it came to weapons of destruction. The papal stipulations were ignored by those militaries that wished to integrate the newer weapons and practice their war craft skills rather than please the pope. At other times, however, the papacy actually stimulated warfare, as when Pope Pius IV rallied Europe to fight the Ottomans before the seminal Battle of Lepanto Gulf in 1571.

This need for receptivity to military innovation is true in the midst of war as well as between them. At the time of the Anglo-American invasion of Sicily in 1943, for example, the Germans used radio-guided bombs (such as the FX-100), which were launched from bombers. These proved to be startlingly effective against ships during the subsequent landings at Salerno on the Italian mainland. But two months later, the U.S. Navy came up with jamming transmitters that drastically reduced the effectiveness of the guided bombs.

We now turn to three somewhat longer examples of societies whose military and political decision makers proved to be hostile to military innovation and paid a considerable price for that failure to appease Mars. These are also examples of non-Western societies that could have more effectively challenged European countries for global supremacy, but by their failure to truly and consistently worship at the shrine of Mars, did not.

China

First, there is the case of the Chinese. Ironically, over time, the Chinese have long proven to be very innovative with weapons, developing some of the most forward-looking and useful. For example, the Chinese had composite bows and crossbows 200 years before the West and gunpowder hundreds of years earlier as well, but they made neither central to their military planning or activities. The Chinese also invented the stirrup, which eventually made European "heavy horse" medieval warfare possible when it was finally adopted by Western horsemen.

The Chinese also were ahead of the West when they married the cannon and the ship, so that by the thirteenth century they were in a position to project force far across the then known world. At the same time, the Chinese seem to have failed to see the true importance of naval gunfire, keeping the number of cannons on ships low and using instead of mass gunfire the technique of firing a single volley or couple of volleys and then closing in to use their manpower advantages to board the other ship. The Chinese simply failed to see the revolution that cannons could make in any naval warfare situation.

The most striking example of the potential of Chinese force projection occurred later under the leadership of the Muslim eunuch, Admiral Zheng He. According to Daniel Boorstin and Felipe Fernandez-Armesto, between 1405 and 1433, Zheng led a series of major Chinese voyages far and wide in the Pacific and Indian Oceans.[23] In his most impressive one, Admiral Zheng took a massive fleet of 62 oceangoing junks together with 225 support vessels and nearly 28,000 men to Indonesia, India, Arabia, and Africa.[24] Some of his ships were 600 feet long, compared with the later ships of Columbus that measured 90–130 feet.

This formidable projection of Chinese power could well have presaged Chinese expansion into the New World, Africa, and Asia. By comparison, Columbus's first voyage was not until 1492, and Magellan did not become the first European to circumnavigate the globe until his 1519–1522 journey.

Some authors claim that Zheng He actually made it to the Americas or into "European" waters.[25] But however far Zheng He traveled, when he returned to China in 1423, conservative Confucian mandarins took over the government and stopped overseas expansion, wanting instead to concentrate on the Inner Kingdom and to rebuild the Great Wall of China.

The mandarins opposed commerce and overseas activities generally. So, by 1474, their decrees had reduced the imperial fleet to 140 ships, and by 1500, the Chinese government had made it a capital offense even to build a seagoing junk with more than two masts. Further, in 1525, coastal officials were ordered to destroy all such ships and arrest mariners who continued to sail in them. Even the records of Admiral He were destroyed. The Chinese were forbidden to go abroad, and even more incredibly, as Boorstin relates, "In 1551 the crime of espionage was redefined to include all who went to sea in multiple-masted ships, even if they went only to trade. The party of the anti-maritime bureaucrats had triumphed. China turned back on itself."[26]

Thus, when Europe was expanding and taking territory and subjugating peoples around the world, China was turning inward and landward, dooming itself to be discovered and preyed upon later by those societies from far away that were proving to be more receptive to military and process innovation, particularly for their navies and merchant marines. The Chinese did not anticipate the long-term implications of turning their back on the ongoing and future challenges of Mars. They paid for that failure, eventually suffering subjugation not only by the Western powers, but also by the Japanese, who were eventually willing to receive new European weapons technology and saw China as a weak, unmilitary, and attractive prey.

Each important military innovation broke the prevailing equilibrium and provoked a phase of rapid transformation and adjustment. The Chinese could have continued to project power across the globe. Instead they chose not to, leaving the field to the European explorers, conquerors, and eventually imperialists. When it came, the great Manchu dynasty expansion of the seventeenth century would therefore have to rely on its army rather than meet the intruding ships with its navy.

Japan

One of China's own adversaries, Japan, itself provides an important example of the failure of a military elite to be receptive to innovation. In chapter two we pointed out the overwhelming revolution that the "fiery weapons" produced, first in Europe and then on the global scene.

In the case of Japan, the Oda clan got muskets from the Portuguese in the 1540s, and for twenty years the Odas trained their soldiers in secret so that when they were attacked by the more powerful Takeda clan, the Odas utilized their new weapons to great effect. In the process of experimenting with firearms prior to the battle, the Odas invented volley fire (the best use of firearms, in which one rank fires, the other stands ready, and then while the first rank reloads, the second rank fires).

The musket importation of the Oda started out as an excellent example of a military showing entrepreneurship by taking a weapon and improving its performance through discipline and innovation. In Europe, for example, the Dutch are credited with developing volley fire in the West but not until the 1590s, underscoring the fact that the Japanese were ahead of the West in this important tactical innovation.

In the important Battle of Nagashino in 1575, the Oda clan deployed 10,000 harquebusiers and destroyed the attacking Takedas. The samurai knights of the Takedas attacked over and over and were slaughtered by the guns of the Oda. It was potentially the dawn of a new age that could have given the Japanese a potentially major power boost in Asia.

Initially, the gun did enable a new polity to evolve out of the previous feudal power diffusion and led to the invasions of Korea and China by the warlord Toyotomi Hideyoshi and Oda Nobunaga in the 1590s.[27] But by 1625, the Japanese government issued severe restrictions on the use of firearms because they threatened the position of the samurai warriors (the equivalent of knights in the West) in society. Because it took years and years to train a samurai, and the guns could enable a peasant with little training

to kill the best-trained and most experienced fighting man, guns represented a threat to the existing social structure itself.[28] This phenomenon was
analogous to the French knight's opposition to usage of the longbow.

As a society, Japan ultimately refused to integrate the new military technology into its society in order to keep the old military and social order in
place even though their use of volley fire as well as pike and gun formations were either ahead of, or contemporary with, these advancements in
the West. As with the French knights and the longbow, it was the samurai
warriors themselves who refused to accept the primacy of the new weapons,
and their opposition ultimately forced the abandonment of firearms.

By contrast, in the West, with the widening use of gunpowder, the predominance of "heavy horse" mounted knights (the basis of feudal warfare) became an anachronism. The Western knights were made obsolete
by events and the rapidly evolving firearms dispersal throughout various
societies in Europe. By opting out of the "fiery weapons" arms race, the
Japanese allowed the West a major advantage in military technology. It
was not until 250 years later when Admiral Peary "opened up" Japanese
ports with raw naval gun fire, that they returned belatedly to the pursuit of
firearms and cannons.

Of course, some in the West were not without such feelings of revulsion
that the lower orders could kill their betters so easily. In his epic poem *Or-
lando Furioso*, the Italian poet Ludovico Ariosto laments the passing of an
era, as Furioso throws a gun into the sea with the words, "To ensure that no
knight will ever again be intimidated by you, and that no villain will ever
again boast himself the equal of a good man because of you, sink here." But
in the West, such lofty sentiments did not change the climate of acceptance
of "these fiery weapons" and their eventual integration into the military life
of the continent as the gunpowder revolution spread across Europe.

Later, in the nineteenth century, when the Japanese decided to innovate
and worship more effectively at the altar of Mars, they ultimately copied
the West with a vengeance, and in the twentieth century defeated Russia,
dominated Britain and France in Asia, occupied major portions of China,
and even threatened the United States from 1941 until 1943. The Japanese
had belatedly decided to follow Mars in accenting receptivity to military
and process innovation. Once they did, their advancement to the top ranks
of military powers proceeded apace. In doing so, they also underscored the
universal aspects of the Template's important ingredient of process and
weapons innovation.

Turkey

A final example of a failure to continually follow Mars and to end up
being militarily eclipsed by others is that of the Turks. Although theirs was

a more ambiguous relationship between military culture and receptivity to military innovation, on balance, there is a marked bifurcation of their attitudes between the period 1500–1700 and that of 1700–1900.

The Turks never made the same continual commitment to military innovation in the second period that many European countries did. Perhaps the difference can best be seen as the Turks' inability to understand just how jealous a god Mars really is, and how worshiping him from time to time—rather than continually—would cost them dearly.

But that is how matters ended, not how they began. If a visitor from another planet had visited Earth in 1522, he or she would have been astonished at the power and military mastery of the Ottoman Empire and its relentless expansion, which had been going on since the middle of the previous century. Ever since Mehmet II seized Constantinople in 1453, the Turks had been on the ascendancy in and around the Mediterranean basin. That year, they also took Serbia; in 1463, Bosnia; and in 1468, Albania; and by the end of fifteenth century, they even threatened Hungary.

In his turn, Selim the Grim (1512–1520) conquered Iran, Iraq, Egypt, and Arabia, and the Turks reached the height of their power under Süleyman the Magnificent (1520–1566) as the Ottoman Empire turned toward Christian Europe, capturing Belgrade in 1521 and seizing Rhodes, the last European military presence in the eastern Mediterranean, in 1522.

Thus, in 1522, the Ottomans seemed poised to conquer the West. As Roger Crowley points out, not since the Roman Empire had there been such an organized, bureaucratic state able to call upon enough wealth and military power to seize and hold the Mediterranean basin.[29]

Across North Africa, Ottoman corsairs based in Tunis, Tripoli, and Algiers raided far and wide, capturing slaves and taking wealth from the coastal areas of Spain, France, Italy, Sicily, and the Dalmatian Coast. Europeans lived in fear of Ottoman power and force projection on a yearly basis. With the Turks in the Balkans and North Africa, the future looked dark indeed. As one observer put it, "Turkish expansion is like the sea . . . it never has peace but always rolls."[30]

But there was always ambiguity in the Ottoman relation to military innovation, even as their campaign successes were piling up. When he seized Constantinople in 1453, Sultan Mehmet II used a Transylvanian cannon foundry's twenty-eight-foot-long cannon (the most powerful of its day) to knock down the walls. Ironically, the Ottoman Turks under Mehmet got those cannons from an Austrian (because the Hapsburgs wouldn't pay him enough for his new weapon). But after he blew down the walls of Constantinople with these big cannons, Mehmet had them dragged to Belgrade, where he eventually—and symbolically—left them lying in the mud.

The Turks thus used the new weapons, but never made their constant improvement and integration into war-making tactics central to their vision of ongoing military supremacy, as did the Europeans. Süleyman the Magnificent crushed the Hungarians at the Battle of Mohacs on August 29, 1526, a battle in which 30,000 European troops lost their lives. But in 1529, when Süleyman invested Vienna with an army of 75,000, we see again the extent to which the Ottomans had an ambiguous relationship with the "fiery weapons." While they had effectively used cannons to knock down the walls of Constantinople and the fortress on Rhodes, in their attempt at the siege of Vienna, they brought only light artillery, not the heavy artillery necessary. Instead they relied on trench and mine warfare. As far as the Turks were concerned, "gunfire was an auxiliary."[31] Lacking the firepower to win the battle quickly, Süleyman was forced to retire to winter quarters, never to return.

Later, when Sultan Mehmed IV returned to besiege Vienna in 1683, he again brought with him light artillery that could kill people and destroy houses. But without heavy artillery to destroy the walls, bastions, and palisades, he was unable to subdue the city before a large Christian relief force showed up and routed his forces.[32]

This Turkish failure to continually embrace military innovation must be seen in light of the successes the Turks had even without following Mars, as well as in relation to their European adversaries. For Crowley, it was a close-run struggle between Turkey and European countries, with the Ottomans checked first in the siege of Malta in 1565 and then six years later at one of the most important sea battles of the age, the 1571 Battle of Lepanto Gulf off Corinth. There Turkish Mediterranean naval expansion was decisively defeated in the largest naval battle ever fought in the Mediterranean, one involving over 600 ships. The Christians fielded 300 ships, with 50,000 rowers and 30,000 soldiers, while the Turks had 100,000 men in 310 ships.

According to Victor Hanson, the mainstay of the Christian effort was the Venetians, who had capital and an arsenal where they mass-produced galleys, keeping the makings on hand so they could build a galley in a couple of hours and a fleet in a week. Although Venice had only 200,000 people, "The Arsenal was a natural expression of Venetian capitalism and constitutional government."[33]

In the ensuing battle, the Turks lost over 200 of their ships. Why? The Christians were successful, Hanson believes, because they were able to field 1,815 guns to 750 for the Turks and because of their entrepreneurship—the Venetians' ability to introduce more and better cannons, including mass-produced heavy iron cannons and smaller swiveling brass cannons. In addition, risk-taking captains cut off the "beaks" of ramming galleys to put on more guns and thus were able to marshal their military innovation to maximum advantage.

For his part, however, John Guilmartin Jr. is less inclined to give total credit to the factors listed by Hanson, seeing a much greater role in the battle played by the leadership and the tactical skill of the Europeans and notes, not without irony, that contrary to many accounts, the battle went amazingly according to plan. In the final analysis, Guilmartin views Lepanto not as some truly decisive turning point in history but rather a chapter ending the Mediterranean galley form of warfare at sea with its reliance on human rowers.[34]

Crowley, also rightly points out that this armada of the Holy League, a marriage of forced convenience among the Hapsburg monarch Philip V, the Venetians, and Pope Clement V (Spain paid for half the Armada, the Venetians a third and the Papacy one-sixth) greatly benefited from the six Venetian galleasses, heavily armed gun platforms that crushed the Turkish center.[35]

He also asserts that it was not the Venetians' inspiration, but the specific orders of Don Juan, the admiral of the fleet and half brother to Philip, to cut off the beaks of the galleys in order to pack more firepower onto their bows that helped to alter the strategic balance.[36] In any case, in terms of receptivity to military innovation, the Turks proved to be relatively less adaptive.

In the ensuing battle, Christian ships collided head-on with the Turkish vessels and destroyed them, and then they killed virtually every Turk in the water. That day, the Turks would suffer their most significant loss in 200 years. Some 40,000 men would die that day. 12,000 Christian slaves were freed, and 137 Turkish ships captured. It came as a huge shock to the Turks as well as to Christian Europe, for as Cervantes wrote of the battle, "That day so fortunate to Christendom . . . all nations were undeceived of their error in believing that the Turks were invincible."

The Turks also had the capacity and the technological skills to project power overseas, but eventually they became resigned to being a land power. "God," an Ottoman official told the English traveler Paul Rycaut in the 1660s, "has given the sea to the Christians, while reserving the land for the Muslims."[37] The Ottoman official was not quite correct in that, for their surrogates in North Africa continued seizing European shipping for more than two centuries as Barbary pirates, who raided as far afield as Ireland in the late 1700s.

Ultimately and unfortunately for their subsequent fortunes, there was a debilitating fatalism in the Turks' response to defeat. Their senior commander, Kapudan Pasha, said simply, "The fleet of the divinely guided Empire encountered the fleet of the wretched infidels, and the will of Allah turned the other way."[38] There was no mention made of the technological, logistical, and strategic advantages of the Christian forces.

As Jason Goodwin points out, "Peoples dedicated to war is not the same thing as peoples dedicated to warcraft." He sees the "down-drag" of religion on military innovation, citing the Koran, "Every novelty is an innovation, every innovation is an error, every error leads to Hellfire."[39] Since for the Ottomans, "Time is circular, not linear" and "Fatalism the ballast of the Ottoman valor," European visitors glorified the Ottoman opposition to machines and the horrors of the industrial revolution, but that revolution enabled the West to conquer the world.[40]

Of course, there can be very important cultural biases (both within the military and the broader society and culture) against innovation in warfare, as in other aspects of life. Yet these observations seem to tell less than the whole story. Niccolo Capponi, for example, documents a number of instances in the earlier period when the Ottomans successfully used artillery and handgun-armed janissaries, especially at the 1526 Battle of Mohacs, and introduced galley artillery fire against the Mytilene.[41]

In any case, worshiping Mars clearly requires dedication and ongoing commitment to his dictates. In retrospect, for the period 1500–1700, the Ottomans were much more likely to follow these rules than they were from 1700–1900. The decline of the Ottoman Empire in this latter period can be seen most clearly within the analytic framework of the Template.

We will take this opportunity to look at the Template as a series of interlocking variables whose cumulative effect can bring success or failure in warfare. Many scholars have looked at the decline of the Ottoman Empire and come to a number of conclusions as to its causes. Let us use the Template to examine the more telling ones.

First, there was the relative failure of the Turks to keep up with military technology. Daniel Goffman, for example, points to the great strides made by the European maritime powers such as the English, Dutch, and French, and their introduction into the world of the Turkish galleys the smaller, faster, and more maneuverable *bertones*.[42]

Daniel Quataert also asserts that the newer military technologies being developed in the West cost more and more to produce and integrate into the armed forces, leaving the Ottomans at a distinct disadvantage due to the great infusion of wealth from the New World upon which the aggressive countries of the West could rely.[43]

Second, there was the Ottoman failure to be receptive, not just to the new military technologies, but also to the bureaucratic revolution taking place in military organization and the loss of central control due to decentralization within the empire. There was a similar and concomitant failure to industrialize and modernize their economy to keep pace with the countries of the West and their growing economic engines.

This failure to modernize their economy was also clearly exacerbated by the absolute and relative failure of the Turks to protect capital from the people even within the confines of their existing spheres of influence. The Turks' loss of vast stretches of territory resulted in the widespread loss of wealth from these areas, a loss that further reduced the total gross domestic product available for military purposes. The result was that by the eighteenth century, the cost of maintaining its army and large fleet became "intolerable."[44]

There was also the failure to protect capital from misuse by the existing military. Instead of the military being a prime force for modernization, it had become a substantial drain on the capital available for both offense and defense. For example, after 1699 when Huseyin Pasa attempted to reform the military, he found that while there were 70,000 janissaries on the rolls and being paid, only 10,000 actually were prepared to fight.[45] Also, the janissaries as a class had become, as Dietrich Jung suggests, a reactionary caste, often seeking to thwart military as well as economic progress. Indeed, various reformers such as Mahmud II, who tried to create a more modern army, were stymied time and again: "At the end of the eighteenth century, the janissaries had degenerated into an idle military caste carefully protecting their traditions and principles."[46]

Third, in the area of will, the Ottoman Empire suffered dramatically relative to the increase in the wills of others, especially from the rise of dynastic powers in Europe and later nationalism in Austria, Poland, and Russia as these peoples increased their self-identity and their willingness to die for that self-identity. Rhoads Murphy, for example, believes that "what had changed in Europe circa 1685 was that individual, entrepreneurial and private and semi-private initiative in the military sphere had begun to be replaced by collective action on a hitherto unprecedented scale."[47]

Fourth, in the element of "there will always be another war," the Ottomans ended up being on the defensive for much of the period under review. Instead of having a forward-looking, aggressive, optimistic frame for that assumption, they began to think more and more defensively, trying to hold on to the status quo. They prepared over and over for what Daniel Quataert has called "the wars of contraction," especially between 1683 and 1798.[48]

Moreover, even as some European powers were gaining in military ability and confidence, loss of martial pride and confidence grew within the Ottoman Empire. The defeats sapped the strength of the Turkish military because it was constantly on the defensive for much of this later period, not just in the Balkans and versus Russia or Austria, but in Iran as well.

Fifth, the Ottoman Empire, which had been so powerfully centralized in the sixteenth century, was by the eighteenth highly decentralized. This meant that even when the political center made correct decisions about military improvements (in discipline, technology, and innovative managerial techniques), and even saw the need to develop and industrialize, the degree of decentralization made it less and less possible that these correct decisions could be implemented throughout the Empire. In this regard, William McNeill adds additional reasons for the decline of the Ottomans.

He believes that the failure of the Sultans to lead their military campaigns in person and the internal discipline of the Sultans' slave households became unreliable, further weakening the political center.[49]

We have only touched on these tantalizing elements here, but a future comparison of the Ottoman Empire in the period 1500–1700 and then from 1700 to 1900 using the Template more extensively and in much greater depth might prove to be of significant assistance comparing the Ottomans against themselves through time and space, as well as with regard to contemporary European developments for similar periods.

In this regard, Geoffrey Parker argues correctly that although war is widespread in most human societies, the societies of the West have proven at least in the past to be particularly adroit at waging war and making it more central to their states over a long period of time.[50] While one can—and should—certainly argue with his thesis over the long course of all human history, he is certainly spot on for the period under review. During this time frame, the European militaries were simply far more open to the new military technologies (and far more willing to pay for them) than were other societies around the world. Europeans got better and better at war making because their rivals in Europe were getting better and better. As William McNeill puts it, "Perennial rivalries among the neighboring states and rulers therefore put a forced draft under the continued evolution of the art of war" and led to what he called "the gunpowder empires."[51]

Thomas Sowell at the Hoover Institute makes a further telling argument:

> The very nature of European dominance evolved in step with the evolution of guns and cannon. Early, crude, inaccurate, and slow-loading firearms had no decisive advantage against fast charging horsemen and fast shooting archers. Although Europeans began making cannons in the first half of the fourteenth century, it was two centuries later before military battles began to be won by field artillery. The immobility of heavy early cannons, which limited their usefulness on land, was not as major of a handicap at sea, however, where the warship itself provided the mobility for its cannon, leading to European dominance on the oceans of the world, long before the mass territorial conquests which created European land empires overseas.[52]

But just because the Chinese, the Japanese, and the Turks at certain times chose to avoid some aspects of the risk-taking of military and societal innovation does not mean that they had to do so, and choosing to avoid military entrepreneurship at one time did not mean they were forever bound to make the same mistakes of avoiding the lessons of Mars again.

Likewise, those states of the West that in the past were willing to dedicate more of their scarce resources to military innovation and for a longer time chose this path and were successful at it. But many countries of Western

Europe are no longer making that set of choices, and it remains to be seen if the military world of the twenty-first century will see them phased out of the good graces of Mars.

In conclusion, during the period before and during the great global expansion of the West, many other societies could have worshiped Mars to a greater extent than they did and thus found themselves in a position of military inferiority. The Chinese, the Japanese, the Ottoman Turks, as well as the earlier African empires of Mali under Mansa Musa (Dark Ages) and Songhai (thirteenth century), and the Aztec (Mexica) and Inca Empires all could have decided to worship Mars more, and more effectively, than they did for long periods of time.

But they did not. And therein lies an important tale.

THE CHOICE OF CHANGE

Whether due to cultural dimensions or simply a lack of leadership and vision—some societies throughout history chose not to remain faithful to the Template of Mars. And Mars made them pay a steep price for their dereliction.

Some may see this process as the tyranny of a particular military or civilian culture, but from the position of success in war, these were cultural and strategic mistakes, regardless of why they were made. The Template of Mars may be shunned because of cultural values, but that does not detract from the efficacy of its elements.

Many authors have argued that this reluctance is overwhelmingly due to cultural inhibitions and patterns. This is a fair assumption, but only up to a point. When any society transcends its previous cultural constraints—either because of a savage defeat or changed international goals—it is free to worship at the shrine of Mars. It is the choice of following the Template of Mars or not following that template that can transcend a society's cultural starting point.

Changes in Strategy and Tactics

The importance of receptivity to military and process innovation is not limited to the weapons themselves. It applies to strategy and tactics as well. Once a new weapon is utilized (such as the rifle as an improvement on the musket), the military tactics must at least take the new equipment into account.

For example, in the First Afghan War, the British, whose "Brown Bess" muskets had a range of only 150 yards, failed to take into account the long-barreled jezails of the Afghanis, which had a range of over 350 yards. When they formed their traditional square on the plains, the Afghanis simply stayed out of range and shot the British soldiers down one after the other. Disaster followed and the British were ignominiously defeated.[53]

In the early years of the American Civil War, soldiers were trained to stand shoulder to shoulder and fire as their opponents advanced. Since the effective range of the musket had been 50–60 yards and now the rifle could effectively kill at 150–200 yards, these standing formations became killing zones, and their continued use produced horrific casualties. In fact, so deadly were the new weapons when melded to the old formations that the casualties were truly staggering, producing the highest ratio of deaths per soldier engaged in the history of American warfare. Whereas in World War II, 6.7 percent of troops engaged in combat were killed, in the American Civil War, that figure was 29 percent.

It was not unusual for units—Northern and Southern—to suffer 50 to 60 percent casualties, and at Gettysburg, some units such as the First Minnesotans suffered 80 percent casualties. This was a high price paid for (among other things) a failure to understand the military change in tactics and strategy required to correlate with innovations. Perhaps, given the problems of command and control of the large formations employed, this is more understandable, but it was not less lethal for the soldiers involved.

In fact, the increased and almost exponential change in firepower from the American Civil War until 1914 brought no major difference in the common tactical approach to frontal assaults during that period. Reading about the failure of strategy to catch up with the newer weapons can be startlingly depressing, as most European armies went into World War I with the notion that attacks were more likely to succeed than defensive strategies.

As a consequence of the failure to change tactics and strategies, the later horrendous slaughter in World War I on the Somme, Verdun, and Passchendaele battlefields occurred on the most heightened of scales as the hypertrophy of war overwhelmed all efforts to reduce lethality. Wave after wave, tens of thousands strong, humans went to their deaths in the face of torrents of machine gun, artillery, and rapid-volley rifle fire. Shelford Bidwell and Dominick Graham rightly underscore the extent to which the "combination of old ideas and new weapons" along with a lack of coordination between the various branches of the armed forces caused such destruction.[54]

In a number of battles, the troops were made to walk rather than run into that maelstrom, with predictably horrible results. At the battle of the Somme in 1916, for example, to calm their nerves and show *sang froid*, British troops were allowed to kick soccer balls ahead of them as they advanced, although as Peter Hart indicates, commanders felt they had to keep a tight reign on their men so they didn't kick the ball too hard or fast and then run after it.[55] The tactic of British troops walking into the maelstrom of the Somme puzzled the Germans: "We were surprised to see them walking. We had never seen that before. . . . When we started to fire we just had to load and reload. They went down in their hundreds. We didn't have to aim, we just fired into them."[56]

In fact, the defense was so strong that the defending side won most of the major battles of World War I on the Western Front. There were no true offensive victories until the Germans finally collapsed from the strain of their final 1918 offensive and the subsequent Allied counterattack prevailed.[57]

Even a cursory study of World War I finds considerable support for the theory that the Allies only won because when both sides were exhausted in 1918 and on the verge of collapse, a million fresh American troops simply tipped the balance in their favor. The Germans had no such additional manpower pool to draw on at the end of the war.[58]

Interestingly enough, in war, when it comes to receptivity to military and process innovation, the losers often learn more than the winners. For example, the Prussians were defeated by Napoleon at Jena in 1806, but they subsequently regrouped to form a national army by 1815. The Prussians transformed their army with advanced training, greatly improved discipline, and modern mobilization methods including the use of railroads. In addition they had the technological advantage of the needle gun and breech-loading artillery, which enabled the Prussians to overpower the Austrians in 1866 and the French in 1870–1871.

Likewise the Germans after World War I, having lost that horrible war of attrition, began to develop the use of shock-troop tactics and rapid movement they had begun to use at the very end of the war. Between World War I and World War II they developed the blitzkrieg that proved to be so successful in the Polish campaign and later against France and Britain, both tactically and strategically.

The American military, which saw the Vietnam War lost in 1975, even though they won every significant battle fought in that war (some very Pyrrhic in nature), completely revitalized their army and air force. The American military introduced new weapons systems, adding greatly advanced training and military professionalism, plus a quantum leap in strategic thinking.

For example, they began to appreciate the writings and insights of Clausewitz. The integration of his theories into twentieth-century warfare resulted in one of their most impressive victories in the 1991 Gulf War. The worshiping of Mars, especially the assumption that "there will always be another war" paid off dramatically and unexpectedly when the military freed itself from the constraints of the past and dedicated itself to the worship of Mars, at least in that war.

Receptivity to military and process innovation obviously differs greatly from military to military, country to country, and age to age, but even a small degree of difference with regard to receptivity can be of enormous consequence when one finds oneself in a new war.

Changes in Intelligence Gathering

There is also a final, very important element in war fighting, which has to do with strategic and tactical reaction to intelligence gathering and its subsequent use in a timely fashion. Sun Tzu put it best in *The Art of War*, "Know the enemy and know yourself; in a hundred battles you will never be in peril."

This receptivity to new information is of enormous importance, since so much information swirls about in the fog of war. Commanders since time immemorial have had to make judgments based on conflicting "evidence." Confusion levels often replicate the image of just "a pig looking at a watch," in intelligence gathering parlance.

Take two examples, one that shows the dangers of the failure to integrate new knowledge into one's battle plans, and a second that shows how knowledge in and of itself can give one side a huge operational advantage. In addition, we will leave for chapter ten a discussion of the situation where previously new knowledge was subsequently "lost" to decision makers and then rediscovered, as in the case of the U.S. experience and knowledge of successful counterinsurgency techniques.

The United States in Korea

In the first instance, we look at the United States/United Nations effort in Korea and compare it with the contending Chinese operations. In October 1950, North Korea had been defeated in its invasion of the South. South Korean troops moved north into North Korea, followed by American and other UN forces. The UN coalition rapidly moved toward the Yalu River, the border between Korea and China. For General Douglas MacArthur and his senior staff, the war was drawing to a close. They did not believe that the Chinese would enter the war to rescue the defeated North Koreans.

In fact, so sure of victory was MacArthur that he had been sending his strategic bombing assets such as the heavy B-29 bomber wings back to the United States. But since July 1950, entire Chinese divisions, indeed, whole armies, had moved from their positions opposite Formosa (now Taiwan) all across China and into Manchuria opposite North Korea.

Mao Tse-tung had decided to intervene in Korea if the U.S. formations moved north of the thirty-eighth parallel, and he communicated that to the United States through the Indian Ambassador K. M. Panikkar to Beijing, so the United States should have expected, or at least not dismissed out of hand, that possibility.[59] Incidentally, Mao also stated to his commanders that he would not intervene if only South Korean forces went north of the thirty-eighth.

In preparation for their possible attack, six Chinese armies moved north from central and coastal China to prepare to intervene across the Yalu River if they were needed. In fact, at the very time General MacArthur and his staff were assuring the president of the United States at their meeting on Wake Island on October 15, 1950, that the Chinese would never enter the war and if they did, it would be "the greatest slaughter in the history of mankind," the Chinese were about to do exactly that. They indeed produced a savage defeat—but one for the UN forces.[60]

When the Chinese attacked, they sent the U.S./UN forces reeling backward. MacArthur was stunned. After all, he had flown over North Korea during the day earlier and had seen no Chinese. He simply refused to believe that the Chinese would ever enter the war.

Because MacArthur's personal mind-set dominated his staff in Tokyo, brooking no alternative interpretation of battlefield reality, it had become their mind-set as well. New information that the Chinese had, in fact, intervened was ignored. In terms of the Template of Mars, the intelligence-gathering apparatus was flawed. It was a very closed system of wishful thinking and disregard for any evidence that didn't fit the hypothesis that the war was over and the Chinese were not going to intervene.

In point of fact, MacArthur had forbidden the U.S. Central Intelligence Agency from intervening in Korea, and they were not allowed to operate in his theater of operations.[61] Even more incredibly, he refused to allow the normal military intelligence (G-2) to operate except though his totally subservient staff. This meant that new information, even accurate new information, coming in from the field was filtered through the existing mind-set of headquarters. MacArthur had said that the Chinese would never intervene, and thus any field information to the contrary was ignored, discarded, or downplayed.

In consequence, as the U.S. forces encountered Chinese forces and in fact captured many, these Chinese prisoners, fearing that they would be turned over to the South Koreans for torture, readily gave their names, their units, and the designations of the other Chinese units near them. The airwaves were full of Chinese-language chatter, and the local U.S. Army and Marine units identified no fewer than six Chinese armies present in Korea. Line units captured Chinese prisoners who were well fed and equipped, and who belonged to known Chinese army units, units that were supposed to be in central China, not Korea.

By November 1, the brilliant Chinese general Peng Dehuai had moved his entire Thirteenth Army Group (eighteen divisions) under General Li Tianyu into Korea, where it was poised to strike the Eighth Army in the west, while the Ninth Army Group (twelve divisions) led by General Song

Shilun was ready to smash the X Corps in the east. Peng was to prove a worthy adversary for the United States. In fact, one could argue that General Peng, along with General Matthew Ridgeway of the United States, turned out to be the premier field commanders of the entire war.

So, there was new and vital intelligence information. That information was valid information. It was flowing to MacArthur's headquarters in Tokyo on a daily if not hourly basis. The "tip of the spear" soldiers were capturing and interrogating Chinese regular unit troops, and they were saying, "we are here and there are many of us." There were, in fact, hundreds of thousands of Chinese from thirty different divisions.

Was the U.S. command receptive to intelligence and responsive to innovation in the form of new, contradictory information? Not at all. In fact, as line units passed their new and vital information up the chain of command, their reports were met with disbelief and derision.

Acknowledging this gross failure to accept valid information not only is one of the most poignant episodes of this, or any other war, it represents a drastic failure to appreciate the dictates of Mars. On November 28, for example, the commander of the U.S. X Corps, General Ned Almond, flew into North Korea and discussed the situation with Colonel Don Faith, the head of Task Force Faith, a unit of the Seventh Division, which was moving up the east side of the Chosin Reservoir as the U.S. First Marine Division was moving up the west side. For days, Colonel Faith's troops had been under heavy attack by three different Chinese divisions and had suffered considerable casualties. For the soldier of Task Force Faith, the Chinese offensive had already begun.

However, when General Almond arrived, he cavalierly dismissed their information out of hand, dispensed three medals to random troops, and told Colonel Faith not to be afraid of a few Chinese stragglers.[62] Almond then flew back to Tokyo that night. Colonel Faith and his entire Task Force would be wiped out within days, Colonel Faith being killed in action trying to get some of his wounded soldiers back to safety.

The point of this Korean vignette is to dramatize a clear failure to adhere to the Template of Mars, a mind-set that penalized the U.S. high command for its unwillingness to integrate new knowledge into its decision-making loop. That failure resulted in what would become in December 1950 the longest military withdrawal in U.S. military history.

On November 26, the Chinese units smashed into the U.S./UN Eighth Army in the west of Korea and decisively defeated it, sending it from close to the Yalu River to the extreme southern portion of the peninsula. Also, across the Korean peninsula, other Chinese formations surrounded the U.S. First Marine Division and U.S. Army Seventh Division and sent the latter, plus the U.S. Third Division and the South Korean ROK Capital Division, on a pell-mell retreat to the port of Hamhung, from which they were all eventually evacuated, while the former had to fight their way out through the encirclement.[63]

From the perspective of Mars, of course, the Chinese deserved to win this battle. The failure to be receptive to new military knowledge doomed the U.S./UN effort in North Korea, suggesting that one ignores this dimension of the Template of Mars at one's peril.

The British in Ireland

By contrast, British receptivity to new information in its war against the IRA in Northern Ireland shows how being open to ongoing intelligence is critical to military success. In this very long war (1967–2007), the British army greatly expanded its information-gathering techniques, centralized that information, and developed a sophisticated database. Each soldier on patrol was expected to know at least thirty suspects' face, name, and address, and there was competition within and among units to secure the best information about individuals, their contacts, and the license plate numbers of the cars they would use.[64] Each soldier became a data gatherer, and the resulting information was highly valuable in determining IRA action patterns, being used extensively to preempt or disrupt operations before they were activated.

Bing West also documented this type of innovative behavior during the climactic turning point in Anbar province in 2006, when American officers on the ground instituted similar data-gathering operations, turning cities such as Ramadi into digital pictures, with profiles of all males using personal computers combined with house-to-house "census" gathering.[65]

Today, in Afghanistan, U.S. forces while on patrol use a small device that takes photos, fingerprints, and an iris scan of people they meet. These are all put into a database so that the next time they are in a village or area, they know who belongs and who does not. Knowledge acquired in this way not only becomes power, it becomes life saving for the troops in the field. In Iraq, U.S. forces also collect biometric data at border points with Iran and Syria in an effort to create an effective database in order to catch would-be insurgents before they enter the country, or to apprehend those who seek to return.

So from the perspective of Mars, receptivity to military innovation involves a number of critical elements that are extremely productive in terms of return on military investment. The first is the development or acquisition of new weapons over time. The second is the integration of those weapons into a production, training, and use processes.[66] The third is the adjustment of tactics and strategy to reflect the impact on war fighting these changes will involve. The fourth is the receptivity to new information before, during, and after a war.

All four are important, even vital, components in the ongoing contest to see whom Mars will reward more. Warfare is never static, and weapons and tactics must always be changed and improved. Motives and goals of countries, leaders, and generals change. Being receptive to new information, new weapons, new processes and changes in any battle space remains a critical element in the Template of Mars. Mars remains, in terms of ongoing change, a most jealous god.

6

The Ability and Willingness
to Protect Capital
from People and Rulers

War is such a lavish consumer that it always makes a great market.

—James Stokesbury

In order to please Mars, it is important that the available capital for new weapons and superior training be kept from those who would spend it on other things, whether they are the people or the rulers. Mars favors states that year in and year out prepare for the eventuality of war (See chapter eight). Gustavus Adolphus liked to say, "War must pay for itself," but in fact, it almost never does. Of course it costs a great deal to be ready to prevail in a future war, but it costs far more to be unprepared.

There has always been wisdom in the saying of the rulers of Meiji Japan, "Rich nation, strong army," which simply and powerfully recognizes the potential correlation between wealth and the ability to afford military power. We say "potential" because as this chapter will illustrate, the society can choose not to pay for the military might it could have afforded. Or it could squander the military portion of its budget on a lavish lifestyle for senior officers. But certainly, having access to more capital is better for a military than having access to less capital. As Marshal Trivulzio put it, "'To carry out war, three things are necessary, money, money and yet more money."[1]

On the surface, this element may seem easy to understand. However, it can sometimes be hard to appreciate its nuances. Especially in democracies, it is often difficult for the elected representatives of the people to resist demands for increases in consumer goods and services. It is much easier in command, hierarchal governmental situations for the political center to appropriate funds for national defense—even if in reality many of those funds go to the military in exchange for regime preservation. But even in command or hierarchal governments, the rulers often may choose to protect capital from people only to spend it on themselves.

One example of this tendency, provided by David Emery, former deputy director of the United States Arms Control Agency, illustrates the need to protect capital from people for defense in a democracy. A few years prior to the second Persian invasion of the Greek Isles by Xerxes I, Themistocles, an Athenian statesman, became convinced that Persia continued to be a serious threat and argued loudly for building a large Athenian fleet.

When Athenians were unmoved by his arguments, preferring to spend their money on other things, he devised a clever ruse, claiming that a serious threat existed to Athenian trade from certain neighboring islands. Losing trade, as opposed to rearming per se, became a more tangible threat in the eyes of Athenians, so large sums were raised and the fleet was subsequently built.

When the Persians did, in fact, attack in 480 BCE, Themistocles was able to soundly defeat the Persian Navy at the Battle of Salamis. He had successfully protected needed military capital from the people.

Conversely, Winston Churchill made a similar argument regarding the rearming of Germany during his "wilderness years." Unfortunately for his country and the world, his arguments for increased military spending and less spending on domestic needs, fell on deaf ears—until the Nazi threat turned out to be as real a threat to Britain as the Persian one had been to Athens.

In the West, military activity and state formation became inextricably linked, and it has long been recognized as such. "Accumulated capital, not forced exactions, is what sustains wars," wrote Thucydides, and Cicero echoes the theme for Rome, "Free capital is the key to making war on any large scale," providing what he called the "sinews of war." Richard Fitz Neal put it equally incisively in his *Dialogus de Scaccario* in 1179, "Money appears necessary not only in time of war but also in peace." From the perspective of Mars, this is still true today.

In addition, those who would make war must always heed the wise words of Allan Millett, "Only amateurs discuss military technology without considering logistics," and logistics require enormous amounts of capital before, during, and after battle.[2] Logistics and the gross domestic product they flow from remain critical to the ability of a people to make war and to reserve the police. We have always to remember that the purpose of many, if not most, armies in the world is not to protect against international predators, nor is it to project force beyond that country's borders. Rather, the role of the armed forces is simply to keep civilian order and to prevent a forced overthrow of the regime.

Since these situations do not involve the notion of international conquest or even defense against outside aggressors, it would appear that the role of the Template is very limited, although it can come into play if the international situation changes and the regime itself is under pressure from another country or armed group outside its own borders. However, the role internal security plays in preventing outside predators from penetrating a state's space and taking its human or natural resources is an important one. Take, for example, the situation in the Congo (formerly Zaire and before that the Congo/Kinshasa), which has existed from the time of its independence in 1960. Because none of its many governments have ever paid or trained the Congolese army properly, in a timely fashion, or enough, the army has never been able or willing to provide much in the way of internal security, much less adequately defend the frontiers of the country.

In fact, its soldiers have invariably turned to extortion and banditry. In the 1960s, when then president Mobutu was stealing literally billions of dollars, the army went unpaid. Not surprisingly, the Congo, which is the size of Western Europe and was the richest country in Africa, has seen incursions from Uganda, Angola, Zambia, Burundi, and Rwanda (as well as local banditry of huge and ongoing proportions) over and over. Today, the country lies in ruins.

Obviously, nations have yearly national budgets, and the military's share of those budgets changes from year to year depending on perceived threats, whether domestic or international. There is also the question of scale, richer countries have more disposable income to put into the coffers of Mars without greatly disrupting the lives of their citizens. But each society has a security bill that is due yearly and must be paid. It is much harder to get a civilian population to support a distant or global effort (even if one is required) rather than an immediate one.

Mars definitely favors those nations and states that allocate *enough* scarce resources to the military to appreciably affect the other elements of the Template. For example, a military may spend funds on new technology or additional training for its armed forces or for new processes and management improvements or all of them. On the other hand, if the military's share is spent on high-ranking officers' salaries and perks rather than for the other important dimensions of the Template—or as in the case of the Congo, providing for simple law and order—the protection of capital from people is not a power multiplier.

There is also the question of task scale. Most countries have limited tasks on reduced scales. The United States, however, has global responsibilities and demands. Since 9/11, the entire world has become a potential battle space for the United States, and with that reality has come an unprecedented need to play chess on 100 or more interlocking chessboards. This is a very expensive challenge but today, the United States is still spending less than 5 percent of its gross domestic product on defense and the two ongoing wars in Afghanistan and Iraq.

In terms of theaters, the United States believes it must also be prepared for the need to deter a potential major threat from a nuclear adversary, such as China or a future, oil-revitalized Russia, which continues to harbor nationalistic goals. At the same time, it must be ready for a confrontation with a middle-range power such as Iran or North Korea. Finally, it needs to combat terrorism on an extremely local and extremely widespread basis.[3]

Early in his book *Hog Pilots and Blue Water Grunts*, Robert Kaplan highlights the stark military choices in the new reality: one F-22 fighter costs the same as putting Special Forces A teams *all over Africa*. The U.S. military thus has a huge demand to place on America's gross domestic product, and a huge responsibility to allocate those scarce resources in the most effective way possible. To compete in the global battle space is both a financial and a strategic burden. General Richard Cody, an American four-star general, has described the overwhelming challenge of preparing for all the possible threats facing the United States in 2009 as like "building an airplane in flight."

There is also the concomitant problem of cost overruns. In addition to protecting capital from the people, the civilian authorities, and misuse by military elites, a polity must protect scarce capital from wasteful military procurement. In 2008, for example, the Pentagon reported that there was almost $300 million in overruns of U.S. weapons programs. Clearly, if the U.S. military faces lean years ahead, either because of task scale or refitting while prosecuting major wars, it is imperative that scarce capital be protected from some military suppliers as well.

But Mars would state categorically that the alternative is likely to be far more costly. From a return on investment perspective, the al Qaeda attack on the World Trade Center was the most cost-effective strike in history. For an outlay of less than $1 million, it inflicted damages and international costs of hundreds of billions of dollars if one includes the subsequent and ongoing wars in Iraq, Afghanistan, and the border regions of Pakistan.

In this endeavor of global supervision and protection against terrorism, the United States could use a great deal more help from its traditional allies in Western Europe and elsewhere. Indeed, if we take Middle East oil as one measuring stick, we see clearly that Europe and Japan are far more dependent on this region than the United States, yet European countries often act as if it is primarily an American responsibility.

In any case, if we look at the societies of Western Europe today through the prism of Mars, we can scarcely find a single one that is putting enough into its military improvements to give any confidence that it will be better prepared to conduct any war in the future than it is in the present. This is a far cry from earlier centuries, when European nations spent much higher percentages of their GDP on the military and its needs.

In centuries past, it was the European states that, by devoting a greater percentage of their national treasure in order to achieve military superiority, prevailed often over richer but less-well-armed states. They chose to do something others did not. Max Boot makes the point quite forcefully that during the global force projection of Europe, "the civilizations of East Asia, South Asia, and the Near East were rich enough, populous enough and sophisticated enough that, unlike the tribes of Africa, Australia, and the Americas, they could have competed with the Europeans on the gunpowder battlefield. Many tried, few succeeded. Their failure made possible the rise of the West."[4]

To further prove his point, Boot argues that the Mogul Emperor Aurungzebe (1658–1707) had ten times the revenues of Louis XIV, but he did not devote enough of those revenues to building up his armed forces to the point where they could defeat the European powers.[5] And even if he had, of course, there would be no guarantee that he and his ministers would have spent that money effectively or in the right military configurations. Now, however, it is the Europeans who are refusing to pay the military price necessary to remain militarily relevant, not just worldwide but in their own theater and potential battle space.

PROTECTING CAPITAL FROM PEOPLE

There are at least three important dimensions of the element of protecting capital from people and rulers. First, there is the size of the gross domestic product, which sets the basic capital pool from which the military can draw. Second, there is the military budget itself as a percentage of the total gross domestic product. And finally, within the military budget there is the percentage of funds spent on new weapons, advanced training, and process updating as opposed to wasting funds on the lifestyles of generals.

Countries in Western Europe that used to devote 3–4 percent of their gross domestic product to military matters, today spend on average only between 1–2 percent of their GDPs on their militaries, leaving them "hollowed out," unable to project force in any appreciable amount beyond the European theater or even in any major conflict in Europe itself.

The inability of the Europeans to do anything meaningful about the war in Kosovo without the United States was a most telling failure for the EU states. Social welfare systems of Europe over the last twenty-five years have diverted billions from defense spending and left their militaries at the point where they cannot manage a major theater crisis. With 63,000

NATO soldiers deployed outside of their home countries, their cumulative collective military capacity is presently stretched very thin.[6]

In the first half of the century, as James Sheehan points out, "European states . . . were made by and for war—the war for which states prepared before 1914 and the two great wars they fought between 1914 and 1945. In the century's second half, European states were made by and for peace."[7] Between 1985 and 1999, France cut its defense budget 7 percent, Germany 15 percent and Great Britain 30 percent, assuming that since the Cold War was over, there would be little need for future military spending at higher levels.[8]

The numbers are even more startling when one considers that although the costs of weapons and weapons systems are rising, the European states have been cutting their defense budgets over the last decade. Moreover, even these reduced numbers do not tell the whole story, since a higher and higher percentage of the military budget in European countries is going simply to pay personnel, not for their training or weapons.

In terms of training, equipment, and operations, most European armies, Sheehan notes, are "more like heavily armed police officers than military units."[9] And they are likely to remain so for the foreseeable future. For example, Germany in 2004 spent only 1.4 percent of its GDP on defense, Italy 1.8 percent, and Spain 1.1 percent.

Today, only Great Britain (2.3 percent of GDP on defense) has shown an ability to project enough force globally to remain even a mid-level player in the rest of the world. And that capability of the United Kingdom has been eroded significantly by ongoing wars in Iraq and Afghanistan. Others, facing even modest force projection requirements, are unable to meet them. For example, in the aftermath of the 9/11 attacks, Germany offered to send peacekeepers to Afghanistan but lacked the airlift capacity to get them there and had to use Ukrainian aircraft to get to the Afghani battle space.[10] Then when the German troops arrived, they were forbidden to fight.

A large part of this problem is, as Sheehan suggests, due to Europe's violent twentieth century and its last fifty years of peace. But it is of considerable importance to Mars that he reports that in 2003, whereas 55 percent of Americans believe that under certain circumstances, war was necessary to obtain justice, in France and Germany, only 12 percent agree.[11] Loss of civilian willingness to even consider war as a viable option suggests to Mars that the future will likely include some dark moments for those who believe they have wished war away.

Another factor to explain this phenomenon is "war weariness." The United States, following the Vietnam debacle, was dispirited and unsure of itself. America's political leadership, as elected in the anti-Nixon, antiwar years of the mid-1970s, wanted no part of war or military preparation for war. There were constant attempts to shrink the military budget, to eliminate military programs such as the MX missile, the B-1 bomber, nuclear aircraft carriers, or new tactical fighter planes. Many on the American Left fought against deployments for any reason anywhere in the world, and the United States saw itself on the defensive from Nicaragua to Angola to Afghanistan.

This antiwar malaise did not ebb until the election of Ronald Reagan in 1980, but even during his term of office and since, there has been no unity of thinking on U.S. defense spending or military strategy. Whereas *before* the Vietnam War, foreign policy and defense policy were largely bipartisan and nonpartisan, *since* the Vietnam War, powerful voices within and out of the government have always been present to contest any policy that might commit American military personnel to a conflict, no matter what the justification.

The obvious reason to avoid war weariness is to recognize that it results directly in subsequent unpreparedness. Nations that will not provide for their own defense are likely to suffer severely at some point. In the present context, therefore, it is ironic that at just the current moment of war weariness there is a pressing need to expand the armed forces of the United States, or shrink its global goals and commitments.

In all societies that go to war—or that try to avoid war by being so strong as to deter attack—it is necessary to protect capital from people in order to finance war-fighting ability over time. Although their subject lies beyond the scope of this book, Jurgen Brauer and Hubert Van Tuyll have made an important study of the relationship between economic and military outcomes, focusing on the opportunity costs of certain strategies (or failure to purse them) and a cost-benefit analysis of a variety of case studies from the High Middle Ages to the twenty-first century.[12]

For example, Europe in the Middle Ages featured many localized polities without adequate capital with which to create protection for themselves. When William the Conqueror came to England in 1066, his force was only 7,500 strong. The *conrois*, the basic combat unit of the Middle Ages consisted of 40–100 knights on horseback, and the expense of outfitting a knight was so considerable as to make small armies the only ones any state could afford. As early as the time of Charlemagne, a single "heavy horse" knight required the following outlay of capital, which it put in terms of cows sold to pay for the item:

Helmet = 6 cows
Coat of mail = 12 cows
Sword = 7 cows
Leg armor = 6 cows
Lance and shield = 2 cows
Horses = 36 cows[13]

Thus a single knight needed the equivalent of 84 cows to be outfitted. Medieval societies simply did not have enough capital to pay for the equipment to put large armies into the field unless the knights brought their own.

But, however impoverished and small were the armies of feudal Europe, it should be noted that from the perspective of Mars, the military was generally not able to protect scarce capital from overconsumption by rulers. Many observers of Middle Age warfare seem to miss this central point that at the same time the "heavy horse" form of war was so expensive, the rulers spent enormous sums on themselves with conspicuous consumption seen as their right and their symbolic duty.[14]

Some observers focus on the class distinctions that enabled Henry III's court to celebrate the Christmas festivities of 1246. In the process, the court consumed 5,000 chickens; 1,100 partridges, hares, and rabbits; 10,000 eels; 36 swans; 54 peacocks; and 90 boars. Later, in 1387 when Richard II dined with John of Gaunt and the Bishop of Durham, he required 120 sheep; 16 oxen; 152 pigs; 210 geese; 900 chickens; 50 swans; 1,200 pigeons, rabbits, and curlews; 11,000 eggs; 120 gallons of milk; and 12 gallons of cream.[15] From the perspective of Mars, however, it is not the mind-boggling consumption per se as much as it is the fact that these rulers spent their scarce resources in this fashion, rather than in building up and equipping a strong standing army.

There was so little accumulated capital in the Middle Ages that when rulers spent much of the national treasure on themselves, they had to rely on their vassals to show up with their forces and were thus often at their mercy. In 1280, for example, when Edward I summoned his knights, of approximately 7,000, only 375 showed up.

By comparison, the very year William the Conqueror came to England with his small force of approximately 7,500 soldiers, the Emperor of Ghana had a huge army believed to number close to 100,000 men.[16] John Reader believes that the figure for the Ghanaian armies was closer to 20,000, but even that estimate dwarfs the largest European armed expedition of that era.[17] Clearly the Ghanaian emperor was sustained by the enormous riches of his kingdom.

The empires of Ghana (and later, Mali and Songhai) were far more extensive than any comparable European entity. In fact, at their heights, Mali and Songhai controlled empires roughly the size of today's United States, and since they sat astride the trade routes for both salt and gold, as well as grain and livestock, they were astonishingly wealthy. Huge caravans, numbering 1,200–2,000 beasts, crossed the Sahel and Sahara carrying precious salt and gold.[18] In fact, by the end of the fourteenth century, two-thirds of the gold in Europe came from Mali.[19]

The rulers of Ghana, Mali, and Songhai could afford a professional standing army many of their neighbors could only dream about.[20] Also, imagine the organization required to sustain such an army in the field, to say nothing of the cost of equipping, training, and maintaining such a huge army, something no European power of that era could hope to match.

When the later Malian King, Mansa Musa, went on the pilgrimage to Mecca in 1324, for example, he brought with him so much gold that its value dropped by half in Egypt and other places through which he traveled. He brought with him a huge entourage numbering 60,000, including 12,000 slaves. The pilgrimage took two years, and while he was gone, one of his generals, Skamania, took the city of Gao and presented it to him as a homecoming gift.

The huge, extremely wealthy, orderly, and powerful savanna kingdoms of Ghana, Mali, and Songhai represent a stark contrast to the European states during the Middle Ages. A contemporary visitor stated, "There is complete security in their country."[21] Their relative size, richness, and military strength raises here an interesting question. How different the relationship between Europe and Africa might have been had Europeans encountered them at their height of power and military might instead of several centuries later when the area had sunk into decline with anarchy and decay in place of the former strong, centralized kingdom.

Of course, lavishing money on military elites and building palaces for the ruler are not the same as lavishing capital on gaining opportunities and weapons innovations. Mars rewards societies that protect scarce capital from both the civilian population *and* its rulers. Money not spent on weapons and training can be squandered by rulers as well as by the people.

PROTECTING CAPITAL FROM RULERS

Princes can take money and spend it on themselves or on arms. Most do spend it on themselves. Different societies take scarce resources and spend it on people. The B-52 or B-1 bomber—or any other complex weapons system for that matter—must always be seen as being symbolically in competition with hot lunch programs, Head Start, and other social welfare programs. Political allocation is, of course, not usually that simple or crude a calculation, but we are so used to hearing the argument that military spending is wasteful that we need to recalibrate our thinking in order to take into account the true demands of Mars.

Because the military can spend its portion of the GDP unwisely as well as wisely, it is important for followers of Mars to make sure that (1) there is enough pay for the troops themselves, not simply the military elites,

(2) there is proper planning and thinking about which weapons systems are truly needed versus those that are politically desirable but militarily marginal, (3) there is a balance between the needs of current wars and future wars, (a military can be focused too far into the future as well as too far into today and yesterday), (4) the warriors themselves are taken care of before battle and after battle through high-quality rehabilitation and retraining efforts, and (5) the military engages its civilian population on a regular and ongoing basis to educate that population as to the importance of the realities of its needs and the value of its protection.

Currently the United States spends between 4 percent and 5 percent of its GDP on the military. Even with the expenses of the current wars in Afghanistan and Iraq, 5 percent of the total GDP of the country is relatively small because although the levels of military spending are at record levels, so too is the GDP, albeit along with the national debt.

In the past, when the U.S. percentage has slipped to 2 percent or less, the country has eventually had to pay a huge price in blood and treasure to catch up to its adversaries when the next war came. For example, the United States had to spend 24 percent of its GDP during World War I because of decades of previous deficiencies in military preparedness. World War II consumed 45 percent of the U.S. GDP, and once again, after the gutting of the American armed forces following that war, the percentage jumped up to 15 percent during the Korean War and 12 percent during the Vietnam War.

But one of the reasons the United States has to spend so much on its military is the high price of its military "tail," that portion of the military needed to support and supply the "tooth," or the actual fighting cohort. Currently, the tail-to-tooth ratios in the United States armed services are: U.S. Army and Marines, twelve to one; U.S. Navy, fifteen to one; U.S. Air Force, thirty-two to one.[22]

It should be noted, however, that as counterinsurgency demands increase, the tail, with its support, military police, and civil affairs units and other aspects, becomes far more relevant and useful to the total war effort. It is important to recognize that this large tail-to-tooth ratio for the United States military is also due to the fact that the United States continues to project force across most of the globe.

Why do nations have to protect weapons and the military from people or their rulers? Because capital is the wellspring of technological innovation. Even in the poverty-stricken Middle Ages, it was seen as essential. Christine de Pizan, in the *Book of Deeds of Arms and of Chivalry* stated,

> What will the wise prince . . . do when . . . he must undertake wars and fight battles? First of all, he will consider how much strength he has or can obtain, how many men are available and how much money. For unless he is well sup-

plied with these two basic elements, it is folly to wage war, for they are necessary to have above all else, especially money.[23]

Richer nations can thus afford better and bigger armies—but only if they can master the self-discipline to do so. To be successful in war and war fighting over time, you have to risk large amounts of capital to develop your capability. This is a very important point: Mars rewards societies that protect capital from people and use that capital for armaments, training, and process innovations.

For example, military historians have rightly focused on Frederick the Great's military genius and sense of timing and his emphasis on Roman-like discipline, but it is rare that one gives proper credit to his father, Frederick William I (1713–1740), who refused a lavish lifestyle and set the stage for Prussia's lead into European war-making credibility: "This he accomplished by more than doubling the Prussian army to c. 81,000 men by the end of his reign, financing it entirely from Prussian resources and amassing a great war-chest of 8,700,000 talers."[24]

Likewise, Tim Blanning perspicaciously gives great credit for England's eventual success in the Napoleonic wars to William Pitt "the Younger" whose "Sinking Fund" was based on taxes such as customs and excise that were indirect, bureaucratically controllable, and relatively hidden. The buildup of capital reserves that could be spent on war was truly astonishing, raising some 440 million pounds during the Revolutionary-Napoleonic Wars until "the stability of the Bank of England [became] equal to that of the British government."[25]

A central lesson thus emerges: it costs money to stay militarily strong, but it is always less expensive than being subjugated yourself. War is work, and work requires capital investments to be effective. As John Keegan suggests, "War is a form of work, and America makes war, however reluctantly, however unwillingly, in a particularly workmanlike way. I do not love war; but I love America."[26]

As Rick Atkinson points out, the United States built 200 planes in 1939, but 86,000 in 1943, along with 18,000 ships, 45,000 tanks, and 648,000 trucks.[27] Functioning as the "Arsenal of Democracy," the United States provided 43,000 planes to its allies during WWII through the Lend-Lease program. In the last eighteen months of the war, for example, Germany produced 70,000 trucks, the Allies, 1 million.

The rise of Western capitalist economies and banking systems allowed states to borrow against their future productivity to finance current wars. Banks lent money to make war profitable. Access to capital is critical when trying to build up armed forces, but the costs of not keeping up with technological, training, and other changes are many times more expensive. Now, oil-rich states can afford almost any weapons they wish and can multiply their military power considerably if they follow the Template and couple their new weapons systems with training and discipline.

From the point of view of Mars, it is very important to protect weapons from people and their rulers. A capital-intensive military system requires the stockpiling of a wide panoply of weapons that, although extremely expensive, may soon become outdated. These may never be used in battle, but their evolution leads inexorably to weapons that will be used; therefore, the process is vital. Being ongoing, moreover, it ensures that the state in question is never too far behind the military advances of its potential adversaries.

Additionally, weapons don't have to be used to be useful. Well-armed and well-trained militaries can scare off potential adversaries in the international community. Preventing a war can be even more advantageous than winning one. Deterrence can actually save money in the long run.

Richer nations can afford better armies, better equipment, better training, and larger force projection, but only if they care to. Some states rise to the occasion by understanding this principle, but others fail to appreciate the importance of technological change or are unwilling to pay for it. As Victor Hanson points out, Venice was once the greatest naval power in the Mediterranean world, with ships powered by oars, well suited for Mediterranean battles of ramming and boarding; but the Venetians were overwhelmed when the cannon went to sea and allowed for stand off battles.[28] Later, the Venetians could not afford the capital to build the larger, more heavily gunned ships of the line, which became the major force projection means of the Portuguese, Dutch, and British. Venice eventually ended up having to be protected by the British and Dutch to avoid domination by Spain. As a small city-state, it simply could not keep up with the emerging nation-states that had so much larger gross domestic products.

After the industrial revolution, weapons became too expensive to be developed and produced except by the state, and over time, by richer states at that. But in and of itself, state development is no guarantee weapons will work the first time they are used. It takes a long time to integrate new weapons systems into contemporary use. Complex weapons systems require lengthy "break-in" periods, and weapon modification is an ongoing process. Today the lead time between development and deployment of most new weapons systems is seven to eight years.

Of course, even a large percentage of a country's gross domestic product can be wasted by the military itself. Interservice rivalries, choleric standard operating procedures, vested interest, and bloated military contracts and bureaucratic infighting can all collide with and undercut Mars's desire to have scarce resources spent on useful equipment.

WAR AND WEALTH

Few states could compete with military developments from the sixteenth century onward by paying out of current accounts; they needed credit. Feeding Mars required new techniques for mobilizing credit: national banks, bank notes, letters of credit and bonds, and creative borrowing strategies to enable the polity to afford the new weapons.

Today this means running a national deficit, as in the United States, or being left behind in the contemporary arms races. A wide range of possible scenarios exist that the United States must prepare for, including possible confrontations in the future with China, Russia, Iran, or North Korea, as well as anti-terrorism activities all around the world. To be able to prevail, the United States constantly needs to modernize militarily.

For example, the B-52 aircraft flying today in the U.S. Air Force are older than the men and women who fly them. The B-52s have been built and rebuilt and rebuilt again at considerable cost, but at a lesser cost than building a comparable complement of B-1 bombers. Newer weapons systems require even larger amounts of capital. The Air Force's air superiority F-22 Raptor, for example, costs almost $200 million apiece, and the fighter-bomber F-35 Lightning costs over $100 million.

Ironically, the United States finds itself in the post-2001 world where it needs greatly enhanced force projection capabilities (with concomitant huge costs). Yet it simultaneously requires more flexible small-group dynamics and regional presences, which are less obtrusive than large "little America" bases with huge footprints. Mars demands a stiff price. But not following Mars for an extended period of time does not mean that that debt is cancelled.

It is often simply postponed. And enlarged.

But let us look at an empire far removed in time and space to see if the Template, in and of itself, can offer insight.

The Empire of Mali

As mentioned previously, there was in the fourteenth century in Africa, one of the richest human collectivities in the world at that time, the Empire of Mali. Mansa Musa presided over the Malian Empire, which, at its height, occupied a landmass larger than the United States. Moreover, it lay astride the two trade routes that were the most valuable in that era. The kingdom of Mali, occupying the savanna region in West Africa, controlled the gold trade coming from the forest kingdoms, such as Ghana going north into Europe, and the salt trade going south into the southern rainforest. As a result, Mali had a huge gross domestic product.

It was a major center of learning, with scholars coming from all over the known world to study at the world-famous universities at Goa and Timbuktu, where Arab mathematics and science was in the forefront of world knowledge.

With such enormous wealth, the empire of Mali thus had the basic capital formation to sustain itself and to provide for a political system so secure that Mansa Musa, a devout Muslim, could leave his kingdom for two years to go on the aforementioned pilgrimage to Mecca and return to find his throne still his. Mansa Musa's margin for error was thus much greater than his potential rivals in Africa, let alone Europe, none of whom could put in the field one-tenth as many soldiers. It is quite likely that Mansa Musa had five to ten times the capital to protect from his people than *any* of his European counterparts in the same era.

How tragic for future African-European relations that most of Europe, mired in the Dark Ages in 1300, had no way of knowing everything about the great African empires of Ghana, Mali, and Songhai, and their centers of learning and scientific accomplishments. By the time Europeans arrived in Africa in the fifteenth century, the great empires of the African savanna had collapsed, and what the newly empowered Europeans encountered was the African equivalent of the Dark Ages.

The Africans in the twelfth and thirteenth centuries had more capital to protect from fewer people, and only the Europeans' rapacious looting of North and South America redressed that fundamental balance. For the African empires, protecting capital from the people simply meant that they could have controlled their own destinies. Ironically, their subsequent disintegration came from the disruption of their trade routes, which provided the capital from which they armed and defended themselves and provided the sinews of war. Without safe trade routes, the gold and salt trades collapsed, and with them, the concomitant revenues they had produced for the savanna kingdoms for so long.

In addition to keeping a weather eye on training and discipline, Mars watches a country or a people's willingness to protect capital from its civilians and its rulers, especially before and during a war.

The Confederacy

This element of the Template can be illuminated by a most interesting case study. A number of historians have focused on the South's attempted protection of capital during the American Civil War and its subsequent failure. Their conclusions are quite startling, as they point out the vast difference between the ways the North protected capital in order to finance its war effort and those of the South.

For example, Mark Grimsley notes that while the Union sold war bonds and instituted an efficient graduated income tax, the South floundered around with promissory notes that couldn't be redeemed unless and until the Confederacy won the war, exempted land and slaves from taxation, and took crops and livestock as "tax in kind."[29] The result was a massive inflationary spiral that drove the value of a Confederate dollar down from ninety-one cents in 1861 to five cents in 1864.[30] The result of the Confederate monetary and fiscal policy was that the military in the South was constantly underfunded and underequipped, leaving Grimsley to conclude,

> The contrast between the North's smooth management of its wartime economy and the Richmond government's wretched handling of its own finance was telling. It is probably too much to claim, as has one recent analyst, that the Confederacy lost the war because of its clumsy fiscal policy, but it is certain that those policies exacerbated difficulties in the Confederate armed forces while radically increasing tensions within Confederate society.[31]

This misguided set of fiscal and economic steps not only hampered the physical equipping of the Confederate armies, it also was important in undermining morale in the South. Paul D. Escott, for example, adds the important dimension that the perceived difference in the burdens shouldered by the planter and yeoman classes resulted in "a quiet kind of rebellion" that helped to cripple the Southern war effort.[32]

Douglas B. Ball sees this collective failure to properly protect capital from people (and to utilize it to provide the wherewithal for Southern efforts) on the part of the Southern authorities as central to their ultimate defeat, "The Confederate government had it well within its power to prolong its resistance to the point where independence or at least a compromise peace might have been achieved."[33] It would appear that when it came to waging the War Between the States, the Template element, "protecting capital from people" played a far more considerable role than had been previously believed.

The Use of Resources

One final image to capture the importance of the element of misused scarce resources prior to a war: remember that all of Sadam Hussein's expensive palaces were of no consequence in either of the Gulf wars, except to provide bombing targets in the first and headquarters for the conquering Americans in the second.

Remember also that when considering this element one has to look at the relative scale of the combatant's gross domestic product and the percentage of that GDP spent on military weapons and training and personnel compared with their adversary's. Protecting capital from people and the whims of rulers remains one of Mars's abiding litmus tests for success in warfare, for it ensures the ability and willingness to finance a continual arms race.

Finally, there is the element of external overreach. A polity, large or small, can engage in activities that, over time, reduce its overall capacity for collective military action. In chapter five, we looked at the rise and eventual fall of the Ottoman Empire in such a context and noted the declining military strength that accompanied declining economic strength due in part to a shrinking empire, both in terms of geographic space and riches, that is, capital accumulation possibilities.

Here we should indicate that even successful powers run the risk of overextending themselves with external (as well as internal) commitments. The "imperial overstretch" identified by Paul Kennedy may lead to even great power decline.[34] Moreover, his assertion that economic health and power is the sine qua non for military health and power seems warranted. From the point of view of the Template, however, such an assertion is subsumed under another dimension of it. Mars expects that success in war warrants necessary expenditures in order to achieve success, but excess in setting goals and "overstretching" (for empires and nonempires) can undermine the ability of that polity to achieve its goals.

Further extensive analysis of this aspect lies beyond the scope of this book, but it remains as a caution and counterweight to the notion that the Template of Mars is unaffected by bad decisions in goal setting over time, no matter how temporarily wealthy a polity may be.

7

The Centrality of Superior Will

There is no idea so absurd that men will not die for it.

—Montaigne

A certain plodding earnestness and strict discipline may keep up military virtue for a long time, but can never create it.

—Carl von Clausewitz

Oh, Mother, I was born to die soon but Olympian Zeus the Thunderer owes me some honor for it.

—Achilles in the Iliad

For Clausewitz, although war is hard to prosecute, it is very simple to understand. War is nothing more than a struggle of wills, "War is thus an act of force to compel our enemy to do our will."

Clausewitz thus accurately captures war's stark duality—"You want, I want." At base, war is simply a struggle between two wills. Or, as B. H. Liddell Hart put it, "In war, the chief incalculable is the human will." This is true for both or all sides in any given conflict. It seems very clear that Clausewitz was correct then and is correct now.

THE NECESSITY OF WILL

Breaking the enemy's will to fight is central to any war.

For example, Colonel Bui Tin of the North Vietnamese army, when asked how Hanoi intended to defeat the Americans, replied, "By fighting a long war which would break their will to help South Vietnam." Ho Chi Minh said, "We don't need to win military victories, we only need to hit them until they give up and get out."[1] The real contest of wills was lost by the United States in Washington, not South Vietnam, making the slogan of the American Yippie Party, "DC for the VC," oddly declarative.

It therefore follows that having a superior will to begin with, or gaining one through actions during the war, will enable that side to gain an important advantage. This is particularly true if it is a strong national will. No matter how strong the will of a country's armed forces, they can be undercut by a lack of will in their nation.

A country with a strong national will can also recover from initial setbacks. Britain was famous in the nineteenth century for losing battles but eventually winning wars, in part because they believed in themselves, and the superiority of their soldiers and sailors. Conversely, a numerically or materially superior side may lack the necessary will to prevail or may, in the course of the contest, lose its will for a variety of reasons. As Leo Tolstoy put it, "Battle is decided not by the orders of a commander in chief, but by the spirit of the enemy."

Whatever the merits of either side's initial will positions, at the end of the Vietnam War, the stronger will of North Vietnam enabled that smaller, numerically and materially weaker country to prevail over the United States. From the perspective of Mars, this stronger will translated into victory where defeat was possible, even likely, when the contest began and for a long time during it.

Interestingly enough, a prominent North Vietnamese military figure, when asked "How could the Americans have won the war?" did not say, "They couldn't." He said, instead, "Cut the Ho Chi Minh trail inside Laos. If Johnson had granted Westmoreland's request to enter Laos and block the Ho Chi Minh trail, Hanoi could not have won the war."[2] Of course, one does not have to accept this statement as military fact to see the element of historical malleability contained in it, as well as the concomitant role of will.

Viewed in this light, will is a potentially decisive power multiplier in any war. Not much can, of course, happen without the other five elements of the Template previously covered, but with them, will enhancement matters a great deal. The will to win enables one side to overcome its material or even numerical inferiority. Or superior will may enable the stronger side to magnify the rate of its victory accomplishment.

Will, in and of itself, is not always the decisive element, although we must always be aware that "the emotional appeal of victory and the repugnance of defeat are endemic."[3] The previous five aspects of the Template of Mars must also be present. For example, even with the strongest will in the world, Iceland could not defeat China in a war. Mars thus sets quantitative and qualitative limits on the power of this element.

Yet in the face of an opponent with roughly equal discipline and technology, will can make a huge difference. A weaker country can defeat a stronger one because of stronger will, as in the North Vietnamese defeating the South and its ally, the United States, or the Afghanis defeating the Soviet Union. Of course, in both cases, there was a great deal of technology supplied by the supporters, both to the North Vietnamese (Soviets, Chinese) and to the Afghanis (United States, Pakistan, Saudi Arabia).

We can think of some simple examples throughout history: the French under Napoleon failed to break the will of the Spanish people (and the Catholic Church) and their British allies and eventually lost the Peninsula campaign. (See chapter ten for a further examination of this illustration.) In the Anglo-Boer War, the British broke the will of the Boers, not just by winning battles but by putting many enemy civilians in concentration camps to break the will of the Boer fighters. The U.S. invasion of Iraq defeated the Iraqi military, but initially did not break the will of the Sunni population. In addition, the American Coalition Provisional Authority made a number of incredibly dysfunctional decisions, including disbanding the Iraqi army and decapitating the Sunni leadership from the government. The French defeated the FLN (*Front de Liberation Nationale*) militarily during the Algerian War, but ended up losing due to a failure of will. Having a stronger will means that being weaker on the battlefield early on does not necessarily spell defeat.

SOURCES OF WILL

Overall, will can be enhanced by nationalism, religion, ideology, or ethnicity. Throughout history, religion has often been used to motivate violence against others. Nationalism then superseded it in many countries as a civic religion, and nationalism has remained a terribly powerful driver of interstate warfare, particularly the nationalism of the post–World War I era. And ideology, as a supranational mind-set, led to the carnage of World War II. Statist ideologies have proven to have had a calamitous impact on the world. Today, we see the rise of religion again as a wellspring for will in war.

With Communism, an intense and deadly civic religion, for example, we are left today with the truly daunting task of trying to discover whether

Communism, as an ideology in the Soviet Union, China, Cambodia, Vietnam, and Cuba, was responsible for 85 or 100 million deaths.[4] Certainly, one and a half million people were killed by the Khmer Rouge in Cambodia alone as the movement under Pol Pot mixed ideological communism-driven massacres with ethnic ones. In 1978, for example, Pol Pot announced, "Each Cambodian is to kill 30 Vietnamese."[5]

How does will serve to enhance military success? It does so because nationalism, ethnicity, religion, ideology, and sociocentric beliefs all can promote what Ward Just describes as "otherness." "Anger," he says, "is the common denominator of all ideology. A belief in the righteousness of your cause and the squalor of all other causes."[6] Or as Frank James writes, "What is war for if it isn't to kill people for a principle?" It is precisely the strength and power of these "principles" that make "nationalism" or "religion" or "ideology" so powerful and so important to Mars. Anything that promotes a suspension of disbelief about the evils of killing large numbers of people in the name of something other than self, and anything that enables a people to do things in wartime and over a long period of time that they would never think of doing in peacetime promotes sustained violence in warfare.

Will uses any of these cloaks to demonize the opposition. And by pushing that opposition into "otherness," it allows for extreme ferocity. Mars seems to reward this demonizing centrifugal force that religion, ideology, or nationalism provides to the host state or people. Motivation can come from small-group solidarity, discipline, or fear of failure, but it is central for both the winning of battles and the winning of wars, especially long wars of attrition.

Most students of war are very familiar with Hitler's Nazi ideology that demonized the Slavic peoples (and others), terming them *Untermenschen*, or subhumans. Perhaps fewer are aware of the extent to which the Soviets, in turn, dehumanized the Germans after the war began. Andrew Nagorski quotes Konstantin Simonov writing in August 1942 in the Red Army newspaper: "Now we know. The Germans are not human. Now the word 'German' has become the most terrible swear word. Let us not speak. Let us not be indignant. Let us kill. If you do not kill the German he will kill you. . . . If you have killed one German. Kill another. There is nothing jollier than German corpses."[7]

Even without demonization, the role of morale or will is crucial. Practitioners of warfare have appreciated this element throughout the ages. Napoleon said simply, "Morale is to force as three is to one." And General James Wolfe in front of Quebec stated, "The Marquis de Montcalm is at the head of a great number of bad soldiers, and I am at the head of a small number of good ones, that wish for nothing so much as to fight him; but the wary old fellow avoids an action, doubtful of the behavior of his army."[8]

What are the sources of will that give one side confidence in the righteousness of their cause and buttress a belief in their eventual triumph? At the outset, let us ask an important question. Is it remotely possible that none of the following would motivate any reader to kill a fellow human? Only the reader can know her or his own heart, but this chapter makes the point that throughout all of human history, many, many humans have followed the siren's song of those given below. There are many notes in that song.

Religion

When the Ayatollah Khomeini said, "War is a blessing to the world and for all nations. It is God who incites men to fight and kill. . . . A religion without war is an incomplete religion," he was going to the heart of religiously inspired violence against others.[9]

Even though cynics sometimes argue that "God is on the side that wins," the notion that "God is with us" has long been a most powerful energizer of those who went to war. Religion, no matter what the intentions of its founders, can turn into a justification for warfare. War is a sin in Christianity and Islam, but both religions can be made to justify it in the form of a crusade (even against other Christians) or a jihad (even against other Muslims).

Consider, for example, the turning of Christianity from the second most pacific major religion in the world (perhaps slightly behind Buddhism) into a religion that sanctifies violence and eventually full-scale war. This would appear to show that any major religion can be turned into a justification for war. After 313 CE, and the adoption of Christianity as the official religion of the Byzantine Empire, war became a central doctrine of the Christian faith, no matter how far the concept was modified from any perceived intent of Jesus of Nazareth.

Ben Kiernan, in his wide ranging *Blood and Soil*, points out that "Christian, Muslim and Buddhist forces in turn all perpetuated genocidal massacres in South East Asia between 1520 and 1800."[10] Citing the harsh melding of ethnicity and religious violence against Cambodian, Javanese, Burmese, and Vietnamese, he argues that religion can be twisted in order to justify interethnic violence bordering on genocide. Kiernan consistently documents the will-multiplying effect of combining religion and ethnicity. In Europe this can be seen most recently in the Serbian wars and ethnic cleansings undertaken against the Bosnians and Albanian Kosovars.[11]

If the pacific dimensions of Christianity and Buddhism can be twisted, turned, and distorted in order to justify going to war, it seems likely that virtually all religions can be used in this way. In fact, the overarching justification for killing that can come from religion is breathtaking, not just a religion or people against another religion or people but the religion can be used to justify killing fellow countrymen and coreligionists.

Consider the Wars of Religion in Europe from the early sixteenth century, as two Christian groups, Catholics and Protestants, slaughtered each other with reckless abandon. Consider also Catholics killing other Catholics as in the 1209 holy war against the Cathars in southern France, which was ordered by Pope Innocent III despite the opposition of the Catholic Count Raymond VI of Toulouse, the most powerful baron in Languedoc. As the marauding "cleansers" came into one village, a knight asked the pope's special legate, Abbot Arnold-Amalric, "But who are the heretics?" Amalric replied, "Kill them all, God will know his own."[12] Later, during the seventeenth century, Protestant and Catholic Christians would slaughter each other in huge numbers during the Thirty Years War, which devastated great portions of the population of what is now Germany.

The initial anti-Muslim wars by Christians began when Pope Urban agreed to absolve the sins of all those who would go the Holy Land to rescue it from the Muslims. On November 17, 1095, in front of a large number of nobles, knights, and clergymen, he called for the liberation of the Eastern churches and the Christian Holy Places, which had fallen to the Muslims. "*Deus hoc vult*," he said ("God wishes it").[13]

The First Christian Crusade, Anthony Pagden argues, was a true watershed in the history of that religion, "For the first time in history, a European people was embarked upon an officially sanctified holy war."[14] The first sanctified holy war in Christian history began rather badly the next year, as the crusaders stopped along their way through Europe to massacre Jewish communities in Mainz, Regensburg, Trier, and Metz in the "first Holocaust."

The bloodshed when they reached Jerusalem in 1099 was truly mind-boggling. Great portions of its population—noncombatant men, women, children—were massacred after the Muslim forces were defeated and they fled the city.[15] The Christian accomplishment of recapturing the holy city was forever stained by the indiscriminate slaughter of Muslims, Jews, and others until, "it was impossible to see without horror that mass of dead and even the sight of the victors covered with blood from head to foot was also a ghastly sight."[16]

Another example of Christian violence is the religious movement of Hung Hsiu-ch'uan and his Kingdom of Heavenly Peace. It led to one of the bloodiest civil wars in human history, taking the lives of over 20 million people between 1850 and 1864. Believing that the millennium was at hand and the Second Coming of Christ imminent, Hung and his Taiping Heavenly Army marauded around southern and eastern China in the name of religion.[17]

Religion was also the wellspring for the massive violence that accompanied the partition of India in 1947 as Muslims, Sikhs, and Hindus slaughtered each other at such a horrendous rate that perhaps as many as 3.4 million people were killed. Subsequent wars between India and Pakistan took place in 1965 and 1971.[18] Similarly Islam's long and aggressively expansionist impulses have killed vast numbers of people on numerous continents and indeed today.[19]

A belief in an afterlife and the role of war in helping one attain a superior place there is a persistent theme in stimulating will throughout great swatches of history. Millions upon millions of people have been motivated to go to war by the inspiration that going to war would get them to heaven. The Vikings' belief that they would be going to the warrior heaven, Valhalla, if they died with a weapon in their hand promoted their willingness not only to go to war, but also to glorify dying in battle.

James Anderson Winn also suggests that the notion of "enemy as comrade" appears again and again in the poetry of war, as in his example of Wilfred Owen's "Strange Meeting," showing the dead warrior meeting his adversary in the afterlife:

> I am the enemy you killed, my friend.
> I knew you in this dark: for you frowned.
> Yesterday through me as you jabbed and killed. I parried; but my hands were
> loath and cold. Let us sleep now.[20]

In the American Civil War, many soldiers on both sides seem to have thought that if they died they would simply "pass over" to the "other side" to see or await loved ones in Heaven. And, as Drew Gilpin Faust has so movingly written in her *This Republic of Suffering: Death and the American Civil War*, this belief not only sustained individual soldiers but many others caught up in the massive scale of its societal repercussions.[21] Indeed, there are very poignant echoes of the horrendous impact of losing a loved one in battle in Jim Sheeler's fine *Final Salute*.[22]

For the purposes of power multiplication, of course, it doesn't really matter if "God" or god actually helps one group triumph over another, it is enough to stimulate superior will that one side *believes* that God is intervening on their side or supporting their cause.

In the case of today's Muslim radical, jihadist Salafists, winning isn't even the point of fighting. Merely enduring in the struggle is what matters. Their cosmology, which encompasses the view that Allah will only bring the end-time when he believes the Salafists are worthy of it, depends not on success in war but in simply waging perpetual war. Those struggling to bring Allah's rule must endure enough to deserve the bringing of end-time. It is important to note in this regard that in the Iraq insurgency, there were important Salafist elements, but many if not most Iraqi insurgents were not Salafists. Many Sunnis, for example, simply wanted the United States out of their areas, the territorial integrity of Iraq not destroyed, and their position in Iraqi society and politics restored. They were fighting for more limited antioccupation goals and to regain their former superior position within the Iraqi political system.

Incidentally, when Osama bin Laden planned the strike on the World Trade Center, he referred to it as "The Hubal of the Age," a reference to the large stone pagan god torn down by Muhammad.[23] He thus interjected an ancient call to arms in his political-religious message.

The use of terrorism as a tactic in war is greatly enhanced by the belief that martyrdom is rewarded with eternal life. Clearly its utter ruthlessness is very effective against those who see suicide as frightening and abhorrent. Most people, for example, can comprehend a soldier going into battle against an enemy, no matter how ferocious the fighting. But how does one fight against a suicide bomber who cares not for his or her own life in pursuit of his political or religious objective? Religious motivation has been, and remains, a great force multiplier in war.

Sometimes the role of religion and nationalism can blur, as in the Spanish uprising against Napoleon where being "Spanish" meant not wanting to be under an imposed "French" king. The Catholic Church in Spain vigorously opposed the French rule and fostered resistance at all levels of society. Other observers have also noted the extent to which this most Catholic of countries resisted the threat from the atheism of the French Revolution.[24]

Nationalism as a Civic Religion

Nationalism is, after all, nothing but a set of learned responses to symbols. We are not born Americans or Chinese or Nigerians. Instead, we are taught to be a particular nationality. But when we are taught that feeling of attachment, the love for country can be a powerful motivator. As Sir Walter Scott wrote in *The Lay of the Last Minstrel*, "Breathes there a man, with soul so dead, / Who never to himself hath said, / This is my own, my native land!"

That feeling of belonging to a country has inspired millions over the years to go to war and go to war gladly. Nationalism can also be an important wellspring of motivation when a country is attacked, as with the Finns during the "Winter War" of 1939–1940, and the Americans after the Japanese attack on Pearl Harbor in December 1941.

Before nationalism as a civic religion took root in Europe during and after the French Revolution, it was quite difficult to put armies of 100,000 into the field by conscription and professional hiring, but after 1789, it became possible to raise armies of 300,000 and 400,000, as "citizens" identified with their country and could easily be conscripted into the armed forces.

The 1793 French *levee en masse* was instrumental in defeating the enemies of the French Revolution by greatly increasing the manpower pool available to the French leadership. That is because the French Constitution of 1793 declared that "All Frenchmen shall be soldiers; all shall be trained in arms." Suddenly the projection of French power beyond its borders became possible in a way Louis XIV could only have dreamed about.

In fact, it is impossible to imagine Napoleon's career without the nationalism that resulted from the French Revolution. Almost as fast as he burned up armies, he could raise new levies of enormous size. Rupert Smith calls the universal service of the French Republic and subsequent Empire where 2 million men served "a colossal number, a force unprecedented in human history."[25]And John A. Lynn is undoubtedly correct when he points out that nationalism in and of itself gave the French the opportunity to pay less attention to their losses. Unlike previous armies where trained professionals were regarded as valuable human capital, the "citizen armies" after the French Revolution would be more recklessly spent.[26]

Eventually, of course, as a reaction to French nationalism, the other countries of Europe responded with nationalism of their own—the English, the Prussians, the Austrians, the Spanish, and the Russians, although some would take longer than others to move to that civic religion. The nineteenth century, then, was both an incubator of nationalism and a witness to a resulting hypertrophy of war, which would later result in the disastrous casualty lists of World Wars I and II.

Nationalism, at best, can be a source of internal unity and cultural pride. It can drive a people to do things and make sacrifices unthinkable without it.[27] The North Vietnamese became committed to *"Dau Tranh,"* or protracted struggle, where the ends justified any means and no price was too great to pay for the victory of the nation. Also, in this case, the ideology of Communism dovetailed nicely with the nationalistic aspects of the Vietnamese struggle. It helped sustain the Vietnamese will to apply sustained ruthlessness regardless of cost until they had won.

For example, when the Viet Cong and NVA overran the old imperial capital of Hue during the February 1968 Tet Offensive, thousands of Vietnamese civilians were executed as "reactionaries," including school teachers, janitors, and other "government" workers. Subsequently, documents were captured in which the Communists claimed to have "eliminated 1,892 administrative personnel, 38 policemen, and 790 tyrants."[28]

Extreme nationalism can also be a hellish multiplier of death and destruction. From the perspective of Mars, nationalism is useful because it gets ordinary people to do horrible things to their fellows that they would not do otherwise. In this regard, fascism can be seen as a hyper nationalism. Ironically, as nationalism faded as a causative factor in some parts of the world during the late twentieth century, the role of religion reemerged, and its validity increased dramatically as a source of will in war.

It should also be noted, as Robert Kagan does so persuasively in his history of America and its place in the world, *Dangerous Nation*, America's nationalism has often been supported by a belief in a transcendent mission, such as Manifest Destiny.[29] Thus, he sees the Spanish American War as both "a new departure" and also "a culmination."[30] Nationalism plus an ideology can be a most potent driver of interstate activity and an enhancer of will. It follows, of course, that diminished nationalism may also diminish power. As fewer and fewer people in the United States and Western Europe strongly identify with their country "right or wrong," waging war on a sustained basis is far more difficult.

Ideology as a Transcendent Force

In the form of communism or fascism, ideology has been a most powerful driver of interstate and intrastate will. Historically, a pronounced ideology has provided dramatic increases in the number of people willing to kill others in the hope of having a better tomorrow. Ideology gives an excuse to promote the most draconian revamping of society, leading Alex Comfort correctly to write, "The smell of burning flesh will not sicken you if they persuade you it will warm the world."

Thucydides, writing in the fifth century BCE captures the essence of this element as he documents the progress of the revolution at Corcyra. He depicts how in revolutionary situations the basest of human behaviors come to the surface, and his description of ideology's dimensions remains relevant today

> During seven days that Eurymedon stayed with his sixty ships, the Corcyraeans were engaged in butchering those of their fellow-citizens whom they regarded as their enemies: and although the crime imputed was that of attempting to put down the democracy, some were slain also for private hatred, others by their debtors because of the monies owed to them. Death thus raged in every shape and, as usually happens at such times, there was no length to which violence did not go; sons were killed by their fathers, and suppliants dragged from the altar or slain upon it; while some were even walled up in the Temple of Dionysus and died there.[31]

"Revolution" can also be thus regarded as a transcendent religion with a utopian vision for a new world. As David Bell suggests, the combination of revolution and nationalism by which we often try to explain the success of France after 1789 and under Napoleon, is not sufficient to explain the extraordinary violence that occurred in putting down the revolts in the Vendee 1793–1794.[32] Rather, the process also depended on the promotion of a "culture of war," the rise of civilian armies, and a concomitant militarism that permeated society. *"Vive the Nation"* became the justification for widespread warfare and most draconian methods. Thucydides would have understood perfectly.

Bell describes the Girondins as thinking the war to defend revolutionary France "would turn into a worldwide war of liberation."[33] The "enemies" would be defeated. But as he relates, "The enemies in question, however, were not England or Austria or Prussia. . . . Instead the torch of total war was first applied to a region of France itself: the Vendee."[34] In the name of "revolution" (which by this time was actually "counterrevolution" since the rebellion was against the revolutionary government recently in control of France), war turned into slaughter. "Hell columns" of government soldiers marauded into the countryside, killing, burning, destroying, with cries for "extermination," "pulverization," and "depopulation."[35]

The result of this murderous total war in the region during 1793–1794 was 220,000–250,000 dead men, women, and children or one-quarter of the entire population of the Vendee. Whole provinces were laid waste, with animals slaughtered or driven off, fruit trees cut down, and wells poisoned.[36] Bell is careful to stop short of calling this a genocide, but it appears to be as close to genocide as one would ever want to get, regardless of the appropriateness of that name for him. Whatever one calls this slaughter of total war, the poisonous brew of nationalism, revolutionary fervor and civil war enabled otherwise normal and rational people to behave in most destructive ways, providing the will to do whatever was necessary to preserve the revolution.

Nazism was another transcendent ideology (as well as a virulent form of racism). Americans, Britons, Russians, and other peoples are rightly proud of the fact that Nazi Germany was defeated by the grand coalition of the United States, Great Britain, and the Soviet Union. But the ultimate triumph of that coalition masks the tremendous but sad fact that fascist ideology and racial beliefs gave the German soldiers the will to fight on against enormous odds for as long as they did.

It is worth noting that when General Charles de Gaulle visited the Soviet city of Stalingrad after World War II, he remarked to his hosts, "How amazing!" The Soviets assumed de Gaulle meant their tremendous victory at that site. But he corrected them, saying "how amazing" it was the Germans got that far. For many German soldiers, belief in the Nazi ideology was the key to success in battle and strengthened their resistance to defeat when the war turned against them.

Ethnicity/Race as a Primordial Attachment

Ethnicity, or tribalism, is another power multiplier. When a people is able to set themselves so far apart emotionally that their opponents become simply "the other," they are able to kill them with dispatch, even enthusiasm. In this regard, Peter Silver makes the very interesting point that the Indian wars from the 1750s to the 1780s in America helped to solidify "white people" out of the previous disparate European religious-based identity, and in turn, "the closing years of the Revolution saw extraordinary anti-Indian violence."[37]

In Rwanda and Burundi, the internal wars of ethnic slaughter are recurring exclamation points to the primacy of primordial attachments energizing ordinary people to take extraordinary action against their fellows. The 1994 Rwandan Hutu genocide against the Tutsi minority, which killed between 500,000 and 800,000 Tutsis between May and July, spurred the fighting spirit of the Tutsi invading army.[38] It should also be noted that Kiernan quite rightly points out that the 1994 genocide by the Hutu was itself presaged by the Tutsi genocide of Hutu in Burundi in 1963 and 1972, which killed perhaps 200,000 Hutus.[39] From the point of view of Mars, however, the key element here is the extent to which the Tutsi Rwandan Patriotic Front (RPF) army utilized the racial genocide as a motivator for its soldiers, defeating and driving from the country the much larger Hutu militias and national army in a 100-day war. Likewise, the Nigerian civil war and the secession of Biafra was due to ethnic hatreds and the desecration of the common good, as Hausas and Fulanis saw value in the demonization of the Igbo and vice versa.

For the Japanese in the period leading up to World War II, racism was not only widespread as a personal belief, it was a doctrine used to instill a sense of will: "Chinese, British, American. We were schooled to regard them as evil, devilish, animalistic."[40] The Chinese, in particular, were looked upon as subhuman, as "murata," or blocks of wood, and 16 million of them died during the war. The Japanese racist ideology justified their taking over Korea and then their thrusts into China.

The Chinese war led to a huge expansion of the Japanese army, from seventeen divisions and 250,000 men in July 1937, to fifty-one divisions and 2.1 million men by December 8, 1941.[41] The expressed Japanese ideology toward the Chinese in 1941 was clearly and succinctly summed up in their extraordinary directive to their soldiers in China: "Three Alls: Kill All, Burn All, Destroy All."

Surely, knowing this, it seems ludicrous to say, as some do, that the Japanese themselves were innocent victims of "racism" during World War II. In fact, it was Japanese racial attitudes toward the Koreans, Chinese, Philippinos, Javanese, Americans, and others that validated their wars of conquest and that were buttressed by their assumptions prior to the war. One could well argue, however, that the Japanese people were punished for the racism of their leaders by others who brought their own racial prejudices into play.

The Japanese high command even routinely referred to their own soldiers as *issen gorin*, the name for the price of a penny postcard, which is what it cost to send a notice to a Japanese family announcing that their son was conscripted into the Imperial Japanese Army. So it was quite easy for the hermetically sealed Japanese society to see the Koreans, the Chinese, Philippinos, Americans, British, French, and others as lesser beings and act accordingly. Even today, there are Japanese apologists who deny that Japan ever committed its many atrocities and argue that the Korean "comfort women" who were raped and brutalized in military brothels were volunteers.[42]

Anyone who fell into Japanese hands, military or civilian, suffered mightily. British and American soldiers, sailors, and airmen died at astonishing rates when in Japanese hands. For example, whereas 4 percent of Allied POWs died in German custody, 37 percent of them died in Japanese custody.[43]

Colonel Masanobu Tsuji, who during the Burma campaign dined on the liver of a dead Allied pilot, berated his men for not joining in, "The more we eat, the brighter will burn the fire of our hatred for the enemy."[44] Not surprisingly, American attitudes hardened toward the Japanese after the attack on Pearl Harbor, and especially during the course of the war. The U.S. Marine colonel "Chesty" Puller, landing on Peleliu, summed up this attitude when he declared, "You will take no prisoners, you will kill every yellow son-of-a-bitch and that's that."[45]

Hastings, marveling at the Japanese unwillingness to accept responsibility for their brutality during the war puts it this way, "War is inherently inhumane, but the Japanese practiced extraordinary refinements of inhumanity in the treatment of those thrown upon their mercy."[46]

In the Philippines during 1945, for example, after Japan had clearly lost the war, Captain Yoshio Tsuneyoski of Cabanatua prisoner of war camp, said to the American prisoners: "We do not consider you to be prisoners of war. You are members of an inferior race, and we will treat you as we see fit. Whether you live or die is of no concern to us. If you violate any of the rules, you will be shot immediately. Your country has forgotten your name. Your loved ones no longer weep for you. You are forever the enemy of Japan."[47]

If there remains any doubt about Japanese war-racism, listen carefully to the War Ministry in Tokyo in August 1944 issuing a directive to the commandant of the various Japanese prisoner of war camps, outlining the final disposition of prisoners of war. This is known as the August 1 "Kill All Order":

Whether they are destroyed individually or in groups, and whether it is accomplished by means of mass bombing, poisonous smoke, poisons, drowning or decapitation, dispose of them as the situation dictates. It is the aim not to allow the escape of a single one, to annihilate them all, and not to leave any traces.[48]

In fact, Kiernan points out that this racism had a long history, quoting orders from the Japanese leaders before their 1597 invasion of Korea, "Kill Koreans one by one, and empty the country." The leaders rewarded individual Japanese soldiers for the heads of officers and the noses of regular soldiers. These were sent back to Japan by the barrelful.[49]

Regardless of who started the race war between Japan and the United States, and regardless of who played the race card most effectively during the war (or now after it), there can be no doubt that racism was a powerful motivator in the Pacific theater, whether Japanese against Korean, Chinese, British, and American, or Allied soldiers against the Japanese.[50]

Greed and Glory

Throughout history, soldiers have fought for the spoils of war, and warriors have joined wars simply for that purpose. When coupled with a "higher" purpose, it becomes a most potent wellspring of military action.

Or, as Lord Krishna put it, "There is nothing more welcome for a warrior than a righteous war. . . . Die and you will enter heaven. Conquer, and you will enjoy the sovereignty of earth." Almost always, of course, those who go to war believe their cause is "righteous," leaving the objective observer to note that "righteousness" may not be found in time or space but in the eye and mind and heart of the beholder.[51]

The Macedonians who followed Alexander the Great and the French Army that followed Napoleon to Italy all were driven by pride in battle and by the hope for material gains for themselves and their families at the end of the campaign. For centuries, the Vikings from Denmark, Sweden, and Norway raided far and wide for gold and glory, eventually taking over huge portions of England, northwest France, and Sicily.

The Venetians in the thirteenth century took the crusaders of the Fourth Crusade to Constantinople in exchange for the sacking of that Christian city. The initial three-day sack in April 1204 took the lives of thousands of men, women, and children with the Venetians and others continuing the looting for years afterward. "Venetians excelled in plundering; they knew all the best religious artifacts, the most precious gems, the most important statuary to carry away. As a visible symbol of conquest, four bronze horses were taken out of Constantinople one to adorn the façade of the Basilica di San Marco; they represented the choicest booty of empire, another stolen treasure that came to reside in Venice."[52]

Many Spanish conquistadors were primarily driven by a desire to attain riches and status that were denied them in the straightjacketed hierarchal society of Spain. They were robbers and plunderers whose sense of self-entitlement overrode other considerations. The conquistadors wanted riches, and when they found those riches, they took them with hardly any thought for the Native Americans they had robbed and murdered in the name of Christ. Hernando Cortez, Francisco Vasquez de Coronado, Hernando de Soto, Ponce de Leon, the Pizarro brothers and their men were driven by greed and gold as much as by a desire for glory.

So too, Napoleon on leading his troops into Italy exhorted them with these words, "Soldiers! You are hungry and naked, the government owes you much but can give you nothing. I will lead you into the most fertile plains on earth. Rich provinces, opulent towns all shall be at your disposal. There you will find honor, glory and riches. Soldiers of Italy! Will you be lacking in courage or endurance?"

In the violent civil wars in the Sudan today, the Janjaweed militia are not paid by the government for its ethnic cleansing in Darfur, but instead are promised unrestricted looting of the villages they terrorize. However venal such exhortations may seem to those of us far removed from the battlefield, it should be remembered that they have rung out with great effect century after century, encouraging many in many cultures to follow the dictates of Mars.

Stern Self-Righteousness

Sometimes warrior-hood responds to a sense of righteousness, or righting a wrong or accomplishing a lofty goal. Over and over in the American Civil War, we see soldiers of the North giving their lives to preserve the Union and/or to free the slaves and soldiers of the South giving their lives to achieve independence or to preserve their way of life. Certainly a major portion of the 33,000 African Americans who died in the Civil War were seeking to right a wrong, free their fellows, and gain the respect of their fellow warriors.

And Victor Hanson makes the excellent point that American soldiers fight best when they have a sense of moral purpose: General W. T. Sherman's men ending slavery, General George Patton's Third Army destroying the evils of Nazi death camps, General Tommy Franks's men and women riding high to remove a psychopathic murderer.

Love of Battle

Closely associated with in-group solidarity is the ancient code of the warrior, which says that war is the *only* fitting occupation for men. From the earliest stirrings of battle lust to the words from World War II, men have

fought (and died) for the love of battle. Hence the motto of the Waffen
SS (Schutzstaffel) Division Liebstandarte Adolf Hitler, "Our Heaven is the
Great War. Our Heaven is the great war on Earth. We live in battle, our
eternal life."

Many warrior societies throughout time and space have venerated war
for its own sake and melted warfare into a rite of passage to manhood.
And warriors of different cultures can recognize their universal common
virtues, as when Winston Churchill, having watched the soldiers of the
Mahdi in action at the Battle of Omdurman in 1898, noted their courage:
"Why should we regard as madness in the savage what would be sublime
in civilized men?"

More recently, in his travels around the globe meeting regular military
personnel, for example, Robert Kaplan over and over encounters men and
women who are having the times of their life and looking forward to getting into battle zones of one kind or another, to participate in war. This
enthusiasm, seldom captured in the popular press, is precisely a major
enhancer of will in the armed forces.

Or, as Martin van Creveld has so aptly put it,

> Just as it makes no sense to ask "why people eat" or "what they sleep for," so fight-
> ing in many ways is not a means but an end. Throughout history, for every person
> who has expressed his horror of war there is another who found it the most mar-
> velous of all the experiences that are vouchsafed to man, even to the point that he
> later spent a lifetime boring his descendants by recounting his exploits.[53]

He goes even further in perceptively turning some contemporary conventional wisdom on its head, "However unpalatable the fact, the real reason
why we have wars is that men like fighting, and women like those men who
are prepared to fight on their behalf."[54]

For his part, Chris Hedges extensively documents the degree to which war
can be "an enticing elixir," much more popular with more people than we
would like to believe. He sees war as a reason in and of itself to gain the
enthusiastic support of people.[55]

Inspirational Leadership

James S. Robbins makes the important point that "Planning, cultural
understanding, leadership, wisdom, the ability to get things done—these
sometimes ineffable qualities will always be central to success in war." He
further notes that leadership quality and the ability to inspire men in battle
is not always apparent in one's grades at their military academy, saying,
"Nothing in one's academic record can predict heroism."[56]

Throughout history there have been men, and more than a few women,
who, in Napoleon's words, were "born for war," humans who inspired,

led, and motivated armies to follow them into battle and subsequent success. Although perhaps not as often as popular history supposes, individual commanders can impart confidence, cohesion, and additional will to their followers.

Peng Dehuai, Tamerlane, Gustavus Adolphus, Subutai, George Washington, Saladin, Süleyman the Magnificent, Hannibal, Scipio Africanus, Sun-Shin Yi, George Patton, Chaka, Ka Sensangakhona, Amina of Hausaland, Nzinga, Oliver Cromwell, Geronimo, Askia the Great, Asoka, Napoleon, Alexander the Great, Zhu Yanzhang (Hongwu), Hitler, Wellington, Crazy Horse, Mao Tse-tung, Tecumseh, Isoroku Yamamoto, Vo Nguyen Giap, and Genghis Khan were all examples of heroic and inspirational leaders who infused their followers with a sense of élan and expectation of inevitable victory, thus enhancing their fighting qualities. Their soldiers believed they were going to win because their leaders told them they were going to win and they believed those leaders.

For example, David Bell indicates how Napoleon was beyond compare when it came to creating a cult of personality in war. He led by example, provided ribbons and rewards to his soldiers, and allowed them to loot when victorious in battle. He also owned his own newspaper, which was devoted to a hyperbolic vision of himself as "a comet cleaving the clouds."[57]

Revenge/Retaliation

A great source of will in warfare is a desire for revenge. The Americans during World War II were willing to do almost anything to defeat the Japanese because of their sneak attack on Pearl Harbor in December 1941. Likewise, after their defeat in the Franco-Prussian War of 1870, and the loss of the provinces of Alsace Lorraine, the French vowed never to stop until they had regained those areas, which they eventually did in 1918.

As mentioned above, the Tutsi Rwandan Patriotic Front (RPF) army attack on Rwanda was also motivated by revenge for the genocide perpetrated by the Hutu government of Rwanda. Likewise, The Yom Kippur War of 1973 can also be seen in this light. Syria and Egypt launched the Yom Kippur war in major part as revenge for the swift and decisive victory of Israel in the Six-Day War of 1967, which had "left a legacy of shame and bitterness on the Arab side."[58] If space permitted, this list could be greatly expanded throughout time and location.

Freedom

A people's desire to be independent or free of outside domination has been a powerful multiplier of will. Whether to escape the shackles of colonialism

(Americans in the eighteenth century, the Haitians and Italians in the nine-teenth century, the Vietnamese or the Algerians in the twentieth), or to make their country's government more democratic, the yearning for freedom adds to the military success of those who are motivated to make sacrifices in its name.

The campaigns of Simon Bolivar, Bernardo O'Higgins, and Jose San Martin, which liberated much of South America from Spanish rule from 1813 to 1825 would be other prime examples of the powerful motivational wellspring of the desire for freedom.

Decolonization was a powerful motivation in the revolutions of Mo-zambique, Guinea-Bissau, and Angola, as well as South Africa and Rhode-sia/Zimbabwe. The desire of Eritreans to be free from Ethiopian rule in the twentieth century was another example from Africa.

More recently, the Bosnian and Kosovar resistance to continued domi-nance by the Serbian government can also be seen as a desire for freedom, although there were strong religious and even racial overtones to the Serbian repression, including the massacre of nearly 9,000 Muslims in Srebrenica in 1995. Obviously, the above sources of will can be mutually reinforcing, as when a people who believe themselves to be a nation are struggling for their freedom as well, such as the Italians during the nineteenth century.

There are innumerable instances of individuals fighting in war in order to obtain their personal freedom. African Americans joined the American revolutionary struggle in large numbers after 1778 (making up perhaps as many as 5 percent of the Continental Army by the end of the war), some already having their personal freedom and wanting to achieve their new nation's, and others joined in order to throw off the shackles of personal servitude.

Will and determination can thus come from a lot of different sources. But how to sustain will over time? All of the motivators mentioned above can increase the will of a society to go to war and to wage war successfully. They are power multipliers in terms of getting both soldiers and civilians to sub-ordinate their needs and wishes to the greater task at hand. But conversely, if will diminishes, so too do the chances of success in any given war. What can sap a country's will? What detracts from its potential power multiplica-tion? Division can hurt, poor leadership can hurt, and the appearance of losing a war can hurt. For in this regard, we should always remember the words of George Orwell, "The quickest way to end a war is to lose it."

The obvious reason to avoid outcomes that lead to "war weariness" is that attrition on the battlefield often results directly in unpreparedness for future conflicts. Nations that will not provide for their own defense are likely to suffer severely at some point. History is littered with such examples of states that were attacked because they were unprepared.

How then does a country sustain a "long war" mentality in a democracy, where a large segment of the population doesn't believe in that war, its length, or the threat it seeks to counter? As Stendhal put it, in *Lucien Leuwan, or the Green Huntsman*, "But to fight with joy, one must feel that one's country is really interested in the combat."

Mars decries disunity, disbelief, and mental or moral despair. Mars rewards unity, belief, and moral optimism. Mars sanctions a variety of ways to enhance will because will is the ultimate power multiplier. Mars applauds the words of Winston Churchill at the start of World War II, "What is our policy? I will say: It is to wage war by sea, land and air with all our might. . . . You ask: What is our aim? I can answer in one word: Victory. Victory at all costs, victory in spite of all terror, victory however long and hard the road may be."

Today, as previously, the will to win, to achieve victory remains central to success in war, and critical to a lasting conflict or an uphill struggle in war.

Clausewitz got that ingredient of the Template very right 150 years ago.

8

The Belief That There
Will Always Be Another War

War is a limitless game that goes on and on.

—Vishnugupta Kautilya

Only the dead have truly known the end of war.

—Plato

Eternal peace is a dream.

—Helmut von Moltke

Peter Paul Rubens's magnificent allegorical painting *Minerva Protects Pax from Mars* represents a long-held hope that wisdom can prevent war. And decent people everywhere can share that hope, but just as Rubens failed in his diplomatic mission to prevent war between England and Spain, unfortunately, too often human wisdom is too weak or too late or simply unable to stop a rush toward war. And the brute fact remains that sometimes war is the best available alternative, the one that wisdom must finally embrace.

Mars seems to smile on countries and states whose leaders believe there will always be another war. Of course, not all countries under all regimes are anxious to go to war or even plan for war or are prepared for war. And many states want to avoid war completely. But those reactions often court disaster.

Over the course of human history, many entities that did not want another war, or thought there would not be a future war, have suffered for such assumptions. In international relations there are always predators and prey. Possible prey are well served to imagine themselves actual prey and act accordingly.

Those individuals and states that wish to avoid war often find themselves up against the awful truth expressed by Leo Tolstoy in *War and Peace*, "Is there any sort of combined action which could not find justification in political unity, or in patriotism, or in the balance of power, or in civilization?" As we saw in chapter seven, it is simply too easy for people, states, organizations, and religions to have a purpose for which to kill for anyone to ever say that war is now ended.

In fact, the assumption that there will be another war seems central to the policies of many nations as well as nonstate actors. This observation remains fundamental to an appreciation of success in future wars, since wars often happen whether the targeted state wants to go to war or not.

There also seems to be a multiplicity of situations where the warriors on competing sides had the same basic equipment and fought with the same degree of enthusiasm, and yet one side consistently won battles and conquered territory because they assumed that today's battle was simply a prelude to tomorrow's.

For example, the Danish conquest of England 980–1016 pitted Danes against Saxons with both having relatively similar weapons, levels of discipline, and training. Also, both sides were equally receptive to military innovation. During their ascendancy, the Vikings always assumed there would be another war and were prepared to start one every summer when they went raiding and conquering.[1] By contrast, the Saxons—and other peoples of coastal Europe—often seemed to take refuge in the hope that the last summer's raid would be the last.

One can reasonably ask, therefore, "How can you preserve the peace unless you prepare for war and make your adversaries *less* likely to attack you than *more* likely"? If a country or a people believe there will always be another war, and act accordingly to prepare for it, they are less likely to be subject to attack. In fact, if there is *any* characteristic that Mars most constantly rewards, it is the assumption that peace, far from being perpetual, is fleeting.

PREPARING FOR THE NEXT WAR

There is a popular bumper sticker that says, "You can't prepare for Peace and War at the same time." Yet despite the pleasant sound of this bromide, the reverse is actually true. You *must* prepare for war during times of peace in order to make it less likely you will have to go to war. Mars truly says:

"Plan for war, you may get peace. If you don't plan for war, you are more likely to get war."

We hear echoes throughout the ages of people who recognized the importance of this element.

Horace: "In peace, as a wise man, he should make suitable preparation for war."

Publilius Syrus: "We should provide in peace what we need in war."

George Washington: "To be prepared for war is one of the most effectual means of preserving peace."

Carl von Clausewitz makes perhaps the most telling argument: "We are not interested in generals who win victories without bloodshed. The fact that slaughter is a horrifying spectacle must make us all take war more seriously, but not provide an excuse for gradually blunting our swords in the name of humanity. Sooner or later someone will come along with a sharp sword and hack off our arms."[2]

Frederick the Great was even more forthright in his *The General Principles of War*: "The wars that I have waged have made me reflect profoundly on the principles of this great art which has made and overturned so many empires. The Roman discipline now exists only with us; in following their example we must regard war as a mediation, peace as a rehearsal."[3]

In most cases, there cannot be total preparation for war. As Andre Beaufre has written, "Through the entire course of history, warfare is always changing." New threats may arise which were not even contemplated. But in any case, it is the peoples and nations which, having won or lost a war, believe that wars are over who then pay the greater prices in the next war.[4]

For example, the United States was incredibly ill prepared for World War I. As mentioned earlier, it even had to get machine guns from the French and British when it entered the war, and had to fly British and French planes. Only the war-weariness of the Germans and the million-person exuberance of the American commitment to the Allied cause turned the tide. But America paid a most-fearful price for its lack of preparation prior to participation, suffering over 53,000 dead.

Again, the United States was totally unprepared for World War II. And following its success in that conflict (but paying a horrific price of over 291,000 dead), it unilaterally disarmed again, finding itself woefully unprepared for the Korean War (which cost over 36,000 lives).

Writing in *An Army at Dawn*, Rick Atkinson captures the true level of unpreparedness of the United States armed forces in 1940: "Equipment and weaponry were pathetic. Soldiers trained with drainpipes for antitank guns, stovepipes for mortar tubes, and brooms for rifles. Money was short, and little guns were cheaper than big ones; no guns were cheapest of all. Only six medium tanks had been built in 1939."[5]

And as if World War I and armored warfare developments in Germany and Great Britain had never happened, and tank-led warfare was not perceived clearly as the wave of the future, American planners still stressed the importance of the horse: "The Army's cavalry chief assured Congress in 1941 that four well-spaced horsemen could charge half a mile across an open field to destroy an enemy machine-gun nest without sustaining a scratch."[6]

After World War II, amazingly enough, history repeated itself as the United States was completely ill prepared for combat in Korea. Even today, the phrase "Remember Task Force Smith" reverberates at the Pentagon in remembrance of the first American unit dispatched from Japan to fight with the South Koreans in June 1950. Named for its colonel, Lt. Colonel Charles B. Smith, Task Force Smith consisted of soldiers thrown together for the first time, soldiers who had never trained together. They were equipped with cast-off weapons, radios that worked poorly if at all, and C-rations from the previous war (imagine eating canned fried eggs that were, at best, five years old).

The 407 soldiers of Task Force Smith were the first Americans sent to Korea, despite the fact that the only reason for being sent was that they happened to the closest soldiers geographically to Korea and closest to Japanese ports.

Cobbled together in a matter of a few days, the soldiers of Task Force Smith went into that situation bravely, even a bit fool-hardily, and they were brushed aside and destroyed piecemeal by the North Koreans. From the point of view of Mars, there was no reason they should have been thrown into battle in that condition, and they paid the ultimate price for their country's lack of preparation for another war.

Ironically, prior to that conflict, the United States previously had feared that it was the South Koreans who might "go North" if they were too well armed, so the South Korean army was given neither aircraft nor tanks nor heavy artillery, the very things that might have enabled the South Koreans to better resist the North's armed forces when the North Korean army, the Inmun Gun, rolled south in June 1950.

For those born in the United States since the great expansion of the American military during the Cold War, this incident seems almost incredible. Yet American unpreparedness for major conflict was emblematic of its military situation throughout the first three wars of the twentieth century. For America, a huge blood price was paid for not believing there would be another war. Of course, one cannot assert categorically that a United States military that was adequately prepared for war would not still have suffered severe casualties in World War I, World War II, or Korea, given the breadth and scope of the tasks each brought.

It may even be possible to argue that the United States would have suffered the same number of war dead in all three contests if it had been prepared for them, but such an assertion seems to fly directly in the face of common sense. Even if the country had not been able to avoid war by being stronger than its potential adversaries, it seems far more likely that fewer American lives would have been lost if the country's military had been prepared before the outbreak of those wars. A military prepared for war, well equipped and well trained, would be far less likely to suffer as grievously and unnecessarily as did the American military at the beginning of those three successive wars.

Leaving aside the question as to whether or not this lack of preparation in fact led to the wars themselves or simply upped the human price paid in those wars, it is clear that the United States paid an enormous price in terms of the lives of its soldiers as well as treasure in order to catch up with its adversaries. For example, the United States ended up spending 45 percent of its GDP to successfully fight World War II, and more than 14 percent of its GDP to fight the Korean War to a draw.

Compared to what could well have happened, the Cold War thus can be looked upon as a cheap war in terms of human lives lost, albeit an expensive one in terms of treasure, because technologically speaking, World Wars III through VI were "fought" without the two principal adversaries, the United States and the Soviet Union, getting into combat directly against each other.

There is an important political/personal dimension to all this. Individual "warriors" believe in evil, and evil exists throughout time. Therefore, evil will always reemerge. To believe anything else is sheer folly, goes this argument. If you do not believe in evil, however defined, you cannot be a warrior, or a true worshiper of Mars. Mars requires a commitment to this essential societal commitment. Even if that evil is war itself, ignoring its possibility can be very costly.

THE FUTURE OF WAR

From the early days of the Republic to this moment, there have been American leaders whose basic assumptions were anathema to Mars. President James Madison, for example, said that the best way to prepare for war was to declare it, suggesting that only after war was declared was it legitimate to prepare for it. What a huge blood price America—and other countries—have paid for similar assumptions. Of course, Madison himself was forced to flee the White House just prior to the British invaders setting it on fire.

If one seriously listens to Mars, one can never say, "We're done with war." Sometimes, victorious countries can and do say "We're done with war for now" or "We can rest on our laurels." Even today, after the entire weight of human history has been factored in, some, like John Mueller, still argue that remaining warfare is "fundamentally trivial."[7] For Mueller, "war is merely an idea, an institution like dueling or slavery, that has been grafted onto human existence."[8]

Thus with the twenty-first century and the decline in appeal for wars, especially among developed societies and democracies, what remains are ethnic conflicts, "criminal war," and other "thuggish remnants," which for reasons unclear, he refuses to call wars. One would not, of course, like to have to explain such "triviality" to the hundreds of thousands, indeed the millions, who recently perished, and who continue to perish in Iraq, Afghanistan, Darfur, the Congo, Rwanda, and other places. It seems that, for some, hope—even dream—has been asked to replace reality.

Despite protestations to the contrary, war as an institution seems alive and well. The complex, multisided war in the Congo (involving forces from Uganda, Rwanda, Burundi, Chad, Angola, Zambia, Zimbabwe, and the Congo) from 1998 to 2002, for example, took over 4 million lives, continuing off and on until the present.[9]

Yet others, such as John Moore, look to "democratic peace" and the spread of democracy to lead to "a future with fewer wars."[10] Moore, a former American ambassador and the founding chairman of the United States Institute of Peace, believes that democracies can effectively reduce the incidence of war across the globe and by working with international institutions, curb any residual urge to war.

This seems, again, a laudatory but unlikely hope, given the whole spectrum of human history. Especially today with authoritarianism seemingly again on the rise across the world, and no sign that "local" wars are diminishing in scope or levels of violence, it seems unlikely that we have seen war's end. It would indeed be wonderful if truly we had seen the end of war; but it is much safer to assume that there will be more wars.

Still others, and Thomas Friedman is perhaps the most erudite exponent of this point of view, argue that gradual globalization, represented by the phrase "the world is flat," will eventually undercut any pushes for war because of the world's interdependence.[11] But on the other hand, of course, the flatter the world, one could argue, the more likely there will be competition and struggle for control of the important resources of the future—oil, water, food, forest canopy, and so on. The oil and mineral reserves of the Arctic and the Antarctic, for example, are likely to attract more than covetous glances in the decades ahead.

Parag Khanna, in an illuminating and wide-ranging analysis of today's world sees three "superpowers" vying for influence: the United States, the

European Union, and China.[12] All three of these economic and military power centers offer examples and rewards to others. For Khanna, this tri-cornered competition somehow results not, as one might imagine, in more wars for resources and influence but fewer. How this can be is not clear.

These views may turn out to be correct, but from the perspective of Mars, that seems highly unlikely. Khanna, for example, starkly overlooks the current role the United States military plays by being deployed across 150 countries as well as on all the world's oceans. One has only to look at the difficulties the UN has in dealing with such ongoing military problems as the pirates of Somalia and the recurring wars in the Congo to see the need for an even larger U.S. role in maintaining security on a worldwide basis.

One could well argue that this is the very presence that has enabled globalization to avoid becoming hostage to the disorder and chaos that would prevent globalism from flourishing. It seems just as likely that increased globalization will promote great (and small) power rivalry for markets, scarce resources, and ultimately the security of trade routes, as to work against them becoming *casus belli*.

In fact, today the arms race goes on at a fast rate. Wars and armed conflicts continue to break out all over the world between and among states and nonstate actors. And "evil" in various forms continues to threaten pacific people all over the globe. Yesterday's defeated adversary prepares for tomorrow's war. Yesterday's victor dares not believe that this war was the war that ends all future conflict.

Think about World War I, "the war to end all wars," which actually led to the worst war in human history, World War II. It is interesting to see what lessons some of the belligerents of World War I drew from that European disaster, showing us that poor judgment was not confined to a single country.[13]

France, of course, made a major strategic mistake in thinking they could fight a future war the same way they had fought a previous war. In Britain, many thought "the war to end all wars" had just passed, although there were some who saw the next war as being different. In any case, the financial constraints on Britain following World War I (which changed from being the world's largest creditor in 1914 to its biggest debtor in 1919), made rearmament doubly difficult even if its leaders had wanted to follow the dictates of Mars.

The United States, having fought "the war to end all wars," unilaterally disarmed. "There will be no future war," said the American people, and the government agreed, or vice versa. And, said the Americans, "If there is one, we'll blunder about and handle it when it comes. There is no need to get ready for another." Not surprisingly, when World War II broke out, the United States had a smaller armed force than Romania, Bulgaria, or Portugal.

Describing this substantial degree of unpreparedness, Ronald Spector states that the U.S. armed forces in the 1920s and 1930s "were obliged to function in a political environment which made it extremely difficult, if not impossible for those organizations to secure the financial, industrial, and human resources which they considered necessary to attain even the minimum level of military capability to carry out their anticipated wartimes missions."[14]

The tragedy in all of this is that if Great Britain, France, and the United States had rearmed and remained firm against the rise of Nazi Germany when it began to expand, World War II might never have happened. Great Britain, in particular, by recoiling from the true horrors of World War I, refused to face the reality of a revived Germany bent on war and revenge, and involuntarily did much to ensure that such a conflict would come about, or at the very least, made it far more costly to defeat Germany when war finally came. As Donald Kagan so clearly puts it: "In Britain, pacifism, isolationism, and other forms of wishful thinking were widespread and contributed to the mood favoring disarmament and concession. The idea of maintaining peace through strength was not in fashion."[15] And further, "Had the French and the British between the wars examined their political and strategic situation objectively and realistically, they would have seen that an offensive element was essential to their very defensive goals of maintaining peace and the security of the new Europe."[16]

Mars could only applaud Kagan's realism and perspicuity. If only France and Great Britain had coupled their World War I experience with a frank assumption that "there will always be another war" (and most likely with a rearmed Germany), there might not have been a worldwide conflagration. There were, of course, risks in French and British action against Hitler as Germany rearmed, but these seem to pale in comparison to the subsequent risks both countries faced for their inaction.

To appreciate the true importance of Mars, one has to always assume there will be another war. Why? Because there always has been another one.

It is true that there is now a United Nations, and having that organization sometimes enables two sides who want to stop fighting to do so without losing face. It is also true that an expanded European Union presages fewer wars between and among its membership. But neither entity is in any position to prevent or stop countries that really wish to go to war. Europeans could only watch as Serbia invaded Bosnia in the 1990s and Russia invaded Georgia in 2008. Until proven otherwise, therefore, from the perspective of Mars, it makes sense to assume there will be another war.

"There will always be another war," strikes most people as a horrible assumption but the penalties for avoiding its conclusions can be monumental. For example, where would the state of Israel be today if it had not always assumed there would always be another war? Likewise, how could its Arab neighbors have made a decision that there would never be another war either? Indeed, while something like peace has been engineered between Israel and Egypt and between Israel and Jordan, the ongoing struggle between Israel and Hamas and Hezbollah suggest that the armed struggle has just morphed into another form, not been eliminated.

No one, even one who supports the full rights of the Palestinians, could reasonably expect Israel to make peace with those who want to wipe it off the face of the earth. Conversely, even one who fully supports the right of Israel to continue to exist could not currently expect Palestinians to accept the status quo or other states such as Iran and Syria to give up the valuable "devil" enemy played by the Israelis in their domestic situations.

Rightly, Israelis say "no more Holocausts." At the same time, many Palestinians and Arabs would be quite correct in saying to Europeans and Americans, "If you truly didn't want a Holocaust or don't want another one, why not let unlimited Jewish immigrants into your country?" Or, "Why let so many Jews go to Palestine?" Or, "Why support them as long as they stay there?" "Why make Arabs pay to assuage European or American guilt over the Holocaust?"

These are legitimate questions for all parties, but these questions underscore the likelihood of further warfare, not less, since it is unlikely that Europe and the United States—let alone the Israelis—would ever be willing to pay such a price for "peace" in the Middle East.

In this regard, when planning for the next war, it is important to note that money spent on weapons is not wasted, even if the weapons are not even used, for they lead to newer, "better" weapons, and the process goes on and on with a dynamic of its own. But a country that stays ahead of the military curve is less likely to be attacked.

WAR AND GLOBALIZATION

In many ways weapons speak for themselves. The weapons a country possesses define what that country's limits are. They show how far it is willing to go to prevent the next war by being strong enough to avoid it. And the inability to constantly upgrade weapons, training, and tactics sends a very clear signal to its opponents, present and future.

However, just when a power thinks it is secure, it may well be at the hour of its maximum danger. As the 1990s began, the United States appeared to be the only remaining superpower, and some observers were asking if this was the "end of history."[17] Yet at that very moment, two colonels in China were highlighting the true vulnerability of the reigning hegemon, and, in the process, underscoring one of the central elements of the Template as they eagerly projected what the next war could and probably would look like.

In a brilliant analysis subsequently published in the West in 1999 as *Unrestricted Warfare*, Qiao Liang and Wang Xiangsui precisely pinpoint the vulnerability of the United States.[18] Despite the lurid title of the American edition, the contribution of its U.S. publisher, the book is actually a very sober and insightful analysis of hegemon vulnerability—and the importance of the Template's assertion, "There will always be another war."

At the time of America's unexpectedly overwhelming victory in the Gulf War of 1991, and in the face of many alternative assumptions by others, these Chinese authors achieved a counterintuitive intellectual breakthrough. Qiao and Wang incisively saw that far from ending wars, the Gulf War of 1991 simply moved the battle space from where big tanks and air power could be dominant to other battle spaces where these weapons would prove to be of little value—if not irrelevant. The authors' perspective is very much that of Mars: there can never be a final hegemon, only placeholders for that title; there is no permanent peace, only interludes of peace.

Qiao and Wang quote General Fu Quanyou, the chief of staff of China's People's Liberation Army, saying, "the inferior can defeat the superior." Their point is that there were challengers who were about to appear and who would focus on what they must do to win the future laurels of Mars. In their book, they enumerate how financial war, cyberspace war, drug war, cultural war, smuggling war, technological war, environmental war, network warfare, computer hacking war, and other forms of nontraditional war were likely to succeed against the Americans, who, they feel, cannot and will not sustain ongoing and high casualties—however they are dealt—without giving up.[19]

Qiao and Wang also see a vital shift to a new paradigm where the entire world is the battle space and the blurring between "military" and "civilian" arenas is of enormous import. Their chapter "Ten Thousand Methods Combined as One: Combinations That Transcend Boundaries," predicts the future of warfare.[20]

This analysis seems almost breathtakingly new, unless one has read *The Peloponnesian War* of Thucydides from the fifth century BCE or the fourth-century BCE writings of Kautilya, especially his *The Arthashastra*.[21] Both these realists capture the essence of the multifarious dimensions of warfare. Thucydides's investigations into war cover the gamut from conventional warfare to revolution, while Kautilya was another ancient theorist who looked at war in its many guises, such as open war, secret war, and undeclared war.

Of course, the Chinese colonels were looking at their own war sage, Sun Tzu, but Kautilya focused on the various aspects of warfare in a similar way. He called "secret war" the "terrorizing, sudden assault, threatening in one direction while attacking in another, sudden assault without specifying time or place."[22] Kautilya also advocated torture, assassination, and destruction of enemies, both foreign and domestic. "War and peace are considered solely from the point of view of profit."[23]

Osama bin Laden also noticed the inability of the American people to sustain their will in a protracted war or to persevere in the face of a relatively small number of casualties. Bin Laden, after the fiasco of the U.S. military efforts in Mogadishu in October 1993, concluded that the United States lacked the will to ever defeat dedicated fighters, fighters who refused to believe that there would ever be "a war to end all wars." As depicted in the book (and subsequent movie by the same title) by Mark Bowden, *Black Hawk Down*, the incident in Somalia was to color war perceptions for a generation.[24] After suffering eighteen dead and dozens wounded, the United States pulled out of Somalia, abandoning its peacekeeping—or peace establishing—mission. Bin Laden, having been part of the successful defeat of the Soviets in Afghanistan, saw this withdrawal from Somalia as a sign of fundamental American weakness.[25] His judgment turned out to be a miscalculation after the United States invaded both Afghanistan and Iraq and remained despite sustaining ongoing casualties.

Regardless of the stimulus, the Chinese, bin Laden, and others saw that there is indeed no "end to history," no end to warfare. This view, of course, is very much in keeping with the dictates of Mars. Everything that has followed has borne out these conclusions.

Since the Chinese have already begun to think about the next series of wars, and al Qaeda has planned specifically for and began another war, the United States itself has embarked on two wars since 1991, one in Afghanistan and another in Iraq. It would appear that there is a great deal of contemporary validity in believing that there will always be another war. And there is scant evidence that this mind-set is changing across the world. We must always remember that what some see as a defensive buildup of military capability looks to others as a prelude to military action.

At least for any country, people, or movement wishing to be prepared for whatever form that war takes, following the Template of Mars seems the best way to ensure survival. There may not "always be another war," but for now, the prudent must assume the centrifugal force still lies with Mars. However much we may individually oppose war, we must accept the words of David Livingstone Smith that, for some, "war is both intensely horrible and exquisitely pleasurable." Mars says, "It will come again. Sooner rather than later."

Thomas Sheehan makes a most powerful and telling point that "the obsolescence of war is not a global phenomenon but a European one."[26] Major segments of the American public seem to have assumed the same unilateral—and incorrect—projection of values onto the world stage. Why this is so unclear except for the fact that large segments of the American intelligentsia seem to believe that because war is harmful and hateful it is not a "natural" condition of humankind but a mere "aberration."

Moreover, it is important to remember that in the post-9/11 world, nonstate actors can prepare for the next war without necessarily assuming they will be punished for their attacks. This means that traditional deterrence theory is greatly undercut. Philip Bobbitt makes a powerful point when he shows that countries and nonstate actors will always feel threatened if they do not have nuclear weapons or other weapons of mass destruction, hence their quest will be ongoing and very dangerous unless constantly checked.[27]

There is also the most stimulating and persuasive analysis of Anthony Pagden on the ongoing struggle between East and West.[28] Pagden underscores the long sweep of human history, the ebb and flow of military action from East to West and West to East that has gone on for century after century. It is a saga that puts in sharp relief the ongoing nature of those military interactions.

Starting with the attempted Persian invasion of Europe, thwarted by the Greeks at Thermopylae, Marathon, Salamis, and Plataea, he sees a back-and-forth "perpetual enmity" fueling an ongoing struggle that alternates between Western incursions (under Alexander the Great and the Romans) into the heartland between Europe and India, and Eastern incursions under the Muslims, Arabs, and Ottomans. There are Western intrusions during the Crusades, but they are eventually overcome by the East, as was the Byzantine Empire. Yet the East in turn falls to Western imperialist intrusions beginning with Napoleon's invasion of Egypt.

Pagden also calls Samuel Huntington's much-maligned and much-praised "Clash of Civilizations" hypothesis "a crude but useful phrase" and the ongoing clash with the forces of the West "an enduring reality of Islamic life."[29] Of course bin Laden himself refers again and again to the "clash of civilizations," as well.[30]

Prophetically, Pagden echoes the power and vibrancy of the "always another war" dimension of the Template of Mars: "It seems unlikely that the long struggle between East and West is going to end very soon. The battle lines drawn during the Persian Wars more than twenty-three centuries ago are still, in the selfsame corner of the world, very much where they were then."[31] In his view, even if the other great civilizations of Asia—China, India, Korea, and Japan—have allowed themselves to reach an accommodation with the West, the Muslim world, the Umma, can never do so: "O Prophet!" the angel Gabriel commanded Muhammad, "Urge the believers to war, if there are twenty patient ones of you they shall overcome two hundred, and if there are a hundred they shall overcome a thousand." The patient ones are patient still.[32]

Today, one can and must ask, "How powerful is the dimension 'There will always be another war' of the Template of Mars?" It can be argued that it is perhaps the most important of all the Template features. Planning for the next war is essential, whether it be new weapons, new techniques, or new constellations of forces.

MASS DESTRUCTION AND DETERRENCE

Concepts such as President Reagan's antimissile shield to guard against ballistic missiles intrigue us. And sensible people might well recoil at the Reagan-era notion that after a nuclear exchange, when the United States had hit the (then) Soviet Union with 6,000 nuclear weapons and the Soviets responded with 5,000 of their own that Secretary of Defense Casper Weinberger would ask the question, "Now who will prevail?" Yet that was and remains the essence of nuclear deterrence. If the outcomes of such a nuclear exchange are so mutually horrific that neither side wishes or dares to take the risk to start a war, there is safety in "mutually assured destruction." *MAY*

But the notion of deterrence is based on the principle of rationality and assumes a rational decision-making model for war. It also assumes a known target state with known state actors and countertargets. Such an assumption would be extremely risky in today's asymmetrical, sub-national world of international terrorism. Failed states such as Somalia and potentially failed states such as Pakistan (in the sense of having no effective control over considerable population and territory nominally included in the country) make excellent spawning grounds for asymmetrical violence. The disasters of nonstate actors using nuclear or radioactive devices may lie in the future.

Writing in 1990, Martin van Creveld accurately asserted that nuclear war between states was not only less and less likely, but so too were multiarmy major wars among the superpowers.[33] At the same time, he recognized that while warfare was morphing away from its interstate form, it was spreading in its sub-national or sub-state incarnations. He concluded that war, far from being phased out of human interaction, was moving into a new and potentially deadly phase: "The nature of the entities by which war is made, the conventions by which it is surrounded, and the ends for which it is fought may change. However, now as ever war itself is 'alive and well' with the result that, now as ever, such communities as refuse to look facts in the face and fight for their existence will, in all probability, cease to exist."[34] He thus prudently underscored the continuing validity of the assumption that for Mars, a key ingredient must remain: "There will always be another war."

But what about arms control and arms reduction? Do they not offer a way to a safer world? Yes, but only under the most unusual and constrained situations. David Emery, former congressman from Maine and deputy director of the U.S. Arms Control Agency during the Reagan years, raises the question as to how "arms control negotiations" fit into the Template of Mars. For him, there are four key ingredients to any successful arms control efforts:

1. The reductions must be militarily significant rather than cosmetic.
2. Both sides must agree to negotiate in good faith and refrain from egregious public relations statements or stunts.
3. The symmetric nature of the forces has to be taken into account in order to maintain an approximate balance of forces during the lifetime of the treaty.
4. Meaningful verification must ensure that each side knows beyond a reasonable doubt that the other side is following the rules.[35]

As these rules indicate, true arms control is very rare (although, in the case of the U.S. and the USSR chemical and nuclear reduction treaties, very important). Just the listing of meaningful conditions suggests how fragile such a process must be unless *both* sides truly want an agreement.

It should also be pointed out that "arms control" can be, and often is, a marriage of convenience, allowing both sides to reduce the cost of maintaining obsolete or less desirable weapons. The result is often that the governments and militaries in question will have more resources available for new technologies and the challenges of different types of new wars.

It should be noted that international treaties are often made to be broken or are being broken before the ink is dry. For example, when the USSR endorsed the Biological Weapons Convention in 1972, it already had the largest and most advanced stockpiles of biological warfare capability in the world. As the former head of the Soviet Union's *Biopreparat*, put it:

> We were among the 140 signatories of the convention, pledging "not to develop, produce, stockpile or otherwise acquire or retain" biological agents for offensive military purposes. At the same time, through our covert program, we stockpiled hundreds of tons of anthrax and dozens of tons of plague and smallpox near Moscow and other Russian cities for use against the United States and its Western allies.[36]

The Soviets would continue to explore both biological agents (including plague, tularemia, brucellosis, anthrax, glanders, melioidosis, Ebola, Marburg, and Bolivian hemorrhagic fever) and the means to deliver them for the next several decades, targeting New York, Los Angeles, Seattle, and Chicago on a scale paralleling the Soviet's nuclear targeting plans.[37] "Ballistic missiles containing stimulants of biological agents were fired in tests over the Pacific Ocean from 1960 to 1980."[38] Even after the ascension to power of Mikhail Gorbachev, the Biopreparat was told to keep its weapons assembly lines one step ahead of inspectors.[39]

When portions of the arms race slow or even die out, new inventions and weapons arrive. For example, the United States is currently working to develop a whole new set of weapons for the next war, including "Rods from God," titanium rods shot from space at 7,300 miles an hour, which can achieve the deep-bunker penetration of a nuclear weapon but without the attendant radiation. This innovation, while exciting to U.S. war planners, could be very destabilizing to others who assume the United States would enjoy a decisive competitive advantage and would hence have to seek their own countermeasures.[40]

At the same time, countries such as Iran seek to develop nuclear-weapons delivery systems that could create massive electromagnetic pulses that would cripple vast portions of the United States by permanently destroying the electrical grid of the country. As Harry Yarger so accurately puts it, "Globalism means different things to different constituencies but what it clearly does not mean is a period of international peace and stability."[41]

Other countries are avidly rushing to make sure the United States does not stay the unchallenged hegemon for long. China, Russia, even India and Iran continue to put scarce resources into their militaries as if they expect there will be future wars.

THE NEXT WAR

The flywheel of Mars continues to spin, providing inertial power for future conflicts. Whatever the new forms of warfare, there seems to be an ongoing and irresistible movement toward war qua war, making Mars smile yet again.

Who or "where" will start the "next" war? An unknown hacker who breaks though a code to start a war? A fanatic; a dedicated nationalist; or a rogue person, cult, or group? A determined group in one of the increasing number of failed states throughout the world? Any number of nonstate actors for whom the ongoing struggle is worth any price to others?

Think of the possible insurgency, terrorist, and secessionist situations that could involve others in a major war: Kosovo, Uganda, Zimbabwe, alQaeda in the Islamic Maghreb in Algeria, Niger, Bosnia, Hezbollah in Lebanon, Montenegro, FARC in Colombia aided by Venezuela, dissident elements in Azerbaijan, Kashmir, Armenia, Nagorno-Karabakh, India, Jaish-e-Moham-med or Hizbul Mujahideen in Pakistan, Yemen, Harkat-ul-Jihad-al-Islami in Bangladesh, Mozambique, the Congo, Chad, Nigeria, Ukraine, the Kurds in Turkey (and Iraq and Iran), Lebanon, Somalia, Tibet, Chiapas, Darfur and/or the southern Sudan, Al-Shabaab in Somalia, southern Thailand, Xinjiang, Chechnya, Kashmir, the Crimea, the Philippines, Sri Lanka and so on.

Also, consider what has happened to the NATO alliance since 1991. On the one hand, it has greatly expanded to twenty-six members and is engaged in out-of-theater activities for the first time in Afghanistan, causing considerable strains between the military and the civilian populations in Europe. Yet on the other hand, NATO's greatly expanded membership, pushing east to include Poland, Croatia, Albania, Hungary, the Czech Republic, Romania, Bulgaria and perhaps most ominously for the future, Estonia, Latvia, and Lithuania, could well provoke a resurgent Russia. Russia might in fact decide to try to destabilize and even occupy its former "territories" or "allies."[42] There is also the vexing potential problem of Kaliningrad, the Russian territory sandwiched in between Poland and Lithuania. The very size of NATO may now make future unified action less, not more, likely and thus cause it considerable problems in the future.

It is hard to imagine that a resurgent Russia in the future would not have military confrontations with one or more of the new members or aspiring members. This could draw the United States and some NATO members into direct military conflict with Russia, but perhaps not with the backing of all members.

As humans, war seems as much a part of our future as our present and our past. That is why Helmut Schmidt's words make so much sense, "to be able to fight, so as not to be compelled to."[43] And William Blake's "War Song to Englishmen" remains even more universal in its poignancy:

> Prepare, prepare the iron helm of war,
> Bright forth the lots, cast in the spacious orb;
> Th'Angel of Fate turns them with mighty hands,
> And casts them out upon the darken'd earth!
> Prepare, prepare!

The current prospects and possibilities for future wars seem nearly endless, which is just how Mars has always wanted it. And so it has been for a long, long time. And so it is most likely to be in the future.

9

Applying the Template: A Battle

The past is never dead. It's not even past.

—William Faulkner

In addition to being a conceptual framework for understanding the patterns of who wins in war and why, the Template of Mars is also an explanatory tool that can help to provide patterns that explain why some armies and states win some battles and lose others, as well as how battles can illuminate long-term trends and project impacts into the far future.

It is very important that future analyses of war and success in war look at the phenomena of wars and battles through the prism of Mars to make sure that centuries of outcomes are not superficially overridden by short-term events and judgments. Battles are windows that, when properly utilized, can offer insights into fundamental changes in power relationships and the degree to which entities have been following the Template of Mars. By applying the Template to important battles, one can see why one side was more likely to lose and the other more likely to win.

USING THE TEMPLATE TO EXPLORE A BATTLE

When one thinks about World War II, and the various key turning points in that war, a number of possibilities arise. Depending on one's perspective, and the importance one ascribes to either the European or Pacific theater and their respective culminating points, there are a number of places one could focus on and that often have been analyzed.

In the European theater, one often sees Stalingrad (1942–1943) or Kursk (1943) being cited as the most important.[1] Still, some recent studies by careful observers have made a case for the Battle of Moscow (1941). Rodric Braithwaite and Andrew Nagorski, for example, make the point that this battle deserves to be reexamined due to the huge battle space involved (an area the size of Western Europe) and the closeness the Germans came to actually capturing the capital of the Soviet Union.[2] Others might offer, from a more traditional Anglo-American perspective, the Allied landings in Normandy (1944) or the Battle of the Bulge (1944). In the Pacific theater, most military historians would point to the campaigns at Guadalcanal, Midway, Okinawa, or perhaps even the fire bombing of the principal cities of Japan.

But in truth, if you combine the theaters and link together their common destinies, then perhaps the most important battle—in terms of the longer time frame implications and eventual outcome of World War II and in terms of impact on both theaters—was the battle of Khalkin-Gol (sometimes spelled "Kolkin Gol") or Nomonhan (sometimes spelled "Nohoma" or "Nomon-Han-Burd-Obo").

As with the terminology of the American Civil War, one side may choose to designate a battle by the closest town (as did the South in First Manassas) or by the river in the middle of the battle, (as did the North in First Bull Run). In this case, the small river was Khalkin Gol, and the nearby, similarly sized town was Nomonhan. For the sake of consistency, I will use the name of the town, Nomonhan, to describe the battle and its impact on world history.

When properly examined, Nomonhan turns out to be a battle of the highest importance, and yet it remains one that has been curiously in the background for many military historians writing about World War II. From the perspective of Mars, however, it appears to be seminal, perhaps even decisive, in determining the subsequent course of World War II in both the Pacific and European theaters. With the advantage of the conceptual framework of the Template of Mars, we can see who won the battle and why, and why it may well have preordained the Japanese attack on Pearl Harbor as well as the eventual defeat of the Germans in front of Moscow in 1941. In this chapter, we will present that battle through the eyes of Mars in order to see why the battle turned out the way it did.

When we examined the Japanese relationship to the Template of Mars as it existed in the early part of the twentieth century, we saw that they had been extremely effective in the Russo-Japanese War of 1905. The Japanese seemed to have mastered the principles of the Template far better than their Russian opponents and crushed them both on land and sea. At the end of that war, the Japanese emerged entirely victorious in the Far East against the Russian Empire and positioned for greater expansion throughout the region.

For their part, the Russians proved themselves to be catastrophically inept. The Russian Czar would go on to lose another war to the Germans and Austrians before being overthrown by the Bolsheviks. The loss to the Bolsheviks, of course, proved fatal to the Romanov family, the monarchy, and its government. One could argue that from the perspective of Mars, the Russian Czarist government and its military deserved their fate.

Given what they perceived to be Russian weakness, Japanese expansion in the twentieth century was initially driven by a strategy of "go north" against the Russians, Korea, and later Manchuria and other parts of China. Such a strategy was predicated on a Japanese desire for raw materials and territorial expansion and by what they assumed to be the inherent weakness of their opposition. Later the Japanese activities also included elements of an anti-Bolshevik crusade (which Japan shared with Nazi Germany), as well as the more pragmatically possible opportunity to eventually cut the Trans-Siberian railroad and isolate the Soviet Far East, making that region more susceptible to Japanese economic and political influence if not outright conquest.

At the time of Nomonhan, the "go south" faction of the Japanese high command (heavily but not exclusively naval in character), whose imperial officers wanted an attack on the Philippines, Singapore, and Indonesia were outnumbered by those favoring the "go north" option (heavily but not exclusively army officer inspired). Thus, as late as 1939, it was by no means certain that Japan would decide to go south and engage the British, Americans, French, and Dutch. In fact, prior to the Battle of Nomonhan in 1939, it seemed far more likely they would indeed go north. The Japanese military was collectively confident that they could defeat the Soviets, just as they had defeated the Russians under the Czar.

Earlier, after the establishment of the Mongolian People's Republic in 1924, the Soviets sought to use Mongolia as a buffer state between themselves and the Japanese-controlled territory. Japan occupied both Korea and Manchuria (forming the puppet state Manchukuo in 1932) and cast their eyes covetously on Soviet territory farther north and west. The Japanese and Soviet forces thus faced off against each other on the very ill-defined and disputed border between Mongolia and Manchuria, clashing in 1938. There were hundreds of border "incidents" in the years running up to our Template's battle.

On the surface, Nomonhan appears to be an obscure, simple battle of short duration. It started out as many previous border incidents had in this huge, desolate area where the border between the two forces was both porous and highly disputed. On May 11, 1939, Soviet-Mongolian forces were attacked by elements of the Kwantung (Sixth) Japanese army in the area of northwest Manchuria on the border with Outer Mongolia. In this initial skirmish, the Soviet-Mongolian units were forced to withdraw to the Khalkin Gol River. The Soviets were outnumbered and the Japanese subsequently dug in one mile from the river.

Following up on this clash and the Soviet retreat, as John Erickson indicates, the Japanese brought up additional forces, and on May 28, they attacked in force with approximately 24,700 men, supported by forty aircraft.[3] The Soviets fought hard to contain the Japanese advance, and in response, during June, Soviet corps commander, General Georgi Zhukov, was assigned to take over the First Army Group.

General Zhukov brought with him "massive reinforcements" of both men and equipment, bringing up large numbers of tanks and armored cars until the Soviets enjoyed a 1.5:1 superiority in infantry, 1.7:1 in machine guns, 2:1 in artillery and aircraft and 4:1 in tanks. Soviet armor included the new and powerful BT-5 (a forerunner of the Soviet T-34, which would be regarded by many experts as the best medium battle tank of World War II).

All this was accomplished with the nearest supply base 200 miles away. The Soviets thus began this phase of the battle with significant attention to their logistical needs, both immediate and projected, and put themselves in a position to prevail in a long struggle against the Japanese. In all, Zhukov pressed 3,000 trucks into service to make sure his forces would be well supplied with ammunition and fuel when he ultimately launched his offensive. By contrast, as Alvin Coox points out, the Japanese moved most of their supplies by horse and mules, and the backs of their soldiers.[4]

By mid-July the Soviets had a force of 70,000 (later 100,000) positioned in the battle space, while the Japanese had 40,000 (later 60,000). But it was the Japanese, believing in their invincibility and suffering from very poor intelligence, who then launched a major assault under Lt. General Komatsubara Michitaro.

The Soviets continued to fight a delaying action until all their potential counterattacking assault divisions were in place. It was the quality of their defensive fighting that enabled the Soviets to absorb the Japanese attacks while building up their forces on the flanks for the eventual counterattack.[5]

For their part, the Japanese were surprised by the extent of Soviet resistance but continued to try to break the Soviet lines even in the face of the Soviet buildup, believing that it was only a matter of time before they broke through and destroyed the Soviet forces. The Japanese were quite convinced that they would prevail and that their superior élan and courage would carry the day.

On August 20, however, Zhukov vigorously attacked with almost 100,000 troops and 500 tanks along a forty-eight-mile front to the north and south of the central portion of the Japanese position. Displaying the ferocity that would distinguish his entire World War II career, Zhukov insisted on offensive action regardless of cost, and soon the Soviets broke through the main Japanese line of resistance and eventually surrounded the main body of them in a classic double envelopment. The Soviets' relentless attack, skillful use of combined arms, and a heavy reliance on massed artillery (over 200 pieces) and armor (500 tanks) backed by 200 bombers succeeded in surrounding the Japanese.

In terms of receptivity to innovation at Nomonhan, the Soviets showed they had mastered the art of combined operations in the era of the tank. Soviet artillery and aircraft proved to be superior to that of the Japanese in terms of rate of fire, altitude, and bomb load. Highly disciplined Soviet formations broke through and encircled the Japanese from the north and the south. This strategy was, with its superior technology, tight discipline, and rapid forward movement with close air support, an ironic albeit brief forerunner of the German blitzkrieg style of warfare.

For their part, the Japanese were stunned by the magnitude of their defeat. They lost as many as 45,000 out of their 60,000-man force while the Soviets on the attack lost 17,000 (they admitted to 6,000).[6] Some historians put the numbers of losses as high as 50,000 for the Japanese and 10,000 for the Soviets; figures vary widely for this under-reported battle. According to Coox, for example, Zhukov said he inflicted 52,000–55,000 total casualties, while Japanese medical records show 20,000 killed, wounded, or captured out of 60,000 troops engaged.[7]

While we shall probably never know the exact casualties on both sides, at the end of the battle, it was a most decisive defeat for the Japanese and a very significant victory for the Soviets. Because of their much greater adherence to the principles of the Template of Mars, the Soviets turned out to be a much tougher foe than the forces of the Russian Czar had been thirty-four years earlier.

Japanese technological superiority at sea, which they displayed so prominently in their victory at Tsushima in 1905, was not duplicated by their land army equipment at Nomonhan. In the Battle of Nomonhan, the Japanese proved to be inferior to the Soviets in terms of tanks, artillery, and air support. The impressive Japanese advances in terms of aircraft carriers and naval aircraft were simply not duplicated in the small arms, tanks, and artillery of this army, and the imbalance showed in stark relief.

Ironically, the magnitude of the Soviet victory at Nomonhan was overshadowed by events elsewhere, and this may well account for its obscurity in the annals of World War II. On September 1, the Germans invaded

Poland from the west, causing the French and the British to declare war on Germany.

For their part, the Soviets would wait to join the Germans until they signed a truce with the Japanese on September 10. Then they would attack Poland from the east on September 17, eventually dividing the country with the Germans and getting a free hand in Estonia, Latvia, and Lithuania in exchange for additional Polish territory going to the Germans.

Applying the Template element by element, we can see the primacy of certain dimensions that turned out to be decisive.

Superior Technological Entrepreneurship

In this regard, the Soviets had much the advantage. Not only did they integrate their artillery, armor, and infantry far better than the Japanese, the Russians had sheer technological superiority with both their armor and their artillery.

The Soviet BT-5, for example, had 45 mm of armor, carried a 76 mm gun, and had a top speed of 55 km per hour while the Japanese main battle tank was the Type 95 with only a 37 mm gun, 12 mm of armor, and a speed of 30 mph. And that was the best Japanese tank. Many of their others were significantly inferior to the Type 95. In all, the Russians utilized almost 500 tanks, including an early version of the T-34, arguably the best medium tank of World War II.[8]

Coox also estimates that 54 percent of Japanese casualties were caused by rapid-firing artillery from which the 200 Soviet field guns could fire 120 rounds per minute, far more than the Japanese. Aircraft losses went from four to one in the Japanese favor during the outbreak of the battle to ten to one in the Soviets' favor in August.[9] The Soviets also used newly developed flamethrowers to great effect. In the air, the Polikarpov 1-15s and 1-16s brought ground support and air-to-air Soviet aviation superiority over the Japanese.

Superior Discipline as an Organizational Principle

For many familiar with World War II, stories of Japanese soldiers showing iron discipline and fighting to the death are widespread and well known. In this case, however, the stronger discipline was on the Soviet side. Although the Japanese displayed initial cohesion when on the attack, once the Soviets counterattacked, Japanese discipline broke down in a number of key places, especially after Soviet armor broke though to their rear.

Certainly, Japanese soldiers provided many examples of courage and the willingness to fight to the death. But it was the Soviet army that more consistently showed stronger small-unit cohesion and discipline, even while taking heavy casualties during the attack phase. The Japanese would continue their reliance on suicidal infantry charges throughout the war in the Pacific with the United States.

Ability and Willingness to Practice Sustained but Controlled Ruthlessness

The Soviets also excelled in the area of sustained ruthlessness. Despite all the horrors and destruction of the Russian Revolution and subsequent civil war, despite the Stalin-inspired purges of the Soviet officer corps in the 1930s, the Soviet military at the Battle of Nomonhan proved up to the task of practicing sustained but controlled ruthlessness to a powerful foreign foe.

Having once penetrated the Japanese outer defenses, they were determined to destroy the entire Japanese force and inflict on them a devastating defeat that would teach the Japanese a savage lesson not to attack Soviet forces again. Later, when the Japanese were surrounded but refused to surrender, Zhukov pounded away until he destroyed their formations with massive heavy artillery and aircraft strikes, annihilating the Japanese Twenty-third Division and its supporting units.

In this battle Zhukov earned a reputation for ruthlessness not only against his enemies but also in the seemingly brutal use of his own troops. For example, he was later to tell General Dwight Eisenhower, "When we come to a minefield, our infantry attack as if it were not there. The losses would be the same regardless of the type of defense."[10] At Nomonhan, he showed his ruthlessness by refusing to let his troops rest until the enemy had been destroyed and insisting they attack even as they suffered heavy casualties during the first phases of the counteroffensive.

Receptivity to Innovation

The Soviet ground forces also proved to be far more receptive to innovation in this battle. Not only were their tanks far better than anything the Japanese had, the Soviets had learned to concentrate their armor while the Japanese still fought ineffectively by sprinkling their tanks out among their infantry. The smashing success of Zhukov's double envelopment was due to the Soviets' receptivity to innovative tactics and strategy as well as the new weapons themselves.

Moreover, the setting up of the complex Soviet supply system was itself innovative. Not only were the Soviets equipped with better tanks and armored cars and able to concentrate their formations better, they also developed the capacity to supply and fuel those tanks and provide the artillery shells necessary to take maximum advantage of their technological superiority with a very long logistics tail.

Coox rightly goes so far as to call this combination a "technical operational revolution."[11] The Soviet preparation for, and execution of, their offensive at Nomonhan reflected considerable learning from their previous tactics and strategy.

Ability and Willingness to Protect Capital from People and Rulers

In the interim between Tsushima Straits and the battle by the river Khalkin Gol, the Soviet Union protected far more of its capital from its civilian population. At the height of its industrialization, Stalin was forcing a reinvestment rate of 25 percent from the society, albeit by draconian means. But looking at this strategy not from a humanitarian or even an ideological perspective, but simply from that of Mars, the Soviet massive investment in arms at the expense of the civilian goods and services meant that the Soviet Union was better prepared for the world war that was to follow than the Japanese or Germans.

In this remote battle space, the Soviets were thus able to amass an incredible advantage in matériel, arms, ammunition, transport, and gasoline, an advantage that the Japanese could only dream about as the battle progressed. The Japanese had failed to develop their army, both in terms of its basic equipment and its ongoing supply system and paid a heavy price in Nomonhan. In the years since 1905, they had failed to put their land forces in a position of superiority versus a modern, well-armed foe.

Superior Will

The Japanese doctrine of the divinity of the emperor and their nationalistic pride had always been two important wellsprings of Japanese will in battle. At Nomonhan, however, the Japanese forces were not only far from home, they also found themselves suddenly fighting a defensive battle for which they had not prepared. And their leadership at the battalion, division, and corps levels was not up to the task of sustaining, let alone enhancing, Japanese collective will during the critical phases of the battle.

For their part, the Soviets not only had the commissar system to ensure loyalty among subordinate troops and to make sure orders were followed, but the personality and domination of General Zhukov was also central to the enhancement of Soviet will. He was insistent that they would win, determined to make them win, and intolerant of any failure to press the attacks with vigor. The force of his personality was itself a key power multiplier in the battle of wills played out in the desolate Mongolian steppes in the summer of 1939.

Assumption That There Will Always Be Another War

In terms of this element, both the Soviets and the Japanese assumed there would always be another war, but whereas the Soviets expected to be attacked, the Japanese assumed they would be the ones deciding where or when to attack. This mind-set undoubtedly gave the Japanese a false sense of security. Having been the aggressors for so long, the Japanese felt they would always be the ones to seize the initiative. This proved to be a drastically mistaken assumption.

Strangely enough, however, Joseph Stalin seems not to have taken the lesson to heart. He wanted desperately to believe that the Germans wouldn't attack until the Soviets were ready and therefore played for time in the European theater. The Soviet military and indeed, the entire Russian nation subsequently paid a huge price for this mistaken assumption. Conversely, the Japanese thought of themselves as masters of battle timing. But they were completely caught off guard by the ability of the Soviets to launch a counterattack.

Thus, as we examine the Template element by element, it is not surprising to see that as the Soviets dominated in the seven categories, so too did they dominate the battle. Metaphorically speaking, Mars was most pleased with Soviet total progress and adequately rewarded them in the dusty, far-off battle space on the Khalkin Gol River.

WHAT WERE THE LONG-TERM
RESULTS OF THE BATTLE?

Prior to their victory over the Japanese, the Soviets had been very reluctant to join the Germans in their invasion of Poland unless and until the situation in the Far East had been resolved. Erickson, in fact, believes that the Battle for Khalkin Gol was "a significant part of the 'difficult situation' in which the Soviet military command found itself."[12] With the overwhelming Soviet victory, Stalin could confidently assure the Germans that the Red Army would join them in the partition of Poland, which they did on September 17, 1939.

Many, although not all, of the Japanese Army's "go north" cohort began to see the "go south" option as far less hazardous and challenging. The Japanese naval (and other services) "go south" advocates were thus greatly strengthened. As a result, the Japanese high command began to plan for a "firecracker" set of attacks on the U.S. forces at Pearl Harbor and the Philippines, British forces in Singapore and Malaya, French forces in Indochina, and Dutch forces in Indonesia.

This action would subsequently turn out to produce disastrous results, not just for the nations the Japanese attacked and conquered, but eventually also for the Japanese themselves when the war turned decisively against them and brought massive destruction to them from one end of the Japanese Empire to the other.

It seems clear that a major part of the Japanese decision to go south, was due to the quality of the Soviet forces and above all their technological entrepreneurship advantages the Japanese encountered at Nomonhan. Within the armed forces and the Japanese government, the Imperial Navy was increasingly seen for what it was—a far more modernized and efficient force when compared to the army units and their old-fashioned equipment, especially in the areas of armor, artillery, and close-support aircraft.

The Japanese reorientation of its major battle plans removed the major threat of an attack on the USSR from the east, enabling the Soviets to shift their forces west, which was to prove decisive in the subsequent battles for Moscow (December 1941) and Stalingrad (August 1942 to February 1943).

How differently World War II might have developed if the Japanese had attacked the Soviet Union instead of the United States, the Philippines, the Dutch Indies, Malaya, and Singapore. A Japanese attack on the eastern Soviet Union would have prevented the Soviets from fighting a single-front war and, given the close-run nature of that single front war, such an attack might have proven decisive in giving the Germans a far better chance to win the war.

One should also remember that the United States was drawn into the European war when and how it was only because Germany foolishly chose to declare war on the United States after the Japanese attack on Pearl Harbor. As much as some American officials—such as President Roosevelt—wanted to go to war against Germany, it was by no means certain that they would prevail in that desire as long as Germany did not attack the United States directly.

In accordance with the Pact of Steel, however, Hitler duly declared war on the United States after Pearl Harbor. He did not wait for a declaration of war from the United States. It is a most interesting historical question whether, with its Pacific battleship and cruiser fleet in ruins, the United States would have declared war on Germany at that time. The declaration of war by Hitler against the United States after the Japanese attack on Pearl Harbor netted him nothing in the way of strategic advantage, only enmity and ultimate defeat.

Ironically, the Japanese high command as a result of the battle considered the Soviets to be a tougher foe than the United States. This not only strengthened the hand of the "go south" faction, but turned over planning for the defeat of the Americans to Japan's navy. Surprisingly, the Japanese learned few other important lessons from the battle and never upgraded their army's artillery, armor, or small-arms capabilities. Nor did they revamp their tactics, perhaps because those involved in the defeat were not anxious to have others revisit the event.

Despite his belief that he and the navy could "run wild" for six months against the United States, Admiral Isoroku Yamamoto predicted that, in the end, the United States would triumph. His reasoning? He had seen the oil wells of Texas and the auto factories of Detroit, and he knew of America's industrial might. He believed that these material advantages would prove decisive in favor of the United States.

But Yamamoto's concerns were brushed aside by the army commanders who believed that the United States soldiers, sailors, and marines would not have the stomach to take the enormous casualties required to recapture all the territories Japan would take in those first six months. They would simply prove less effective and dangerous than their Soviet counterparts had been at Nomonhan. Japanese military leaders did not want further warfare with the Soviets.

Zhukov's successful use of the double envelopment at Nomonhan was to presage his similar use of this maneuver in the pivotal battles on the Eastern Front that were to come in the fight against Nazi Germany. As mentioned, his victory at Nomonhan and the subsequent Japanese lunge to the south and east enabled the Soviets to transfer large numbers of the Siberian and other trans-Ural armies to assist in the battle for Moscow in December 1941, and it was the arrival of these forces that set in motion the first Soviet counteroffensive against the Germans.

Although the 1942–1943 Battle of Stalingrad was fought on an east-to-west axis rather than the west-to-east axis featured at Nomonhan, the Soviets again used the center of their line to absorb the initial attacks by the Germans while Zhukov built up massive reserves on the flanks to break through and surround the enemy forces, putting them in a "cauldron."

Strangely enough, other than deciding on a strategy not to fight the Soviets, the Japanese high command learned few enduring lessons from the battle itself. Its leaders failed to see the importance of newer armor and artillery formations, and they failed to alter their strategy or tactics, continuing to rely largely on the bravery and commitment of their foot soldiers. The Japanese turned a blind eye to the obvious deficiencies in their army's equipment, tactics, logistics, and leadership.

In the two years between Nomonhan and Pearl Harbor, the Japanese army did virtually nothing to enhance its competitive position in the ground war. Japanese tanks, artillery, machine guns, and small arms remained inferior to the Americans' weaponry. Failing to learn the lesson of Nomonhan turned out to be but part of a pattern in which, as Carl Boyd so aptly puts it, "The Japanese military was a prisoner of its own arrogant past."[13]

Equally ironic, Zhukov's strategic massing of armor and his use of combined operations at Nomonhan, while stunningly successful, were subsequently dismissed by members of the Soviet General Staff. Zhukov was demoted to Deputy Commander of the Ukrainian Military District and only reemerged when appointed chief of staff to General Semyon Timoshenko in late 1940 after the disastrous beginning of the Soviet Winter War against Finland.[14]

For his part, Zhukov himself credits the lessons he learned at Nomonhan with inspiring his extremely successful later military career.[15] Certainly, Zhukov's later triumphs were duplicates of the double envelopment he achieved there.

The application of the Template to the Battle of Nomonhan thus indicates the extent to which it can provide a useful overarching analysis of a battle by showing what ingredients were central to both victory and defeat. In the next chapter, we apply the Template to a type of warfare widely regarded as "new" and "redefined."

10

Applying the Template: A War

We consider a general insurrection as simply another means of war in its
relation therefore to the enemy.

—Carl von Clausewitz

The more things change the more they are the same.

—Alphonse Karr

Counterinsurgency is a thinking man's war.

—Peter R. Mansoor

In this concluding chapter, we turn to a possible challenge to the Template
of Mars that could come from an assumption that the world of war has
changed dramatically and drastically since 1991 and that these changes
obviate its explanatory characteristics. Some argue that the "old rules" of
war no longer apply. We are living, they say, and will continue to live, in a
"new world" of war with concomitant changes that make previous forms of
warfare (and the Template for success in those forms) obsolete.

Has warfare indeed changed since 1991 to such a considerable extent as
to render the Template useless? This is a reasonable question, and one that
needs to be examined, for it is true that 1991 appears to be a watershed
year for world politics and international relations (and assumptions about
them). There have been major structural and belief-system changes that
flow forward from its events.

For example, 1991 was the year the United States and its coalition
partners decisively defeated Iraq and restored the government of Kuwait,

confirming and underscoring America's position as the only remaining superpower. Moreover, the sweeping nature of that victory and the near "perfect working" of the land-air battle strategy of the United States gave rise to the assumption that there might never be another major set-piece-battle war fought.

As a result of such an overwhelming victory, there was a concomitant rush in the United States to spend "a peace dividend," an effort that reduced military spending to below any yearly percentage of its GDP since before World War II. The United States seemed to be in a race with Europe to see who could disarm more and faster, perhaps for economic competition reasons.[1]

The subsequent cutting of the American defense budget, of course, flew directly in the face of the seventh element of the Template, "There will always be another war." That element was studiously ignored by many, including the U.S. Congress. The centuries-old U.S. pattern of "win a war and substantially cut the defense budget," again held sway, as it had after the Revolutionary War, the Civil War, World War I, and World War II.

The year 1991 also saw the collapse of the Soviet Union, ending forty years of a bipolar international system under which many smaller, less powerful state actors had to maneuver politically, diplomatically, and strategically between the two super powers. The year also seemed to signal an end to an era of the superpowers fighting each other by using proxies, which had stimulated warfare in Asia, Latin America, Africa, and the Middle East.

The economic and military dominance of the United States now looked unchallenged, as the Soviet Union lost not only all of its previous satellite states in Eastern Europe (East Germany, Czechoslovakia, Albania, Bulgaria, Poland, Romania, and Hungary), but also, a considerable portion of its former territory. Estonia, Latvia, Lithuania, Georgia, Ukraine, Kigiristan, Kazakhstan, Turkmenistan, and Uzbekistan all declared themselves free of the former "Union of Soviet Socialist Republics."

Indeed, these developments came at a time when some believed that warfare was over and that liberal democracies had banished war to the side-lines for all time. Some even believed that nation-states were losing—and would continue to lose—their power to control history to nonstate actors. There were even claims made—and believed—that this new era was "the end of history."[2] This new era, it was felt, would bring the end of the nation state. It would also bring the end of warfare as we had known it for many centuries.

However, at the same time, 1991 was the year in which Osama bin Laden launched his movement, al Qaeda, declaring the primacy of the clash of civilizations now that one "Great Satan" (the United States) had replaced

"Two Great Satans" (the United States and the Soviet Union). His declaration seemed to fly in the face of the seemingly major structural changes taking place. But it also suggested that the new era might indeed have some important repercussions from the previous one. Bin Laden's pronouncement suggested that war, perhaps even war as previously understood, would go on.

But even if wars did not become historical relics, many argued that the Gulf War of 1991 was the last "old style" war, one with large military formations in divisional form. Indeed, General Rupert Smith suggests that from that moment on, the old paradigm of interstate, industrial-based war "no longer exists" and has been replaced by a new paradigm of "war amongst the people."[3] He argues that while conflicts will continue to rage across the world, they will not fit the previous pattern of interstate activity. For him, even the Second Gulf War of 2003 was simply an echo of a dying model, not a continuation of it.

Instead, based on his extensive experience in Iraq, Kosovo, Northern Ireland, and Bosnia, Smith postulates that a new form of warfare will have malleable objectives. And this "new war" will take place in every living room in the world as well as on the streets and fields of the conflict zones; it will be timeless in the sense of taking years or decades to be resolved, and will be fought by forces that will seek to preserve themselves rather than risk them in an all out battle.[4]

Moreover, Smith feels these conflicts will require new weapons, technology, and techniques and that the actors in these fights will be mostly nonstate in character.

Smith's hypothesis is both stimulating and open to challenge. He may well be right about changes in the nature of some wars, but at the same time, it seems more likely that *both* forms of warfare—"war among the people" and "war between states"—will continue to exist.

Certainly Smith's thesis seems undercut by the Russian dismemberment of Georgia during the summer of 2008, when old style tanks, armored personnel carriers, and artillery from one sovereign state went across an international border in order to defeat and partially dismember another sovereign state. Reports of the demise of the international nation state system seem, at best, premature.

But in any case, even if Smith's hypothesis is true, would any such paradigm shift obviate the use of the Template? While the initial, short, and ultimate answer is "no," it remains now for us to reexamine the Template in terms of this asserted "paradigm shift," to see if it continues to have efficacy in the age of insurgency and counterinsurgency.

Has Clausewitz become irrelevant? Has the Template of Mars been turned upside down?

Is there some primordial advantage in warfare that now belongs to "insurgents" and those who would practice "war among the people," irrespective of their time and place and objectives? Of course, all terrorists are not engaged in insurgency, and all insurgents do not practice extensive terror (although this is rarer). But for our purposes, are "terrorists" capable of taking the concept of "insurgency" and turning it into some new form of war where the "old" rules no longer apply?

We argue here the very reverse: nothing truly basic has changed about warfare, even though many aspects of it may have changed, and many new strategies and tactics will be required to win both wars among the people and wars between states. But because the modes and aspects of war have changed, at least at some times and in some places, this does not mean that the core of warfare has indeed mutated so as to obviate the previous assumptions about it.

Indeed, for both expanded "terrorism" and "insurgency," Clausewitz's basic premise is even more true and at its core, even more relevant. War remains nothing more than a contest of wills—deadly, hurtful, and enormously cruel but a contest of wills nevertheless. Many aspects of war have changed, but not its central character. Breaking the enemy's will to continue the struggle—however arrived at—remains the central ingredient in warfare. It is just that the means of, obstacles to, and time frame of will breaking has changed. Therefore, the Template, as a framework for analysis has not lost validity; rather, it maintains its power and efficacy for uncovering and assessing fundamental patterns.

Certainly, the current terrorist model for warfare is transnational, decentralized, civilian-interspersed, and potentially ultraviolent in character. Therefore, the insurgent/terrorist model stands as a fundamental challenge to the historical interstate system that has been in place since the 1648 Treaty of Westphalia. But that does not mean that the essential struggle of wills that lies at the heart of all warfare has been altered. Nor has the basic way of conflict analysis changed. In fact, as Alan Springer has argued, after 9/ll, perhaps only states can mount an effective counterchallenge to transnational terror organizations such as al Qaeda.[5]

Much has changed, including the ability of nonstate actors to obtain weapons of mass destruction—anthrax, saran, radioactive material, nuclear weapons, and so on—so that we may be stampeded into thinking that the fundamental characteristics of war, and hence the means to success in war, have changed.

Because of globalization and the Internet, the current terrorist challenge has access to an international marketplace for weapons, personnel, information, propaganda, and "real time" reaction possibilities. Rupert Smith is quite right about various aspects of insurgency; we often have "real-time" knowledge of changes in the battle space, wherever that may be. But whether these changed modalities constitute a truly changed framework for war practice remains in doubt.

Philip Bobbitt, in his perspicacious *Terror and Consent*, grapples with all of these changes, including the domestic and international dimensions and their implications for counterterror activities, and he concludes that "the market states" (the United States, the EU, Japan, and India) are not winning the war against terror.[6] While some of Bobbitt's theorizing is open to question, he does raise the question of what can ever be considered "winning" against global terrorism. Bobbitt also rightly points out that, should these market states eventually "win" against the terrorists, it will be a "victory without parades."[7] So again, it looks as if this is truly a new war, one in which the traditional landmarks of success, victory and defeat are lacking.

But at base, Bobbitt too remains faced with the underlying conundrum that war and success in war have not changed. The British success in the much earlier counterinsurgency wars in Malaya, Borneo, Sarawak, and Brunei, for example, under generals like Walter Walker resulted in victories that "did not involve a set-piece battle, the capture of territory and prisoners or a formal surrender by the enemy. It was question of preventing the enemy from achieving his objectives to the point where these are abandoned."[8]

Interestingly enough, as Amos Eno suggests, the ultimately successful British defeat of the insurgency in Malaya (and later Eastern Malaysia) was due in large part to their antecedent actions of World War II. When the British, under General William Slim, were defeated and driven out by the Japanese, they retreated back to India but eventually counterattacked and won a major double victory over the Japanese Fifteenth Army at Imphal and Kohima in the spring of 1944. As the war continued, and the British drove farther into Burma, they themselves, especially the Chindits fighting under General Orde Charles Wingate, practiced a very effective insurgency against the Japanese as well as simultaneous more conventional mobile warfare strategy.[9]

In the process, what the British learned in practicing insurgency became extremely useful when it later became necessary to practice counterinsurgency. Their ultimate success under Generals Walter Walker and Gerald Templer in Malaya, Sarawak, Brunei, and Borneo could—and should—have been a model for the Americans and South Vietnamese in the early stages of that insurgency. But the American military in Vietnam under General William Westmoreland was not receptive to this "new knowledge" that the British had gained by hard experience.

As Tom Pocock underscores, included in that packet of "new information" was (a) the need to win the hearts and minds of the people while (b) providing reliable security until the local people learned to provide their own, and (c) the need to move quickly and ruthlessly within the insurgents' decision-making and action cycles, especially by light, fast-moving small counterinsurgency units, rather than by ponderous, large-scale units alone.[10]

General Gerald Templer, who served in Malaya 1952–1954, in particular deserves credit for developing the integrated military and civilian program for winning the hearts and minds of those initially sympathetic to, or afraid of, the insurgents. Stressing heightened intelligence gathering, expanding and retraining the Home Guard, using the army for local development projects, involving Malay women as well as men in finding local and regional solutions, and following a strategy of "clear and hold," he developed the approach that eventually won the day for the counterinsurgent cause.[11]

Certainly, the Template of Mars still explains who wins in that type of warfare and why. The hermeneutic properties of the Template remain vibrant and useful. Why is this so?

INSURGENCY IS NOT NEW

Let us take the example of "postmodern" insurgency, particularly that of the radical jihadist Salafists. Because of the ideology and cosmology of religious terrorists, they would seem to offer the greatest challenge to the assumption that war today is susceptible to the same analysis as war earlier.

This challenge in part stems from their possible potential numbers, but far more important is their potential access to weapons of mass destruction and their willingness to use them. Weapons of mass destruction were a *casus belli* when the invading Americans went into Iraq. They failed to find them; however, today bioterrorism and radioactive materials continue to remain a most viable option for those beyond the reaches of the hegemonic nation-state.

But are insurgencies, especially terrorist-inspired insurgencies, truly "unique" or even "unusual" or "new"? Beyond having potential access to weapons of mass destruction, are today's insurgencies somehow "different" from insurgencies in the past? The truth is, of course, that insurgencies and revolutions are as old as human societies. Thucydides and Kautilya both saw a need for every ruler to keep his eye on potential insurgents, especially those who would practice terror. Over 2,500 years ago, Kautilya wrote extensively about "revolts and rebellions," not seeing them as "different" but as simply war under another guise. He specifically enumerated and specified a large number of types of rebellions, concluding that "an internal rebellion is more dangerous than one in the outer regions because it is like nurturing a viper in one's bosom."[12]

Thucydides also gave us a most incisive introduction to the violence of revolution and counterrevolution in his powerful description of the Corcyraean Revolution, stating that violence was likely to persist in the human experience: "The sufferings which revolution entailed upon the cities were many and terrible, such as have occurred and always will occur, as long as the nature of mankind remains the same, though in a severer or milder form, and varying in their symptoms according to the variety of the particular cases."[13]

Insurgencies and revolutions have been part of the human condition for thousands of years. Moving far ahead to the Spanish insurgency against Napoleon (from which we get the term "guerilla warfare" or "little war"), we find European corollaries to the many, many uprisings and insurgencies that have plagued so many rulers all across the world for so long. Ronald Fraser captures the true extent of that conflict, involving as it did, the intervention of the British and the Portuguese, who assisted the popular uprising against Napoleon. For him the role of ordinary people and their heart-rending sacrifices, indeed their truly national uprising, lie at the heart of the successful struggle.[14]

Indeed, Clausewitz provides us with some fundamental insights into insurgency in his often-overlooked chapter in *On War*, "The People in Arms."[15] In that chapter, he states clearly that we must "consider a general insurrection as simply another means of war—in its relationship, therefore to the enemy."[16]

As to the "inevitability" of insurgencies, that is by no means certain. We know that since history is written by the victors, it is not surprising that revolutionaries—the most successful insurgents—are often glorified and their triumphs assumed to be inevitable. Certainly, the Russian Revolution, the Chinese revolution, the Algerian Revolution, the French Revolution, the Vietnamese Revolution, the American Revolution, even the Haitian and Cuban revolutions, have all cast long, powerful and popular shadows. With hindsight, they seem to have been "inevitable" to many. Yet a careful examination of those revolutions yields far different conclusions. The American Revolution, for example, was, as John Ferling describes it in his recent and most incisive military history of that war, "almost a miracle." And Jeremy Black quite rightly asserts, "It is only too easy to assume that the war was a forgone conclusion, that the British could not conquer the Thirteen Colonies and that their defeat was inevitable."[17] At various times during the eight-year struggle, he correctly argues, the revolution looked stillborn. As late as the first months of 1781, the colonials were "bankrupt with a mutinous army," the British were on the ascendancy in North Carolina and Virginia, and France was wavering in its support of the Americans. In fact, many American revolutionaries were convinced they would have to settle for less than independence.[18]

It would take a number of surprisingly unlikely victories by the rebel armies and strategic mistakes by Great Britain to lead to the outcome we now take for granted. The American and French victory at Yorktown in October 1781 was very far from preordained.[19]

In fact, as the American Revolution indicates, successful revolutions are neither inevitable nor actually very widespread when one considers the ratio of failed insurgencies in relation to successful ones. Historically, counterinsurgency succeeds many times and in many places as well as within and among many cultures. Interested readers should consult the end of this chapter for a wide sampling of successful and unsuccessful insurgencies as well as a number of ongoing ones to get a relative sense of their seeming ubiquity, diversity, and lack of inevitability.[20] Moreover, a review of the more recent insurgencies in Iraq and Afghanistan suggests they are not sufficiently different from those previously encountered in history to warrant any sweeping assertion that "war will never be the same."

Nor are suitable and effective counterinsurgency techniques lacking. Writing in 1906, C. E. Callwell, wrote *Small Wars: Their Principles and Practice*, a detailed study of counterinsurgency strategies, tactics, and analysis, highlighting the successful "crushing" of insurrectionary movements.[21] While Callwell perhaps pays too little attention to the political dimensions of counterinsurgency, his work serves as a strong reminder that there is marked lack of inevitability to insurgencies, despite the pronouncements of Mao and others.

Also, contrary to some widely held views, the United States itself has had a long and varied history of waging counterinsurgency warfare, and indeed, winning counterinsurgency struggles.[22] Not applying the lessons of the past is not the same as arguing there are no applicable lessons from the past. Writing in *Baghdad at Sunrise*, Peter Mansoor chillingly describes how the U.S. Special Operations School at Fort Bragg was ordered to throw away their counterinsurgency files in the 1970s.[23]

HOW INSURGENCIES WORK

While there are some new dimensions and aspects to the twenty-first-century "wars among the people," they readily give themselves over to analysis by the persistence of the paradigms presented in the Template. Thus we would set forward two propositions: (1) most insurgencies and rebellions throughout history have failed and (2) those that succeed have special factors such as outside assistance and the availability of sanctuaries that often come into play. For example, the successful North Vietnamese takeover of South Vietnam depended upon billions of dollars in equipment, weapons, and supplies from the Soviet Union and China, as well as substantial amounts of manpower, and ultimately the crucial contributions of the U.S. government's deficient strategies as well as the American antiwar Left role in undermining the collective American will to prosecute the war.[24]

General Franco's rebellion against the Spanish Republic, for example, was aided by Italy and Germany (even while the Republic was aided by the USSR). It is hard to imagine his being successful in overthrowing the Spanish Republic without that aid, especially the physical movement of his troops from North Africa to Spain proper and superior weaponry provided by outside forces. Of course, his rebellion was essentially a conventional war in addition to a civil insurrection, but it is most doubtful he would have succeeded without the outside aid.

There are, of course, exceptions to the notion of outside aid. The Chinese, Cuban, and French revolutions were primarily internal, as was the Russian revolution. But the much-vaunted Spanish insurgency against Napoleon and the French depended for its final triumph on multiple major British armed interventions, as did the American revolution, which required massive French aid and troops and especially the French navy.

But most importantly, insurgencies are still wars and wars remain to be decided by Clausewitz's rule of will. Insurgencies succeed when they break the will of the enemy and fail when their enemy breaks theirs. The breaking of the enemy's will by either insurgents or counterinsurgents remains the independent variable in warfare.

Nothing changes in this fundamental axiom.

Winning Hearts and Minds

In the case of insurgencies, of course, since we are talking about influencing whole populations, there thus needs to be a strategic and tactical emphasis on "carrots" as well as "sticks." With different situations and different opponents, different tactical and strategic innovations are required, but at the end of the day, in Clausewitzian terms, insurgencies are simply "small" wars.

When the Allies were liberating France, for example, they were welcomed. When they crossed the Rhine, they were not generally welcomed, but as long as there was not armed resistance from the general population, the Allies could and did concentrate on defeating the Nazi military and its government.

In insurgencies, or Rupert Smith's "war among the people," the winning over of the civilian population takes on much greater tactical and strategic importance. Naturally this requires nonmilitary strategies as well as military ones and continually introduces politics, even at the tactical level of military operations. However, establishing security remains a most intrinsic part of that process, and convincing the civilian population that their support of the insurgents will not succeed is critical to winning that war.

Major portions of the European and American intelligentsia suggest that "there is no military solution" to insurgency. But to the contrary, when Mao Tse-tung wrote, "Power comes out of the barrel of a gun," he was simply stating the obvious. While insurgencies can rarely be defeated by military force alone, the intelligent use of counterinsurgency military force combined with a civilian retention strategy is the sine qua non for creating the situation where other factors such as reconciliation and political development can come into play.

A statement widely attributed to John Paul Vann puts it best, "Security might be 10 percent of the solution or 90 percent of the solution, but it was the first 10 percent or the first 90 percent."[25] There can be no defeat of insurgencies without military force and the security it provides for those the government wants on its side (or already has on its side) and would lose if security were not provided through force of action. Certainly those who say that fighting terrorism is—at some point—a "police matter" are correct in that local intelligence gathering and societal control are critical to eventual success, but when the police and other local officials are severely outgunned, the regular military must step into the vital role of protection and strategic intervention.

Indeed, as heretical as it may sound to many, the American/South Vietnamese anti-insurgency strategy from 1968 to 1972 can serve as a model—albeit only if one is intellectually capable of separating the counterinsurgency efforts from the efforts to defeat the regular North Vietnamese army units. The counterinsurgency strategy developed by General Creighton Abrams and used in Vietnam from the middle of 1968 until the end of 1972 showed enormous progress when carrots (the Chu Hoi program granting amnesty to former Viet Cong) and sticks (assassination of Viet Cong leaders at the village level and the arming of the local South Vietnamese; all told, upward of 500,000 villagers were armed between 1968 and 1972) were combined.[26]

It should be emphasized, of course, that this degree of counterinsurgency progress was made after the Tet Offensive of 1968 discussed below. As a result of this multipronged effort, by 1972 as much as 90 percent of the South Vietnamese population was under government control.[27] The eventual, total Communist victory lay three years in the future. And this victory, it must be said, was not due to failed counterinsurgency techniques, but rather because the United States was unable to break the will of the North Vietnamese government and dissuade them from their goal of taking over South Vietnam by using main-force, regular army units.

By contrast, the North Vietnamese were able to break the will of the American people and government and overrun the forces of South Vietnam *after* the United States no longer supplied air and artillery support for the army it had trained to depend on these additional elements of force. By way of a historical parallel, it is hard to imagine the South Koreans in 1953 being able to successfully hold off any renewed assault by the North Koreans and Chinese without air and artillery support as well as massive aid from the United States. It should be noted in this context that even today, the United States' substantial presence in South Korea is essential to maintaining peace on the peninsula.

By 1972, together with its South Vietnamese ally, the United States military had already broken the back of the Viet Cong insurgents. As Colonel Bui Tin of the North Vietnamese military said, about the 1968 Tet Offensive,

> Our losses were staggering and a complete surprise. . . . The second and third waves in May and September were, in retrospect, mistakes. Our forces in the South were nearly wiped out by all the fighting in 1968. It took us until 1971 to re-establish our presence but we had to use North Vietnamese troops as local guerillas. If the American forces had not begun to withdraw under Nixon in 1969, they could have punished us severely. We suffered badly in 1969 and 1970 as it was.[28]

RELIGIOUS INSURGENCY

If Vietnam and other counterinsurgencies show the power and the vulnerability of insurgents, what about the present situation with radical Muslim jihadists seeking to overthrow many Muslim governments as well as to drive the United States from its territories? Does this phenomenon offer insights into the future? Does the melding of insurgency with religion rather than with ideology and nationalism make a difference in our assessment?

It may be as Anthony Pagden suggests in his *Worlds at War*, that West and Islamic peoples have been at war long and hard for centuries, but, he rightly notes, it is not Christians versus Muslims but some Christians versus some Muslims, with many Christians and many Muslims rooting for their coreligionists and many against them—depending on the era. While Rome was not distraught when Byzantium fell to the Turks, and Venice played a double game for a very long time seeking to weaken the Byzantium Empire, by and large Pagden is correct; there was a longer and more enduring pattern of Christian versus Muslim warfare.

But going back to the Arab invasions of the West, which were turned back at the Battle of Tours in 751 and later by the Normans in Sicily and the Spanish in Spain, and the subsequent invasions of Arab lands by the West, there has been an ebb and flow here that suggests a more deep-seated and longer-lasting phenomenon, a phenomenon that helps to cast the present situation in harsh relief. There has also been a long tradition of widespread accommodation between West and East, and mutual acceptance or peaceful competition interwoven with the patterns of thrust and counterthrust.

The true radical jihadist Salafists, however, have a belief system that does not lend itself to accommodation or eradication except with sustained ruthlessness and sense of purpose. The term *radical jihadist Salafists* is carefully chosen. Obviously, not all terrorists are Muslim. So too, not all Muslim terrorists are Salafists and many Salafists are peaceful and content to live their lives according to "pure" Muslim principles without imposing them on others.

But "radical jihadist Salafists" are committed to use violence to overthrow any and all governments, including Islamic regimes, that do not practice strict adherence to the principles of eighth-century Islam. Thus the radical jihadist Salafists ultimately challenge not only the present world order but the nation-state system itself, based as it is on national sovereignty.

Moreover, this challenge can be ferociously delivered. In Algeria, the ongoing struggle between the government and radical Salafists has cost 150,000 dead in a long-running civil war. The gratuitous violence of the insurgents against innocent Muslim civilians eventually cost it popular support, as did its harsh view of society, government, and religion. In an attempt to revitalize its fortunes, the insurgents subsequently renamed themselves "al Qaeda in the Islamic Maghreb." It remains to be seen whether the Algerian government continues to have the will to suppress the insurgents' goals in its own version of "the long war."

It seems unlikely that most people, indeed most Muslims, would want to go back to a society existing 1,200 years ago. Yet that is exactly what al Qaeda, the Taliban, and other Salafists are offering, albeit over the barrel of a gun. It is not as if the people of a particular country will be allowed any freedom of choice, as the insurgents are intent upon forcing their vision of the past upon all those who fall under their sway.

The radical jihadist Salafists are in essence fighting the Western nation-state model that has been the essence of political reality dating back to 1648 when the Treaty of Westphalia, in order to stop the religious wars of Europe, said that the religion of the sovereign ruler would be the official religion of the country and that the state should have a monopoly over the use of force within its territory.

After the Treaty of Westphalia, Catholics and Protestants no longer needed to fight and kill and pillage in order to impose their religions on all Christians, and others, in their jurisdiction. The official religion of the entity in question would be the religion of the sovereign, although other religions could be practiced at his or her tolerance. But the present-day radical jihadist Salafists have, by rejection of the tenets of Westphalia as well as by their actions and universal worldview, made "the whole world a battle space," as Robert Kaplan puts it in his very important book, *Hog Pilots, Blue Water Grunts*. Their potential terrorist targets are now global in scope and recognize no "state" except their own.

Assessing the Threat of Radical Jihadist Salafists

Let us try to understand the potential reach of the radical jihadist Salafists who believe that killing someone who disagrees with their belief in a specific supreme deity is justified and to be welcomed. Virtually all the world's major religions contain a certain extreme or fringe element whose views run counter to the essence of their chosen religion and who also believe that killing those who don't believe in their version of God or his vision should be killed.

Is this number 1 percent or 2 percent or 5 percent of any given religion? We do not—indeed cannot—know for certain, but as long as assumptions are parallel in nature, it seems fair as well as prudent to examine them. Let us take the lower figure of 1 percent and apply it to all the major religions. If 1 percent of Christians, Hindus, Buddhists, Shintoists, and Muslims believe so strongly that their personal religion is the *only* truly worthy religion, and that it should be imposed by force on those who do not so believe, then that 1 percent probably represents a threat to most others of all faiths and must be taken most seriously wherever their advocates persist.

We obviously do not know how many people share this radical jihadist Salafist ideology, but if it were to be only 1 percent, and there are 1.8 billion professed Muslims today, that would mean almost 18 million potential recruits, or at least supporters.[29] Given the size of that potential cohort, it is not surprising that some projections today speak of a "long war" of forty or fifty or a hundred years between the forces of radical jihadist Salafist Islam and forces of both moderate Islam and the West. Seen in that context, the Salafist threat seems current, widespread throughout the battle space, and likely to remain relevant into the foreseeable future.[30]

Given such a potential pool for recruits, there is enormous opportunity for insurgents in many countries to exist, develop, and flourish. Therefore, "insurgency" can now seem suddenly and powerfully, a phenomenon of concern. Bear in mind that it is their cosmology, not just their current actions and dedication to destroy the almost 500-year-old interstate system that should give many across the globe pause. Al Qaeda, the most prominent and well known of the radical jihadist Salafist groups, is currently operating in at least sixty countries, and as the Salafist Cleric Suleiman Abu Ghaith put it in June of 2002, they truly do mean harm to others: "Al Qaeda has the right to kill 4 million Americans, including 1 million children, displace double that figure and insure and cripple hundreds of thousands."[31]

Using the Template helps to cast in sharp relief the intertwined and ongoing relationship between insurgents and counterinsurgents.

HOW THE TEMPLATE OF MARS
APPLIES TO INSURGENCY WARFARE

Let us, therefore, look at the phenomenon of insurgency through the lens of Mars, with some special emphasis on al Qaeda as the global terrorist insurgency with the most ubiquitous, worldwide positioning. It also has the most potential for causing disruption in the international community and remains the most valid threat to the international interstate system since international Communism tried, but failed, to create a universal Marxist-Leninist transcultural "jihad" for its values. It is also the entity most committed to the notion "There will always be another war."

Superior Technological Entrepreneurship

Generally, insurgents are usually perceived as having less access to advanced military technology. This may or may not be true, looking at all of their capabilities. But in a series of "plays within plays," outlined earlier in chapter four, they may actually have technological advantages in certain situations. These may prove to be decisive in a given theater of operations—unless the more dominant side learns from its mistakes and proves receptive to innovation.

For example, early in the Iraqi insurgency of 2003, the Sunni insurgents and their new al Qaeda allies had a big local advantage in the widespread availability of discarded artillery shells and other munitions. They needed no foreign sources. These intertwined insurgents did not need to give battle to obtain the military resources necessary to pursue their struggle.

There were hundreds of thousands of artillery and mortar shells and millions of other small-arms munitions lying around, thanks to Sadam Hussein's predilection for putting vast amounts of ordnance in and among the population—in schools, mosques, local party headquarters, and so on. The insurgents were able to move swiftly and effectively to utilize the potential of these weapons. They even inherited a raft of AS-7, SA-14, and SA-16 surface-to-air missiles with which they would shoot down dozens of U.S. helicopters.

The Sunni portion of the insurgency was also fueled by the disastrous decisions of the Coalition Provisional Authority, which disbanded the army and police and decapitated the Baathist leadership of the government, thereby providing over 100,000 newly unemployed Sunnis with a grudge against the Americans and the Shiites. Thus, the emergent Sunni participation in the insurgency appears to be more like a traditional insurgency than the newer, transnational terrorist version as represented by al Qaeda.

The insurgents made improvised explosive devices (IEDs) their weapon of choice, blowing up American Humvees and even tanks with powerful explosive charges. The United States countered with more explosive-resistant armored vehicles and electronic countermeasures to either prevent detonation or to disarm these munitions from a safe distance. In turn, the insurgents countered with propelled projectiles of greater force and potency. The technological entrepreneurship in the area of suicide bombers, more powerful roadside bombs, and their countermeasures continues.

On the other hand, as a result of fighting insurgency wars in Afghanistan and Iraq, the United States has developed a very advanced weapons system, the Predator drone, which, when coupled with two Hellfire missiles, is like virtually no other weapon in the history of warfare[32] Flown by an operator thousands of miles safely away from the battle space, it can see and kill, unobserved, from 30,000 feet, day or night. Operationally, one can anticipate greater and greater use of the Predator (and the next generation and larger Reaper) going forward in future insurgencies. The potential future impact of this weapons system to destroy in "real time" isolated and remote targets cannot be ignored. In fact it is likely that these weapons will be seen as so successful that the insurgents will make stopping their use through political pressure on the host countries a top priority.

It should also not be forgotten that the nineteen-ton Strikers, the eight-wheeled armored vehicles with state-of-the-art graphics and data provided by tactical drones, turned out to be a huge improvement on the lighter-armed Humvees in terms of urban warfare and putting boots safely on the ground. Mars looks upon such a technological breakthrough as an enduring revolution in military advantage, even though such improved technology is, in and of itself, not the ultimate answer to defeating either conventional or insurgent forces.

Think also of the imperative that propelled the American military to develop and deploy the Excalibur XM982 artillery shell (which using GPS tracking can hit within thirty feet of a target fourteen miles away) in order to minimize civilian casualties when the insurgents hide among them. Costing $89,000 per shell compared with $300 for a conventional shell, the Excalibur is yet another indication of the need to protect military capital from people.

At the same time, one cannot assume that insurgents will not be able to figure out how to obviate any technological advantage enjoyed by the counterinsurgents. On balance, however, the insurgents may not have the time, ability, or capital to prevail technologically unless will is lacking on the part of the counterinsurgency partners. Still, from the perspective of Mars, the struggle between insurgent and counterinsurgent is by no means settled, especially in the most fluid of battle spaces such as the tribal areas of Pakistan. Superior technology is but one facet of the counterinsurgency effort, albeit an important one.

Superior Discipline as an Organizational Principle

Superior discipline is one area of the Template that is very useful when one looks at insurgency. Superior discipline remains vital in struggles between the armed combatants, but it is also extremely important in getting the civilian population to support one's goals, especially in "wars among the people." For the insurgents, this means not raping, looting, or killing indiscriminately, lest the population turn against you—as it did in the Sunni heartland when al Qaeda operatives behaved very badly toward the civilian population and, over time, made them more accepting of counterinsurgent strategies, even those projected by a foreign, occupying power.

Maoist revolutionary theory places much emphasis on the idea of the people as the sea in which the insurgents swim. Mao's forces were told to pay for the food they got from the peasants, to always be courteous so as to gain the support of the people, and to be kind and just to those they captured. Think of Mao as an ironic forerunner of the current archetype of the "warrior gentleman" of current U.S. military doctrine, even though he and his forces often ignored its ideal.[33] It is as important for the counterinsurgents to live among the people as it is for the insurgents.

Mao was quite right to assert that the counterinsurgents must themselves practice heightened discipline. Rogue torture, false imprisonment, or ongoing humiliation of the civilian population often will backfire—as it did when the less-than-stellar discipline among a small number of American military personnel tasked with running Abu Ghraib forgot the purpose of their mission and were foolish enough to record their malfeasance.[34]

Keeping tight discipline thus remains one of the most important keys to any successful counterinsurgency effort. For example, as Anthony Jones rightly points out, it was increased discipline on the part of the American counterinsurgency forces in the Philippines from 1899 to 1902 that made a huge difference in their effectiveness.[35] Conversely, the Soviet defeat at the hands of the Afghani insurgents was aided immeasurably by the terrible discipline problems within the Soviet military, as its poorly trained recruits and even regular army personnel looted, killed indiscriminately, and traded their weapons and ammunition for alcohol, food, and clothing from 1980 to 1989.

So there are more dimensions to superior discipline in a situation where insurgency is involved that could shift advantage to either side in such a conflict, and superior discipline remains at the very heart of a Mars-favored strategy of success. Whichever side adheres to strong discipline and self-control usually wins in the end.

It is true that radical jihadist Salafists, who not only are not afraid to die but actually wish to achieve personal martyrdom, represent a somewhat different foe than many other insurgents, but again, it is more a difference of degree than kind. Suicide bombers can be very effective weapons, both in specific tactical situations and cumulatively, but they do not alter the nature of war.

The Ability and Willingness to Practice Sustained but Controlled Ruthlessness

This is one area where the Template is of even more assistance in judging a particular characteristic. The insurgents and the counterinsurgents must both balance sustained ruthlessness with taking care not to overdo it.

In this regard, the insurgents have far more leeway to act. Rolling a grenade into a crowded marketplace or blowing up a mosque with worshipers in it is ruthless and sometimes undertaken for its own sake as well as with particular targets in mind. Such a tactic is both a strength and a weakness. It is a strength because the perpetrators have the self-righteousness to kill civilians without qualms, but it is a weakness because it underscores their inability to strike true military targets. Unfocused violence can also undercut the legitimacy of the insurgents and even, as in Iraq and Afghanistan, stimulate counterinsurgency.

Causing chaos is usually easier than trying to create stability and calm. In fact, the extent to which random ongoing violence destabilizes a government is emblematic of the upside potential for the insurgents because the target government is automatically seen as weaker than it really is simply because it is unable to prevent it. Sustained ruthlessness can obviously be carried too far, causing a backlash among the very population one is trying to win over, however. As indicated earlier, the Salafists in Algeria (*Groupement Islamique Arme*, or GIA, now renamed al Qaeda in the Islamic Maghreb) have been responsible for the deaths of over 150,000 men, women, and children, 99.9 percent of whom were Muslims.[36] This wholesale and often untargeted slaughter and the effective (but also often brutal) counterinsurgency activities by the Algerian government have turned many Algerians against the insurgents. Ordinary men and women who might have been attracted to a purer religious life, did not necessarily want to live and have their children live under a rule as onerous as proscribed by the Salafists such that one would fear for one's life daily.

We should note here that the Algerian military has been successful enough (reducing the number of its operatives from 27,000 to 1,500) that

American Special Forces now go there to learn how to defeat al Qaeda.[37] Still, the latest incarnation, al Qaeda in Islamic North Africa continues to exist, showing that while it is possible to defeat insurgents in some commonsensical way, it is almost impossible to totally eliminate them. Merely reducing them to an "acceptable" level of diminished violence, however, should not be disheartening as long as it is accepted as a fact at the outset of the campaign.

There is also evidence from other parts of the Muslim world that al Qaeda's indiscriminate terror attacks on Muslims were, by 2007, beginning to cause a backlash among previous supporters or neutrals. The respected Saudi religions scholar, and one of Osama bin Laden's heroes, Sheikh Salman al Qudah, on the sixth anniversary of the September 11, 2001, attack on the World Trade Center condemned the bloody path of al Qaeda in killing so many Muslims in Jordan, Afghanistan, and Iraq: "My brother Osama, how much blood has been spilt? How many innocent people, children, elderly, and women have been killed . . . in the name of al Qaeda? Will you be happy to meet God Almighty carrying the burden of these hundreds of thousands or millions on your back?"[38]

For insurgents, "war among the people," means using civilians as human shields and placing their assets of war among civilians—in homes, schools, hospitals, and mosques. These tactics guarantee high levels of collateral damage when the government counterinsurgency forces attack. Thus, a battle of wills is unfortunately conducted among the innocent and the nonbelligerent.

The element of ruthlessness also puts enormous pressure on the counterinsurgency forces not to overreact to enemy provocations and create exactly the type of public disillusionment the insurgents are seeking. The Template, far from being obviated by insurgent warfare, enables us to focus on the differences and similarities between different forms of sustained ruthlessness in that context and to judge the extent to which one side rather than another is properly adhering to the Template. It can thus be an effective framework into which to put the dimensions of both insurgency and counterinsurgency.

Receptivity to Military and Process Innovation

Here we see one of the most important ingredients of the Template in action. How fast do insurgents learn and innovate in the battle space? How do they overcome the initial advantages enjoyed by their opponents? How fast do the counterinsurgents adjust their tactics to those of the insurgents?

Certainly in the post-Saddam era in Iraq the insurgents proved to be extremely innovative and quick to make tactical and strategic adjustments:

In just twelve months the insurgent had surpassed the level of bomb-making ability achieved by the IRA over thirty years. In Iraq there were over two thousand IED attacks a month, using every type of electronic gizmo imaginable, including car alarms, wireless doorbells, cell phones, pagers, and encrypted radios. Global jihadist from Chechnya, Afghanistan, the Balkans, and the Middle East were sharing technologies, tactics, and procedures at a lightning-fast pace, via the Internet, terrorist training camps and CD-ROM. The IED became one of the most dangerous and effective weapon systems we'd ever faced, and the insurgent's weapon of choice.[39]

The rapidity and effectiveness with which the insurgents used the existing munitions (250,000 *tons* of which went unsecured by coalition forces), gave them an enormous advantage, one that would subsequently take years to overcome. In this regard, what would Mars say about leaving a million pieces of military ordnance lying around on the battlefield to be picked up by one's opponents? It is difficult to understand how the United States military could allow such a blunder.

The insurgents, however, both in this situation and many others, are subject to the same successful strategies employed in other dimensions of warfare. For example John Boyd, one of the most important and innovative military thinkers of the twentieth century, sees "an unequal distribution [of forces] as the basis for local supremacy and decisive leverage to collapse adversary resistance."[40] In its simplest incarnation, Boyd's OODA, as discussed in chapter five, stands for "observe, orient, decide, and act." But in fact, it is a very elegant process consisting of a hundred feedback loops all designed to get "inside" an enemy's decision-making loop and make your own decisions better and faster and more continuous.

This rapid-fire, nimble decision making is precisely the essence of both insurgency and counterinsurgency. It is essential for exploiting local unequal distribution of forces, and the selection of these targets becomes an ongoing OODA loop with myriad permutations cumulatively of enormous consequences.

In other words, regardless of the total forces for defensive and offensive operations in the entire theater, the key for success lies in producing a preponderance of force at specific times and places within the theater. Successful insurgents avail themselves of this principle, but so too do successful counterinsurgents.

The so-called surge in American forces in Iraq during 2007–2008 was such a success precisely because the counterinsurgency brought enough troops to bear (both in terms of manpower, firepower, and political power) to make the unequal distribution of forces an advantage for the defense at strategically selected geographic positions at precisely the time many Sunni insurgents were looking for protection from al-Qaeda (the Anbar Awakening). Using existing units as well as those newly arriving in new ways was thus critical to its success.

"Beneficial asymmetry," whereby one side has an overwhelming local tactical advantage in soldiers and equipment, can come into play to assist the counterinsurgency forces as well as what Boyd calls "faster tempo or rhythm," putting "learning" at the heart of counterinsurgency.[41] Innovation in asymmetrical warfare thus works both ways, from possible insurgent advantage to possible counterinsurgent advantage.

This emphasis on "faster tempo or rhythm" has echoes throughout the history of insurgency. For example, commentators have always focused on physical speed in examining guerrilla movements. Ronald Fraser, for example, commenting on the Spanish guerrillas in their war against the French highlighted correctly, "Mobility, rapidity, surprise was their strength in attack, retreat and dispersal. A lion's heart, a fly's stomach, and a hare's feet—this was their self-image. Their speed of light in different directions was as important as their surprise in attack."[42]

Yet Fraser also saw the success in the counterinsurgency situations of the French under the highly successful General Jean de Dieu Soult, who employed "battle-trained soldiers used to fighting in small units, lightly equipped and rapid, acting by surprise and led by experienced officers who were both audacious and prudent."[43] These observations, of course, highlight physical speed in a given battle space. But Boyd's incisive OODA loop also accents the mental dimension and the need for insurgent or counterinsurgent to get inside the decision-making loop of one's opponent.

Looking at the war in Vietnam through this lens, for example, it becomes readily apparent that the United States (except perhaps during the Christmas bombing campaign against Hanoi and Haiphong in 1972) never "got inside" the decision-making loop of the North Vietnamese. At virtually all other times, American steps in escalation were way behind the existing thought patterns of the North Vietnamese, who always expected greater steps and ended up being contemptuous of America's actual smaller, less effective steps.

There is also another way to look at the insurgency-counterinsurgency dynamic. When dealing with insurgencies, there are basically two distinct military strategies that can be used to defeat them by those seeking to remain in ascendancy (or to reestablish it in zones of the battle space where it has been lost).

The first, which is known as "enemy-centric" (often called "search and destroy"), focuses on sending overwhelming military force where the insurgents are thought to be in order to force them into a set-piece battle where the counterinsurgents have greater firepower and can likely destroy them. This was the strategic imperative followed by the British in first dealing with the Malayan Emergency (which lasted from June 1948 until July 1960). In the first phase, from 1948 to 1950, the British sought pitched battles with the Malayan Races Liberation Army (MRLA). This also was the U.S. military strategy in Vietnam from 1965 until mid-1968, and the Soviet approach during much of the war in Afghanistan from 1980 to 1989.

The second strategy, termed "population-centric" (often called "clear and hold"), focuses not on trying simply to find and destroy the insurgents as a military force, but on driving them from areas of concentrated civilian population and gradually expanding the number of civilians under government control. It requires more "boots on the ground" and greater efforts to create local forces to assist in protecting those under the government's control.

This approach was originally (and to some extent today still is) known as the "hearts and minds" approach, first espoused after World War II by the British in Malaya from 1951 until the final defeat of the Communists by 1960.[44] Another antecedent of this strategy, ironically enough, was the successful "oil spot" expansion of French rule in Indochina during the nineteenth century.

The strategy of clear and hold also requires an important shift in the military's mind-set. As Sir Robert Thompson writes:

> The army's role here is to clear the main insurgent units out of the area over which the government is attempting to regain control, and keep them out. Elimination of the units and the killing of insurgents is a secondary consideration at this stage. After clearing, it is the role of the police field units, supported by the regular police and civilian government departments, to hold the area, restore government authority and win the people to the side of the government.[45]

This was the highly successful strategy directed by General Creighton Abrams that the United States belatedly adopted in Vietnam from mid-1968 until 1973, when the United States effectively withdrew from ground actions. By the end of 1972, the South Vietnamese with American air support defeated the regular North Vietnamese army's major offensives, and by the end of that year, they controlled as much as 90 percent of the South Vietnamese population.[46]

This degree of South Vietnamese governmental control is so deleteriously—even disastrously—lost in intellectual time and space that it often makes any objective analysis of the Vietnam War impossible, as most conventional histories of that war exhibit. Far from using the Template as a means of analysis, these accounts often stop considering any potential historical malleability after 1968. This seems quite odd when, in fact, the balance of forces moved dramatically and consistently against the insurgents during the next four years.

For example the Tet Offensive of February 1968, widely regarded as the reason why the United States public gave up on the war, was actually a crushing military defeat for the Viet Cong and the North Vietnamese. After undertaking a major offensive against the northern Marine base at Khe Sanh in I Corps near the demilitarized zone between the two countries, the North Vietnamese and Viet Cong launched a series of simultaneous attacks all over the country, overrunning several provincial capitals, including the old imperial city of Hue and striking within Saigon, even attacking the American Embassy. Pictures of that facility under fire lit up the nightly TV news. It appeared that defeat was imminent.

But over the next few days and weeks, the attackers were decimated by counterattacking American and South Vietnamese forces. Estimates of Viet Cong and NVA casualties run from 40,000 out of 80,000 attackers to more than 72,000 Communists killed.[47] The Viet Cong suffered grievous losses, and thereafter, the North Vietnamese had to do the bulk of the fighting.

Nevertheless, the Tet Offensive provided a huge political victory for the North Vietnamese. In terms of the battle of wills, so central to Mars, it was absolutely critical to their eventual success. The resulting images and sense of national despair drove President Johnson from office and stimulated those opposed to the war in Vietnam, and the growth of that opposition in turn greatly encouraged the North Vietnamese. As the former Viet Cong colonel, Bui Tin, put it, "The Mau Than Offensive caused a disastrous turnabout in U.S. policy that gave Hanoi breathing room at just the moment when we were hardest-pressed in South Vietnam! So, on the political, strategic, and psychological fronts, we had won a major and spectacular victory.[48]

Despite the success of the "clear-and-hold" strategy during the latter stages of the war in Vietnam, the United States high command, when confronted with the Sunni–al Qaeda insurgency in Iraq in 2003, reverted to the traditional—and some would say discredited—search-and-destroy approach. Only when that unimaginative strategy failed to produce enough positive results did General David Petraeus and other area commanders insist that their troops relearn the lessons of Vietnam and other insurgencies and introduce the clear-and-hold approach.

Listen to the advice Petraeus gave his troops in March of 2007:

> Improving security for Iraq's population is . . . the over-riding objective of your strategy. Accomplishing this mission requires carrying out complex military operations and convincing the Iraq people that we will not just "clear" their neighborhoods of the enemy, we also stay and help "hold" the neighborhoods so that the "build" phase that many of their communities need can go forward.[49]

In this, it is important to give credit not only to General Petraeus, who carried the innovational reforms through the minefields of the American political system and forced its implementation in the field, but also to these lower-ranking officers who, against all odds, solved the question of how to win the war against the insurgents.

As Bing West and Linda Robinson narrate, the war on the ground turned in rural Anbar, urban Anbar, Diayala, and Baghdad, led by the efforts of those junior officers practicing *auftragstakik* before the changes were recognized by many in Washington.[50] As indicated in chapter five, it was the lieutenants, captains, and lieutenant colonels in the field who redesigned the "war among the people" counterinsurgency that was ultimately successful in Iraq.

Even then, and in the succeeding months, there continued to be widespread opposition to the surge and disbelief in the notion of progress in Iraq. See, for example, the opposition that Bob Woodward most ironically documents in *The War Within*.[51] Woodward finds opposition to the idea of the surge virtually everywhere, not only among Democrats but Republicans, Secretary of State Condoleezza Rice, and even within the Joint Chiefs of Staff. After this major strategy shift occurred in Iraq during 2007, the security situation greatly improved, although at the time of this writing it is by no means clear that the American people have the will or the desire to see this highly successful counterinsurgency strategy through to its successful conclusion.

While the clear-and-hold approach has proven very successful not just in Vietnam and Iraq but in many other insurgency situations such as Malaya, Oman, and Kenya, it requires the soldiers on the ground to adopt some unconventional (to their traditional training) approaches and to be open to nontraditional military approaches such as cooperating with civilian populations. This, as well as the subtle interplay between insurgent and counterinsurgent activity, is well covered by David Galula in his 1964 work, *Counter-Insurgency Warfare: Theory and Practice*.[52]

The ability of the armed forces to learn "carrot" as well as "stick" methods is clearly seen in all three examples above, but it often does not fit the traditional training of the military. As Williamson Murray and Robert Scale Jr. put it, in these situations: "Attitudes will be influenced less by demonstrations of fighting strength than by the emotional security that comes from safe streets, employment, electricity and fresh water."[53]

In the case of Oman, for instance, the Dhofar insurgency in Oman, led by the Marxist Dhofar Liberation Front and backed by the Soviets, China, and Yemen, raged from 1962 until 1975. But it was ultimately defeated by a combination of Omani Sultan Qaboos' enlightened outreach efforts and offer of amnesty and substantial public-works projects, as well as a strong military clear-and-hold strategy backed by British Special Air Service (SAS) units, and Iranian troops, including paratroopers and the Imperial Iranian Battle Group.[54] Here is another example where the forces of counterinsurgency successfully changed their tactics in the middle of the war.[55]

In terms of success against insurgents, much depends on the culture of the military force in question. Today, for example, there are military cultural crosscurrents that tend to make the U.S. Marines and Special Forces more receptive to this way of war fighting than some other branches, such as the regular army. People often forget how much bureaucratic inertia and ballast underline every army, with large portions of that bureaucracy's leadership resistant to change. Bureaucracies prefer to deal with what they know, with what they are most familiar with, but Mars judges armies on their ability to change as circumstances in the battle space require. As MacGregor Knox so aptly puts it, "They are happiest with established wisdom and incremental change. They cherish the myth that virtually all strategic problems are soluble in and through their own element."[56]

To judge the likely success or failure of any given counterinsurgency effort, it is necessary therefore to use the Template to examine the defending armed forces' receptivity to military process innovation. Likewise, the insurgents must adjust to changed circumstances and learn from the battle conditions. In the case of Vietnam, the North Vietnamese learned early in the war that the Viet Cong guerrilla operation would not be strong enough to overcome the South Vietnamese and American forces, and they therefore made a conscious decision to move main-force North Vietnamese units south in a more conventional assault. Indeed it was that conventional assault with tanks and heavy artillery and main-force divisions that eventually overwhelmed the South Vietnamese after the United States removed its air and artillery support from the battle space.

How the "War on Terror" (or its functional equivalent in terms of counterinsurgency) finally turns out on its many battle fronts—and we may not know that for a generation—will be determined in large part by the ability of one side or another to continually adjust to the changed battle space realities as they develop.[57]

Ability and Willingness to Protect Capital from the People and Rulers

Here we see the incredible imbalance of asymmetrical warfare as evidenced by the cost-effectiveness of the attack on the World Trade Center on September 11, 2001. For a campaign costing less than $1 million, al Qaeda cost the American government and its people upwards of $1 trillion both in terms of immediate losses and subsequent counteroffensive costs in Afghanistan, Iraq, and Pakistan.[58] Insurgents do not always have the opportunity to launch such a painful and costly strike against their opponents, and from the perspective of Mars, the 9/11 attack was stupendous in its implications. Yet, as in any counterinsurgency effort, the costs will almost always be higher for that effort than for the insurgents because of the host country's widespread need to protect more locations, populations, and infrastructures.

In this regard, suicide bombers become extremely cost-effective weapons for the terrorist-insurgents. For a tiny fraction of the cost of a plane, a tank, an artillery piece, or even a modern machine gun, the suicide bomber can provide an enormous psychological as well as military advantage to the insurgents. Acquiring, training, and directing suicide bombers is an ongoing and always potentially disruptive element in insurgency. But in and by itself, the use of suicide bombers cannot necessarily cross the threshold to taking, rather than simply disrupting power, although its presence in the battle space requires major tactical adjustment by the counterterrorists.

It should be reiterated here that few revolutions are both self-generated and self-sustaining. The Cuban, Russian, and Chinese revolutions appear to be something of an anomaly in this regard, with most of the weapons and ammunition used to sustain the insurgency coming from captured government sources. Most insurgencies and revolutions require infusions of vast amounts of ongoing supplies from outside.

The North Vietnamese insurgency, for example, and its subsequent main-force invasion of South Vietnam, for example, required massive resources from beyond its borders. The USSR and China provided billions of dollars worth of supplies, including very sophisticated radars, antiaircraft missiles, and air-superiority planes such as the MIG 21 over a twenty-year period. The weapons and ammunition that enabled North Vietnam to overrun South Vietnam were not picked up on the battlefield but were inserted into a multinational pipeline stretching tens of thousands of miles.

With regard to the Sunni and al Qaeda insurgency in Iraq after 2004, it needs to be pointed out that there were large numbers of volunteers coming from Syria as well as extensive and sophisticated antipersonnel and antitank devices and other material coming from Iran.

Superior Will

In the previous examples, the Template shows clearly how the complexities of an insurgency form of war can be sharply reduced to a Clausewitzian formulaic assertion, "War is thus an act of force to compel our enemy to do our will." In the end, success in war often comes down to which side has the stronger will.

The North Vietnamese government was prepared to pay any price for victory; the American people and their government were not. Whether those choices were a good or a bad thing obviously lies beyond the scope of this book. But from the perspective of Mars, it was a very good thing for the North Vietnamese. In the case of Vietnam, the North Vietnamese wanted victory more than the American people did (not necessarily, but perhaps, even more than the American military did). It should also be noted that many Americans thought the war was wrong in the first place, and they were eventually joined by others who decided the war was not worth fighting at the prices it was demanding. Still others thought the war was worth fighting and worth additional costs, but was already lost.

Looking at the world situation today, the role of will again remains paramount. Here the Template sees a substantial contemporary and possibly ongoing advantage for the Salafists. But in other situations, the stronger will turned out to reside with the counterinsurgents.

In the case of the long-running insurgency in Northern Ireland (1967–2007), the British will overcame the will of the Provisional Irish Republican Army. As Daniel Marston puts it: "Carrying out a successful counterinsurgency campaign takes a substantial amount of money, and even more importantly, a substantial amount of political will. This may include an undertaking that such a campaign could last for decades, and that casualties are inevitable in providing security and holding cleared areas."[59]

For the Salafists, in particular, war is existential. For them, war has no beginning, no middle, and no end (until Allah brings the end of time). Losses in battle, tactical or strategic, have no meaning as long as the struggle continues. This places a huge burden on the will of those determined to "defeat" the Salafists wherever the Hydra rises.

Anti-Salafist counterinsurgencies require great patience, and that patience can only be sustained by superior will. T. E. Lawrence states in the *Seven Pillars of Wisdom*, "To make war upon rebellion is messy and slow, like eating soup with a knife." Perhaps no finer metaphor for counterinsurgency has been penned. The length of time required to defeat any insurgency based within the population needs to be clearly stated: the average insurgency that is successfully eliminated has taken a dozen or more years to suppress.

For example, there has been a forty-year-old insurrection in Colombia and only in the last few years has the central government in Bogotá begun to get control over the situation and limit the influence of *Fuerzas Armadas Revolucionarias de Colombia* (FARC).[60]

Patience, a steadfast will, and perseverance are critical to counterinsurgency success. So the question best asked by the counterinsurgents in any ongoing situation is not "Are we winning?" It is "are we not losing fast enough?" For the insurgents the most important question is "Even if we are losing, can we lose slowly enough to break our opponents will?" Mao Tsetung based not only the war against the Japanese but also the war against the central government of China on the notion of a "protracted war" that he believed favored the defense because it could sustain itself easier than the offensive.[61]

At base, it ultimately comes down to will, in insurgent warfare as in traditional warfare between nation-states. Nowhere is this aspect seen to be more critical than in the U.S. experience in Iraq, where by 2006, the war appeared to many to be lost and the insurgency triumphant. But as Bing West has so clearly shown, it was precisely at this most critical of culminating points that patience on the ground with small-unit commanders on the frontlines turned the course of the war around from the bottom up and brought about a broadly successful counterinsurgency.

Against overwhelming odds, the Americans and their Iraqi allies succeeded where only failure had been predicted. Anyone seeking to understand the dynamic tension inherent in any insurgency-counterinsurgency situation needs to carefully read West's incisive account of what turned the tide in Iraq from favoring the insurgents to defeating them.[62]

An Ongoing Assumption That There Will Always Be Another War

This remains the essence of radical jihadist Salafist warfare and what gives them a considerable advantage over time. As an element in the Template, it is particularly relevant when one looks at the will quotient of the insurgents. For the Salafists such as al Qaeda, "Salafism is an Islamic umbrella doctrine embracing all Muslims who reject the concept of the state and seek only a universal kingdom of believers, who deny the right of mortals to make policy or frame laws, insisting that all they need to know of public life can be found in the Koran."[63]

It is their cosmology that sustains them. Rarely is the following analysis seen, but it seems extremely relevant and perspicacious when looked at through the lens of the Template. For Mars, the Salafist cosmology is made to order, "While we embrace death, the Americans fear it." The radical jihadist Salafists are not simply always preparing for the next war, they are simply always engaged in warfare, for which their opponents and potential targets must always be ready.

Radical jihadist Salafists can be endlessly patient, for time has no meaning, since only Allah can bring the end-time; and he will only do that when the Salafists have proven themselves worthy of his judgment. Thus victory is not essential, only enduring is. Succeeding is an ongoing process that has no end until the very end of time. Salafists believe they cannot lose as long as they are still warring.

Whereas the counterinsurgents seek "progress" in their wars against the Salafists, the Salafists are not concerned with process or outcome. The outcome has already been decided by Allah. The war by and against the Salafists is thus an existential war. To defeat it, their opponents must accept the actuality of what it is, and see that from that cosmology comes great strength. To defeat dedicated adherents to its doctrines requires providing an alternative present as well as an alternative future. Those who would mount counterinsurgency campaigns must understand and accept the reality of that cosmology and see why it is necessary to diffuse its appeal in the present.

It is interesting to note that the United States, or at least its military, has had a long history of successfully dealing with insurgencies, whether they be against Native Americans for most of the eighteenth and nineteenth centuries or the Moros (1899–1902) and later the Huks in the Philippines (1946–1951). Indeed, Bruce Gudmundsson makes a telling point that "in Haiti (1915–34), the Dominican Republic (1916–24) and Nicaragua (1927–33), U.S. Marines operated against forces using classic guerilla tactics, conducted sustained counterinsurgency campaigns, formed local constabularies, and engaged in various nation-building programs."[64]

But the American military—like many other militaries—has not always remembered the lessons of one successful counterinsurgency campaign by the time the next insurgency crisis has come about. For many years, policy makers in Washington, civilian and military, focused on a large, quick, and decisive war against the Soviet Union, rather than a long, drawn-out counterinsurgency. For example, in 1997, the National Security Strategy of the United States firmly stated, "Everything is staked on a short, decisive war."[65]

However, the American military—and even its civilian counterparts—have proven they can learn patience (at least in certain theaters). For example, the highly successful Colombian operations against the FARC rebels (assisted and guided by the U.S. military) shows how successful such a patient counterinsurgency strategy can be. In short, insurgencies have been a part of human warfare since the inception of war, they can and have been defeated for that long.

THE ENDURING TEMPLATE

As we have seen, applying the Template of Mars to both individual insurgencies and the notion of insurgencies as a military typology can assist in analyzing both. Insurgencies, like all wars, can be examined, explained, and projected based on the framework of the Template.

Two things remain true simultaneously: aspects of war continue to change; the essence of war does not.

War has always had changed modes, styles, and dimensions, but at base—even in its recent terrorist/insurgency incarnation—it remains susceptible to understanding, logic, and incisive analysis, all of which can be aided by a judicious use of the Template of Mars. Insurgencies have been a part of human warfare since its inception, and they continue to be only one mode among many. The basic character of war and its intrinsic relationship to humankind remain constant. As General Gordon Sullivan notes, "War is an iterative process."

Mars and humankind remain jointed at the hip. This may be upsetting to many, but comforting to others. In any case, war remains an enduring legacy of the human condition.

Notes

PREFACE

1. Robert Sheckley, *Pilgrimage to Earth* (New York: Bantam Books, 1957), 1–11.

2. Sheckley, *Pilgrimage to Earth*, 4.

3. Max Boot, *War Made New* (New York: Gotham Books, 2007), 469. Or as Tim Travers puts it, "Military history is not a separate entity, but warfare, and ideas about warfare, are socially produced and vary with the evolution of society." Tim Travers, *The Killing Ground* (London: Allen and Unwin, 1987), xxii.

4. Raymond Aron, *Peace and War: A Theory of International Relations* (Garden City, NY: Doubleday and Company, 1966).

5. Hans Morgenthau, *Politics among Nations: The Struggle for Power and Peace* (New York: Alfred A. Knopf, 1967).

6. Robert Ardrey, *The Territorial Imperative* (New York: Atheneum, 1966); Desmond Morris, *The Naked Ape* (New York: Dell, 1969); and Konrad Lorenz, *The Natural Science of the Human Species: An Introduction to Comparative Behavioral Research* (Cambridge, MA: MIT Press, 1969).

7. Alexander Alland (ed.), *The Human Imperative* (New York: Columbia University Press, 1972); D. Hard and R. W. Sussman, *Man the Hunted: Primates, Predators and Human Evolution* (New York: Westview Press, 2005).

8. David Livingstone Smith, *The Most Dangerous Animal: Human Nature and the Origins of War* (New York: St. Martin's Press, 2007).

9. Smith, *The Most Dangerous Animal*, 43.

10. Williamson Murray provides most meaningful insights into who wins in war and why. See especially his *The Making of Strategy: Rulers, States and War* (Cambridge: Cambridge University Press, 1994); *The Past as Prologue: The Importance of History to the Military Profession* (Cambridge: Cambridge University Press, 2006); and his enduring "Military Culture Does Matter," *Strategic Review* 27 (Spring 1999): 32–40. For his part, Geoffrey Parker, *The Military Revolution: Military Innovation and the Rise of the West*

1500–1800 (Cambridge: Cambridge University Press, 1988) and his edited work, *Warfare: The Rise of the West* (Cambridge: Cambridge University Press, 1995) provide an incisive look at the military ascendancy of the West. See also Victor Hanson's many works, including *Carnage and Culture* (New York: Doubleday, 2001) and *The Western Way of War* (New York: Alfred A. Knopf, 1989). Surprisingly, although he is a most engaging and knowledgeable writer on matters military, John Keegan's works are of less help in trying to create meaningful cross-cultural archetypes. See John Keegan, *The Face of Battle* (New York: Viking Press, 1976); *The Mask of Command* (New York: Viking Press, 1987); *A History of Warfare* (New York: Alfred A. Knopf, 1993); *War and Our World* (London: Pimlico, 1999); and *Intelligence in War: The Value—and Limitations—of What the Military Can Learn about the Enemy* (New York: Vintage Books, 2004).

11. There are many, many works dealing with battles large and small, some of which were important in determining the course of human history and some of which were not. Among the most holistic of these is Tony Jaques's three-volume set, *Dictionary of Battles and Sieges: A Guide to 8500 Battles from Antiquity through the Twenty-First Century* (Westport, CT: Greenwood Press, 2006). More focused works include: Edward Creasy, *Fifteen Decisive Battles of the World: From Marathon to Waterloo* (London: R. Bentley, 1851); J. F. C. Fuller, *The Decisive Battles of the Western World: 1792–1944* (London: Paladin,1970); Paul Davis, *100 Decisive Battles from Ancient Times to the Present* (London: Oxford University Press, 1999); Samuel Crompton, *100 Battles That Shaped World History* (San Mateo: Bluewood Books, 1997); Ian Hogg, *Battles* (New York: Harcourt Brace, 1995); R. G. Grant, *Battle: A Visual Journey through 5,000 Years of Combat* (London: DK, 2005); Jeremy Black, *Introduction to Global Military History: 1775 to the Present Day* (London: Routledge, 2005); and Charles Messenger, *Wars That Changed the World* (New York: Book Sales, 2008). Interested readers may want to apply the Template to some of the battles and wars included in these works.

CHAPTER ONE: INTRODUCTION: THE TEMPLATE OF MARS

1. See for example, Greek Ares, the Etruscan Maris, the Aztec Huitzilopochtli, the Celtic Camulus and Loucetios (sometimes "Leucetios"), the Pharaonic Maahes and Menthu, The Hindu Shiva and Durga, the Maori Tumatauenga, the Mesopotamian Ninurta, the Norse Odin, the Confucian Guandi, the Philippine Apolake and Mandangan, the Buddhist Bishamon-ten (also the god of happiness), the Slavic Perun and, Svetovid (also god of fertility and abundance), the Prussian tribes' Pikullos, the Chinese Chi You, and many others in cultures throughout time and space. For a more benign view of human cosmologies, as well as enduring archetypes and their relevance for humanity, see Joseph Campbell, *The Hero with a Thousand Faces* (New York: Pantheon Books, 1949) and Mircea Eliade's classic, *The Sacred and the Profane* (New York: Harcourt, Brace and Company, 1959).

2. Mao Tse-tung, *The Art of War* (El Paso, TX: El Paso Norte Press, 2005), 5.

3. Geoffrey Parker, *The Military Revolution: Military Innovation and the Rise of the West 1500–1800* (Cambridge: Cambridge University Press, 1988) and *Warfare: The Rise of*

the West (Cambridge: Cambridge University Press, 1995). William C. Martel provides useful background on modern thinking about war in his *Victory in War: Foundations of Modern Military Policy* (Cambridge: Cambridge University Press, 2007).

4. Hans Delbruck, *The Dawn of Modern Warfare* (Lincoln: University of Nebraska Press, 1990).

5. Baron de Jomini, *The Art of War* (El Paso: El Paso Norte Press, 2005), 34.

6. Williamson Murray, "Military Culture Does Matter," *Strategic Review* 27 (Spring 1999): 32–40.

7. Jeremy Black, *Warfare in the Eighteenth Century* (London: Cassell, 1999), 32.

8. Geoffrey Parker, "The Western Way of War," in Geoffrey Parker (ed.), *The Cambridge Illustrated History of Warfare* (Cambridge: Cambridge University Press, 1995), 2.

9. Walter Millis, *Arms and Men: A Study in American Military History* (New York: G. P. Putnam's Sons, 1956), 131–210. Bevin Alexander also provides an interesting list of elements essential for winning battles and war, ranging from "feigned retreat" to "strike at the weak spot," in his *How Wars Are Won: The 13 Rules of War—from Ancient Greece to the War on Terror* (New York: Crown Publishing, 2002).

10. See especially Williamson Murray and MacGregor Knox, "Thinking about Revolutions in Warfare," in their edited work, *The Dynamics of Military Revolution 1300–2050* (Cambridge: Cambridge University Press, 2001), 1–14.

11. Quoted in Geoffrey Parker (ed.), *Warfare* (Cambridge: Cambridge University Press, 1995), 372. In any society throughout history, however, there is a functional limit on how much of that society's gross domestic profit can go to the military, with or without war. John Childs, looking at the seventeenth century, comes up with some astounding numbers. He believes France spent 65 percent of its government expenditure on the army and 9 percent on its navy. In Russia, that amount was 60 percent for the Russian army and navy. See his *Warfare in the Seventeenth Century* (London: Cassell, 2001), 105.

12. Mao, *The Art of War*.

13. I am indebted to Jeff Selinger for bringing this term into focus for me.

14. See, for example, John Keegan's excellent analysis of the sea war in the North Atlantic, "The Battle of the Atlantic," in his *The Price of Admiralty* (New York: Penguin, 1980, 251–328; Donald Macintyre, *The Naval War against Hitler* (New York: Charles Scribner's Sons, 1971); and S. W. Roskill, *White Ensign: The British Navy at War 1939–1945* (Annapolis: U.S. Naval Institute, 1960).

15. See Carl von Clausewitz, *On War* (New York: Alfred A. Knopf, 1993), 228–32.

16. For example, Parker sees that the West has triumphed in warfare because of its emphasis on a subtle interplay among (a) technology and discipline, (b) the continuity of an aggressive Western military tradition, (c) the challenge-and-response military dynamic that includes an ability to change and the power to finance those changes, and (d) the export of violence and its dominant military tradition to the rest of the world: Geoffrey Parker, "Introduction: The Western Way of War," in his edited volume *Warfare: The Rise of the West* (Cambridge: Cambridge University Press, 1995), 2–11. See also his *The Military Revolution: Military Innovation and the Rise of the West 1500–1800* (Cambridge: Cambridge University Press, 1988). Parker's assertion of such a lengthy revolution, however, is challenged by John Childs in his *Warfare in the Seventeenth Century* (London: Cassell, 2001), especially

on pages 17 and 208–12. See also, Clifford J. Rogers (ed.), *The Military Revolution Debate: Readings on the Military Transformation of Early Modern Europe* (Boulder, CO: Westview Press, 1995) for a further exploration of these issues.

17. Robert A. Doughty, "The French Armed Forces, 1918–40," in Allan Millett and Williamson Murray (eds.), *Military Effectiveness*, volume 2: *The Interwar Period* (Boston: Allen and Unwin, 1988), 66.

18. Gwyn Jones, *A History of the Vikings* (Oxford: Oxford University Press, 1968), 317–18. For a concise overview of the interaction between Viking traditional religion and the subsequent adoption of Christianity by the Scandinavians, see Else Roesdahl, *The Vikings* (London: Penguin Books, 1987). With regard to the enduring power of a "heaven" of perpetual warfare, it is interesting to note that in 2009, U.S. Secretary of Defense, Robert Gates seemed to recognize the appeal of such a notion when he asserted, "If we set ourselves the objective of creating some sort of Central Asian Valhalla over there, we will lose."

19. Hanson, *Carnage and Culture*, 279–33. Hanson would be on firmer ground if he had used examples from the American Plains and upper Mississippian Indian cultures, many of which promoted and prized warrior-hood over soldier-hood (see chapter three of *Winning at War*).

20. John Sowell, *Conquests and Culture: An International History* (New York: Basic Books, 1998).

21. Dennis Showalter, "European Power Projection," *MHQ: The Quarterly Journal of Military History* 20, no. 2 (Winter 2008): 46–55.

22. Quoted in Clifford J. Rogers, "As If a New Sun Had Arisen": England's Fourteenth-Century RMA," in MacGregor Knox and Williamson Murray (eds.), *The Dynamics of Military Revolution 1300–2050* (Cambridge: Cambridge University Press, 2001), 15.

23. The Italian debacle in the Horn of Africa is particularly telling: Christian P. Potholm, *Liberation and Exploitation: The Struggle for Ethiopia* (New York: RF Publishers, 1976). Also, the Carlo Ponti film *Girasoli* (Sunflower) graphically captures the pain and suffering of the Italian soldiers who died in distant lands due to poor leadership, poor equipment, and poor training. Seen in this light, the Italian governmental and military command performance in World War I can be viewed as something of a dress rehearsal for later disasters: Mark Thompson, *The White War: Life and Death on the Italian Front 1915–1919* (New York: Basic Books, 2008).

24. See MacGregor Knox, *Hitler's Italian Allies* (Cambridge: Cambridge University Press, 2000), 170.

25. Knox, *Hitler's Italian Allies*, 170. For his part, Brian Sullivan believes that the "disastrous" performance of Italy in World War II was due to the uneasy relationship between the civilian and military authorities, Italy's limited resources, lack of a critical central command structure, continuous military operations after 1935, and Mussolini's personal alliance with Hitler. See Brian Sullivan, "The Italian Armed Forces, 1918–1940," in Millett and Murray, *Military Effectiveness*, 169. Also, as Tim Woodcock suggests, the Italians were most unlucky to have Mussolini as a leader. Il Duce got carried away by his own sense of destiny and the charisma of Hitler. By contrast, in this regard at least, the Spanish were fortunate to have General Franco, who although a Fascist and one who owed Hitler more than one favor from the days of the Spanish Civil War, nevertheless had the sense to keep Spain from formally

joining with Germany in World War II. Franco did send the "Blue Division" of "volunteers" to fight against the Soviets but kept Spain out of the wider war, resisting Hitler's call for them to attack Gibraltar and engage the British directly.

26. Alan Beyerchen, "Clausewitz, Nonlinearity, and the Unpredictability of War," *International Security* 17, no. 3 (Winter, 1992–1993): 59–90. I an indebted to Williamson Murray for this most useful reference.

27. For example, John Keegan arrives at a rather simple dichotomy between "Western" and "Oriental" forms of warfare. See his *The History of Warfare* (New York: Vintage Books, 1994).

28. See John Masefield, *Gallipoli* (New York: The Macmillan Company, 1916); Philip J. Haythronthwaite, *Gallipoli 1915, Frontal Assault on Turkey* (New York: Osprey Publishing, 1991); Michael Hickey, *Gallipoli* (London: John Murray Publishers, 1995); and Alan Morehead, *Gallipoli* (New York: Harper Classics, 2003).

29. Edward J. Erickson, "Strength against Weakness: Ottoman Military Effectiveness at Gallipoli, 1915," *Journal of Military History* 65, no. 4 (2001): 981–1011; Otto Liman von Sanders, *Five Years in Turkey* (Baltimore, MD: Williams and Wilkins, 1918); and Kevin Fewster and Vecihi Basarin, *Gallipoli: The Turkish Story* (New South Wales: Allen and Unwin, 2003).

30. I am indebted to Amos Eno for this striking example: Centuries after the Mongols swept through Poland, in Cracow, a trumpet sounded *every hour* from the tower of St. Mary's Church to memorialize "the death of the city watchman who was pierced through the throat by a Mongol arrow as he raised the alarm," Norman Davies, *God's Playground: A History of Poland* (New York: Columbia University Press, 1982), 2:87). The savage defeat of the Hungarians at the Battle of Liegnitz in April 1241, is likewise remembered today as a huge "victory" in Hungary although the Mongols were called back upon the death of the Khan, not because they were defeated by the Europeans.

31. There was disorder along the "Silk Road" (as it became known much later), but as the Polos discovered, it mostly occurred when Mongol fought Mongol for control of various areas. See Laurence Bergreen's sprightly account of the adventures of the Polos, *Marco Polo: From Venice to Zanadu* (New York: Alfred A. Knopf, 2007), especially 1–140.

32. Bergreen, *Marco Polo*, 34.

33. Thomas Conlan, e-mail to the author, July 8, 2008. His book, *State of War: The Violent Order of Fourteenth-Century Japan* (Ann Arbor: University of Michigan Center for Japanese Studies, 2003) gives the reader an insightful portrait of Japanese society and military.

34. See *The Secret History of the Mongols: A Mongolian Epic Chronicle of the Thirteenth Century*, translated by Igor de Rachewiltz (Boston: Brill, 2004); David Morgan, *The Mongols* (Cambridge, MA: Blackwell, 1990); Timothy May, *The Mongol Art of War* (Yardley, PA: Westholme Publishing, 2007); David Nicolle, *The Mongol Warlords* (Pool, Dorset, UK: Firebird Books, 1990); Erik Hildinger, *Warriors of the Steppe* (New York: Sarpedon, 1997); James Chambers, *The Devil's Horsemen* (New York: Atheneum, 1985); S. R. Turnbull and Angus McBride, *The Mongols* (London: Osprey Books, 1980); Rene Grousset, *Conqueror of the World: The Life of Chingis-khan* (New York: Viking Press, 1972); Morris Rossabi, *Khubilai Khan: His Life and Times* (Berkeley: University of California Press, 1988); Peter Jackson, *The Mongols and*

the West: 1221–1410 (London: Longmans, 2005); R. P. Lister, *Genghis Khan* (New York: Cooper Square Press, 2000); Richard A. Gabriel, *Subotai the Valiant: Genghis Khan's Greatest General* (Westport, CT: Praeger Publishers, 2004); Ata-Malik Juvaini, *Genghis Khan: The History of the World Conqueror,* translated by J. A. Boyle (Seattle: University of Washington Press, 1997); Robert Marshall, *Storm from the East: From Genghis Khan to Kublai Khan* (Los Angeles: University of California Press, 1993); Bamber Gascoigne, *The Great Moghuls* (New York: Harper and Row, 1971); Thomas T. Allser, *Mongol Imperialism* (Berkeley: University of California Press, 1987); David Woolman, "Primitive Warriors or Not, the Hardy Mongols of the 12th and 13th Centuries Used the Most Advanced of Tactics," *Military History* (October 1995): 12–18; and John Saunders, *The History of the Mongol Conquests* (London: Routledge and Kegan Paul, 1971). For his part, Brian Fagan offers a provocative thesis in his *The Great Warming* (New York: Bloomsbury Press, 2008), 48–65 claiming that the expansion of the Mongols was not driven by a desire for loot or domination, but instead was closely attuned to the rhythm of the steppe grasses. Fagan believes that when the steppe grasses were rich and abundant, the Mongols stayed put, and when the steppes were drought stricken, the Mongols advanced outward seeking new grazing lands.

35. R. E. Dupuy and T. N. Dupuy, *The Encyclopedia of Military History* (New York: Harper and Row, 1977), 345.

36. Jean-Paul Roux, *Genghis Khan and the Mongol Empire* (New York: Harry Abrams, 2002).

37. Timothy May, "The Training of an Inner Asian Nomad Army in the Pre-Modern Period," *The Journal of Military History* 70 (July 2006): 621.

38. William H. McNeill, *The Age of Gunpowder Empires 1450–1800* (Washington, DC: American Historical Association, 1989), 3.

39. Justin Marozzi, *Tamerlane: Sword of Islam, Conqueror of the World* (New York: Da Capo Press, 2004), 103.

40. Niccolo Machiavelli, *The Discourses on Livy,* translated by Harvey Mansfield and Nathan Tarcov (Chicago: University of Chicago Press, 1996), III.40.1, 299.

41. Ken Alibek, *Biohazard* (New York: Random House, 1999), 166–67.

42. Parag Khanna, *The Second World: Empires and Influence in the New Global Order* (New York: Random House, 2008), 67.

43. Marozzi, *Tamerlane,* 79.

44. Paul Ratchnevsky, *Genghis Khan: His Life and Legacy* (Oxford: Blackwell, 1991).

45. The sacking of Baghdad was a major exception but one that had the approval of the top Mongol commanders because the Caliph of Baghdad had refused to submit. See Thomas T. Allsen, *Mongol Imperialism* (Berkeley: University of California Press, 1987), 83.

46. James D. Tracy, *The Rise of Merchant Empires: Long-Distance Trade in the Early Modern World, 1350–1750* (Cambridge: Cambridge University Press, 1990), 356.

47. Marozzi, *Tamerlane,* 91.

48. John A. Lynn, *Battle: A History of Combat and Culture* (Boulder, CO: Westview Press, 2003). See especially his chapter "Written in Blood," 1–27.

49. See especially Reuven Amitai-Preiss, *Mongols and Mamluks: The Mamluk-Ilkhanid War, 1260–1281* (Cambridge: Cambridge University Press, 1995) and his *The*

Mongols in the Islamic Lands (Cornwall, UK: TJ International, 2007); Judith Kolbas, *The Mongols in Iran* (New York: Routledge, 2006); Benjamin Arbel, *Latins and Greeks in the Eastern Mediterranean after 1204* (London: Frank Cass and Co., 1989); and Jason Mason Smith, "Ayn Jalut: Mamluk Success or Mongol Failure?" *Harvard Journal of Asiatic Studies* 44, no. 2 (December 1984): 314–20. I am also indebted to Amos Eno for bringing to my attention the Mongols' destruction of the radical Islamic sect "the Assassins." See Bernard Lewis, *The Assassins: A Radical Sect in Islam* (New York: Basic Books, 1968).

50. Amy Chua, *Day of Empire* (New York: Doubleday, 2007), 121–25.

CHAPTER TWO: SUPERIOR WEAPONS AND TECHNOLOGY ENTREPRENEURSHIP

1. See Michael Hodges, *AK47: The Story of the People's Gun* (New York: MacAdam/Cage, 2008); Larry Kahaner, *AK-47: The Weapon That Changed the Face of War* (New York: Wiley, 2007); and Elena Joly and Mikhail Kalashnikov, *The Gun That Changed the World* (New York: Polity, 2006). By contrast, the American M-16 (5.56 mm) is much harder to keep clean, more likely to misfire, and doesn't have as much stopping power as the previous M-14 version or the more powerful 7.62 mm AK-47. At the same time, the M-16 is more accurate at longer range and lighter to carry. For the long history of the American rifle, see Alexander Rose, *American Rifle: A Bibliography* (New York: Delacorte Press, 2008). Rose also makes a strong case for the qualities of the M-16, "especially after subsequent modifications rectified many of the Vietnam version's flaws" (392). It is important to remember, however, that in terms of military technology, not all "updates" are preferable to existing models.

2. Felipe Fernandez-Armesto, *The Pathfinders: A Global History of Exploration* (New York: Norton, 2007), 142.

3. See especially John Laband, *The Rise and Fall of the Zulu Nation* (New York: Arms and Armour, 1997); Donald R. Morris, *The Washing of the Spears* (New York: Simon and Schuster, 1965); Angus McBride, *The Zulu War* (London: Osprey Publishing, 1976); and Ian Knight, *The Zulus* (London: Osprey Publishing, 1989). For the persistence of the warrior tradition among the Zulus, consult Thembisa Waetien, *Workers and Warriors: Masculinity and the Struggle for Nation in South Africa* (Champaign: University of Illinois Press, 2004).

4. Leonard Thompson, "The Zulu Kingdom and the Mfecane," in his *A History of South Africa* (New Haven, CT: Yale University Press, 1996), 80–87.

5. See especially Neil A. Silberman, "The Coming of the Sea Peoples," *MHQ: The Quarterly Journal of Military History* 10, no. 2 (1998): 6–13. Also, Robert Drews, *The End of the Bronze Age: Change in Warfare and the Catastrophe, ca. 1200 B.C.* (Princeton, NJ: Princeton University Press, 1993).

6. Ben Kiernan, *Blood and Soil: A World History of Genocide and Extermination from Sparta to Darfur* (New Haven, CT: Yale University Press, 2007), 105.

7. Scott Farrell, "Terrorized by Trebuchets," *MHQ: The Quarterly Journal of Military History* 19, no. 1 (Autumn 2006): 18–21.

8. James M. Burns, *A History of Sub-Saharan Africa* (Cambridge: Cambridge University Press, 2007), 88.

9. Geoffrey Parker, *The Military Revolution: Military Innovation and the Rise of the West 1500–1800* (Cambridge: Cambridge University Press, 1996).

10. Peter Padfield, *Maritime Supremacy and the Opening of the Western Mind* (Woodstock, NY: Overlook Press, 2000). This view, of course, is central to the thesis of the nineteenth-century American admiral, Alfred Thayer Mahan, whose strategic brilliance asserted the importance of mastery of the seas to victory on land. See his seminal *The Influence of Sea Power upon History* (Annapolis, MD: Naval War College Press, 1991).

11. Keegan accents the impact of the American Civil War on British Admiralty thinking in his *The Price of Admiralty: The Evolution of Naval Warfare* (New York: Penguin, 1990), 111.

12. John Keegan, *The First World War* (New York: Random House, 1998), 259.

13. Keegan, *The First World War*, 259.

14. Andrew Gordon, *The Rules of the Game: Jutland and British Naval Command* (Annapolis, MD: Naval Institute Press, 1996), 9–15; Keegan, *The Price of Admiralty*, 111.

15. Forest McDonald, *The Presidency of Thomas Jefferson* (Lawrence: University Press of Kansas, 1976), 43.

16. McDonald, *The Presidency of Thomas Jefferson*, 43–44. Reginald Horsman, *The War of 1812* (New York: Alfred A. Knopf, 1969) further asserts that "By 1811, only 16 ships, the largest of them frigates could be put into commission for the regular American Navy" (18). Horsman also notes that on January 11, 1811, when the Naval Committee of the U.S. House finally recommended the building of twelve ships of the line and twenty-four frigates, it was defeated sixty-two to fifty-nine. See also J. Mackay Hitsman, *The Incredible War of 1812: A Military History* (Toronto: University of Toronto Press, 1966). Hitsman firmly states that the Jeffersonian coastal gunboats were "ineffectual" (42). However, Albert Marrin does claim that three of the American frigates—*Constitution, United States,* and *President*—were "super-frigates, the best of their class anywhere in the world." See his, *The War of 1812: The War Nobody Won* (New York: Atheneum, 1985), 52; as well as Bradford Perkins, *Prologue to War* (Berkeley and Los Angeles: University of California Press, 1963).

17. Stephen Budiansky, "Giant Killer" *MHQ: The Quarterly Journal of Military History* 21, no. 3 (2009): 52.

18. For an in-depth look at the British attack on Baltimore and the American response, see Christopher T. George, "The Defense of Baltimore," in *Terror on the Chesapeake: The War of 1812 on the Bay* (Shippensburg, PA: White Mane Books, 2000), 126–57.

19. Max Boot, "Triumph of Prussian Technology and Tactics," *MHQ: The Quarterly Journal of Military History* 19, no. 1 (Autumn 2006): 56–57. Dennis E. Showalter quite rightly puts these changes in a broader context in his "The Prusso-German RMA, 1840–1871," in Williamson Murray and MacGregor Knox, (eds.), *The Dynamics of Military Revolution 1300–2050* (Cambridge: Cambridge University Press, 2001), 92–113.

20. Max Boot, *War Made New* (New York: Gotham Books, 2007), 168. For a more nuanced look at the battlefield of the twentieth century and the dilemmas faced by the generals who confronted it, see Shelford Bidwell and Dominick Graham, *Fire Power: British Army Weapons and Theories of War 1904–1945* (London: Allen and Unwin, 1982).

21. Thomas Pakenham, *The Boer War* (New York: Avon Books, 1979).

22. Williamson Murray and Allan R. Millett (eds.), *Military Innovation in the Interwar Period* (Ithaca, NY: Cornell University Press, 1989), 19.

23. Maxim earned 271 patents on everything from a hair-curling iron to a locomotive headlight, and even demonstrated the possibility of flight with a plane that ran off railroad tracks.

24. See John Ellis, *The Social History of the Machine Gun* (New York: Random House, 1975). The American relationship between its military bureaucracy and the machine gun is extensively covered in David A. Armstrong, *Bullets and Bureaucrats: The Machine Gun and the United States Army, 1861–1916* (Westport, CT: Greenwood Press, 1982).

25. For an elaborate investigation of the history of the Gatling gun and its inventor, see Julia Keller, *Mr. Gatling's Terrible Marvel* (New York: Viking, 2008).

26. Ellis, *The Social History of the Machine Gun*, 34.

27. Ellis, *The Social History of the Machine Gun*, 96.

28. Boot, *War Made New*, 147.

29. Boot, *War Made New*, 198.

30. George Raudzens, "War-Winning Weapons: The Measurement of Technological Determinism in Military History," *The Journal of Military History* 54 (October 1990): 403–33. See also Heidi Holz, "Complementary Keys to Naval Victory," *Naval History* (August 2009): 50; Stephen Turnbull, *Samurai Invasion: Japan's Korean War 1592–98* (London: Cassell and Co., 2002).

31. In fact, it was Admiral Togo's nighttime raid on Port Arthur that crippled and bottled up the Russian Far East Fleet, paving the way for the eventual capture of Port Arthur. See John M. Taylor, "The 'Japanese Nelson' Crushes the Russians," *MHQ: The Quarterly Journal of Military History* 21, no. 2 (Winter 2009): 8–19.

32. Darrell H. Semitis, "Japanese Naval Transformation in the Battle of Tsushima," *Military Review* (November–December) 2004: 261–319. By contrast, the Russian fleet was in great, even fatal disarray, even before it made it halfway from Europe to Japan: Constance Pleshakov, *The Tsar's Last Armada: The Epic Voyage to the Battle of Tsushima* (New York: Basic Books, 2005); Richard Hough, *The Fleet That Had to Die* (London: Birlinn, 2004); and Peggy Warner, *The Tide at Sunrise: A History of the Russo-Japanese War, 1904–5* (London: Frank Cass, 1974).

33. See also Rotem Kowner (ed.), *Rethinking the Russo-Japanese War, 1904–1905* (Kent, UK: Global Oriental, 2007).

34. Barrie Pitt (ed.), *The Military History of World War II* (New York: The Military Press, 1986), 93.

35. Michel believes the Navy F-8 Corsair proved to be the top air-superiority fighter for the United States, in large part because of the superior training, tactics, and experience of its pilots: Marshall L. Michel III, *Clashes: Air Combat over North Vietnam 1965–1972* (Annapolis, MD: Naval Institute Press, 1997), 51.

36. See the extensive descriptions of the North Vietnamese antiaircraft defenses depicted in Marshall L. Michel III, *The 11 Days of Christmas: America's Last Vietnam Battle* (San Francisco: Encounter Books, 2002), especially 139–63.

37. Michel, *Clashes*, 4. Michel's in-depth analysis of the entire course of the air war is outstanding and quite possibly definitive.

38. George Crile, *Charlie Wilson's War: The Extraordinary Story of the Largest Covert Operation in History* (New York: Atlantic Monthly Press, 2003), 427. For a more extensive analysis of all the factors (including the billions in aid from the Saudi government) at work in the Soviets' defeat and a less exuberant view of both Charlie Wilson and the Stinger, see Gregory Feifer, *The Great Gamble: The Soviet War in Afghanistan* (New York: HarpersCollin, 2009). Feifer carefully documents all of the Soviet mistakes in counterinsurgency, which makes it a classic in what not to do when facing guerilla warfare.

39. Boot, *War Made New*, 328.

40. See Brian M. Carney, "Air Combat by Remote Control," *Wall Street Journal*, May 12, 2008, A-13; and Robert D. Kaplan, "The Big Glider and the Jagged Boomerang," in his *Hog Pilots, Blue Water Grunts: The American Military in the Air, at Sea, and on the Ground* (New York: Random House, 2007), 329–336. P. W. Singer adds greatly to our knowledge of robotics and future weapons and conduct of war: *Wired for War: The Robotics Revolution and Conflict in the 21st Century* (New York: Penguin, 2009). He not only deftly sketches the avalanche of new and future weapons, such as long-range acoustic devices (LRADs), war robots, and autonomous robotic fighting vehicles, he also helps us to understand the moral, ethical, legal, and military difficulties of integrating them into war fighting.

41. Kaplan, *Hog Pilots*, 330.

42. Of course, Mars-worship being what it is, there are efforts already underway to find weapons to destroy these unmanned aerial vehicles. As of 2009, for example, Boeing had developed the "Laser Avenger," which is already capable of shooting down the much smaller battlefield drones.

43. Singer, *Wired for War*, 363–64.

CHAPTER THREE: SUPERIOR DISCIPLINE

1. Williamson Murray, "Military Culture Does Matter," *Strategic Review* (Spring, 1999): 36. It is important to note that in war situations, units with the best discipline can show startling success in comparison to other less-disciplined ones. For example, in the Russian Civil War during its initial phases, two units, the Latvian Riflemen and the Czech Legion, had a military impact out of proportion to their numbers; and it was not until the Bolsheviks developed iron discipline that they were able to bring other units up to this level of cohesion. See Evan Mawdsley, *The Russian Civil War* (New York: Pegasus Books, 2008), especially 3–44. For a graphic depiction of the contemporary Russian army lacking such discipline, see Arkady Babchenko, *One Soldier's War* (New York: Grove Press, 2006).

2. For a concise overview of many of the major military thinkers and writers throughout history, see Martin van Creveld, *The Art of War: War and Military Thought* (London: Cassell, 2000); as well as Gerard Chaliand, *The Art of War in World History* (Berkeley: University of California Press, 1994).

3. Nicolo Machiavelli, *The Art of War* (Indianapolis, IN: Bobbs-Merrill, 1965).

4. Felix Gilbert, "Machiavelli: The Renaissance of the Art of War," in Peter Paret, *Makers of Modern Strategy: From Machiavelli to the Nuclear Age* (Princeton, NJ: Princeton University Press, 1986), 1–31.

5. Gilbert, "Machiavelli," 25.

6. Gilbert, "Machiavelli," 25. See also Christopher Lynch's fine translation and edition of Niccolo Machiavelli's *Art of War* (Chicago: University of Chicago Press, 2003) for Machiavelli's own in-depth analysis of Roman discipline, training, and ferocity as a model for contemporary princes.

7. Martin van Creveld, *Fighting Power: German and U.S. Army Performance, 1939–1945* (Westport, CT: Greenwood Press, 1982), 3.

8. Josephus, *The Jewish War*, quoted in J. E. Lendon, "Roman Siege of Jerusalem," in *MHQ: The Quarterly Journal of Military History* 17, no. 4 (Summer 2005): 7. See also G. A. Williamson's translation, Flavius Josephus, *The Jewish War* (New York: Penguin Books, 1959). Of course, like all generalizations, the extent of Roman training varied from commander to commander. In the case of Julius Caesar, for example, "his men were allowed considerable leeway in their behavior" during peacetime, although his discipline was very, very firm during wartime writes Adrian Goldsworthy, *Caesar: Life of a Colossus* (New Haven, CT: Yale University Press, 2008), 234.

9. Lendon, "Roman Siege of Jerusalem," 8. For an overview of Roman military dimensions, see Paul Erdkamp (ed.), *A Companion to the Roman Army* (Oxford: Blackwell, 2007).

10. Williamson Murray, MacGregor Knox, and Alvin Bernstein (eds.), *The Making of Strategy: Rulers, States, and War* (Cambridge: Cambridge University Press, 1994), 61.

11. Gunther Rothenberg, "Maurice of Nassau, Gustavus Adolphus, Raimondo Montecuccoli, and the 'Military Revolution' of the Seventeenth Century," in Peter Paret (ed.), *Makers of Modern Strategy from Machiavelli to the Nuclear Age* (Princeton, NJ: Princeton University Press, 1986), 32–63.

12. John A. Lynn, "Soul of the Sepoy," *MHQ: The Quarterly Journal of Military History* 17, no. 2 (Winter 2005): 46–55. See also his *Battle: A History of Combat and Culture* (Boulder, CO: Westview Press, 2003), an excellent work. His emphasis on the East India Company's side of the equation should be examined in light of Kaushik Roy's important use of the prism of military synthesis, which accents the "defective military synthesis in the Indian armies, 1770–1849," especially among the Marathas and Sikhs in his "Military Synthesis in South Asia: Armies, Warfare, and Indian Society, c. 1740–1849," in *The Journal of Military History* 69 (July 2005): 651–90.

13. For some important insights into his military career and willingness to engage in "wars of annihilation," see Alan Marshall, *Oliver Cromwell—Soldier: The Military Life of a Revolutionary at War* (London: Brassey's, 2004).

14. Robert B. Asprey, *Frederick the Great: The Magnificent Enigma* (New York: Ticknor and Fields, 1986). Discipline as an independent variable is widespread as well in Frederick's, *The Art of War* (New York: Da Capo Press, 1999).

15. Carl von Clausewitz, *On War* (New York: Alfred A. Knopf, 1993), 138.

16. Clausewitz, *On War*, 145.

17. Jared Diamond, *Guns, Germs and Steel: The Fates of Human Societies* (New York: Norton, 1999), 67–82. Note that when the Spanish fought highly disciplined and innovative Native Americans such as the Chilean Araucanians, they were defeated over and over for several hundred years.

18. Diamond, *Guns, Germs, and Steel*, 73.

19. Max Boot, *War Made New* (New York: Gotham Books, 2007), 77–102. Likewise, Alex von Tunzelmann makes a similar point that at the end of the sixteenth century, the Mogul emperor Akbar the Great ruled an Indian empire of 100 million people, an empire that was far richer, far more cosmopolitan, far more tolerant, and far more prosperous than England, whose 2.5 million inhabitants were poorer, more superstitious, more wracked by religious warfare, and for the most part, tied indelibly and perniciously to the land. See her *Indian Summer: The Secret History of the End of an Empire* (New York: Henry Holt, 2008), 11–12. For some important background on the Battle of Panipat, see L. F. Williams, *An Empire Builder of the Sixteenth Century* (New York: Longmans, Green, 1918); Bamber Gascoigne, *The Great Moghuls* (New York: Harper and Row, 1971); Mohibbul Hassan, *Babur: Founder of the Mughal Empire in India* (New Delhi: Manohar, 1985); and Roy Kaushik, *India's Historic Battles from Alexander the Great to Kargil* (Delhi: Permanent Black 2004).

20. Lynn, "Soul of the Sepoy," 50.

21. Juliet Barker, *Agincourt: Henry V and the Battle That Made England* (New York: Little, Brown and Company, 2005), 26.

22. Tim Blanning, *The Pursuit of Glory: Europe 1649–1815* (New York: Viking, 2008), 398.

23. Blanning, *The Pursuit of Glory*, 397.

24. Bruce Condell and David Zabecki (eds.), *On the German Art of War: Truppenfuhrung* (Boulder, CO: Lynne Riener, 2001), 17.

25. Condell and Zabecki, *On the German Art of War*, 19.

26. Jon Latimer, *El Alamein* (Cambridge, MA: Harvard University Press, 2002), 30. Perhaps no writing captures the essence of the leadership qualities of the German NCO better than Willi Heinrich's legendary portrayal of Sergeant Rolf Steiner in his novel *Cross of Iron* (London: Cassell Military, 1999).

27. Stephen Fritz, *Frontsoldaten* (Lexington: University of Kentucky Press, 1995), 24; Hans von Luck, *Panzer Commander* (New York: Dell Books, 1989), introduction. Max Boot also echoes this point and puts the casualty ratio at 100–120 for the Germans against the British and Americans, and 100–200 against the Russians, see his *War Made New*, 238.

28. Michael Reynolds, *Men of Steel* (New York: Sarpedon, 1999), 22. See also, Max Hastings: *Armageddon: The Battle for Germany, 1944–1945* (New York: Alfred A. Knopf, 2004).

29. General Paik Sun Yup, *From Pusan to Panmunjom* (Dulles, Virginia: Brassey's, 1992), 119.

30. Nathaniel Fick, *One Bullet Away: The Making of a Marine Officer* (New York: Houghton Mifflin, 2005), 143. See also Evan Wright, *Generation Kill* (New York: G. P. Putnam's Sons, 2004). Wright was on the same drive to Baghdad with Fick's unit. Bing West and Gary L. Smith, *The March Up: Taking Baghdad with the 1st Marine Division* (New York: Bantam Books, 2003) was inspired by, and reminds one of, the classic story of Xenophon's *Anabasis* as the authors rode with various regimental combat teams of the First Marine Division: "The Anabasis is an account of tough characters bound by an unflinching warrior code" (2).

31. John Ferling, *Almost a Miracle: The American Victory in the War of Independence* (Oxford: Oxford University Press, 2007), 5.

32. Fick, *One Bullet Away*, 369.

33. Fick, *One Bullet Away*, 351.

34. For a most useful overview of what constitutes warrior cultures see Shannon E. French, *The Code of the Warrior: Exploring Warrior Values Past and Present* (Lanham, MD: Rowman and Littlefield, 2005). French looks at Greek, Roman, Arthurian, Viking, Plains Indian, Shaolin, and Samurai examples in considerable depth.

35. William Manchester, *Goodbye, Darkness: A Memoir of the Pacific War* (New York: Random House, 1988), 12. A recent study by Dora L. Cost and Matthew E. Kahn stresses the in-group solidarity shared by soldiers from the same socioeconomic background and area and the desertion dangers of demographic diversity: Dora L. Cost and Matthew E. Kahn, *Heroes and Cowards* (Princeton, NJ: Princeton University Press, 2008).

36. French, *The Code of the Warrior*, 241.

37. See U.S. Marine Corps, *Warfighting*, 2nd ed. (Washington, DC: Department of the Navy, 1997), which integrates lessons from Sun Tzu and Carl von Clausewitz with U.S. Marine experiences for over a hundred years and accents the flexibility and leadership qualities of noncommissioned and junior officers.

38. Condell and Zabecki, *On the German Art of War*, 18. See also the more contemporary views of General Charles C. Krulak, "The Strategic Corporal: Leadership in the Three Block War," *Marines* 28, no. 1 (January 1999): 26–33.

39. See especially John Shay, "Jomini" in Peter Paret (ed.), *Makers of Modern Strategy from Machiavelli to the Nuclear Age* (Princeton, NJ: Princeton University Press, 1986), 143–85.

40. Van Creveld, *Fighting Power*, 163. Somewhat wistfully and surely ironically, van Creveld puts the Israeli armed forces in the 1967 war in the German category but notes that they fought for six days, not six years. It is also worth pointing out in this regard that the German Wehrmacht gave its recruits sixteen weeks of training (at least up until 1944, when the number dropped to twelve to fourteen weeks), considerably higher than their American, British, or Russian counterparts. See Richard Holmes, *Acts of War: The Behavior of Men in Battle* (New York: The Free Press, 1985), 37.

41. Bing West, "The Turnaround Begins: Fall 2006," in *The Strongest Tribe* (New York: Random House, 2008), 73–186. His Tolstoy quote is from page xviii.

42. Boot, *War Made New*, 45.

CHAPTER FOUR: SUSTAINED BUT CONTROLLED RUTHLESSNESS

1. John McCain, "There is No Substitute for Victory," *Wall Street Journal*, October 26, 2001, A. 14.

2. Carl von Clausewitz, *On War* (Princeton, NJ: Princeton University Press, 1976), 83–84.

3. J. E. Lendon, "Roman Siege of Jerusalem," *MHQ: The Quarterly Journal of Military History* 17, no. 4 (Summer 2005): 6–15.

4. But it is not violence for its own sake, it is violence for a purpose.

5. R. J. Rummel, *Death by Government* (London: Transaction Publishers, 1995), 291. Victor Hanson, *Culture and Carnage* (New York: Doubleday, 2001), 424–25,

claims that 40,000 Vietnamese civilians were killed by U.S. air raids, compared to 400,000 targeted by the Viet Cong and NVA. Unfortunately for the historian trying to be truly objective, most estimates of civilian casualities during the twenty-year Vietnam war are wildly divergent, depending on the source, the comprehensiveness of their study, and their political bias. In one specific and well-documented case, the Viet Cong and NVA massacred 6,000 civilians when they briefly took over Hue in 1968: James Warren, *American Spartans* (New York: The Free Press, 2005), 261, quoted in James Corum, *Bad Strategies: How Major Powers Fail in Counterinsurgency* (Minneapolis, MN: Zenith Press, 2008), 155.

   6. C. Dale Walton, *The Myth of Inevitable U.S. Defeat in Vietnam* (London: Frank Cass, 2002), 112. Walton rightly calls this tale, "The Superpower That Defeated Itself," 157–61. See also James H. Willbanks, *Abandoning Vietnam: How America Left and South Vietnam Lost Its War* (Lawrence: University Press of Kansas, 2008).

   7. Walton, *The Myth of Inevitable U.S. Defeat*, 123.

   8. Thomas M. Coffey, *Iron Eagle: The Turbulent Life of General Curtis LeMay* (New York: Thomas Crown, 1986), 429.

   9. Coffey, *Iron Eagle*, 429–30.

   10. John McCain, *Faith of My Fathers* (New York: Random House, 1999), 185–86. Certainly both McCain and LeMay were correct when they indicated the utter failure of the American policy (pushed by Secretary of Defense Robert McNamara and the head of the Joint Chiefs of Staff, General Maxwell Taylor) of "prudent" escalation that, far from providing the desired effect, actually had the opposite impact on North Vietnamese decision makers, encouraging them to believe the United States would not do what was necessary to defeat them.

   11. Note: We are not asserting that the United States "should" have gotten involved in Indochina in the 1960s, nor are we asserting that winning the war in Indochina "would" have been worth the ultimate price to do so. But once the United States had gotten involved in Indochina, there was no a priori reason it was "doomed" to lose the war. Vietnam was never central to U.S. interests and therefore probably was not worth its ultimate costs of involvement, but once the United States made it a central interest by massive investments of blood and treasure, it made little sense to then lose the war through faulty strategy and broken will.

   12. Fred Anderson, *Crucible of War: The Seven Years War and the Fate of Empire in British North America 1754–1763* (New York: Alfred A. Knopf, 2000).

   13. Charles Mann, *1491* (New York: Alfred A. Knopf, 2005). For a more inclusive work dealing with the impact of disease on various cultures, see William McNeill, *Plagues and Peoples* (New York: Anchor Books, 1977).

   14. Leslie Shaw, email to author, June 25, 2008.

   15. J. H. Elliott, *Empires of the Atlantic World: Britain and Spain in America 1492–1830* (New Haven, CT: Yale University Press, 2008), 274.

   16. Ian K. Steele, *Warpaths: Invasions of North America* (New York: Oxford University Press, 1994). The role of diversity in Native American culture and indigenous warfare is explored in Richard J. Chacon and Ruben G. Mendoza (eds.), *North American Indigenous Warfare and Ritual Violence* (Tucson: University of Arizona Press, 2007). For some engaging accounts of the shifting and ongoing kaleidoscope of Indian groups warring with and displacing one another on the High Plains and in the Southwest, see George E. Hyde, *Indians of the High Plains* (Norman: University

of Oklahoma Press, 1959); Francis Haines, *The Plains Indians* (New York: Thomas Crowell, 1976); John C. Ewers, *Plains Indian History and Culture* (Norman: University of Oklahoma Press, 1997); Stan Hoig, *Tribal Wars of the Southern Plains* (Norman: University of Oklahoma Press, 1993).

17. Paul Allen, "Subduing the Seminoles," *The Quarterly Journal of Military History* 12, no. 3 (Spring 2000): 54–63. James S. Robbins points out that the Second Seminole War was the deadliest in American military history with the army suffering a 14 percent mortality rate: *Last in Their Class: Custer, Pickett and the Goats of West Point* (New York: Encounter Books, 2006), 52.

18. Leslie Shaw, email to author, June 25, 2008. See also, Patrick M. Malone, *The Skulking Way of War: Technology and Tactics among the New England Indians* (Lanham, MD: Madison Books, 2000).

19. Steven LeBlanc with Katherine E. Register, *Constant Battles: The Myth of the Peaceful, Noble Savage* (New York: St. Martin's Press, 2003). See also John E. Freling, *A Wilderness of Miseries: War and Warriors in Early America* (Westport, CT: Greenwood Press, 1980).

20. Fred Anderson, *Crucible of War* (New York: Alfred A. Knopf, 2000), 103.

21. Howard Russell, *Indian New England Before the Mayflower* (Hanover, NH: University Press of New England, 1980), 188; and Colin G. Calloway (ed.), *Dawn Encounters: Indians and Europeans in Northern New England* (Hanover, NH: University Press of New England, 1991), 135.

22. Samuel de Champlain, for example, observed this practice in the 1609 Northern Alliance war against the Mohawks, see David Hackett Fisher, *Champlain's Dream* (New York: Simon and Schuster, 2008), 273–74.

23. Francis Jennings, *The Invasion of America: Indians, Colonials and the Cant of Conquest* (Chapel Hill: University of North Carolina Press, 1975).

24. See Wayne E. Lee, "Peace Chiefs and Blood Revenge: Patterns of Restraint in Native American Warfare, 1500–1800," *Journal of Military History* 71 (July 2007): 701–41.

25. Jennings, *The Invasion of America*, title page.

26. Armstrong Starkey, *European and Native American Warfare, 1675–1815* (Norman: University of Oklahoma Press, 1998).

27. For example, during the nine religious civil wars fought between Protestants and Catholics from 1562 and 1598 in France, between 2 and 4 million people were killed: Fisher, *Champlain's Dream*, 53.

28. Tony Horowitz, *A Voyage Long and Strange: Rediscovering the New World* (New York: Henry Holt, 2008), 265–92.

29. T. R. Fehrenbach, *Fire and Blood* (New York: Da Capo Press, 1995), 125.

30. See the many instances of intra-Indian betrayal in William H. Prescott, *The History of the Conquest of Mexico* (London: Swan Sonnenschein and Company, 1890, The Folio Society edition, 1994). Ross Hassig accents the extent to which the Tlaxcalans initially saw the Spaniards not as conquerors, but as vital allies against the encroaching power of the Aztecs. "Better the devil unknown than the devil known" seems to have been their attitude. Ross Hassig, "Aztec Flower Wars," *MHQ: The Quarterly Journal of Military History* 9, no.1 (1996): 8–20. Since, according to M. L. Brown, Cortes had come with only 110 sailors and 508 soldiers (only 12 of whom had guns), without these Indian allies, his expedition would have been destroyed:

M. L. Brown, *Firearms in Colonial America* (Washington, DC: Smithsonian Institution Press, 1980, 310–24, quoted in *American Rifle*, 3. See also Bernal Diaz, *The Conquest of New Spain* (New York: Penguin Books, 1963), 353–14.

31. J. H. Elliott, *Empires of the Atlantic World: Britain and Spain in America 1492–1830* (New Haven, CT: Yale University Press, 2008).

32. Starkey, *European and Native American Warfare*, 33.

33. James Fennimore Cooper, *The Last of the Mohicans: A Narrative of 1757* (Albany: State University of New York Press, 1983).

34. Cooper, *The Last of the Mohicans*, xxxv.

35. Adam Hirsch, "The Collision of Military Cultures in Seventeenth-Century New England," *The Journal of American History* 74, no. 4 (March 1988): 1187–1212, quote from page 1201.

36. Nathan Philbrick, *Mayflower* (New York: Viking, 2006), 178.

37. Alan Taylor, *American Colonies: The Penguin History of the United States* (New York: Viking, 2001), 192. It should be noted that many Puritan groups were willing to accept individual Indians as "Christian," but by the time of the events of 1675, collective punishment was the rule by both Native Americans and Europeans. See James Warren, "Total War Comes to the New World," *MHQ: The Quarterly Journal of Military History* 11, no. 1 (1998), 28–39.

38. Hirsch, "Collision of Military Cultures," 1208.

39. See especially Louis Craft, "Between the Army and the Cheyennes," *MHQ: The Quarterly Journal of Military History* 14, no. 2 (Winter 2002): 48–55; Robert Utley, *The Last Days of the Sioux Nation* (New Haven, CT: Yale University Press, 1963); and Dee Brown, *Bury My Heart at Wounded Knee: An Indian History of the American West* (New York: Holt Paperbacks, 2001).

40. Philbrick, *Mayflower*, 332.

41. Quoted in Starkey, *European and Native American Warfare*, 80.

42. Fred Anderson, *Crucible of War: The Seven Years' War and the Fate of Empire in British North America, 1754–1766* (New York: Alfred A. Knopf, 2000), 344.

43. Anderson, *Crucible of War*, 542.

44. Quoted in Bruce Catton, *This Hallowed Ground* (Garden City, NY: Doubleday, 1956), 151.

45. Mark Grimsley, *The Hard Hand of War* (Cambridge: Cambridge University Press, 2008). See also, Catton, *This Hallowed Ground*, 145–53.

46. See James M. McPherson, "Was It More Restrained Than You Think?" *New York Review of Books*, February 14, 2008), 42–42; and Mark Neely Jr., *The Civil War and the Limits of Destruction* (Cambridge, MA: Harvard University Press, 2008).

47. Victor Hanson, *The Soul of Battle* (New York: The Free Press, 1999). See especially part 2, 123–262.

48. Henry T. Woods, *American Sayings* (New York: Duell, Sloan, Pearce, 1945), 154. Sherman said, "War is cruelty and you can't refine it."

49. Ulysses S. Grant, *Memoirs and Selected Letters: Personal Memoirs of U.S. Grant, Selected Letters 1839–1865* (New York: The Library of America Edition, 1990), 246.

50. Buck Foster, "Sherman's First Campaign of Destruction," *MHQ: The Quarterly Journal of Military History* 19, no. 4 (Summer 2007): 58–67. See also his *Sherman's Mississippi Campaign* (Tuscaloosa: University of Alabama Press, 2006).

51. Foster, "Sherman's First Campaign," 63. John F. Marszalek, in his biography of Sherman, quotes him as seeing civilians as enemies, fitting with his view of col-

lective responsibility, "In war everything is right which prevents anything," John F. Marszalek, *Sherman: A Soldier's Passion for Order* (New York: The Free Press, 1993), 303. For an almost hour-by-hour account of the entire operation, see Noah Andre Trudeau, *Southern Storm: Sherman's March to the Sea* (New York: Harper and Row, 2008).

52. Marszalek, *Sherman: A Soldier's Passion*, 66.

53. Marszalek, *Sherman: A Soldier's Passion*, 65.

54. John Y. Simon (ed.), *The Papers of Ulysses S. Grant*, vol. 2 (Carbondale: Southern Illinois University Press, 1969), 242–43; also quoted in Mark Grimsley, *The Hard Hand of War: Union Military Policy toward Southern Civilians, 1861–1865* (Cambridge: Cambridge University Press, 1995), 167.

55. Michael Fellman (ed.), *The Memoirs of W. T. Sherman* (New York: Penguin Books, 2000), xiii.

56. Hanson, *The Soul of Battle*, 34–35.

57. Hanson, *The Soul of Battle*, 211.

58. Hanson, *The Soul of Battle*, 234.

59. Quoted in James L. Stokesbury, *A Short History of the Civil War* (New York: Morrow, 1995), 262.

60. Charles Bracelen Flood, *1864: Lincoln at the Gates of History* (New York: Simon and Schuster, 2009).

61. Flood, *1864*, 379. Flood states that Atlanta was set on fire once in August by the retreating Confederates and again by the Union forces when they destroyed the commercial and manufacturing areas of the city before departing.

62. Lance Janda, "Shutting the Gates of Mercy: The American Origins of Total War, 1860–1880," *The Journal of Military History* 59, no.1 (January 1995): 7–26.

63. Janda, "Shutting the Gates of Mercy," 25.

64. For a holistic examination of the role of the buffalo in Indian life and cosmology, see Tom McHugh, *The Time of the Buffalo* (New York: Alfred A. Knopf, 1972). It should be noted that not all American generals adopted the most ruthless of solutions. For example, as Tim Woodcock reminds, General George Crook took a considerably different approach from that of General Nelson A. Miles when dealing with the Plains Indians.

65. Bill Yenne, *Indian Wars: The Campaign for the American West* (Yardley, PA: Westholme, 2006), 307.

66. Robert Charles Padden, "Cultural Change and Military Resistance in Araucanian Chile, 1550–1730," *Southwestern Journal of Anthropology* 13, no. 1 (Spring, 1957): 103–21.

67. Padden, "Cultural Change," 119; and David Weber, *Barbaros: Spaniards and Their Savages in the Age of Enlightenment* (New Haven, CT: Yale University Press, 2005), 56, also 54–61 for further information.

68. Padden, "Cultural Change," 119.

69. Padden, "Cultural Change," 121.

70. Padden, "Cultural Change," 121. The Spanish ultimately failed to subdue the Araucanians despite fighting them for over a century, and it was not until 1883 that the Chilean government, working with the Argentines, was finally able to complete their military conquest of the Araucanians. Weber, *Barbaros*, 173.

71. Pekka Hamalainen, *The Comanche Empire* (New Haven, CT: Yale University Press, 2008). On page 69 Hamalainen astutely points out that at the end of the

French and Indian War, in the Treaty of Paris, the Spanish were "given" all of the Comanche territory. However, the Comanches had other plans. "Rather than New Spain absorbing the southern plains into its imperial body, Comanches had reduced the Spanish borderlands to a hinterland for an imperial system of their own." For a look at their eventual decline, see T. R. Fehrenbach, *Comanches: The Destruction of a People* (New York: Alfred A. Knopf, 1979).

72. Larry McMurtry, "The Conquering Indians," *New York Review of Books*, May 29, 2008), 24–25.

73. Rick Atkinson, *The Day of Battle: The War in Sicily and Italy, 1943–1944* (New York: Henry Holt, 2007), 118.

74. See, for example, the highly impressionistic book by Nicholson Baker, *Human Smoke: The Beginning of World War II, the End of Civilization* (New York: Simon and Schuster, 2008). Baker tries to make the case that not only was World War II not worth fighting by the Allies, it didn't even help anyone who needed help and, moreover, the leadership of the United States and Great Britain was about as bad as that of Hitler. It would be most illuminating if his statement were ever read to the survivors of the Holocaust to get their reaction. Moreover, as Michael Korda has written about British raids of German cities after the Battle of Britain, "it would be difficult to overstate the enthusiasm of the British public for giving the Germans a taste of their own medicine after the Blitz began in earnest in the autumn of 1940 and the winter of 1941," Michael Korda, *With Wings Like Eagles: A History of the Battle of Britain* (New York: Harper, 2009), 284. Throughout the war, RAF Air Marshal Sir Arthur "Bomber" Harris steadfastly pushed for an almost total focus on the flattening of German cities, even opposing an emphasis on specific strategic targets such as oil production or ball bearing manufacturing facilities.

75. Williamson Murray and Allan R. Millett, *A War to Be Won: Fighting the Second World War* (Cambridge, MA: Belknap, Harvard University Press, 2000), 335.

76. J. Adam Toose, *The Wages of Destruction: The Making and Breaking of the Nazi Economy* (New York: Viking, 2007), 626–27, 638–39. See also, Alfred C. Mierzejewski, *The Collapse of the German War Economy 1944–1945* (Chapel Hill: University of North Carolina Press, 1988). German aircraft production also peaked during the summer of 1944. For one inside view of how Germany was able to maintain its military production capacity for so long, see Albert Speer, *Inside the Third Reich* (New York: Macmillan, 1970), bearing in mind that Speer is not always a totally reliable source, even on production matters: Gita Sereny, *Albert Speer: His Battle with Truth* (New York: Alfred A. Knopf, 1995).

77. Max Hastings, *Retribution: The Battle for Japan, 1944–1945* (New York: Alfred A. Knopf, 2007), 305. Hastings gives the higher figure.

78. Richard B. Frank, *Downfall: The End of the Imperial Japanese Empire* (New York: Random House, 1999), 77.

79. Max Boot, *War Made New* (New York: Gotham Books, 2007), 293.

80. Boot, *War Made New*, 484.

81. Richard Frank, *Downfall*, 189. Frank also correctly points out that, at the time of these devastating attacks, the so-called "Volunteer Enlistment Law" in Japan applied to all men ages fifteen to sixty and all women ages seventeen to forty. School children were issued awls and told, "Even killing just one American soldier will do.

You must prepare to use the awls for self-defense. You must aim at the enemy's abdomen."

82. Hastings, *Retribution*, 7.

83. Frank, *Downfall*, 286, although Frank himself writes, "The best approximation is that the number is huge and falls between 100,000 and 200,000" (287).

84. Frank, *Downfall*, 145.

85. Frank, *Downfall*, 143.

86. Victor Hanson, "The Wages of Suicide: Okinawa April 1–July 2, 1945," in his *Ripples of Battle*, (New York: Doubleday, 2003), 12.

87. Frank, *Downfall*, 195.

88. See Haruko Taya Cook, "Nagano 1945: Hirohito's Secret Hideout," *MHQ: The Quarterly Journal of Military History* 10, no. 3 (1998): 44–47. For Japan and Germany's search for their own atomic bomb, see Andrew J. Rotter, *Hiroshima: The World's Bomb* (New York: Oxford University Press, 2008).

89. Hastings, *Retribution*, xix.

90. Hastings, *Retribution*, 513.

91. There continue to be books written second-guessing the dropping of the first atomic bomb and declaring its use unnecessary. See, for example, Rotter, *Hiroshima: The World's Bomb* cited above.

92. Thomas B. Allen and Norman Polmar, "Gassing Japan," *MHQ: The Quarterly Journal of Military History* 10, no. 1 (1997): 38–45.

93. Samuel Eliot Morison, *The Two-Ocean War: A Short History of the United States Navy in the Second World War* (Annapolis, MD: Naval Institute Press, 1963), 572.

94. Morison, *The Two-Ocean War*, 573.

95. It would take quite a leap of faith to suggest that German and Japanese production accomplishments would have been *lower* if the bombing had not taken place. In any case, the central point here is that for the British and the Americans, the unleashing of strategic bombing and its concomitant sustained ruthlessness signaled that they were prepared to do whatever was necessary in order to win the war, and beyond that, strategic bombing worked in both campaigns.

CHAPTER FIVE: RECEPTIVITY TO MILITARY AND INTEGRATIVE INNOVATION

1. Stephen Rosen, *Winning the Next War: Innovation and the Modern Military* (Ithaca, NY: Cornell University Press, 1999); and Barry Watts and Williamson Murray, "Military Innovation in Peacetime," in Williamson Murray and Allan R. Millett (eds.), *Military Innovation in the Interwar Period* (Cambridge: Cambridge University Press, 1996), 415.

2. Holger H. Herwig, "The Battlefleet Revolution, 1885–1914," in Williamson Murray and MacGregor Knox (eds.), *The Dynamics of Military Revolution 1300–2050* (Cambridge: Cambridge University Press, 2001), 115.

3. Clifford J. Rogers, "'As If a New Sun Had Arisen': England's Fourteenth-Century RMA," in MacGregor Knox and Williamson Murray (eds.), *The Dynamics of Military*

Revolution 1300–2050 (Cambridge: Cambridge University Press, 2001), 15–34. Thomas Arnold narrates a most interesting account of the diffusion of gunpowder and gunpowder weapons throughout Europe in his *The Renaissance at War* (London: Cassell, 2001).

4. Philippe Contamine, *War in the Middle Ages* (London: Basil Blackwell, 1984), 217.

5. Juliet Barker, *Agincourt: Henry V and the Battle That Made England* (New York: Little, Brown and Company, 2005), 88.

6. Hugh D. H. Soar, *The Crooked Stick: A History of the Longbow* (Yardley, PA: Westholme Publishing, 2004), xi.

7. Juliet Barker, *Agincourt*, 27. The longbow has achieved mythic status in military writings in the West: Robert Hardy, *Longbow: A Social and Military History* (London: Sutton, 2006). For a global perspective on it and other bows throughout history, see Charles E. Grayson, Mary French, and Michael J. O'Brien, *Traditional Archery from Six Continents* (Columbia: University of Missouri Press, 2007).

8. Contamine, *War in the Middle Ages*, 217.

9. Juliet Barker, *Agincourt*, 25.

10. John K. Thornton, *Warfare in Atlantic Africa 1500–1800* (London: UCL Press, 1999), 21.

11. Max Boot, *War Made New* (New York: Gotham Books, 2007), 128–29. Alexander Rose reports that Brigadier General James Ripley head of the U.S. Ordinance Department was also appalled at the "wastage" produced by the much-desired Sharps repeating rifle: Alexander Rose, *American Rifle: A Biography* (New York: Delacorte Press, 2008), 140. See also Joseph G. Bilby, *Revolution in Arms: A History of the First Repeating Rifles* (Yardley, PA: Westholme Publishing, 2006).

12. Michael Korda, *Ike: An American Hero* (New York: HarperCollins, 2007), 132.

13. Korda, *Ike*, 152–53.

14. Boot, *War Made New*, 23.

15. Others sing the Sherman's praises, seeing it as superior to the German and Russian tanks in important dimensions such as versatility and ease of maintenance. Allan Millett and Williamson Murray, for example, describe it as "a wonderful armored fighting vehicle in some respects—more reliable than anything in the German inventory" except for its low-velocity gun. The authors point out that when up-gunned in the British "Firefly" version, the Sherman acquitted itself well in the battle for Normandy: Williamson Murray and Allan R. Millett, *A War to Be Won: Fighting the Second World War* (Cambridge, MA: Belnap, Harvard University Press, 2000), 417, 423. However, they do point out that in 1944, the Third Armored Division lost 648 tanks in combat and had a further 700 damaged (463). For a comprehensive overview of the Sherman tank and its many permutations, see the definite work by R. P. Hunnicutt, *Sherman: A History of the American Medium Tank* (Novato, CA: Presidio Press, 1978).

16. Thomas M. Coffey, *Iron Eagle: The Turbulent Life of General Curtis LeMay* (New York: Crown, 1986), 391. See also Barrett Tillman, *LeMay* (New York: Palgrave Macmillan, 2007). LeMay, for example, was opposed to the use of American ground troops in Vietnam, advocating instead heavy use of air power against strategic targets, telling Coffey: "If you stop the supplies coming in, there can't be too much of a war" (429). Ironically, when he was nearing retirement, LeMay received a highly controversial decoration from the Japanese government for his efforts to help build up Japan's postwar defenses (437).

17. Coffey, *Iron Eagle*, 45.

18. Kenneth Werrell, *Blankets of Fire* (Washington, DC: Smithsonian, 1998).

19. Coffey, *Iron Eagle*, 63.

20. Coffey, *Iron Eagle*, 102.

21. See especially Grant T. Hammond, *The Mind of War: John Boyd and American Security* (Washington, DC: Smithsonian Books, 2001); and Robert Coram, *Boyd: The Fighter Pilot Who Changed the Art of War* (New York: Little, Brown and Company, 2002). Boyd himself wrote little, preferring to give long and engaging "briefings" lasting five or more hours. For an insight into those briefings, see John Boyd, *A Discourse on Winning and Losing* (mimeographed, 1987). Boyd continues to remain relevant to the study of warfare, particularly to students of chaoplexic warfare, see, for example, Antoine Bousquet, *The Scientific Way of Warfare: Order and Chaos on the Battlefields of Modernity* (New York: Columbia University Press, 2009), 187–96.

22. For these and other views about the reasons for U.S. dominance in the air during the Korean War, see Kenneth Werrell, *Sabres over MiG Alley: The F-86 and the Battle for Air Superiority in Korea* (Annapolis, MD: Naval Institute Press, 2005).

23. Daniel Boorstin, *The Discoverers* (New York: Random House, 1983); and Felipe Fernandez-Armesto, *The Pathfinders: A Global History of Exploration* (New York: Norton, 2007). See also Edward L. Dreyer, *Zheng He: China and the Oceans in the Early Ming Dynasty, 1405–1433* (London: Longmans, 2006) for a much more in-depth examination of this era.

24. Felipe Fernandez-Armesto, *Pathfinders*, 109.

25. Anatole Andro, *The 1421 Heresy: An Investigation into the Ming Chinese Maritime Survey of the World* (New York: Authorhouse, 2005).

26. Boorstin, *The Discoverers*, 200.

27. See Ben Kiernan, "Japan's Unification and Its Invasions of Korea, 1567–98," in his *Blood and Soil: A World History of Genocide and Extermination from Sparta to Darfur* (New Haven, CT: Yale University Press, 2007), 112–32.

28. For this fascinating story, see Noah Perrin, *Giving Up the Gun: Japan's Reversion to the Sword 1543–1879* (Boston: David R. Godine Publishing, 1979); Stephen R. Turnbull, *Samurai Warfare* (London: Cassell, 1996) and his *Nagashino: 1575* (London: Osprey Publishing, 2005). A concise but very readable account of the importance of Nagashino is found in Charles Hilbert's "Samurai Slaughtered at Nagashino," *Military History* (October 1996): 63–68.

29. Roger Crowley, *Empires of the Sea: The Siege of Malta, The Battle of Lepanto, and the Contest for the Center of the World* (New York: Random House, 2008), xiv. He also makes the point that the Hapsburg king, Charles V (who was also the Holy Roman Emperor), was in a powerful position with the new wealth from the Spanish possessions in North and South America, but his hegemony was undercut by both the rise of Protestants and the enmity of the French. Crowley does seem to overlook the Mongol Empire, which at its height rivaled or exceeded the scope and power of the Roman one.

30. Crowley, *Empires of the Sea*, 192.

31. John Stoye, *The Siege of Vienna* (London: Collins, 1964), 159.

32. Anthony Pagden, "Turning the Ottoman Tide," *MHQ: The Quarterly Journal of Military History* 20, no. 4 (Summer 2008): 8–17. See also, Niccolo Capponi, *Victory of the West: The Great Christian-Muslim Clash at the Battle of Lepanto* (New York: Da Capo Press, 2006).

33. See Victor Hanson, "The Market—Or Capitalism Kills," in his *Carnage and Culture* (New York: Doubleday, 2001), 260.

34. John F. Guilmartin Jr., *Gunpowder and Galleys: Changing Technology and Mediterranean Warfare at Sea in the Sixteenth Century* (Cambridge: Cambridge University Press, 1974), especially 221–73.

35. Crowley, *Empires of the Sea*, 265. See also G. P. Stokes, "Last Galley Battle," *Military History* (August 1989): 27–33.

36. Crowley, *Empires of the Sea*, 259.

37. Quoted in Felipe Fernandez-Armesto, *Pathfinders*, 139.

38. Bernard Lewis, *What Went Wrong? Western Impact and Middle Eastern Response* (London: Oxford University Press, 2002), 11.

39. See Jason Goodwin, *Lords of the Horizon* (New York: Henry Holt, 1998), 304; and Albert H. Lybyer, *The Government of the Ottoman Empire in the Time of Suleiman the Magnificent* (New York: Russell and Russell, 1966).

40. Thus the Ottoman ambiguity toward military innovation would eventually take a huge toll, a toll that increased with every year of industrialization among the European powers.

41. Capponi, *Victory of the West*, 7–45. I am grateful to Amos Eno for his persistent challenges to the notion that the Ottomans were not receptive to guns and artillery, especially in the earlier period of their expansion.

42. Daniel Goffman, *The Ottoman Empire and Early Modern Europe* (Cambridge: Cambridge University Press, 2002), 194.

43. Daniel Quataert, *The Ottoman Empire, 1700–1922* (Cambridge: Cambridge University Press, 2000), 37–38.

44. Capponi, *Victory of the West*, 321.

45. Stanford J. Shaw, *History of the Ottoman Empire and Modern Turkey*, 2 vols. (Cambridge: Cambridge University Press), 226, and especially 217–79).

46. Dietrich Jung, *Turkey at the Cross Roads: Ottoman Legacies and a Greater Middle East* (London: Zed Books, 2001), 29. See also M. Sukru Hanioglu, who documents the impeding role played by the janissaries in the Empire's efforts to create "New Order Troops" in his *A Brief History of the Late Ottoman Empire* (Princeton, NJ: Princeton University Press, 2008), 45.

47. Rhoads Murphy, *Ottoman Warfare 1500–1700* (New Brunswick, NJ: Rutgers University Press, 1999), 10.

48. For a comprehensive overview of the decline of the Ottomans, see Martin Sicker, *The Islamic World in Decline: From the Treaty of Karlowitz to the disintegration of the Ottoman Empire* (Westport, CT: Praeger, 2001).

49. William H. McNeill, *The Age of Gunpowder Empires 1450–1800* (Washington, DC: American Historical Association, 1989), 35–36.

50. See Geoffrey Parker, "The Western Way of War," in Geoffrey Parker (ed.), *The Cambridge Illustrated History of Warfare* (Cambridge: Cambridge University Press, 1995), 2–9.

51. McNeill, *The Age of Gunpowder Empires*, 1.

52. Thomas Sowell, *Conquests and Cultures: An International History* (New York: Basic Books, 1998), 10. Certainly there was far more ongoing ambiguity toward firearms, especially heavy artillery, within the Ottoman military than in their coun-

terparts in the West, especially by the end of the eighteenth and into the nineteenth century.

53. There were many more blunders associated with this campaign, but the failure to adjust to the technology of their opponent certainly symbolizes British ineptitude in the First Afghan War. See especially, Carl Meyer, "To the Last Man: The Rider Bore Shocking News—The Annihilation of a British Army in Afghanistan," *MHQ: The Quarterly Journal of Military History* 11, no. 4 (1999): 6–17.

54. Shelford Bidwell and Dominick Graham, *Fire-Power: British Army Weapons and Theories of War 1904–1945* (London: Pen and Sword Classics, 2005), quoted in Tim Travers, *The Killing Ground: The British Army, the Western Front, and the Emergence of Modern Warfare, 1900–1918* (London: Allen and Unwin, 1987), xviii. Travers further points out that the British officer corps went off to World War I expecting "that the war would be short in duration, tactically simple, and structured in well-understood stages" (251).

55. Peter Hart, *The Somme* (London: Weidenfeld and Nicolson, 2005), 104.

56. Quoted in John Mosier, *The Myth of the Great War: How the Germans Won the Battles and How the Americans Saved the Allies* (New York: HarperCollins, 2001), 235. Mosier also cites the British captain who remarked, "Meanwhile, on the left, long lines of British infantry, at a few yards interval and in perfect order, were slowly advancing. Wave after wave sprang forward from the trenches, joining in the parade, for that is what it looked like. And they provided magnificent targets" (235).

57. Travers suggests that the prevailing view that the war was won in the last 100 days is incorrect, or at least incomplete, because the German Army began to disintegrate earlier, between the end of March and mid-July: Tim Travers, *How the War Was Won: Command and Technology in the British Army on the Western Front, 1917–1918* (London: Routledge, 1992), 179.

58. See especially John Keegan's "The Breaking of the Armies," and "America and Armageddon," in his *The First World War* (New York: Alfred A. Knopf, 1999), 309–71 and 372–428 respectively. Other works helpful to understanding World War I include Martin Gilbert, *The First World War: A Complete History* (New York: Henry Holt, 1994); Barbara Tuchman, *The Guns of August* (New York: Macmillan, 1962); Holger Herwig, *The First World War, Germany and Austria-Hungary 1914–1918* (London: Arnold, 1997); Byron Farwell, *Over There: The United States in the Great War, 1917–1918* (New York: Norton, 1999); Llewellyn Woodward, *Great Britain and the War of 1914–1918* (London: Methuen, 1967); Hew Strachan, *The First World War* (London: Oxford University Press, 2001); A. H. Farrar-Hockley, *Death of an Army* (New York: W. Morrow, 1968); John Toland, *1918: The Last Year of the Great War* (New York: Smithmark, 1980); Niall Ferguson, *The Pity of War: Explaining World War I* (New York: Basic Books, 1999); and Norman Stone, *World War One: A Short History* (New York: Basic Books, 2009).

59. For an examination of the Chinese strategic thinking up to this point, the interested reader should consult Sergei Goncharow, John Lewis, and Xue Litai, *Uncertain Partners: Stalin, Mao and the Korean War* (Stanford, CA: Stanford University Press, 1993); Chen Jian, *China's Road to the Korean War* (New York: Columbia University Press, 1994); Patrick C. Roe, *The Dragon Strikes* (Novato, CA: Presidio Press, 2000); and Russell Spurr, *Enter the Dragon* (New York: Newmarket Press, 1998).

60. David Halberstam, *The Coldest Winter: America and the Korean War* (New York: Hyperion, 2007), 367. The problem of too much information or not enough information, or erroneous information as well as the importance of the time frame in acquiring that information is handled efficaciously by Geoffrey Parker, "Philip II, Knowledge and Power," *MHQ: The Quarterly Journal of Military History* 11, no. 1 (Autumn 1998): 104–11.

61. The accuracy of the CIA's information on this matter remains debatable, even if MacArthur had been highly receptive to it. Halberstam believes that Carleton Swift, a CIA officer under diplomatic cover in Seoul, "knew" the Chinese were coming (Halberstam, *The Coldest Winter*, 379). But Halberstam's work is almost rabidly anti-MacArthur. A more recent study by Tim Weiner believes that the new CIA was utterly clueless about what was going on in China. See Tim Weiner, *Legacy of Ashes: The History of the CIA* (New York: Anchor Books, 2008), 58–59.

62. Roy Appleby, *East of Chosin: Entrapment and Breakout in Korea, 1950* (College Station: Texas A&M University Press, 1987), 108. See also his *Escaping the Trap: The US Army X Corps in Northeast Korea, 1950* (College Station: Texas A&M, 1990), *Disaster in Korea: The Chinese Confront MacArthur* (College Station: Texas A&M, 1989), and especially his official U.S. Army history of the war, *The United States Army in the Korean War: South to the Naktong, North to the Yalu (June–November, 1950)* (Washington, DC: Office of the Chief of Military History, Department of the Army, 1961) as well as Shelby Stanton, *Ten Corps in Korea: 1950* (Novato, CA: Presidio Press, 1989).

63. There have been many books written about the U.S. Marines' fight from the Chosin Reservoir to the port of Hamhung. Among the most gripping are Martin Russ, *Breakout: The Chosin Reservoir Campaign, Korea 1950* (New York: Fromm International, 1999); and Bob Drury and Tom Clavin, *The Last Stand of Fox Company* (New York: Atlantic Monthly Press, 2009).

64. Richard Iron, "Britain's Longest War: Northern Ireland 1967–2007," in Daniel Marston and Carter Malkasian (eds.), *Counterinsurgency in Modern Warfare* (London: Osprey, 2008), 167–84.

65. Bing West, *The Strongest Tribe: War, Politics, and the Endgame in Iraq* (New York: Random House, 2008), 140.

66. There is also the question of interservice rivalry and a lack of imagination, both of which can hurt the pace and spread of military innovation. I am grateful to Gil Barndollar for this example: It is widely held that the German 88 was the best antitank weapon of World War II, and it also was an excellent antiaircraft weapon. According to Barndollar, however, the British had a better antiaircraft gun, the 3.5-inch gun, but because of a lack of imagination and politics, the British did not end up using it in an antitank role, leaving them with the very inferior two-pounder. See Corelli Barnett, *The Desert Generals* (London: Cassell, 2007), 105; also, Paddy Griffin, *World War II Desert Tactics* (London: Osprey, 2007).

CHAPTER SIX: THE ABILITY AND WILLINGNESS TO PROTECT CAPITAL FROM PEOPLE AND RULERS

1. Roger Crowley, *Empires of the Sea: The Siege of Malta, the Battle of Lepanto, and the Contest for the Center of the World* (New York: Random House, 2008), 193.

2. Allan R. Millett, "Patterns of Military Innovation," in Williamson Murray and Allan R. Millett (eds.), *Military Innovation in the Interwar Period* (Cambridge: Cambridge University Press, 1996), 349.

3. Robert Kaplan does an exceptional job of describing U.S. military activities and the balancing of these various missions in over 150 countries. See his *Imperial Grunts* (New York: Random House, 2004) and *Hog Pilots and Blue Water Grunts* (New York: Random House, 2006). See also Thomas P. M. Barnett, *The Pentagon's New Map: War and Peace in the 21st Century* (New York: G. P. Putnam's Sons, 2004). Not all observers are pleased with the imperial reach of the American armed forces. See especially, James Carroll, *The House of War* (Boston: Houghton Mifflin, 2006), who sees the American military on a never-ending search for new enemies.

4. Max Boot, *War Made New* (New York: Gotham Books, 2007), 100. The figures listed below are drawn from Boot as well.

5. Boot, *War Made New*, 99.

6. For an interesting account of why this phenomenon has developed, see James J. Sheehan, *Where Have All the Soldiers Gone?* (New York: Houghton Mifflin, 2008).

7. Sheehan, *Where Have All the Soldiers Gone?* 221.

8. Sheehan, *Where Have All the Soldiers Gone?* 217.

9. Sheehan, *Where Have All the Soldiers Gone?* 217.

10. Sheehan, *Where Have All the Soldiers Gone?* 218.

11. Sheehan, *Where Have All the Soldiers Gone?* xvi.

12. Jurgen Brauer and Hurbert Van Tuyll, *Castles, Battles, and Bombs: How Economics Explains Military History* (Chicago: University of Chicago Press, 2008).

13. H. W. Koch, *Medieval Warfare* (Barnes and Noble, 1995), 40. Koch only quotes twelve cows for one horse, but the heavily armored knight required three horses at twelve cows a horse: one horse to ride to the battle and normally (palfreys), two larger war horses bred for battle and a weapon in themselves (destriers), plus a cart, horse, and driver to carry the knight's equipment and supplies for an additional fifteen horses.

14. For some important overviews of warfare in the Middle Ages, see Constance Britain Bouchard, *Strong of Body, Brave and Noble* (Ithaca, NY: Cornell University Press, 1998); Nicholas Hooper and Matthew Bennett, *Warfare: The Middle Ages* (Cambridge: Cambridge University Press, 1996); Peter Brown, *The Rise of Western Christendom* (Oxford: Blackwell Publishing, 1996); Christopher Gravett and Christa Hook, *Norman Knight* (London: Osprey Publishing, 1993); Edward Hulme, *The Middle Ages* (New York: Henry Holt, 1929); Philippe Contamine, *War in the Middle Ages* (Oxford: Basil Blackwell, 1984); Bernard Bachrach, *Warfare and Military Organization in Pre-Crusade Europe* (Burlington, VT: Ashgate Publishing, 2002); Christopher Dyer, *Standards of Living in the Later Middle Ages* (Cambridge: Cambridge University Press, 1989); Eric Jager, *The Last Duel* (New York: Broadway Books, 2004); Maurice Keen, *Medieval Warfare* (London: Oxford University Press, 1999); Maurice Keen (ed.), *Medieval Warfare: A History* (Oxford: Oxford University Press, 1999); Hans Delbruck, *Medieval Warfare* (Lincoln: University of Nebraska Press, 1999); Jean DeJoinville and Geoffroy De Villehardouin, *Chronicles of the Crusades*, translated by Margaret Shaw (Baltimore, MD: Penguin Classics, 1963); A. V. B. Norman, *The Medieval Soldier* (New York: Barnes and Noble Books, 1971); R. Ewart Oakeshott, *A Knight and His Castle*

(Chester Springs, PA: Dufour Books, 1997) and his *A Knight in Battle* (London: Lutterworth Press, 1971); Edouard Perroy, *The Hundred Years War* (New York: Capricorn Books, 1965); Matthew Strickland, *War and Chivalry: The Conduct and Perception of War in England and Normandy 1066–1217* (Cambridge: Cambridge University Press, 1996); Barbara Tuchman, *A Distant Mirror: The Calamitous 14th Century* (New York: Alfred A. Knopf, 1978); Philip Warner, *The Medieval Castle* (New York: Barnes and Noble Books, 1971); William Chester Jordan, *Europe in the High Middle Ages* (New York: Penguin Books, 2001); Alison Weir, *Eleanor of Aquitaine* (New York: Ballantine, 1999); and Jean Froissart, *Chronicles*, translated by Geoffrey Brereton (New York: Penguin Classics, 1978). For the changes in medieval warfare that can be considered evolutionary as well as revolutionary, see Andrew Ayton and Leslie Price (eds.), *The Medieval Military Revolution* (London: I.B. Tauris, 1998).

15. Warner, *The Medieval Castle*, 195.

16. Kevin Shillington, *History of Africa* (New York: St. Martin's Press, 1989) quotes Arab scholar Al-Bakri (86) putting the number at 200,000, although that number seems excessive. For the ability of the much richer kingdoms of the African savanna to sustain large standing armies, see also, Philip Curtin, Steven Feierman, Leonard Thompson, and Jan Vansina, "Ghana, Mali, Songhai," in their *A History of Africa* (Boston: Little, Brown and Company, 1978), 108–13.

17. John Reader, *Africa: A Biography of the Continent* (New York: Alfred A. Knopf, 1998), 24.

18. Brian Fagan, *The Great Warming: Climate Change and the Rise and Fall of Civilizations* (New York: Bloomsbury, 2008), 73.

19. Fagan, *The Great Warming*, 66.

20. See Emmanuel Kwaku Akyeampong (ed.), *Themes in West African History* (Athens: Ohio University Press, 2006); William Fage with William Tordoff, "The Development of States and Trade in the Sudan," in their *A History of Africa* (London and New York: Routledge, 2002), 55–77; as well as Erik Gilbert and Jonathan Y. Reynolds, *Africa in World History* (Upper Saddle River, NJ: Pearson/Prentice Hall, 2004), 91–95.

21. Akyeampong, *Themes in West African History*, 100.

22. Boot, *War Made New*, 434.

23. Quoted in Juliet Barker, *Agincourt: Henry V and the Battle That Made England* (New York: Little, Brown and Company, 2005), 101.

24. Tim Blanning, *The Pursuit of Glory: Europe 1649–1815* (New York: Viking, 2008), 229.

25. Blanning, *The Pursuit of Glory*, 598.

26. John Keegan, *Fields of Battle* (New York: Alfred A. Knopf, 1996), 334. For a more holistic account of this "evolutionary" revolution, see Holger H. Herwig, The Battlefleet Revolution, 1885–1914," in Williamson Murray and MacGregor Knox (eds.), *The Dynamics of Military Revolution 1300–2050* (Cambridge: Cambridge University Press, 2001), 114–131.

27. Atkinson, *The Day of Battle: The War in Sicily and Italy, 1943–1944* (New York: Henry Holt, 2007), 450.

28. Victor Hanson, "The Market—Or Capitalism Kills," in *Carnage and Culture*, 233–75.

29. Mark Grimsley, "Surviving Military Revolution: The U.S. Civil War," in MacGregor Knox and Williamson Murray (eds.), *The Dynamics of Military Revolution 1300–2050* (Cambridge: Cambridge University Press, 2001), 74–91.

30. Grimsley, "Surviving Military Revolution," 86.
31. Grimsley, "Surviving Military Revolution," 89.
32. Paul D. Escott, *After Secession: Jefferson Davis and the Failure of Southern Nationalism* (Baton Rouge: Louisiana State University Press, 1978), cited in Grimsley, "Surviving Military Revolution," 89.
33. Douglas B. Ball, *Financial Failure and Confederate Defeat* (Urbana: University Press of Illinois, 1991), cited in Grimsley, "Surviving Military Revolution," 89.
34. Paul Kennedy, *The Rise and Fall of the Great Powers* (New York: Random House, 1987).

CHAPTER SEVEN: THE CENTRALITY OF SUPERIOR WILL

1. "How North Vietnam Won the War," *Wall Street Journal* (August 3, 1995), A8.
2. "How North Vietnam Won the War,", A8. Despite claims to the contrary, the Cambodian port of Sihanockville was not a meaningful logistical alternative to the Trail.
3. Raymond G. O'Connor, "Victory in Modern War," *Journal of Peace Research* 6, no. 4 (1969): 380.
4. Stephane Courtois, Nicolas Werth, Jean-Louis Panne, Andrzej Paczkowski, Karel Bartosek, and Jean-Louis Margolin, *The Black Book of Communism: Crimes, Terror, Repression* (Cambridge, MA: Harvard University Press, 1999).
5. Ben Kiernan, *Blood and Soil: A World History of Genocide and Extermination from Sparta to Darfur* (New Haven, CT: Yale University Press, 2007), 553.
6. Ward Just, *Forgetfulness* (Boston: Houghton Mifflin, 2006), 189.
7. Andrew Nagorski, *The Greatest Battle* (New York: Simon and Schuster, 2007), 247. For a similar racial stereotyping and vilification of the Japanese during the Russo-Japanese War, see Jennifer E. Berry, "Seeing Yellow," *MHQ: The Quarterly Journal of Military History* (Winter 2009): 20–25.
8. From General James Wolfe's last letter to his mother, August 31, 1759 as quoted in Francis Parkman, *Montcalm and Wolfe: The French and Indian War* (New York: Da Capo Press, 2001), 463.
9. David Livingstone Smith, *The Most Dangerous Animal, Human Nature and the Origins of War* (New York: St. Martin's Press, 2007), 10. For an insightful examination of the "peace" and "war" ambiguities in the Qur'an, see T. P. Schwartz-Barcott, *War, Terror, and Peace in the Qur'an and Islam: Insights for Military and Government Leaders* (Carlisle, PA: Army War College Foundation Press, 2004). In this regard, one should also read the Qur'an for oneself, *The Qur'an* (London: Oxford University Press, 2004), translation by M. A. S. Abhel Haleem.
10. Kiernan, *Blood and Soil*, 133.
11. An interesting counterpoint to this argument, at least in one important case, is provided by Michael Burleigh, who shows the nonviolent impact of religion in the defeat of the ideology of Communism. See Burleigh's "'We Want God. We Want God': The Churches and the Collapse of European Marxist-Leninism 1970–1990," in his *Sacred Causes: The Clash of Religion and Politics from the Great War to the War on Terror* (New York: HarperCollins, 2007), 415–49. See also John Micklethwait and Adrian Wooldridge, *God Is Back: How the Global Revival of Faith Is Changing the World* (New York: Penguin Press, 2009), especially "The New Wars of Religions,"

297–321. The authors assert, for example, that since 2000, 43 percent of civil wars have been religious in character.

12. Douglas Hill, "Kill Them All . . . God Will Recognize His Own," *MHQ: The Quarterly Journal of Military History* 9, no. 2 (1997): 98–109. Hill also gives the example of the Crusades' death toll of Catholics. Although the Cathar population of Beziers was only around 200, 12,000 people were slaughtered (102). William Chester Jordan makes a good point in his *Europe in the High Middle Ages* (New York: Penguin Books, 2001), 204. He points out that the Albigensian Crusade—named for the town of Albi near Toulouse—was the first deliberate Christian crusade against other Christians.

13. Anthony Pagden, *Worlds at War: The 2,500 Year Struggle between East and West* (New York: Random House, 2008), 224. See also Norman Housley, *Fighting for the Cross: Crusading to the Holy Land* (New Haven, CT: Yale University Press, 2008).

14. Pagden, *Worlds At War*, 225.

15. David Livingstone Smith, *The Most Dangerous Animal*, 55.

16. William of Tyre quoted in Regine Pernoud, *The Crusades* (London: Secker and Warburg, 1962), 91.

17. Jonathan D. Spence, *God's Chinese Son: The Taiping Heavenly Kingdom of Hong Ziuquan* (New York: Norton, 1996), xxi.

18. See Dominique Lapierre and Larry Collins, *Freedom at Midnight* (New York: Viking, 2001); Yasmin Khan, *The Great Partition* (New Haven, CT: Yale University Press, 2007); Pani Grahi, *India's Partition, The Story of Imperialism in Retreat* (London: Routledge, 2004); Mushirui Hasan, *India's Partition* (London: Routledge, 1994); and Sumit Ganguly, *The Origins of War in South Asia: Indo-Pakistani Conflicts Since 1947* (Boulder, CO: Westview Press, 2003).

19. Efaim Karsh, *Islamic Imperialism: A History* (New Haven, CT: Yale University Press, 2007).

20. James Anderson Winn, *The Poetry of War* (Cambridge: Cambridge University Press, 2008), 181.

21. Drew Gilpin Faust, *This Republic of Suffering: Death and the American Civil War* (New York: Alfred A. Knopf, 2008).

22. Jim Sheeler, *Final Salute* (New York: Penguin Press, 2008).

23. Burleigh, *Sacred Causes*, 466. In the case of Islam, it is important to note that Muhammad was not simply a prophet and writer of the Qur'an but also a warrior in his own right, conquering cities and defeating tribes. See, for example W. Montgomery and W. Watt, *Muhammad at Medina* (Oxford: The Clarendon Press, 1956); Tariq Ramadan, *In the Footsteps of the Prophet: Lessons from the Life of Muhammad* (Oxford: Oxford University Press, 2007); A. Richard Gabriel, *Muhammad: Islam's First Great General* (Norman: University of Oklahoma Press, 2007); and Fred M. Donner, *The Early Islamic Conquests* (Princeton, NJ: Princeton University Press, 1981). In this regard, how important was Muhammad's triumph in the Battle of the Trenches (627 CE), when the combination of Arab tribes from Mecca failed to wipe out his small sect, and Muhammad went on to inspire a religious crusade that was carried by the sword across three continents.

24. Tim Blanning, *The Pursuit of Glory: Europe 1649–1815* (New York: Viking, 2008), 660, and for the intertwined nature of the popular uprising, the nationalism and the role of religion, see also Ronald Fraser, *Napoleon's Cursed War: Popular*

Resistance in the Spanish Peninsular War (London: Verso, 2008), 19. Fraser perhaps gives too little credit to the military assistance of the British during that struggle, but nevertheless makes valid points about the broad and popular nature of the Spanish uprising.

25. Rupert Smith, *The Utility of Force: The Art of War in the Modern World* (New York: Alfred A. Knopf, 2007), 33. It should be noted the Frederick the Great instituted compulsory military service in 1732, but the French total mobilization after 1789 went far beyond it in both scope and practice.

26. John A. Lynn, *Battle: A History of Combat and Culture* (Boulder, CO: Westview Press, 2003), 189.

27. See John Keegan, *Victory at Any Cost: The Genius of Vietnam's General Vo Nguyen Giap* (London: Recon Press, 1976).

28. Peter Macdonald, *Giap*, quoted in James H. Wilbanks, *The Tet Offensive: A Concise History* (New York: Columbia University Press, 2007), 101.

29. Robert Kagan, *Dangerous Nation* (New York: Alfred A. Knopf, 2006).

30. Kagan, *Dangerous Nation*, 416.

31. Thucydides, *The Peloponnesian War* (New York: The Modern Library, 1951), 188–89.

32. David Bell, *The First Total War: Napoleon's Europe and the Birth of Warfare as We Know It* (Boston: Houghton Mifflin, 2007). See also MacGregor Knox, "Mass Politics and Nationalism as Military Revolution: The French Revolution and After," in MacGregor Knox and Williamson Murray (eds.), *The Dynamics of Military Revolution 1300–2050* (Cambridge: Cambridge University Press, 2001), 57–73.

33. Bell, *The First Total War*, 419.

34. Bell, *The First Total War*, 153.

35. Bell, *The First Total War*, 159.

36. Bell, *The First Total War*, 156.

37. Peter Silver, *Our Savage Neighbors: How Indian War Transformed Early America* (New York: W.W. Norton, 2008), xxiii.

38. For some background understanding of these multiple genocides, see Rene Lemarchand, "Stratified Kingships: Rwanda and Burundi," in Rene Lemarchand (ed.), *African Kingships in Perspective* (London: Frank Cass, 1977), 67–128. For further insights into this horrific and long-running tragedy, see also Daniela Kroslak, *The French Betrayal of Rwanda* (Bloomington: Indiana University Press, 2008); Nigel Eltrimingham, *Accounting for Horror: Post-Genocide Debates in Rwanda* (London: Pluto Press, 2004); and Alan J. Kupermann, *The Limits of Human Intervention: Genocide in Rwanda* (Washington, DC: Brookings Institution Press, 2001).

39. Kiernan, *Blood and Soil*, 557.

40. Max Hastings, *Retribution: The Battle for Japan, 1944–1945* (New York: Alfred A. Knopf, 2007), 32.

41. Herbert Bix, *Hirohito and the Making of Modern Japan* (New York: HarperCollins, 2000), 396.

42. See Ikuhiko Hata, *No Organized or Forced Recruitment: Misconceptions about Comfort Women and the Japanese Military* (Tokyo: Society for the Dissemination of Historical Fact, 2007).

43. Bix, *Hirohito and the Making of Modern Japan*, 346.

44. Hastings, *Retribution*, 53.

45. Hastings, *Retribution*, 114.

46. Hastings, *Retribution*, 368.

47. Hampton Sides, *Ghost Soldiers* (New York: Doubleday, 2001), 106.

48. Sides, *Ghost Soldiers*, 24.

49. Kiernan, *Blood and Soil*, 129.

50. For a more extensive examination of this "undeniable hatred," see John A. Lynn, "The Merciless Fight: Race and Military Culture in the Pacific War," in his *Battle*, 219–80. Also useful in this regard are Meirion and Susie Harries, *Soldiers of the Sun* (New York: Random House, 1991); Yuri Tanaka, *Hidden Horrors: Japanese War Crimes in World War II* (Boulder, CO: Westview Press, 1996); John Dower, *War without Mercy: Race and Power in the Pacific War* (New York: Pantheon, 1987); Mark Felton, *Slaughter at Sea: War Crimes of the Imperial Japanese Navy* (Annapolis, MD: U.S. Naval Institute, 2008); Iris Chang, *The Rape of Nanking: The Forgotten Holocaust of World War II* (New York: Penguin, 1998); Ronald Takai, *Double Victory: A Multicultural History of America in World War II* (Boston: Little, Brown and Company, 2000); David Bergamini, *Japan's Imperial Conspiracy* (New York: William Morrow, 1971); John Toland, *The Rising Sun: The Decline and Fall of the Japanese Empire* (New York: Random House, 1970); and Gruhl Werner, *Imperial Japan's World War Two 1931–1945* (New Brunswick, NJ: Transaction Publishing, 2000). Werner believes (86) the Japanese were responsible for the deaths of 15 million Chinese civilians. See also Michael Norman and Elizabeth M. Norman, *Tears in the Darkness: The Story of the Bataan Death March and Its Aftermath* (New York: Farrar, Straus and Giroux, 2009).

51. Congressman David Emery, e-mail to the author, April 11, 2008.

52. Laurence Bergreen, *Marco Polo: From Venice to Xanadu* (New York: Alfred A. Knopf, 2007), 23.

53. Martin van Creveld, *The Transformation of War* (New York: The Free Press, 1991), 161. See also Martin van Creveld, *The Art of War: War and Military Thought* (Washington, DC: Smithsonian Press, 2000).

54. Van Creveld, *The Transformation of War*, 221.

55. Chris Hedges, *War Is a Force That Gives Us Meaning* (New York: Public Affairs Publishers, 2002). This is also an intermittent theme in Tim Newark's *Women Warlords: An Illustrated Military History of Female Warriors* (London: Blandford/Cassell, 1989), especially in his portrait of Artemisia, "Braver Than Her Husband," 53–74.

56. James S. Robbins, "The Too-Much-Information Age (War Made New: Technology, Warfare, and the Course of History: 1500 to Today)," *National Review*, January 29, 2007, 52. See also his *"Last in Their Class": Custer, Pickett and the Goats of West Point* (New York: Encounter Books, 2006), 411. An interesting look at the differing leadership styles of Alexander the Great, the Duke of Wellington, Ulysses S. Grant, and Adolph Hitler is provided by John Keegan, *The Mask of Command* (New York: Penguin Books, 1988). It would have been interesting to have Robbins and Keegan apply their imperatives to the leadership of Julius Caesar. For an excellent but essentially descriptive overview of Caesar's style of leadership, see Adrian Goldsworthy, *Caesar: Life of a Colossus* (New Haven, CT: Yale University Press, 2007). See also Martin van Creveld, *Command in War* (Cambridge, MA: Harvard University Press, 2003).

57. Bell, *The First Total War*, 199.

58. John G. Stoessinger, *Why Nations Go to War* (New York: Wadsworth, 2005), 212.

CHAPTER EIGHT: THE BELIEF THAT THERE WILL ALWAYS BE ANOTHER WAR

1. See especially Jack Coggins, *The Fighting Man* (Garden City, NY: Doubleday, 1966), 94–95.
2. Carl von Clausewitz, *On War* (Princeton, NJ: Princeton University Press, 1976), 309.
3. Quoted in Robert B. Asprey, *Frederick the Great: The Magnificent Enigma* (London: Ticknor and Fields, 1986), 369.
4. Just because many states do not prepare for the next war does not mean that other states should follow their lead *if* rearming can deter international predators.
5. Rick Atkinson, *An Army at Dawn* (New York: Henry Holt, 2001), 9. I am grateful to Tim Woodcock for pointing me in the direction of this most useful quote.
6. Atkinson, *An Army at Dawn*, 9.
7. John Mueller, *The Remnants of War* (Ithaca, NY: Cornell University Press, 2004), 4. Yet the human desire for peace is a long-held and deep-seated wish with strong contemporary resonances. See, for example, David Cortright, *Peace: A History of Movements and Ideas* (Cambridge: Cambridge University Press, 2008).
8. Mueller, *The Remnants of War*, 2.
9. Tim Butcher, *Blood River: A Journey to Africa's Broken Heart* (New York: Grove Press, 2008), 14.
10. John Moore, *Solving the War Puzzle: Beyond Democratic Peace* (Durham, NC: Carolina Academic Press, 2004).
11. Thomas Friedman, *The Earth Is Flat* (New York: Farrar, Straus and Giroux, 2005).
12. Parag Khanna, *The Second World: Empires and Influence in the New Global Order* (New York: Random House, 2008). For his part, Eric Hobsbawm rather blithely discounts the critical role played by American "hard power" fearing it may promote "not the advance of civilization but of barbarism," Eric Hobsbawm, *Empire: America, War and Global Supremacy* (New York: Pantheon, 2008), 91.
13. For an important synopsis of the interwar period from a variety of country perspectives, see also Williamson Murray and Allan R. Millett, "The Revolution in Military Operations 1919–1939," in their *A War to Be Won: Fighting the Second World War* (Cambridge, MA: The Belknap Press of Harvard University Press, 2000), 18–43.
14. Ronald Spector, "The Military Effectiveness of the US Armed Forces, 1919–39," in Allan R. Millett and Williamson Murray (eds.), *Military Effectiveness: Volume II: The Interwar Period* (Boston: Allen and Unwin, 1988), 70.
15. Donald Kagan, *On the Origins of War* (New York: Doubleday, 1995), 414. Brian Bond and Williamson Murray echo this sentiment, asserting that Britain's "Ten Year Rule actually discouraged the services from preparing for war." See Brian Bond and Williamson Murray, "The British Armed Forces, 1918–1939," in Millet and Murray, *Military Effectiveness*, 124.
16. Kagan, *On the Origins of War*, 415.
17. See Francis Fukuyama, "The End of History?" in *The National Interest* 16 (Summer, 1989): 3–18 and his follow-up piece, "Reflections on the End of History, Five Years Later," *History and Theory* 34, no. 2 (May 1995): 27–43. For a contemporary

counterpoint, see Samuel Huntington, "The Clash of Civilizations?" *Foreign Affairs* (Summer 1993): 22–49. The reader interested in this subject should also enjoy the wry response to these notions by Robert Kagan in his *The Return of History and the End of Dreams* (New York: Alfred A. Knopf, 2008).

18. Colonel Qiao Liang and Colonel Wang Xiangsui, *Unrestricted Warfare: China's Master Plan to Destroy America* (Panama City: Pan American Publishing, 2002). Many of their insights parallel the thinking of Osama bin Laden during the same era.

19. There is much dynamic tension in this assumption. For example, before the U.S. invaded Iraq in 2003, Sadam Hussein put the threshold for U.S. casualties at 3,000 dead, after which the United States would stop the war. Ironically, Hussein thought that that milestone would be reached by the time the U.S. forces had reached Basra in their drive on Baghdad.

20. Qiao and Wang, *Unrestricted Warfare*, 153–96.

21. Thucydides, *The Peloponnesian War* (New York: The Modern Library, 1951); and Kautilya, *The Arthashastra*, translation and commentary by L. N. Rangarajan. (Baltimore, MD: Penguin Books, 1987).

22. Kautilya, *The Arthashastra*, 568–69.

23. Roger Boesche, *The First Great Political Realist: Kautilya and His Arthashastra* (Lanham, MD: Lexington Books, 2002), 77.

24. Mark Bowden, *Black Hawk Down: A Story of Modern War* (New York: Atlantic Monthly Press, 1999).

25. For the ousting of the Soviets from Afghanistan, see George Crile, *Charlie Wilson's War* (New York: Atlantic Monthly Press, 2001).

26. Sheehan, *Where Have All the Soldiers Gone?*, xvii.

27. Philip Bobbitt, *The Shield of Achilles* (New York: Alfred A. Knopf, 2002.), 677–91.

28. Anthony Pagden, *Worlds at War: The 2,500 Year Struggle between East and West* (New York: Random House, 2008). For a more positive view of Muslim-Christian sporadic cooperation in war throughout the ages, consult Ian Almond, *Two Faiths, One Banner: When Muslims Marched with Christians Across Europe's Battlegrounds* (Cambridge, MA: Harvard University Press, 2009).

29. Pagden, *Worlds at War*, 538.

30. Michael Burleigh, *Sacred Causes: The Clash of Religion and Politics from the Great War to the War on Terror* (New York: HarperCollins, 2007), 468.

31. Pagden, *Worlds At War*, 538.

32. Pagden, *Worlds At War*, 538.

33. Martin van Creveld, *The Transformation of War* (New York: The Free Press, 1990).

34. Van Creveld, *The Transformation of War*, 222.

35. David E. Emery, e-mail to the author, May 3, 2008.

36. Ken Alibek, *Biohazard: The Chilling True Story of the Largest Covert Biological Weapons Program in the World—Told from Inside by the Man Who Ran It* (New York: Random House, 1999), x.

37. Alibek, *Biohazard*, 7.

38. Alibek, *Biohazard*, 43.

39. Alibek, *Biohazard*, 145.

40. Max Boot, *War Made New* (New York: Gotham Books, 2007), 444. Robert Kaplan puts the current hierarchy in perspective as of 2007. The United States has a current defense budget of $571 billion, or 4.17 percent of its GDP and an active-duty soldier population of 1.5 million. This compares with $46.7 billion, or 1.39 percent of GDP and 2.1 million soldiers for China, and $33 billion or 1.65 percent of GDP and 1 million soldiers for Russia. See his important article "Power Play" in the *Wall Street Journal* (August 30–31, 2008), W1ff.

41. Harry R. Yarger, *Strategy and the National Security Professional: Strategic Thinking and Strategy Formulation in the 21st Century* (New York: Praeger, 2008), 1. For an overview of some truly terrible possible futures, see Andrew F. Krepinevich, *7 Deadly Scenarios: A Military Futurist Explores War in the 21st Century* (New York: Bantam Dell, 2009), especially "The Collapse of Pakistan," 30–62.

42. The Russian assault on Georgia during August 2008 suggests that an ongoing "overreach" of NATO is more than possible, especially if the Russians were to apply the same strategy to Ukraine. For an examination of revived Russian potential due to its energy supplies, see Marshall Goldman, *Petrostate: Putin, Power and the New Russia* (London: Oxford University Press, 2008).

43. Quoted in van Creveld, *Fighting Power: German and U.S. Army Performance, 1939–1945* (Westport, CT: Greenwood Press, 1982), 175.

CHAPTER NINE: APPLYING THE TEMPLATE: A BATTLE

1. For some overviews of the Stalingrad and Kursk campaigns and the war in the East, see Antony Beevor, *Stalingrad: The Fateful Siege: 1942–1943* (New York: Viking, 1998); Joel S. A. Hayward, *Stopped at Stalingrad* (Lawrence: University of Kansas Press, 1998); Christian P. Potholm, *Strategy and Conflict* (Washington, DC: University Press of America, 1980); Catherine Merridale, *Ivan's War: Life and Death in the Red Army, 1939–1945* (New York: Metropolitan Books, 2006); Heinz Schroter, *Stalingrad* (New York: E. P. Dutton, 1958); David M. Glantz and Jonathan House, *When Titans Clashed: How the Red Army Stopped Hitler* (Lawrence: University Press of Kansas, 1995), Evan Mawdsley, *The Nazi-Soviet War 1941–1945* (London: Hodder Headline, 2005); Martin van Creveld, *Fighting Power: German and U.S. Army Performance, 1939–1945* (Westport, CT: Greenwood Press, 1982); Evan Maudsley, *Thunder in the East* (London: Hodder Arnold, 2005); Victor Kamenir, *The Bloody Triangle: The Defeat of Soviet Armor in the Ukraine, June 1941* (Minneapolis: Zenith Press, 2008), 18; and Tim Ripley, *Elite Units of the Third Reich* (London: Lewis, 2002). For an engrossing account of Soviet retribution during the final battle for Germany, see Max Hastings, *Armageddon: The Battle for Germany, 1944–1945* (New York: Alfred A. Knopf, 2004).

2. Rodric Braithwaite, *Moscow 1941: A City and Its People At War* (New York: Alfred A. Knopf, 2006); and Andrew Nagorski, *The Greatest Battle: Stalin, Hitler, and the Desperate Struggle for Moscow That Changed the Course of World War II* (New York: Simon and Schuster, 2007).

3. John Erickson, *The Soviet High Command: A Military-Political History 1918–1941* (London: Frank Cass, 2001), 519.

4. Alvin D. Coox, *Nomonhan: Japan against Russia 1939* (Stanford, CA: Stanford University Press, 1985), 456. This two-volume work remains the most comprehensive and definite account of this often-overlooked but vital battle. Coox's work is drawn primarily from the Japanese materials, however, as the Soviet archives were still closed when he wrote it. We await further research on this important subject.

5. Christopher D. Bellamy and Joseph S. Lahnstein, "The New Soviet Defensive Policy: Khalkin Gol 1939 as Case Study," *U.S Army War College* 20, no. 3 (1990): 24.

6. See Larry W. Moses, "Soviet-Japanese Confrontation in Outer Mongolia: The Battle of Nomonhan-Khalkin Gol," *The Journal of Asian History* (1967): 79.

7. Coox, *Nomonhan*, 914. Some sources suggest that the Japanese army in the field wanted to revenge these losses but were forbidden by the Emperor: Earl F. Ziemke, *The Red Army 1918–1941* (London: Frank Cass, 2004), 223.

8. Erickson, *Soviet High Command*, 533.

9. Erickson, *Soviet High Command*, 1089, 684.

10. Georgi Zhukov, *Marshal Zhukov's Greatest Battles* (New York: Harper and Row, 1969), 7.

11. Coox, *Nomonhan*, 994–95. The interested reader will want to examine Zhukov's strategic and tactical innovations in the much broader context of the Soviet theory of "deep battle" as presented by Mary R. Habeck in her *Storm of Steel: The Development of Armor Doctrine in Germany and the Soviet Union, 1919–1939* (Ithaca, NY: Cornell University Press, 2003).

12. Erickson, *Soviet High Command*, 538.

13. Carl Boyd, "Japanese Military Effectiveness: The Interwar Period," in Allan R. Millett and Williamson Murray (eds.), *Military Effectiveness: Volume II: The Interwar Period* (Boston: Allen and Unwin, 1988), 164.

14. Zhukov, *Marshal Zhukov's Greatest Battles*, 9. For important insights into that conflict, see William R. Trotter, *A Frozen Hell: The Russo-Finnish Winter War of 1939–1940* (Chapel Hill, NC: Algonquin Paperbacks, 1991); and Roger R. Reese "Lessons of the Winter War: A Study in the Military Effectiveness of the Red Army, 1939–1940," *The Journal of Military History* 72, no. 3 (July 2008): 825–52.

15. Zhukov, *Marshal Zhukov's Greatest Battles*.

CHAPTER TEN: APPLYING THE TEMPLATE: A WAR

1. I am grateful to Allen Springer for this observation about the importance of economic competition.

2. Francis Fukuyama, "The End of History?" *National Interest* (Summer 1989): 3–18. Fukuyama likewise asserted the triumph of secularism and downplayed the ongoing role of religion in international relations. Earlier, John Keegan stated, "But the suspicion grows that battle has already abolished itself" in his *The Face of Battle* (New York: The Viking Press, 1976), 336, and "politics must continue; war cannot" in his *A History of Warfare* (New York: The Viking Press, 1974), 91.

3. Rupert Smith, *The Utility of Force: The Art of War in the Modern World* (New York: Alfred A. Knopf, 2007), 7. C. E. Callwell puts it a somewhat different way when he asserts, "The conduct of small wars is in fact in certain respects an art by

itself, diverging widely from what is adapted to the conditions of regular warfare." Quoted in James Corum, *Bad Strategies: How Major Powers Fail in Counterinsurgency* (Minneapolis, MN: Zenith Press, 2008), 241.

4. Smith, *The Utility of Force*, 19–20.

5. See also Robert Jackson, "Sovereignty and Its Presuppositions: Before 9/11 and After," *Political Studies* 55 (2007): 271–73; and his *Sovereignty: The Evolution of an Idea* (Cambridge, MA: Polity, 2007).

6. Philip Bobbitt, *Terror and Consent: The Wars for the Twenty-First Century* (New York: Alfred A. Knopf, 2008). His earlier work looks at the evolution of the state and its relationship to war: Philip Bobbitt, *The Shield of Achilles* (New York: Alfred A. Knopf, 2002).

7. Bobbitt, *Terror and Consent*, 180.

8. Tom Pocock, *Fighting General: The Public and Private Campaigns of General Sir Walter Walker* (London: Collins, 1973), 218.

9. Field-Marshal Viscount Slim, *Defeat into Victory: Battling Japan in Burma and India, 1942–1945* (New York: Cooper Square Press, 2000). Fascinatingly, there were plans to have the British people turn to guerrilla and insurgency warfare had the Germans conquered Britain during World War II, see especially "Yank" Levy, *Guerilla Warfare* (New York: Penguin Books, 1942).

10. Pocock, *Fighting General*.

11. John Cloake, *Templer: Tiger of Malaya* (London: Harrap Limited, 1985), 188–328. The British also successfully applied these techniques in Kenya during that colony's insurgency from 1952–1960.

12. Kautilya, *The Arthashastra* (London: Penguin Books, 1987), 160. See also, Roger Boesche, *The First Great Political Realist: Kautilya and His Arthashastra* (Lanham, MD: Lexington Books, 2002).

13. Thucydides, *The Peloponnesian War*, 184–92.

14. Ronald Fraser, *Napoleon's Cursed War: Popular Resistance in the Spanish Peninsular War* (London: Verso, 2008).

15. Carl von Clausewitz in his *On War* (Princeton, NJ: Princeton University Press, 1976), "The People in Arms," 578–84.

16. Clausewitz, *On War*, 578. Interestingly enough, Jomini, whose experience with Napoleon included seeing the Spanish and Russian national efforts against the French, concluded that these wars of an entire people were both "dangerous and deplorable," and he had little to say about the correct strategy for fighting them. See Antoine-Henri de Jomini, *The Art of War*, translated by G. H. Mendell and W. P. Craighill (El Paso, TX: El Paso Norte Press, 2005). For his part, B. H. Liddel Hart saw guerrilla war as a "form of aggression suited to exploit the nuclear stalemate" in his *Strategy* (New York: Praeger, 1967), 379.

17. John Ferling, *Almost a Miracle: The American Victory in the War of Independence* (Oxford: Oxford University Press, 2007); and Jeremy Black, *Warfare in the Eighteenth Century* (London: Cassell, 1999), 118. It should also be noted that some recent scholarship has rightly accented the tactical "learning" of the British as they fought the American insurgents: see Mark Urban, *Fusiliers: The Saga of a British Redcoat Regiment in the American Revolution* (London: Walker and Company, 2008). The Fusiliers fought in the American Revolution from Lexington to Yorktown.

18. Ferling, *Almost a Miracle*, 478.

19. This is not to say, of course, that the American colonies could *never* have been successful in revolting from Great Britain, it is just that the outcome of the rebellion of 1776 was problematical until the very end of the war.

20. Here is a sampling (but by no means an exhaustive one) of successful and unsuccessful insurgencies, and those whose outcomes have yet to be determined:

Some Successful Insurgencies and Rebellions

Maccabean Revolt against the Greek Seleucid Dynasty (167 BCE)
American Revolution (1775-1783)
French Revolution (1789)
Haitian Revolution (1791-1798)
Spanish against Napoleon and his brother (Peninsular War, 1808-1814)
Montenegrin Revolution against Ottoman Turks (lost control in 1878, Balkan Wars in 1912-1914)
Russian Revolution (1918-1921)
Chinese Revolution (1927-1949)
Franco and the Nationalists against the Spanish Republic (1935-1936)
Vietnam Revolution (1954-1975)
Algerian Revolution (1954-1962)
Sandinistas in Nicaragua (1979-1989)
Algerian Revolution (1954-1962)
Cyprus Insurgency (1955-1959)
Eritrean Revolution against the Ethiopians (1961-1989)
Cuban Revolution (1956-1959)
MPLA in Angola (1956-1975)
FRELIMO in Mozambique (1962-1974)
Mujahideen in Afghanistan (1980-1989)

Some Failed Insurgencies and Rebellions

Boudica and her rebels against Roman Britain (60-61 AD)
Jewish War against the Romans (70 AD)
Owain Glyndwr's Welsh Rebellion (1400-1409)
Muskogee Native Americans against United States (The Red Stick Revolt) (1812-1813)
Rural and urban uprisings: Austria, Italy, Germany, Poland, France (1848)
Indian Uprising/Mutiny (1857) (Note: This was many things: a mutiny, a peasant's revolt; an urban revolution; a war of independence; and a religious jihad with Muslim, Hindu, and Christian elements)
Confederate States versus the United States (1860-1865)
Navajos against the United States (1863-1864)
Massingire Rebellion in Mozambique (1874)
Boers in South Africa (1880-1881)
Aguinaldo's Moro Guerillas in the Philippines following the Spanish American War (1898-1902)
Boer War (1899-1902)
Boxer Rebellion in China (1900)
Herero Rebellion in German South West Africa (1904-1908)

Maji Maji uprising in German East Africa (1905–1907)
Decembrist Revolt against Russian Government (1905)
Koreans against Japanese (1910–1912)
Macedonians versus Ottoman Empire (1912–1913, Balkan Wars)
Cretans versus Ottoman Empire (1913)
Haitian insurgency (1915–1934)
Dominican insurgency (1916–1924)
IRA in Northern Ireland (1916–1997)
Afghanistan insurgency (1919–1920)
Iraqi revolt (1920–1929)
Nicaraguan insurgency (1927–1933)
Christeros Movement in Mexico (1928)
Palestine revolt (1929–1936)
Communist Rebels in El Salvador (1932)
Spanish Saharans against Morocco (1936–1937)
The Ukrainian insurgency (*Ukrainska Poustanska Armiya* or UPA) fought from 1942 to 1950 first against the Germans and later against the Soviets
The Home Army in Poland (1942–1945)
Greek Communists after World War II (1944–1945), (1946–1950)
Huk (People's Army against Japan, *Hukbalahap* in Tagalog) Rebellion in the Philippines (against Japanese 1942–1944 and after World War II against the Americans and the Philippine government 1946–1954)
Malay insurgency against British (1948–1960)
Korean insurgency against South Korea (1950–1953)
The Resistance Army in Tibet (1950–1974)
Mau Mau uprising in Kenya (1952–1960)
ETA Basques versus Spain (1959–2006 complete ceasefire)
Tupamaro insurgency in Uruguay (1960s and 1970s)
Congo Rebellion (1960, 1964)
Bolivia in time of Che (1967)
Biafra (1967–1970)
UNITA Rebels in Angola (formed in 1966, after independence in 1975, they remained a guerilla organization fighting the central government until 2002)
Kurds against Iranians (1978–1979)
Contra Rebels in Nicaragua (1980s)
Shining Path in Peru (1980–1992)
Southern Sudanese versus Northern Sudanese second war 1983–2000)
Sikh "Golden Temple" uprising (1984)
Kurds against Turks (1984–1999)
Chechnyans against Russians (1994–1996)
Northern Alliance versus the Taliban (1996–2001)
Chechnyans against Russians (1999–2000)
Tamil Tigers in Sri Lanka (1983–2009)

Some Ongoing Insurgencies and Rebellions

Kashmiri separatists (1947–present)
Muslim separatists in southern Thailand (1959–present)

FARC in Columbia (1964–present)
Muslim separatists in the Philippines (1971–present)
Intifada in Palestine (1987–1993, 2000–present)
Kurds in Iraq, Turkey, and Iran (1988–present)
Salafists against Algerians (1991–present)
Chiapas Zapatista insurgents in Mexico (1994–present)
Maoists in Nepal (1996–present)
Taliban insurgency in Afghanistan 2001–present)
Iraq (al Qaeda/Sunnis) (2003–present)
Salafists in Somalia (2007–present)

21. C. E. Callwell, *Small Wars: Their Principles and Practice*, reprinted by EP Publishing, 1976 (London: His Majesty's Station Office, 1906). For an overview of many of the wars and insurgencies from which Callwell extrapolated, the interested reader should consult Donald Featherstone, *Colonial Small Wars 1837–1901* (London: David and Charles, 1973).

22. See Keith B. Bickel, *Mars Learning: The Marine Corp's Development of Small Wars Doctrine, 1915–1940* (Boulder, CO: Westview Press, 2001) as well as the subsequent U.S. Marine Corps' Manual itself, *U.S. Marine Corps FM 12–15 Small Wars Manual* (Washington, DC: United States Government Printing Office, 1940).

23. Peter R. Mansoor, *Baghdad at Sunrise: A Brigade Commander's War in Iraq* (New Haven, CT: Yale University Press, 2008), 347.

24. Chinese records indicate that between 1965 and 1969, 320,000 Chinese served in North Vietnam, freeing up hundreds of thousands of North Vietnamese for the war in the south: C. Dale Walton, *The Myths of Inevitable U.S. Defeat in Vietnam* (London: Frank Cass, 2002), 95.

25. For an overview of Vann's illustrious and ultimately tragic career, see Neil Sheehan, *A Bright Shining Lie: John Paul Vann and America in Vietnam* (New York: Vintage Books, 1989).

26. A most useful biography of General Abrams is Lewis Sorley, *Thunderbolt: General Creighton Abrams and the Army of His Times* (New York: Simon and Schuster, 1992).

27. William Colby claims that 90 percent of the South Vietnamese population was under government control, at least in villages ranked A, B, and C in terms of security by the end of 1969, but the later date seems more accurate. James McCarjar, *Lost Victory: A Firsthand Account of America's Sixteen-Year Involvement in Vietnam* (Chicago: Contemporary Books, 1989), 278. William Sorley believes that by the end of 1970 due to the success of pacification, "the war was won." See his *A Better War: The Unexamined Victories and Final Tragedy of America's Last Years in Vietnam* (New York: Harcourt, 1999), 217. Certainly the ability of the South Vietnamese to repel the countrywide attacks during the Easter, 1972 offensive lends credibility to claims of both the degree of government control and the ability of the South Vietnamese to fight effectively *when* provided with U.S. air and artillery support. See Stephen P. Randolph, *Powerful and Brutal Weapons: Nixon, Kissinger, and the Easter Offensive* (Cambridge, MA: Harvard University Press, 2007).

28. Bui Tin, "How North Vietnam Won the War," *Wall Street Journal*, August 3, 1995, A8.

29. If, however, the number of potentially radical jihadi Salafists is 5 percent, this would constitute a possible cohort of 50–60 million people. That population size would be roughly the size of the population cohort commanded by Nazi Germany or Imperial Japan during World War II.

30. See, for example, Richard H. Shultz Jr. and Andrea J. Dew, *Insurgents, Terrorists, and Militias: The Warriors of Contemporary Combat* (New York: Columbia University Press, 2006); and Lee Harris, *The Suicide of Reason: Radical Islam's Threat to the West* (New York: Basic Books, 2007).

31. George Tenet, *At the Center of the Storm: My Years at the CIA* (New York: HarperCollins, 2007), 266. By contrast, as Ralph Peters puts it, "We approach war in terror of lawsuits and criminal charges. Our enemies are enthusiastic killers. Who has the psychological advantage?" quoted in P. W. Singer, *Wired for War: The Robotics Revolution and Conflict in the 21st Century* (New York: The Penguin Press, 2009), 391. There is an additional element of import in the anti-Semitism of some practitioners of Islam. See for example, Andrew G. Bostom (ed.), *The Legacy of Islamic Anti-Semitism: From Sacred Texts to Solemn History* (New York: Prometheus Books, 2008). For his part, however, David Levering Lewis sees Islam as much more positive, playing a very important role in the development of European civilization. See also David Levering Lewis, *God's Crucible: Islam and the Making of Modern Europe, 570–1215* (New York: Norton, 2008). And for another look at the complexity and ambiguity of the relations between Christian and Muslim states, see Ian Almond, *Two Faiths, One Banner: When Muslims Marched with Christians Across Europe's Battlefields* (Cambridge, MA: Harvard University Press, 2009).

32. The Predator as drone was used in Bosnia and Kosovo but *not* as an armed weapons system.

33. See for example, "The Three Rules and the Eight Remarks" of the Eighth Route Army which included "Do not steal from the people," and "Be neither selfish nor unjust," Mao Tse-tung, *On Guerrilla Warfare*, translated by Samuel B. Griffith (Urbana: University of Illinois Press, 2000), 92. For a very interesting insight into counterinsurgency thinking along these lines, see Charles C. Krulak, "Strategic Corporal: Leadership in the Three Block War," *Marines* 28, no. 1 (January 1999): 26–33; and Robert M. Cassidy, "The Long Small War: Indigenous Forces for Counterinsurgency," *Parameter: U.S. Army War College* 36, no. 2 (Summer 2006): 61. David Kilcullen is also adroit at making the point that the counterinsurgent forces always have to be careful to distinguish between their implacable enemies and those who are fighting simply because the counterinsurgents are "in their space." See David Kilcullen, *The Accidental Guerrilla* (London: Oxford University Press, 2009) for a fuller exploration of the socioeconomic, ethnic, tribal, and other dimensions that influenced the situation on the ground in various insurgency situations in Afghanistan, Iraq, Indonesia, and Pakistan.

34. Bing West points out that all the horrendous negative publicity and aid to insurgent recruiting was due to the actions of virtually a single rogue squad and the massacre of twenty-four civilians at Haditha due to those of one other individual squad as well. Two incidents are, of course, two incidents too many, but hardly "a pattern" during six years of war. See Bing West, *The Strongest Tribe: War Politics and the Endgame in Iraq* (New York: Random House, 2008), 152–53. Peter Mansoor, quite rightly, also puts the blame on poor information as to who was an insurgent

and who was not: *Baghdad at Sunrise*, 347. Of course, considerable anti-American sentiment was also generated by the many civilian casualties due to use/misuse of air power.

35. Anthony Jones, "Counterinsurgency in the Philippines 1898–1954," in Daniel Marston and Carter Malkasian (eds.), *Counterinsurgency in Modern Warfare* (Oxford: Osprey Books, 2008).

36. For the interwoven connections among jihadists worldwide, see Olivier Roy, *Globalized Islam: The Search for a New Ummah* (New York: Columbia University Press 2004). The exponential growth in their ability to cause harm to others lies in the possibility of their obtaining nuclear arms and other weapons of mass destruction. See, for example, William Langewiesche, *The Atomic Bazaar: The Rise of the Nuclear Poor* (New York: Farrar, Straus and Giroux, 2007).

37. Robert Kaplan, "NATO's Ragged Southern Edge," in his *Hog Pilots and Blue Water Grunts* (New York: Random House, 2006), 174–207.

38. Quoted in Peter Bergen and Paul Cruickshank, "The Unraveling: Al Qaeda's Revolt against bin Laden," *The New Republic* 238: 10 (June 11, 2008): 17. In this regard, the Sufi sect of Islam may also serve to counter the thrust of al Qaeda and other militant espousers of jihad in a number of countries from Morocco to Iran.

39. Chris Hunter, *Eight Lives Down* (New York: Delacorte Press, 2007), 19. Hunter was a British bomb expert who served in Northern Ireland and Bosnia before Iraq. Williamson Murray points out, however, that Saddam Hussein had already trained a large number of special operatives to use massive car bombs.

40. John Boyd, *A Discourse on Winning and Losing* (mimeographed, 1987), 24.

41. Boyd, *A Discourse on Winning and Losing*, 5. See also John Kiszely, "Learning about Counterinsurgency," *Military Review* 87, no. 2 (March/April 2007): 5–11.

42. Fraser, *Napoleon's Cursed War*, 342.

43. Fraser, *Napoleon's Cursed War*, 424.

44. Richard Stuffs, "From Search and Destroy to Hearts and Minds: The Evolution of British Strategy in Malaya 1948–1960," in Daniel Marston and Carter Malkasian (eds.), *Counterinsurgency in Modern Warfare* (Oxford: Osprey Books, 2008), 113–30. Gil Barndollar rightly points out, however, that this strategy also included massive relocation of the population into New Villages. There has always been a persistent military bias against a defensive posture, as captured by Callwell in his *Small Wars* (195), "A defensive attitude is almost always to be deprecated, and only under certain special circumstances is it to be recommended."

45. Robert Thompson, *Defeating Communist Insurgency: Experiences from Malaya and Vietnam* (New York: Praeger, 1966), 106, quoted in Daniel Marston, "Lessons in 21st-Century Counterinsurgency: Afghanistan 2001–07," in Daniel Marston and Carter Malkasian (eds.), *Counterinsurgency in Modern Warfare* (Oxford: Osprey Books, 2008), 220–40. Obviously successful counterinsurgency requires the training and deployment of a well-trained police force as well. See also, John Nagl, *Learning to Eat Soup with a Knife: Counterinsurgency Lessons from Malaya and Vietnam* (Chicago: University of Chicago Press, 2007).

46. James H. Wilbanks, *The Tet Offensive: A Concise History* (New York: Columbia University Press, 2007), 81. For other realistic assessments of what actually happened in Vietnam *after* the Tet Offensive of 1968, see Lewis Sorley, *A Better War: The Unexamined Victories and Final Tragedy of America's Last Years in Vietnam* (New York:

Harcourt Brace, 1999); Mark Moyar, *Triumph Forsaken: The Vietnam War 1954–1965* (London: Cambridge University Press, 2006); and Lt. Gen. Phillip Davidson, *Vietnam at War: The History 1946–1975* (Novato, CA: Presidio Press, 1988). While Colonel Harry Summers, *On Strategy: A Critical Analysis of the Vietnam War* (Novato, CA: Presidio Press, 1995) provides a most useful overview, I do think Summers misses what should be one of the central lessons of that war from the perspective of Mars, namely that the United States and South Vietnam would have been more successful earlier had they adopted a "clear and hold" strategy rather than a "search and destroy" approach from 1965 to 1968. For a graphic depiction of the demoralizing aspects of "search and destroy," see the powerful film, *Hamburger Hill* about operations in the Ah Shau Valley or read Harold Moore and Joseph Galloway, *We Were Soldiers Once and Young* (New York: Random House, 1992), about operations in the Ia Drang Valley. Depending on one evaluation of the first battle of the Ia Drang Valley, the United States did or did not win most of the major battles of the Vietnam War. On the other hand, Summers is right in arguing that the United States broke many important strategic rules of Clausewitz during the war, ignoring the fact that the centers of gravity for the North Vietnamese were always in the north, never in the south. Because the Americans and the South Vietnamese were now fighting both a diminished insurgency and a conventional war, an amalgam of both strategies was needed. Perhaps Paul Hendrickson has it correct when he says "Vietnam is our great national myth . . . what makes it so terrible a tragedy and so fine a myth is its impenetrability" quoted in Marshall L. Michel III, *The 11 Days of Christmas: America's Last Vietnam Battle* (San Francisco: Encounter Books, 2002), 232. For a rare, and often overlooked South Vietnamese ARVN perspective, see Lam Quang Thi, *The Twenty-Five Year Century* (Denton: University of North Texas Press, 2001); Andrew Wiest, *Vietnam's Forgotten Army: Heroism and Betrayal in the ARVN* (New York: New York University Press, 2007); and James H. Willbanks, *Abandoning Vietnam* (Lawrence: University Press of Kansas, 2004).

47. Wilbanks, *The Tet Offensive*, 181.

48. Bui Tin, "How North Vietnam Won the War," A8. Andrew F. Krepinevich Jr. perceptively calls it "Tet: Defeat in Victory," in his *The Army and Vietnam* (Baltimore, MD: The Johns Hopkins University Press, 1986). For a contemporary reprise of the more simplistic, "it was inevitable" view of the war, see John Prados, *Vietnam: The History of an Unwinnable War, 1945–1975* (Lawrence: University Press of Kansas, 2009).

49. Quoted in Carter Malkasian, "Counterinsurgency in Iraq May 2003–January 2007," in Daniel Marston and Carter Malkasian (eds.), *Counterinsurgency in Modern Warfare* (Oxford: Osprey Books, 2008), 258. See also, David H. Petraeus and James N. Mattis, *FM 3–24: Counterinsurgency* (Washington, DC: Department of the Army, 2006).

50. Bing West, "The War Turns: November 2006," in his *The Strongest Tribe*, 208–15; and Linda Robinson, "The Knights of America" and "The Sons of Iraq," in her *Tell Me How This Ends: General David Petraeus and the Search for a Way Out of Iraq* (New York: Public Affairs, 2008), 217–70.

51. Bob Woodward documents the array of opposition to the surge in his *The War Within: A Secret White House History 2006–2008* (New York: Simon and Schuster, 2008).

52. See especially his "The Insurgency Doctrine" in *Counter-Insurgency Warfare: Theory and Practice* (New York: Praeger, 1964), 43–62.

53. Williamson Murray and Robert H. Scale Jr., *The Iraq War: A Military History* (Cambridge, MA: Belknap Press, 2005), 237.

54. Calvin Allen, *Oman: The Modernization of the Sultanate* (Boulder, CO: Westview Press, 1987), 73; J. E. Petersen, *Oman in the Twentieth Century: Political Foundations of an Emerging State* (New York: Barnes and Noble, 1978), 192; and John Townsend, *Oman: The Making of a Modern State* (New York: St. Martin's Press, 1977), 169. The Iranian forces were particularly important in the crucial battles of December 1974 and January 1975.

55. See also John Peterson, *Oman's Insurgencies: The Sultanate's Struggle for Supremacy* (London: SAQI, 2007); Calvin Allen and W. Lynne Rigsbee, *Oman Under Qaboos: From Coup to Constitution 1970–1996* (London: Frank Cass, 2000); John Akehurst, *We Won a War: The Campaign in Oman 1965–1975* (Southampton: Wilton, Salisbury, Wiltshire, 1982); Ranulph Fienner, *Where Soldiers Fear to Tread* (London: Hodder and Stoughton, 1975); and Tony Jeapes, *SAS Secret War: Operation Storm in the Middle East* (Mechanicsburg, PA: Stackpole Books, 2006).

56. MacGregor Knox, "Conclusion: Continuity and Revolution in the Making of Strategy," in Williamson Murray, MacGregor Knox, and Alvin Bernstein (eds.), *The Making of Strategy: Rulers, States and War* (Cambridge: Cambridge University Press, 1994), 615.

57. For some insights in the America military's efforts to innovate on the fly, see Steven Metz and Frank Hoffman, "Restructuring America's Ground Forces: Better, Not Bigger," *The Stanley Foundation Policy Analysis Brief* (September 2007); Benjamin Buley, *The New American War of War: Military Culture and the Political Utility of Force* (London: Routledge, 2008); as well as even more incisive twin works of Robert Kaplan, *Imperial Grunts: The American Military on the Ground* (New York: Random House, 2005); and *Hog Pilots.*

58. This "return on investment" ratio is attributed to John Mueller and quoted rather exuberantly in John Robb's *Brave New War: The Next Stage of Terrorism and the End of Globalization* (New York: John Wiley and Sons, 2007).

59. Marston, "Lessons in 21st-Century Counterinsurgency," 240. See also H. John Poole, *Phantom Soldier: The Enemy's Answer to U.S. Firepower* (Emerald Isle, SC: Posterity Press, 2001). Poole indicates the many advantages of the "eastern way of war" over conventional U.S. tactics and how they can be countered and defeated in the future. In any case, Linda Robinson is correct when she quotes General Petraeus as saying "the big idea is you can't kill your way out of an insurgency": Robinson, *Tell Me How This Ends*, 97.

60. See Robert Kaplan, "SOUTHCOM Colombia, Winter, 2003" in his *Imperial Grunts*, 39–91, and his later, "Timbuktu, Soviet Stonehenge, and Gnarly-Ass Jungle," in *Hog Pilots*, 303–28. Kaplan documents considerable progress by the Colombian government, and a big reversal of fortune for FARC since the United States began to seriously assist that country's counterinsurgency efforts.

61. Mao Tse-tung, *Selected Military Writings of Mao Tse-tung* (Peking: Foreign Languages Press, 1967), see especially "On Protracted War," 187–268. Mao saw three phases—the period of strategic defense, the period of strategic stalemate, and the period of strategic counteroffensive—as playing out over a long period of time.

Preserving his forces in the face of a superior enemy became his sine qua non for success, declaring "The first law of war is to preserve ourselves and destroy the enemy," Mao Tse-tung, *On Guerilla Warfare*, 20.

62. Bing West, *The Strongest Tribe* (New York: Random House, 2008). This turnabout in events (and their origins) are also captured in Mansoor's *Baghdad at Sunrise*, 188–192; Robinson's *Tell Me How This Ends*, especially 217–305; and Thomas E. Ricks, *The Gamble: General David Petraeus and the American Military Adventure in Iraq, 2006–2008* (New York: Penguin, 2009). Ricks's somewhat grudging account is particularly telling since his previous book was so highly critical of previous U.S. counterinsurgency operations. Still, he insists U.S. forces will be in combat in Iraq until "at least 2015"(325), and he believes the United States can't leave Iraq without disastrous consequences (314). Even more pessimistic in this regard is Dexter Filkins's *The Forever War* (New York: Alfred A. Knopf, 2008).

63. Robert A. Pape, however, in *Dying to Win: The Strategic Logic of Suicide Terrorism* (New York: Random House, 2005), 106, makes the important amendment that not all Salafists are prepared to resort to terrorism to accomplish their goal of reviving "ancient authority over modern interpretations of Islam." This underscores why I have chosen the more limited and specific term "radical jihadist Salafist" to distinguish those who want ancient Islam used as a societal norm and those who would blow up others to achieve that focus.

64. Bruce Gudmundsson, "The First of the Banana Wars: U.S. Marines in Nicaragua 1909–12," in Daniel Marston and Carter Malkasian (eds.), *Counterinsurgency in Modern Warfare* (Oxford: Osprey Books, 2008), 69.

65. Quoted in Thomas K. Adams, *The Army after Next: The First Postindustrial Army* (Stanford, CA: Stanford University Press, 2008), 65. James Corum does an excellent job of highlighting this problem in the early U.S. counterinsurgency efforts in Iraq. See his *Bad Strategies: How Major Powers Fail in Counterinsurgency* (Minneapolis, MN: Zenith Press, 2008).

Index

About the Author

Christian P. Potholm is the DeAlva Stanwood Alexander Professor of Government at Bowdoin College. The author of a dozen books, he has studied, lectured, and written about war for more than forty years.